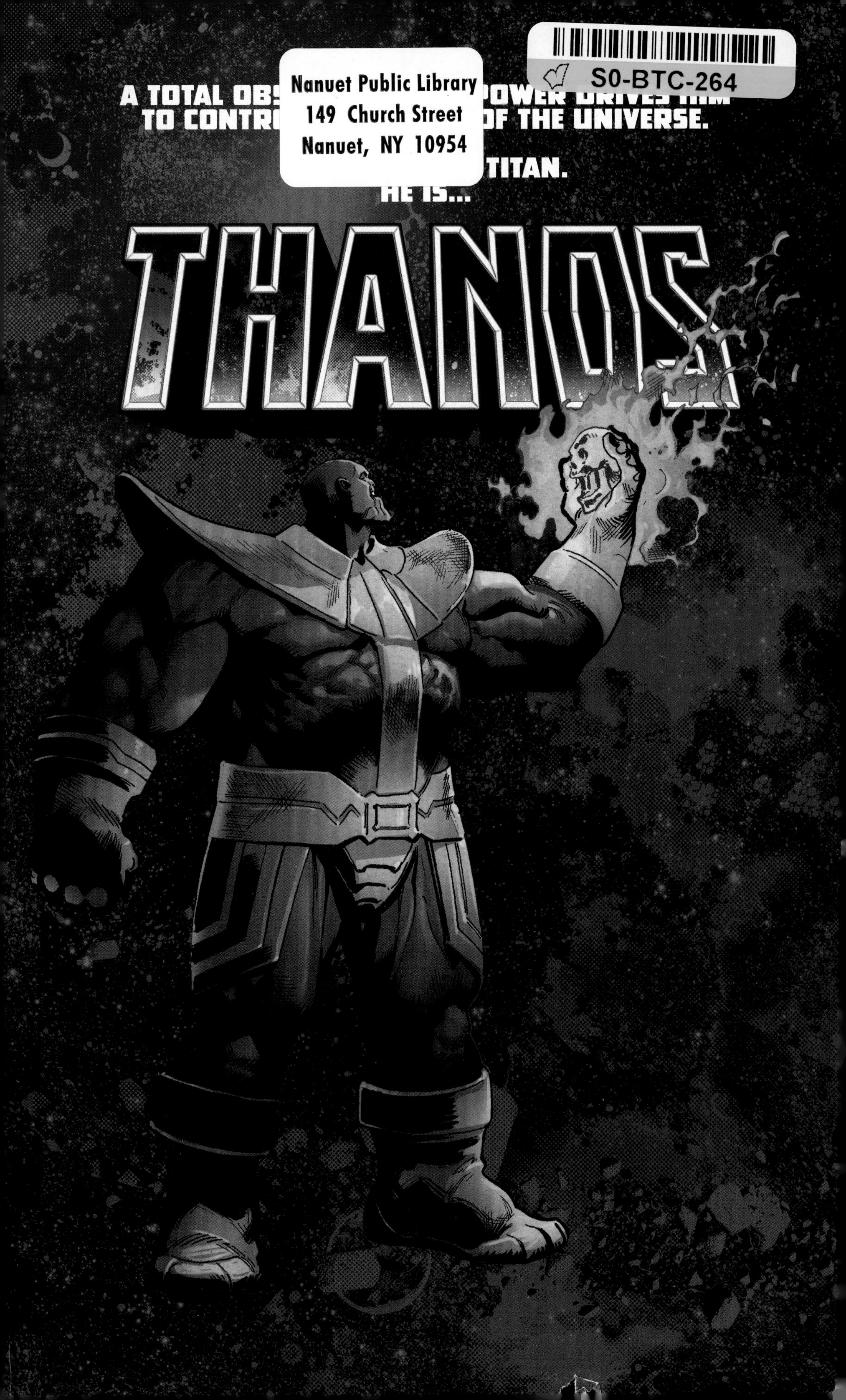
A TOTAL OBS POWER DRIVES HIM
TO CONTR OF THE UNIVERSE.
TITAN.
HE IS...
THANOS

THANOS

THANOS WINS

DONNY CATES
WRITER

GEOFF SHAW
ARTIST

ANTONIO FABELA
COLOR ARTIST

THANOS ANNUAL #1

DONNY CATES, CHRIS HASTINGS, KIERON GILLEN, KATIE COOK, RYAN NORTH & AL EWING
WRITERS

GEOFF SHAW, FLAVIANO, ANDRÉ LIMA ARAÚJO, KATIE COOK, WILL ROBSON & FRAZER IRVING
ARTISTS

ANTONIO FABELA, FEDERICO BLEE, CHRIS O'HALLORAN, HEATHER BRECKEL, RACHELLE ROSENBERG & FRAZER IRVING
COLOR ARTISTS

GEOFF SHAW & ANTONIO FABELA
COVER ART

VC'S CLAYTON COWLES
LETTERER

ANNALISE BISSA
ASSISTANT EDITOR

JORDAN D. WHITE
EDITOR

COLLECTION EDITOR **JENNIFER GRÜNWALD**
ASSISTANT EDITOR **CAITLIN O'CONNELL**
ASSOCIATE MANAGING EDITOR **KATERI WOODY**
EDITOR, SPECIAL PROJECTS **MARK D. BEAZLEY**
VP PRODUCTION & SPECIAL PROJECTS **JEFF YOUNGQUIST**
SVP PRINT, SALES & MARKETING **DAVID GABRIEL**
BOOK DESIGNERS **JAY BOWEN WITH ADAM DEL RE**
EDITOR IN CHIEF **C.B. CEBULSKI**
CHIEF CREATIVE OFFICER **JOE QUESADA**
PRESIDENT **DAN BUCKLEY**
EXECUTIVE PRODUCER **ALAN FINE**

THANOS WINS BY DONNY CATES. Contains material originally published in magazine form as THANOS #13-18 and ANNUAL #1. First printing 2018. ISBN 978-1-302-90559-0. Published by MARVEL WORLDWIDE, INC., a subsidiary of MARVEL ENTERTAINMENT, LLC. OFFICE OF PUBLICATION: 135 West 50th Street, New York, NY 10020. Copyright © 2018 MARVEL No similarity between any of the names, characters, persons, and/or institutions in this magazine with those of any living or dead person or institution is intended, and any such similarity which may exist is purely coincidental. **Printed in Canada.** DAN BUCKLEY, President, Marvel Entertainment; JOHN NEE, Publisher; JOE QUESADA, Chief Creative Officer; TOM BREVOORT, SVP of Publishing; DAVID BOGART, SVP of Business Affairs & Operations, Publishing & Partnership; DAVID GABRIEL, SVP of Sales & Marketing, Publishing; JEFF YOUNGQUIST, VP of Production & Special Projects; DAN CARR, Executive Director of Publishing Technology; ALEX MORALES, Director of Publishing Operations; DAN EDINGTON, Managing Editor; SUSAN CRESPI, Production Manager; STAN LEE, Chairman Emeritus. For information regarding advertising in Marvel Comics or on Marvel.com, please contact Vit DeBellis, Custom Solutions & Integrated Advertising Manager, at vdebellis@marvel.com. For Marvel subscription inquiries, please call 888-511-5480. **Manufactured between 5/4/2018 and 6/5/2018 by SOLISCO PRINTERS, SCOTT, QC, CANADA.**

10 9 8 7 6 5 4 3 2 1

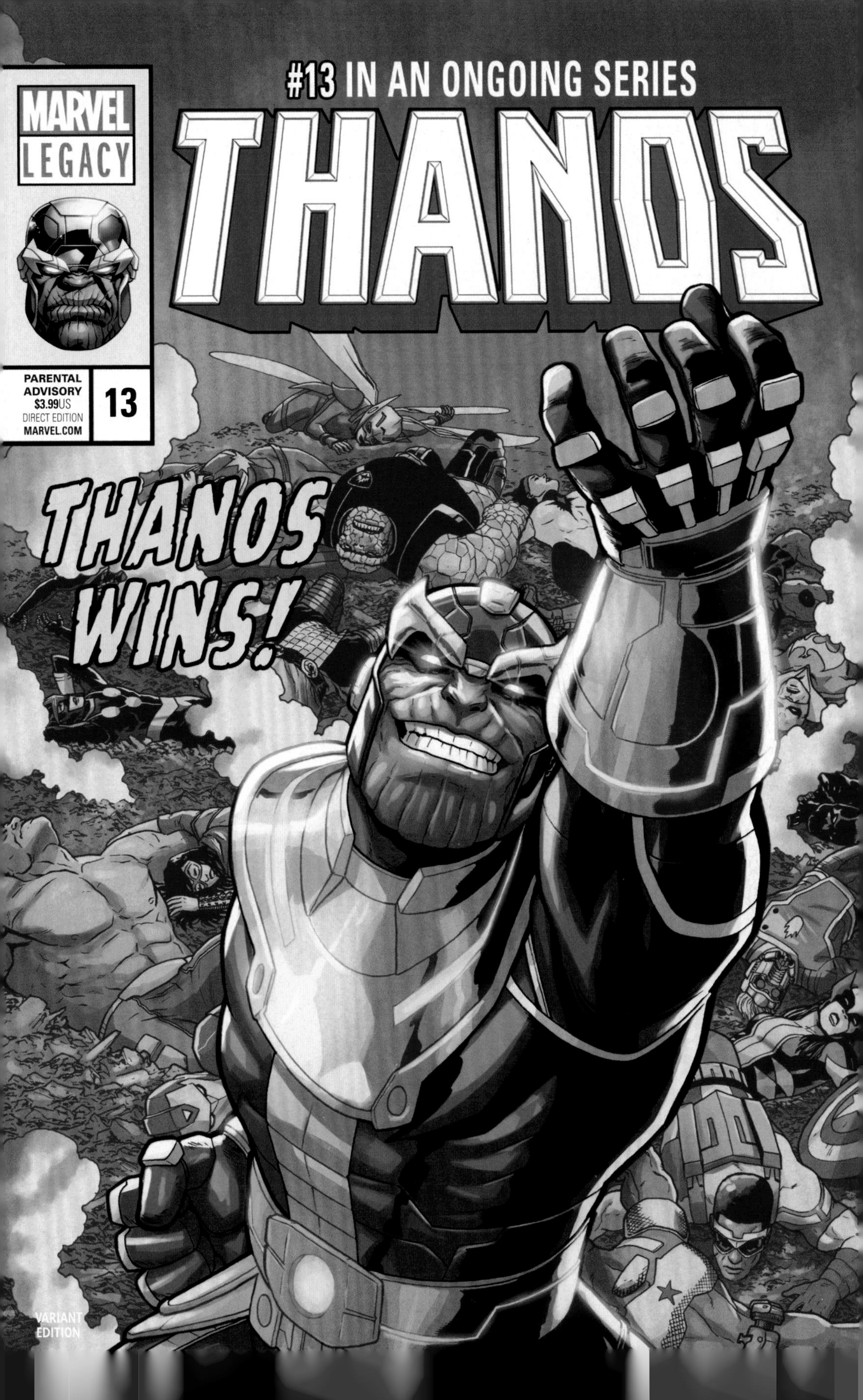

#13 IN AN ONGOING SERIES
THANOS
MARVEL
LEGACY
PARENTAL ADVISORY
$3.99US
DIRECT EDITION
MARVEL.COM
13
THANOS WINS!
VARIANT EDITION

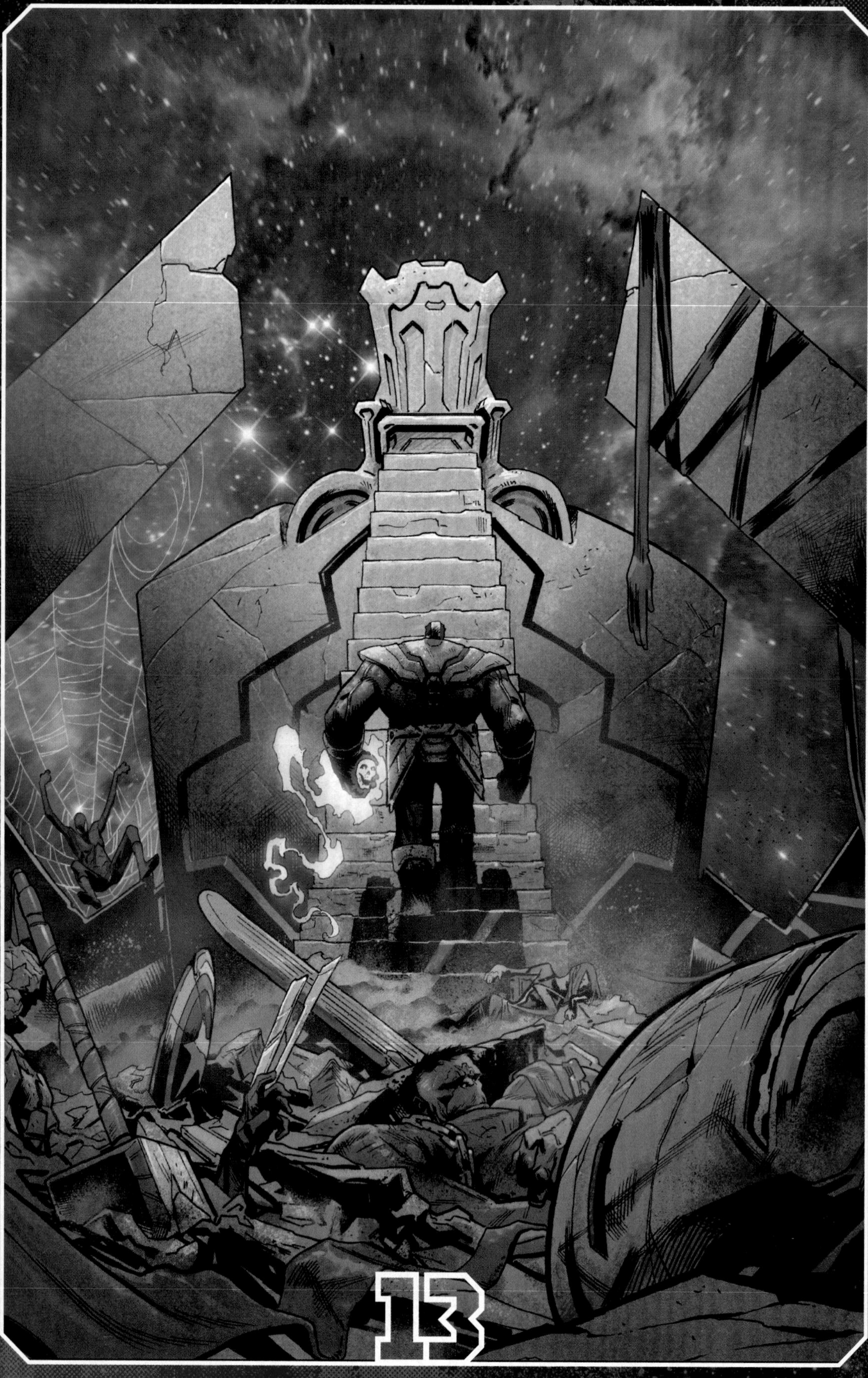
13

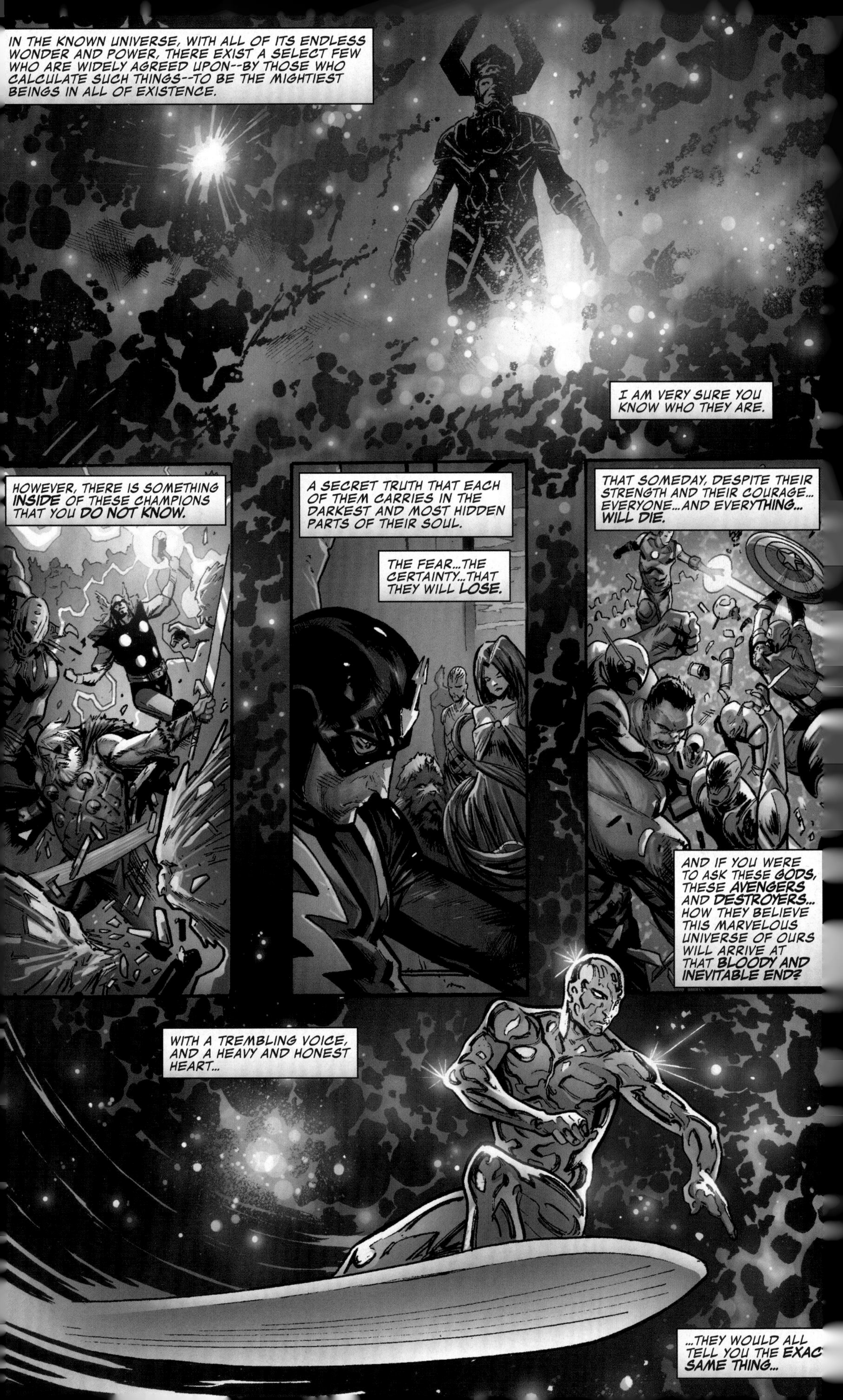
IN THE KNOWN UNIVERSE, WITH ALL OF ITS ENDLESS WONDER AND POWER, THERE EXIST A SELECT FEW WHO ARE WIDELY AGREED UPON--BY THOSE WHO CALCULATE SUCH THINGS--TO BE THE MIGHTIEST BEINGS IN ALL OF EXISTENCE.
I AM VERY SURE YOU KNOW WHO THEY ARE.
HOWEVER, THERE IS SOMETHING INSIDE OF THESE CHAMPIONS THAT YOU DO NOT KNOW.
A SECRET TRUTH THAT EACH OF THEM CARRIES IN THE DARKEST AND MOST HIDDEN PARTS OF THEIR SOUL.
THE FEAR...THE CERTAINTY...THAT THEY WILL LOSE.
THAT SOMEDAY, DESPITE THEIR STRENGTH AND THEIR COURAGE... EVERYONE...AND EVERYTHING... WILL DIE.
AND IF YOU WERE TO ASK THESE GODS, THESE AVENGERS AND DESTROYERS... HOW THEY BELIEVE THIS MARVELOUS UNIVERSE OF OURS WILL ARRIVE AT THAT BLOODY AND INEVITABLE END?
WITH A TREMBLING VOICE, AND A HEAVY AND HONEST HEART...
...THEY WOULD ALL TELL YOU THE EXAC SAME THING...

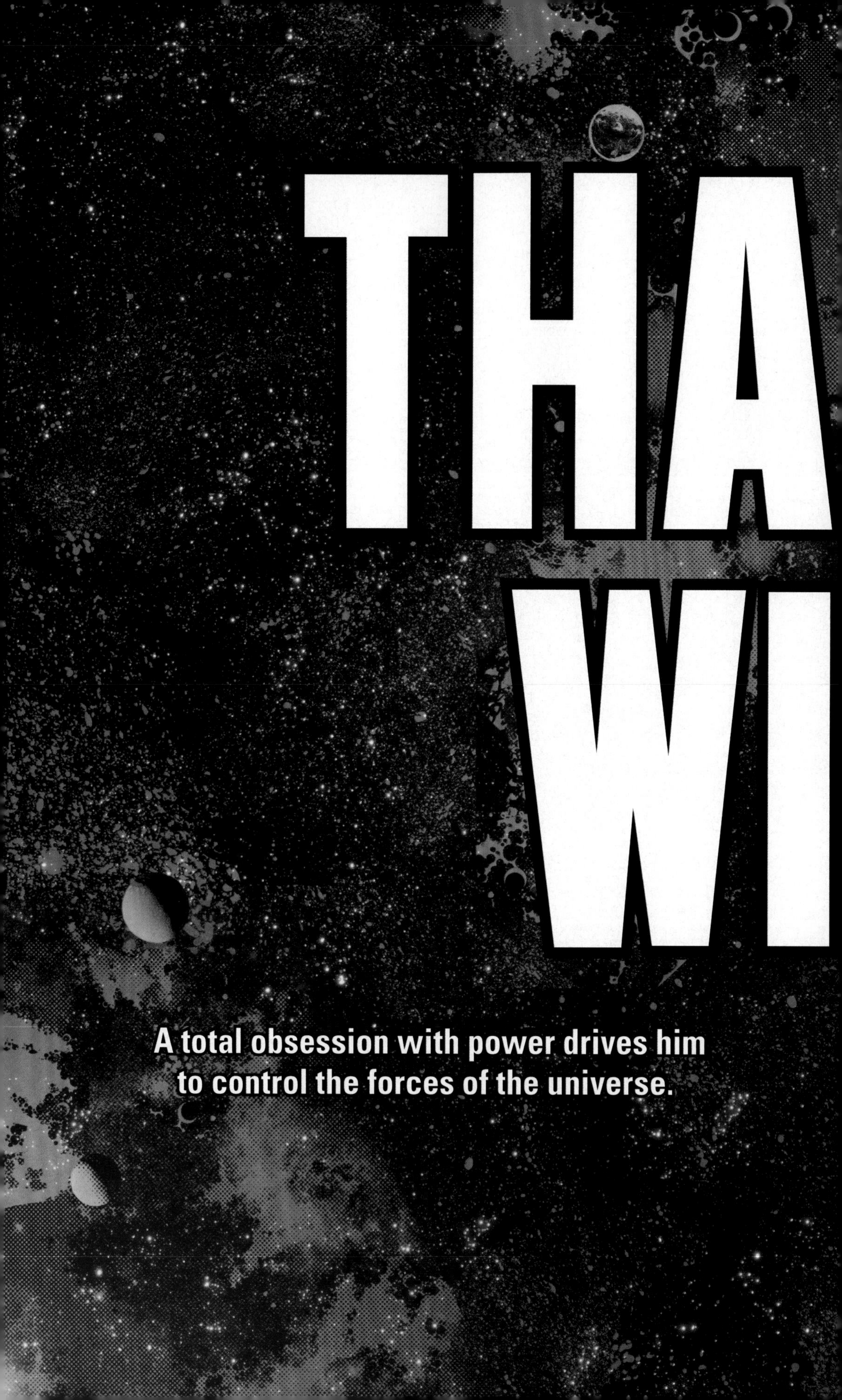
THA
WI
A total obsession with power drives him to control the forces of the universe.

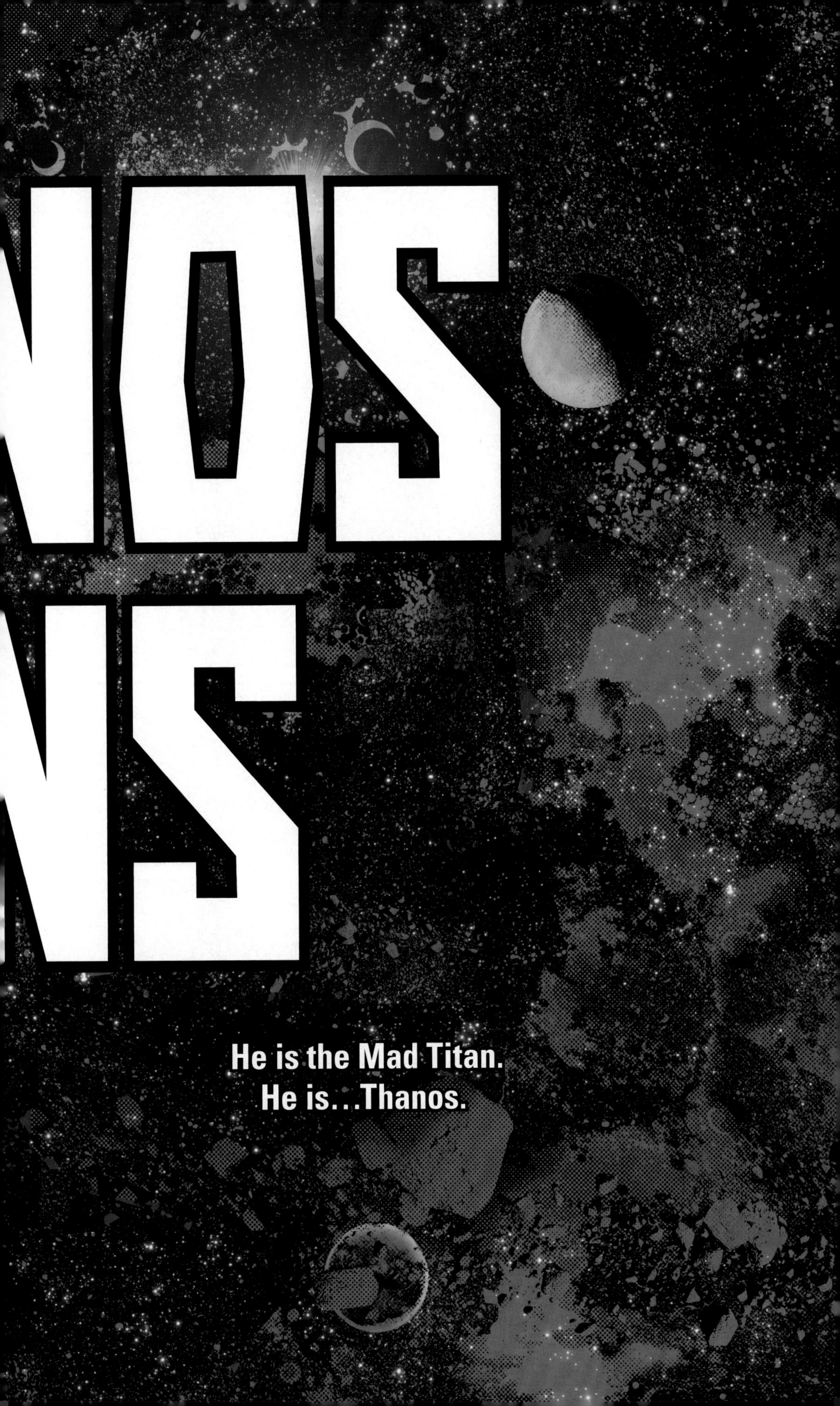
NOS
NS
He is the Mad Titan.
He is...Thanos.

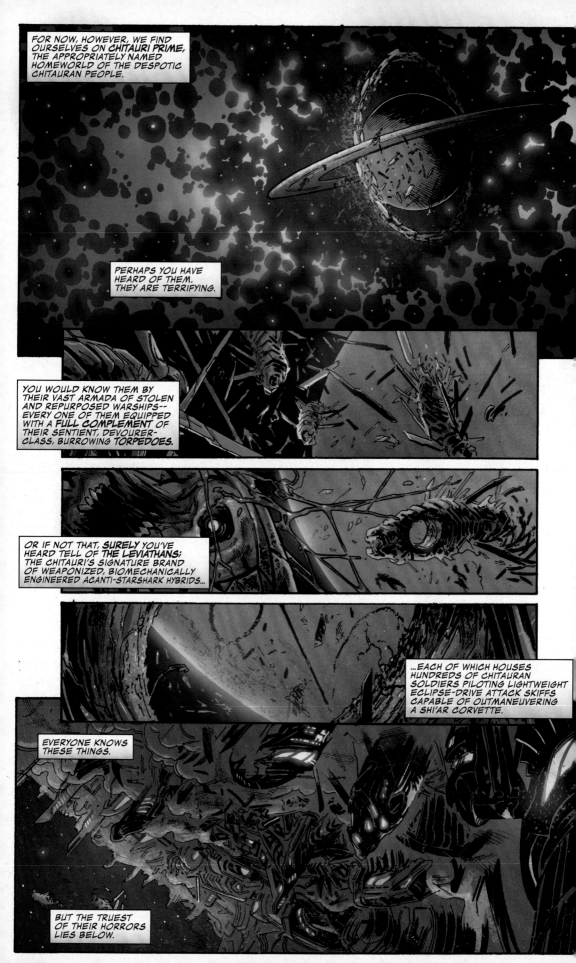

FOR NOW, HOWEVER, WE FIND OURSELVES ON **CHITAURI PRIME,** THE APPROPRIATELY NAMED HOMEWORLD OF THE DESPOTIC CHITAURAN PEOPLE.

PERHAPS YOU HAVE HEARD OF THEM. THEY ARE TERRIFYING.

YOU WOULD KNOW THEM BY THEIR VAST ARMADA OF STOLEN AND REPURPOSED WARSHIPS-- EVERY ONE OF THEM EQUIPPED WITH A **FULL COMPLEMENT** OF THEIR SENTIENT, DEVOURER-CLASS, BURROWING **TORPEDOES.**

OR IF NOT THAT, **SURELY** YOU'VE HEARD TELL OF **THE LEVIATHANS;** THE CHITAURI'S SIGNATURE BRAND OF WEAPONIZED, BIOMECHANICALLY ENGINEERED ACANTI-STARSHARK HYBRIDS...

...EACH OF WHICH HOUSES HUNDREDS OF CHITAURAN SOLDIERS PILOTING LIGHTWEIGHT ECLIPSE-DRIVE ATTACK SKIFFS CAPABLE OF OUTMANEUVERING A SHI'AR CORVETTE.

EVERYONE KNOWS THESE THINGS.

BUT THE TRUEST OF THEIR HORRORS LIES BELOW.

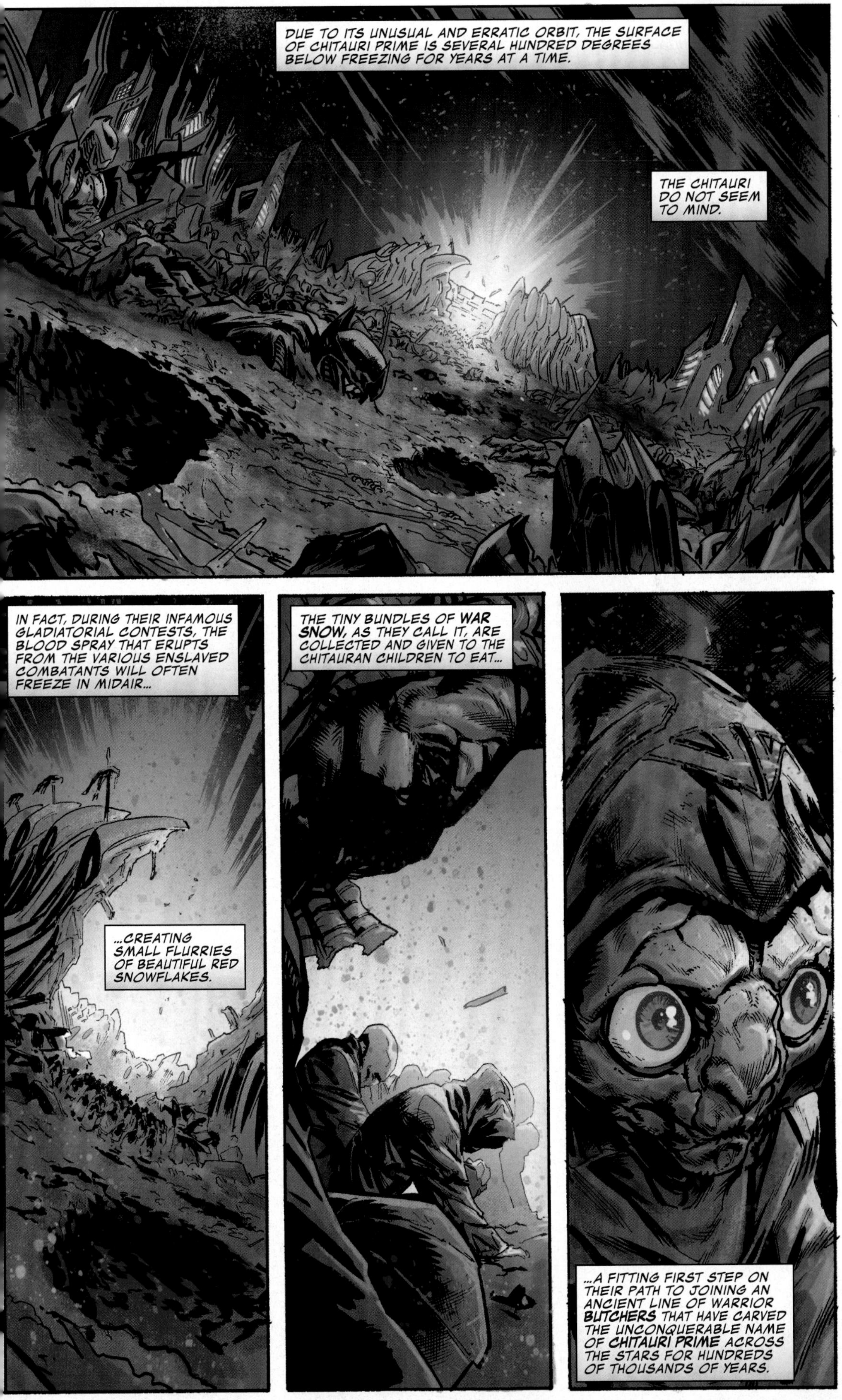
DUE TO ITS UNUSUAL AND ERRATIC ORBIT, THE SURFACE OF CHITAURI PRIME IS SEVERAL HUNDRED DEGREES BELOW FREEZING FOR YEARS AT A TIME.
THE CHITAURI DO NOT SEEM TO MIND.
IN FACT, DURING THEIR INFAMOUS GLADIATORIAL CONTESTS, THE BLOOD SPRAY THAT ERUPTS FROM THE VARIOUS ENSLAVED COMBATANTS WILL OFTEN FREEZE IN MIDAIR...
...CREATING SMALL FLURRIES OF BEAUTIFUL RED SNOWFLAKES.
THE TINY BUNDLES OF WAR SNOW, AS THEY CALL IT, ARE COLLECTED AND GIVEN TO THE CHITAURAN CHILDREN TO EAT...
...A FITTING FIRST STEP ON THEIR PATH TO JOINING AN ANCIENT LINE OF WARRIOR BUTCHERS THAT HAVE CARVED THE UNCONQUERABLE NAME OF CHITAURI PRIME ACROSS THE STARS FOR HUNDREDS OF THOUSANDS OF YEARS.

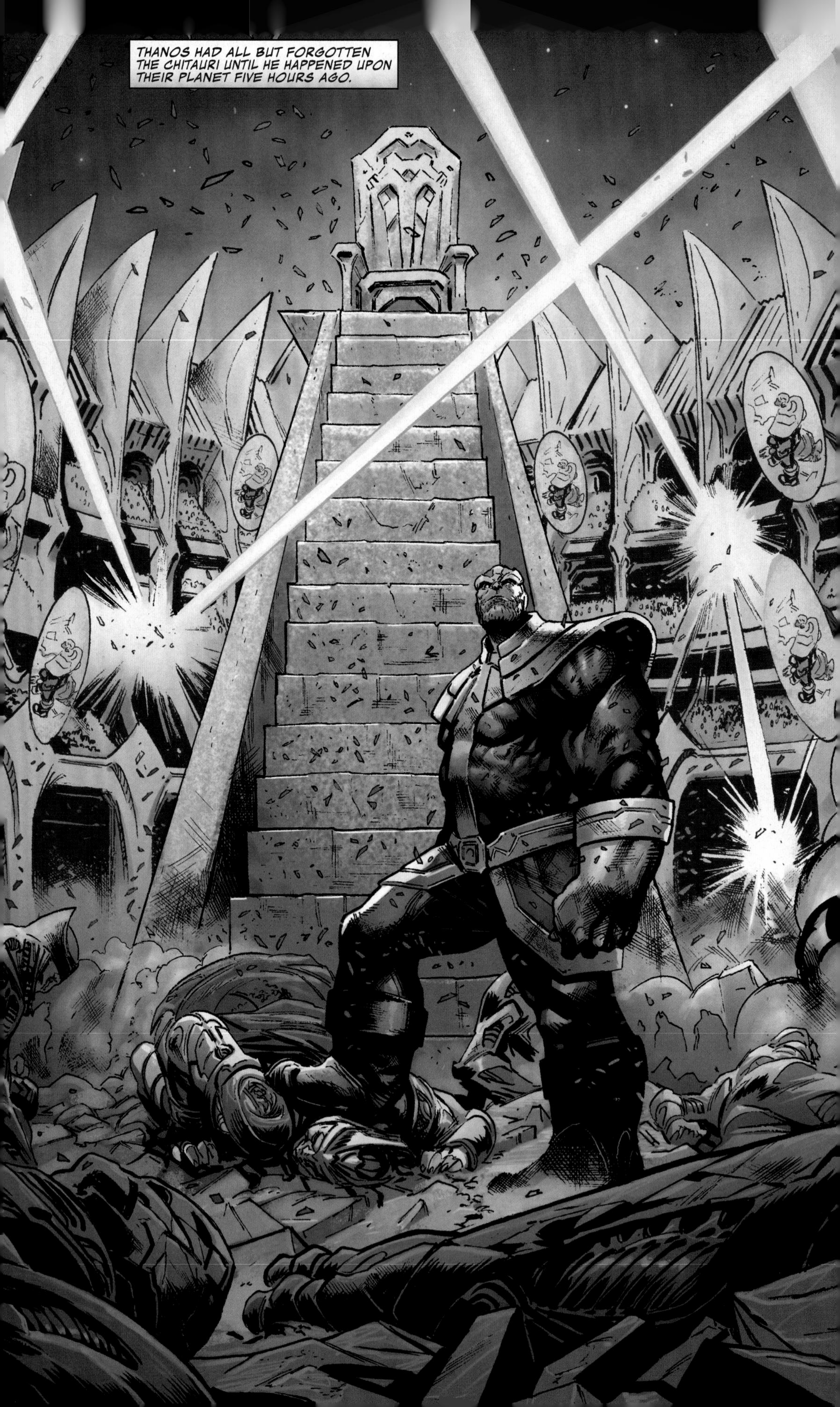
THANOS HAD ALL BUT FORGOTTEN THE CHITAURI UNTIL HE HAPPENED UPON THEIR PLANET FIVE HOURS AGO.

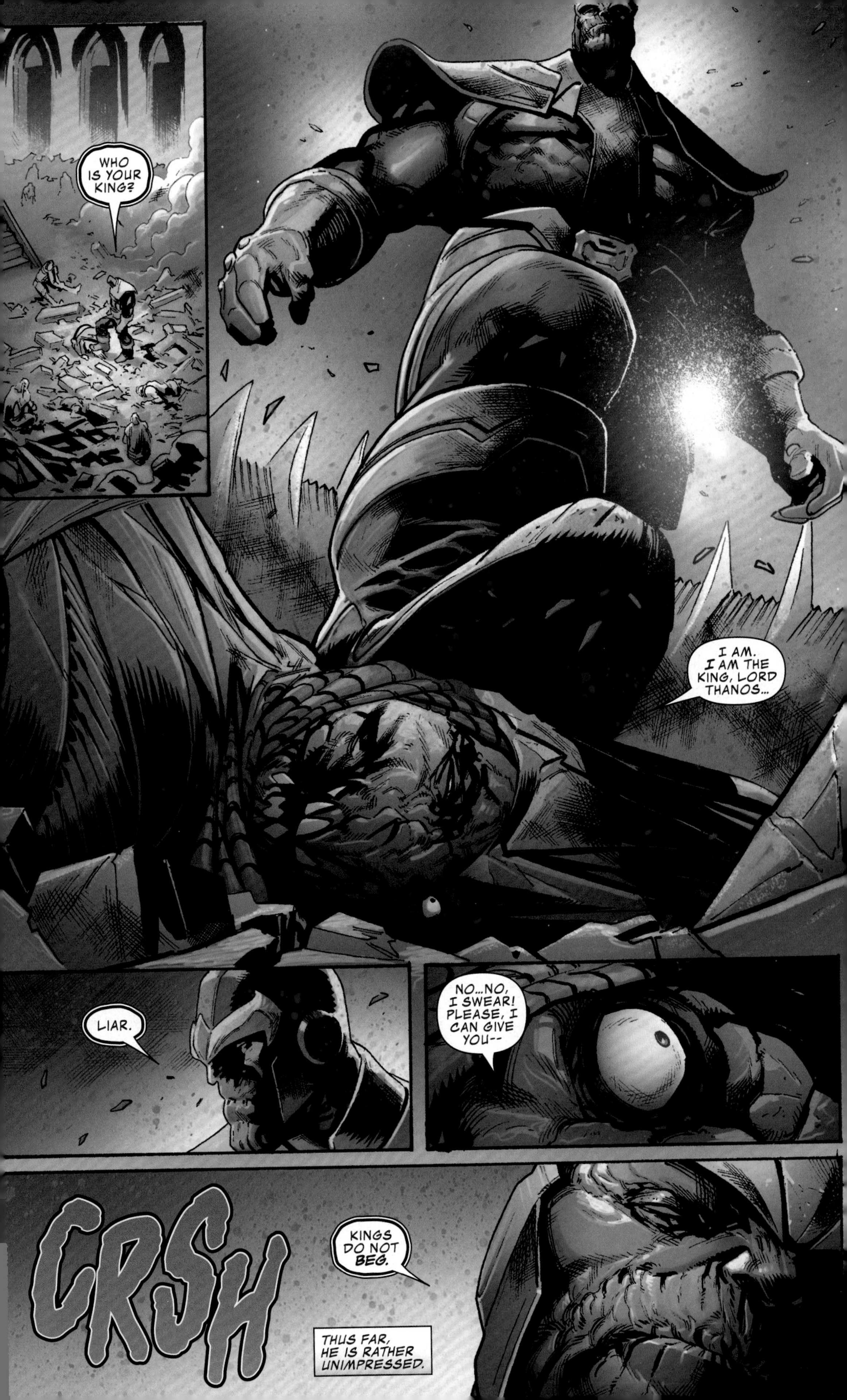
WHO IS YOUR KING?
I AM. I AM THE KING, LORD THANOS...
LIAR.
NO...NO, I SWEAR! PLEASE, I CAN GIVE YOU--
CRSH
KINGS DO NOT BEG.
THUS FAR, HE IS RATHER UNIMPRESSED.

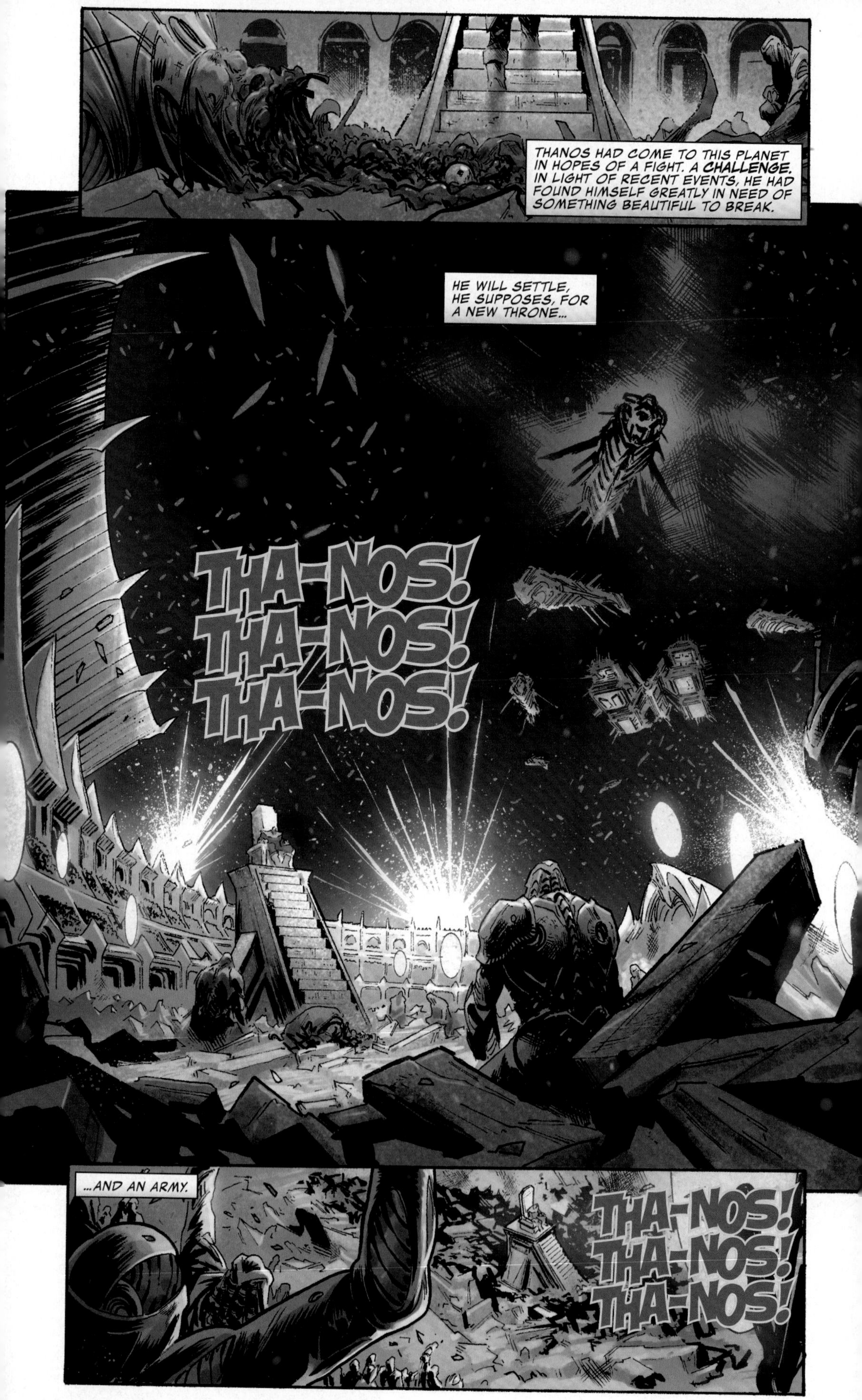
THANOS HAD COME TO THIS PLANET IN HOPES OF A FIGHT. A CHALLENGE. IN LIGHT OF RECENT EVENTS, HE HAD FOUND HIMSELF GREATLY IN NEED OF SOMETHING BEAUTIFUL TO BREAK.
HE WILL SETTLE, HE SUPPOSES, FOR A NEW THRONE...
THA-NOS! THA-NOS! THA-NOS!
...AND AN ARMY.
THA-NOS! THA-NOS! THA-NOS!

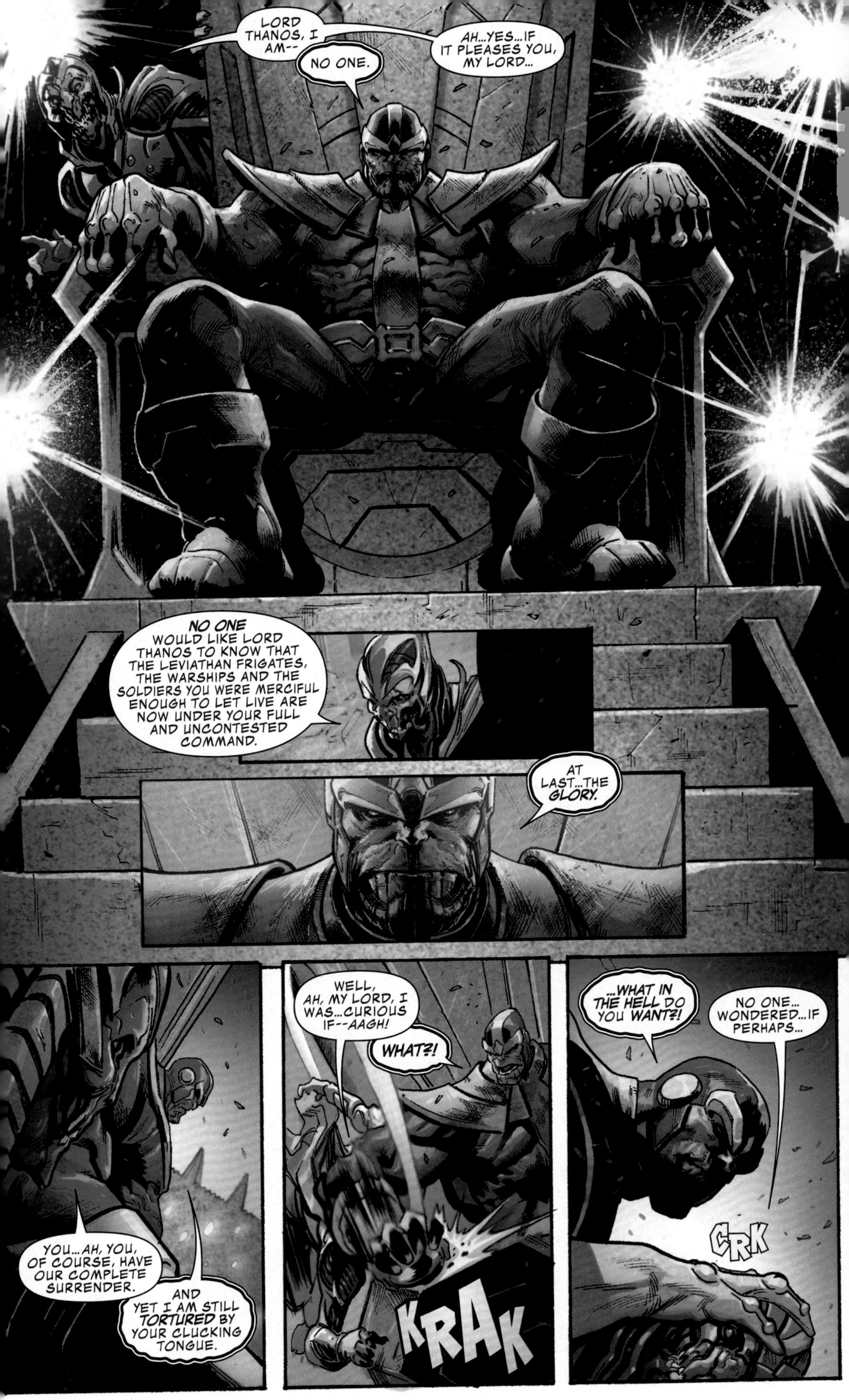

LORD THANOS, I AM--
NO ONE.
AH...YES...IF IT PLEASES YOU, MY LORD...
NO ONE WOULD LIKE LORD THANOS TO KNOW THAT THE LEVIATHAN FRIGATES, THE WARSHIPS AND THE SOLDIERS YOU WERE MERCIFUL ENOUGH TO LET LIVE ARE NOW UNDER YOUR FULL AND UNCONTESTED COMMAND.
AT LAST...THE GLORY.
YOU...AH, YOU, OF COURSE, HAVE OUR COMPLETE SURRENDER.
AND YET I AM STILL TORTURED BY YOUR CLUCKING TONGUE.
WELL, AH, MY LORD, I WAS...CURIOUS IF--AAGH!
WHAT?!
KRAK
...WHAT IN THE HELL DO YOU WANT?!
NO ONE... WONDERED...IF PERHAPS...
CRK

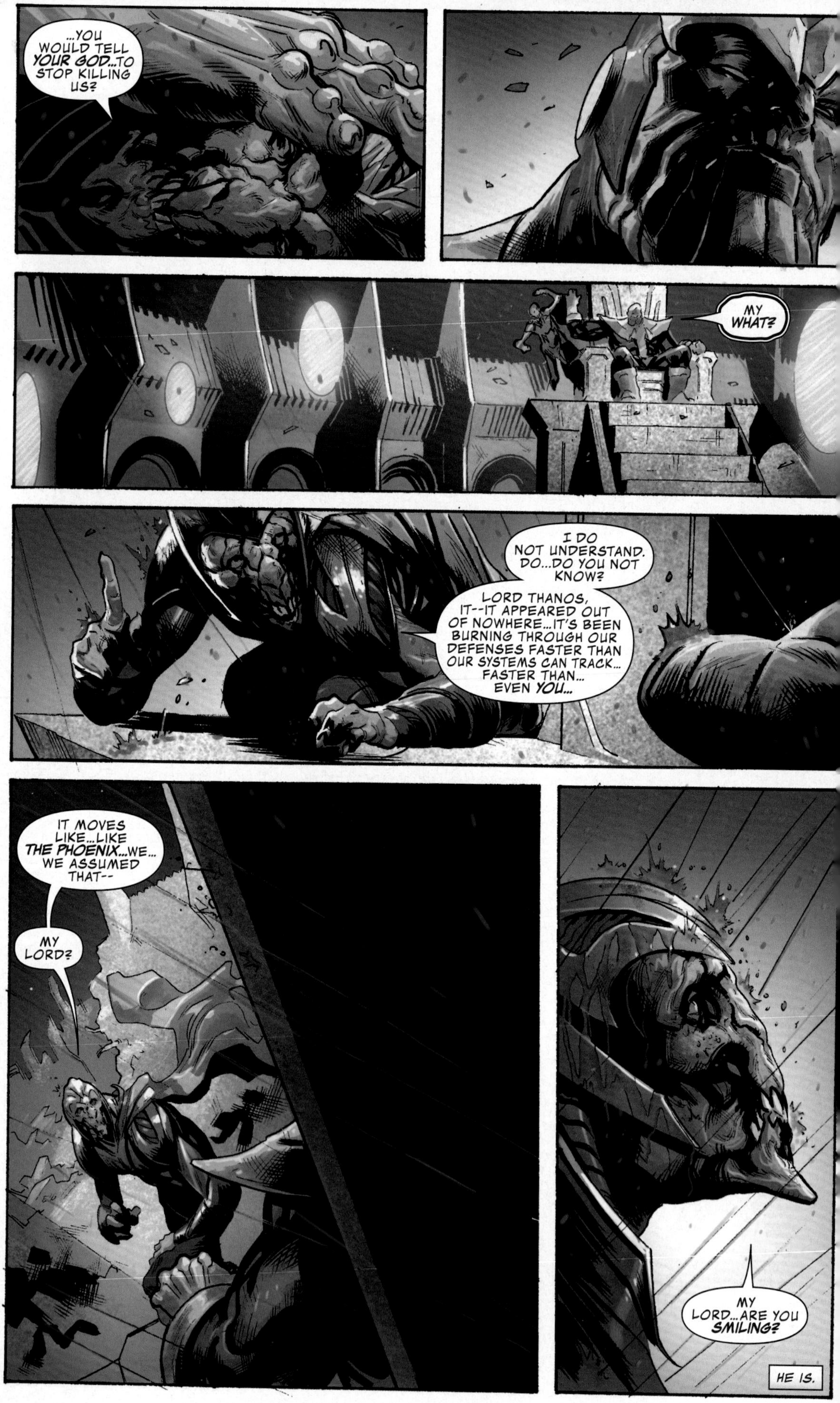
...YOU WOULD TELL YOUR GOD...TO STOP KILLING US?
MY WHAT?
I DO NOT UNDERSTAND. DO...DO YOU NOT KNOW?
LORD THANOS, IT--IT APPEARED OUT OF NOWHERE...IT'S BEEN BURNING THROUGH OUR DEFENSES FASTER THAN OUR SYSTEMS CAN TRACK... FASTER THAN... EVEN YOU...
IT MOVES LIKE...LIKE THE PHOENIX...WE... WE ASSUMED THAT--
MY LORD?
MY LORD...ARE YOU SMILING?
HE IS.

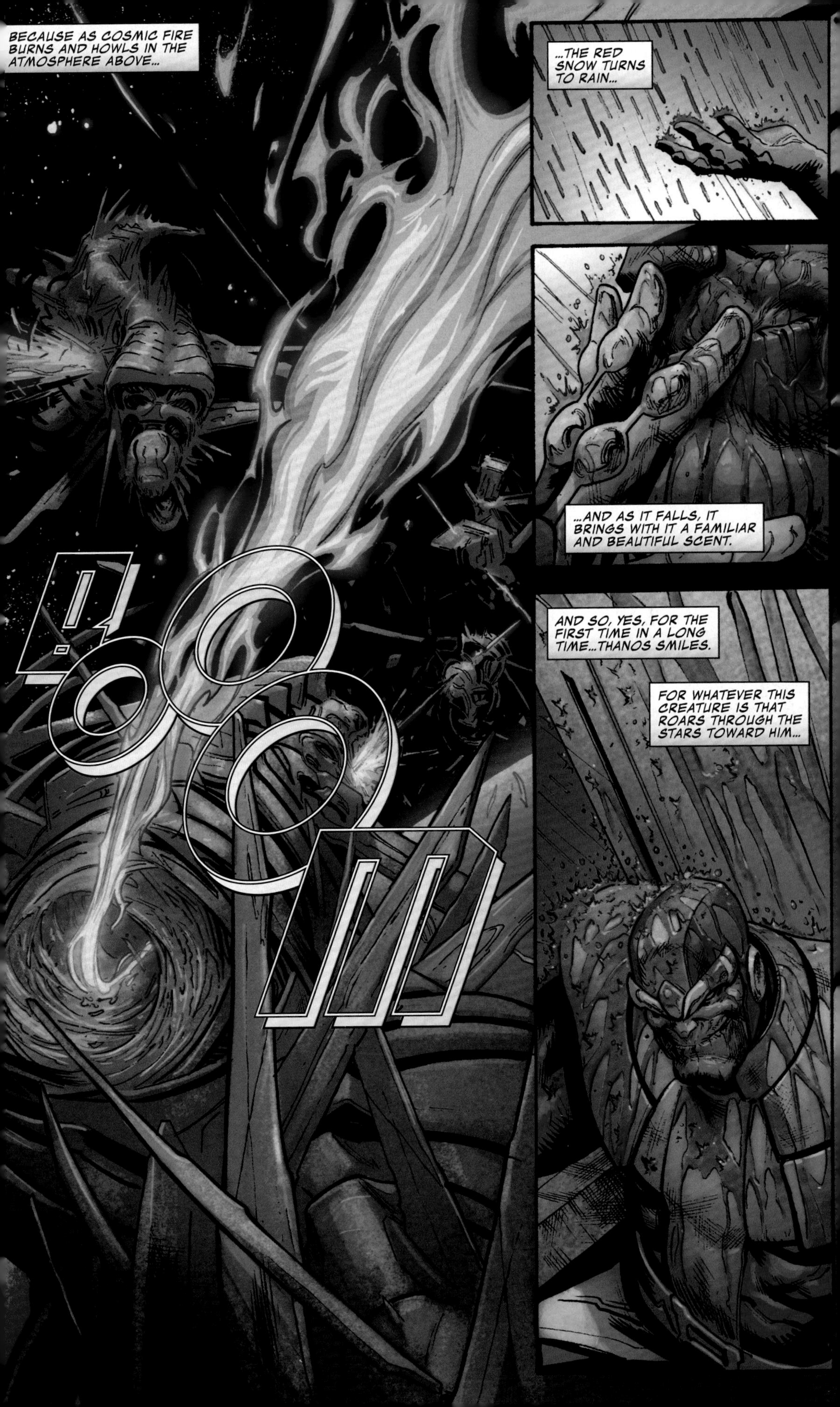
BECAUSE AS COSMIC FIRE BURNS AND HOWLS IN THE ATMOSPHERE ABOVE...
...THE RED SNOW TURNS TO RAIN...
...AND AS IT FALLS, IT BRINGS WITH IT A FAMILIAR AND BEAUTIFUL SCENT.
BOOOM
AND SO, YES, FOR THE FIRST TIME IN A LONG TIME...THANOS SMILES.
FOR WHATEVER THIS CREATURE IS THAT ROARS THROUGH THE STARS TOWARD HIM...

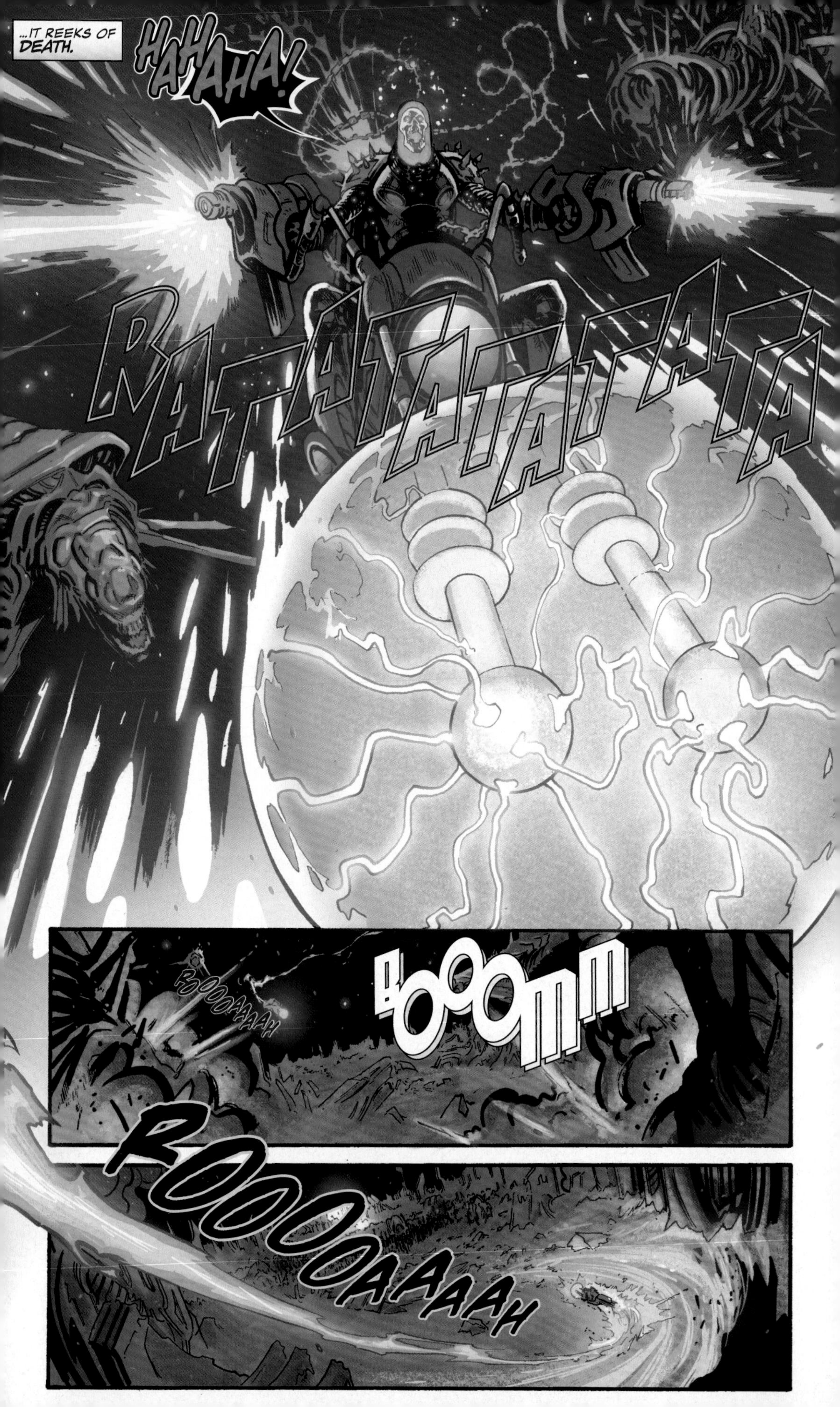
...IT REEKS OF DEATH.
HAHAHAHA!
RATATATATATA
ROOOAAAAH
BOOOMM
ROOOOAAAAAH

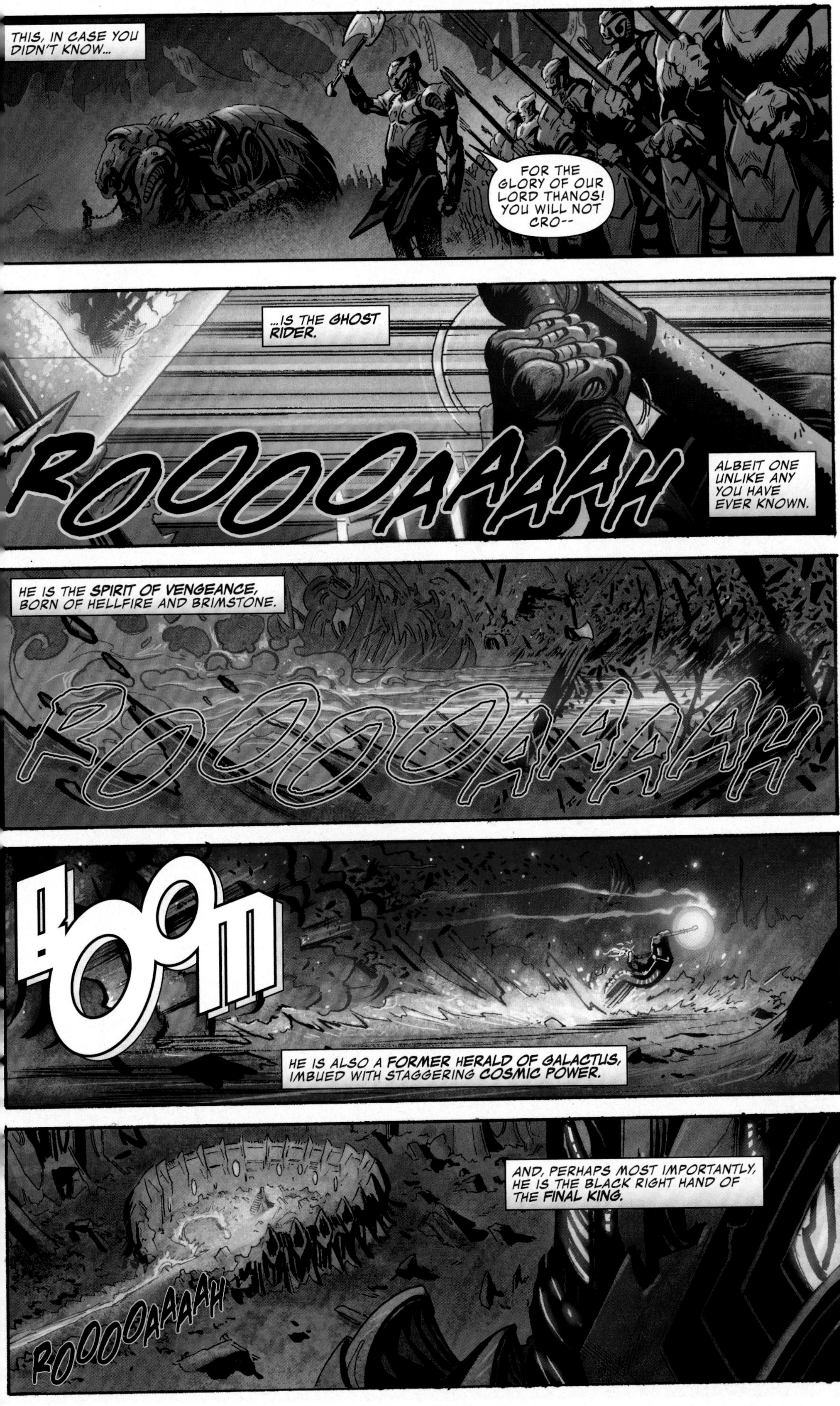
THIS, IN CASE YOU DIDN'T KNOW...
FOR THE GLORY OF OUR LORD THANOS! YOU WILL NOT CRO--
...IS THE GHOST RIDER.
ROOOOAAAAH
ALBEIT ONE UNLIKE ANY YOU HAVE EVER KNOWN.
HE IS THE SPIRIT OF VENGEANCE, BORN OF HELLFIRE AND BRIMSTONE.
ROOOOOAAAAAH
BOOM
HE IS ALSO A FORMER HERALD OF GALACTUS, IMBUED WITH STAGGERING COSMIC POWER.
AND, PERHAPS MOST IMPORTANTLY, HE IS THE BLACK RIGHT HAND OF THE FINAL KING.
ROOOOAAAAAH

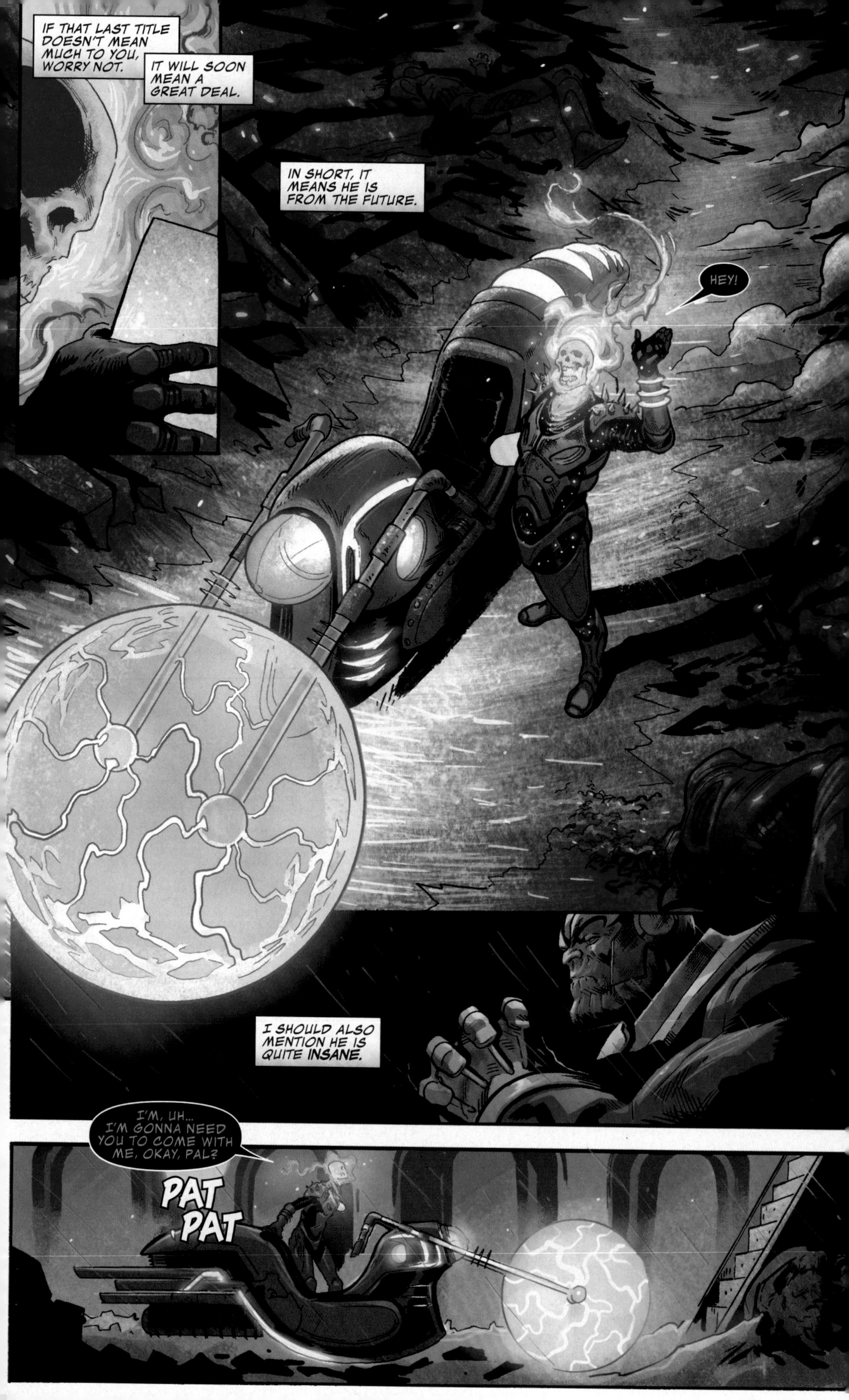
IF THAT LAST TITLE DOESN'T MEAN MUCH TO YOU, WORRY NOT.
IT WILL SOON MEAN A GREAT DEAL.
IN SHORT, IT MEANS HE IS FROM THE FUTURE.
HEY!
I SHOULD ALSO MENTION HE IS QUITE INSANE.
I'M, UH... I'M GONNA NEED YOU TO COME WITH ME, OKAY, PAL?
PAT PAT

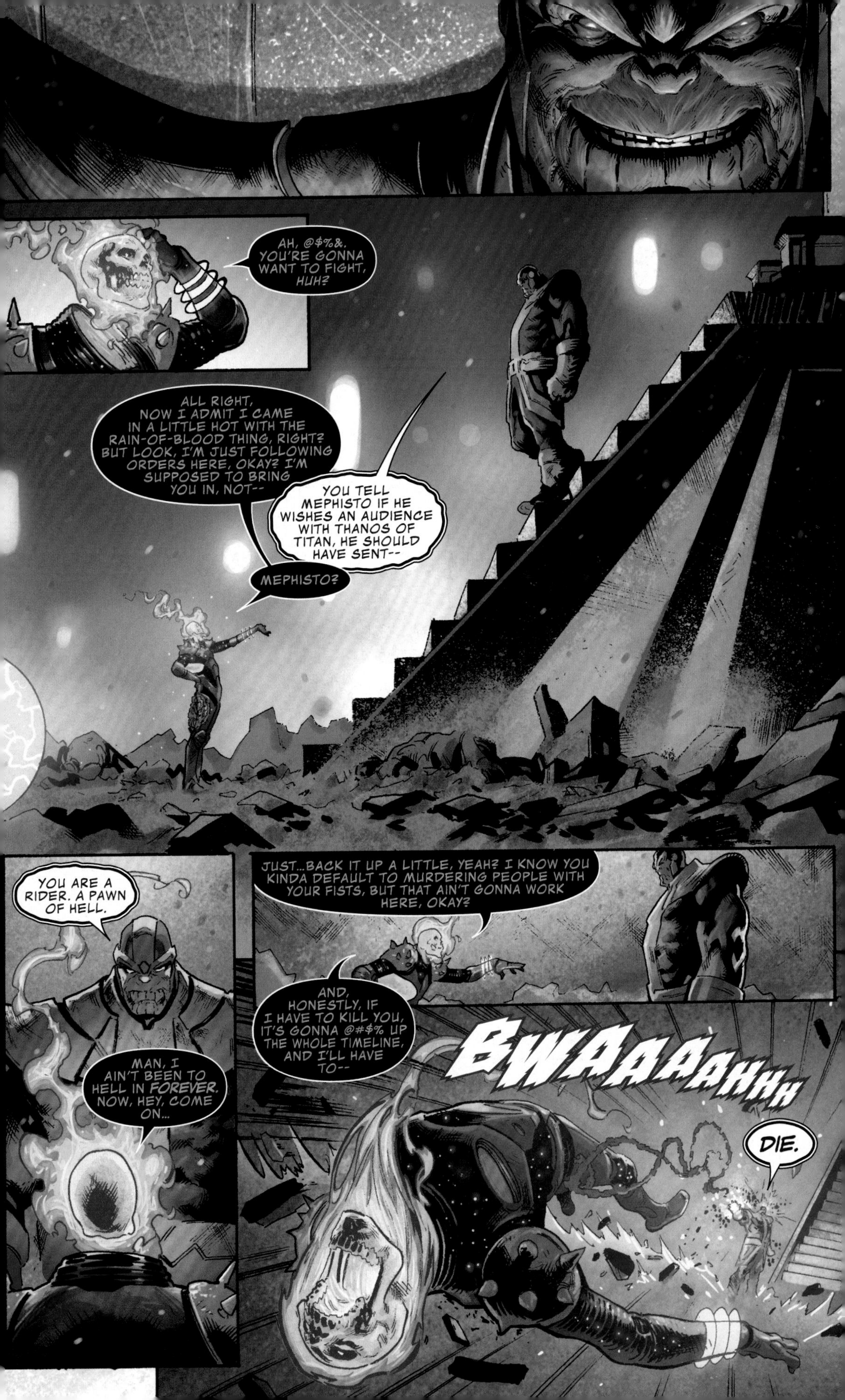

AH, @$%&. YOU'RE GONNA WANT TO FIGHT, HUH?
ALL RIGHT, NOW I ADMIT I CAME IN A LITTLE HOT WITH THE RAIN-OF-BLOOD THING, RIGHT? BUT LOOK, I'M JUST FOLLOWING ORDERS HERE, OKAY? I'M SUPPOSED TO BRING YOU IN, NOT--
YOU TELL MEPHISTO IF HE WISHES AN AUDIENCE WITH THANOS OF TITAN, HE SHOULD HAVE SENT--
MEPHISTO?
YOU ARE A RIDER. A PAWN OF HELL.
MAN, I AIN'T BEEN TO HELL IN *FOREVER*. NOW, HEY, COME ON...
JUST...BACK IT UP A LITTLE, YEAH? I KNOW YOU KINDA DEFAULT TO MURDERING PEOPLE WITH YOUR FISTS, BUT THAT AIN'T GONNA WORK HERE, OKAY?
AND, HONESTLY, IF I HAVE TO KILL YOU, IT'S GONNA @#$% UP THE WHOLE TIMELINE, AND I'LL HAVE TO--
BWAAAAAHHH
DIE.

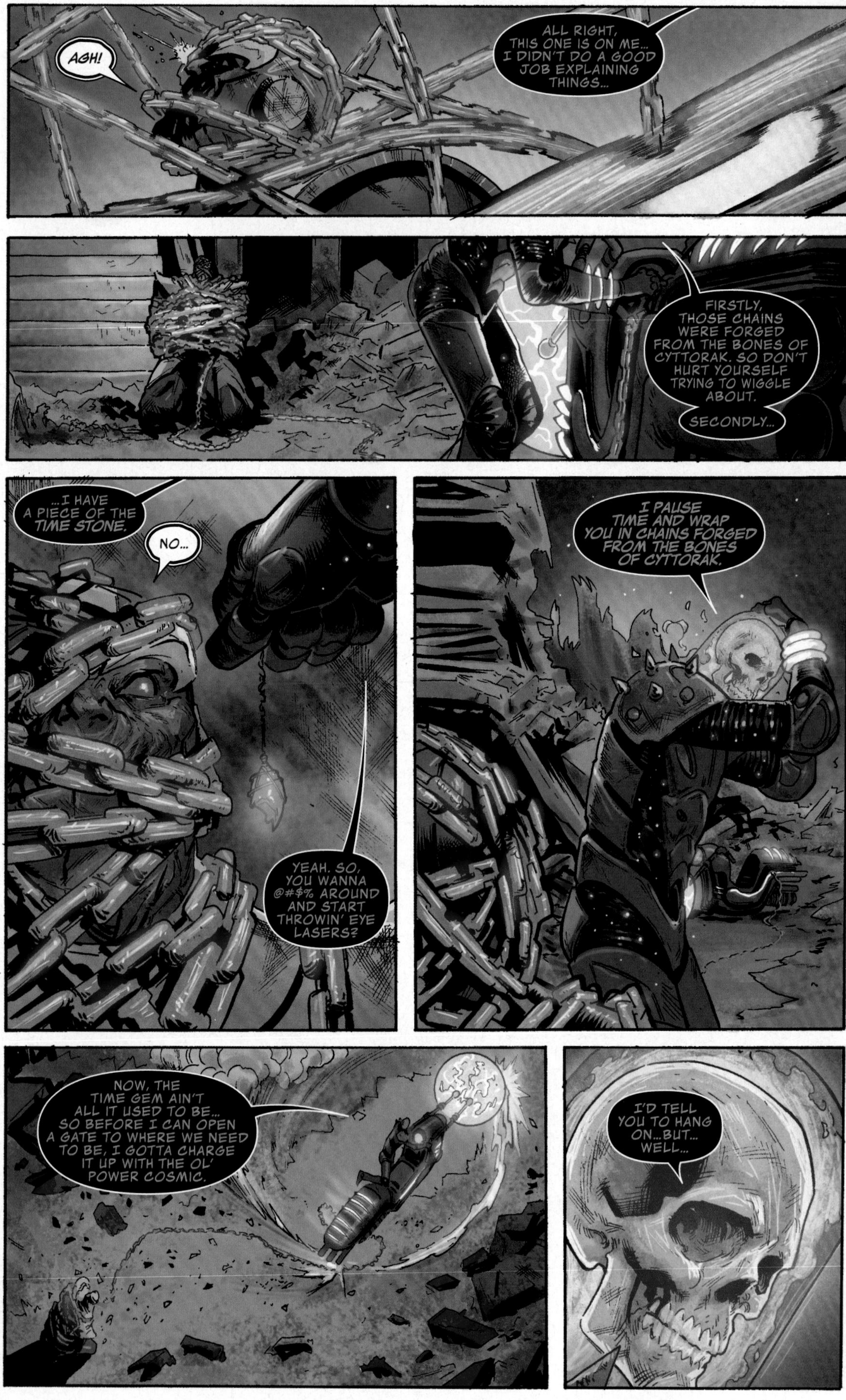
AGH!
ALL RIGHT, THIS ONE IS ON ME... I DIDN'T DO A GOOD JOB EXPLAINING THINGS...
FIRSTLY, THOSE CHAINS WERE FORGED FROM THE BONES OF CYTTORAK. SO DON'T HURT YOURSELF TRYING TO WIGGLE ABOUT.
SECONDLY...
...I HAVE A PIECE OF THE TIME STONE.
NO...
YEAH. SO, YOU WANNA @#$% AROUND AND START THROWIN' EYE LASERS?
I PAUSE TIME AND WRAP YOU IN CHAINS FORGED FROM THE BONES OF CYTTORAK.
NOW, THE TIME GEM AIN'T ALL IT USED TO BE... SO BEFORE I CAN OPEN A GATE TO WHERE WE NEED TO BE, I GOTTA CHARGE IT UP WITH THE OL' POWER COSMIC.
I'D TELL YOU TO HANG ON...BUT... WELL...

OH, THANK GOD.

THE GHOST RIDER IS, AND HAS BEEN, MANY THINGS. IN FACT, WHEN HE WAS STILL ALIVE, YOU MAY HAVE EVEN KNOWN HIM BY ANOTHER NAME.

BUT IT IS IMPORTANT TO NOTE THAT HE IS NOT, IN FACT, A LIAR...

...BECAUSE AS HIS COSMIC ENGINES ROAR TO LIFE...THE INFINITY STONE IN HIS SKELETAL FIST BEGINS TO GLOW ONCE MORE...

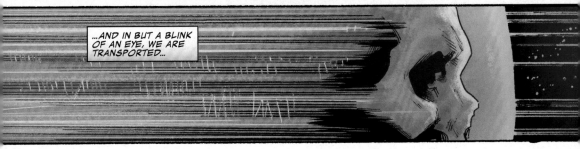

...AND IN BUT A BLINK OF AN EYE, WE ARE TRANSPORTED...

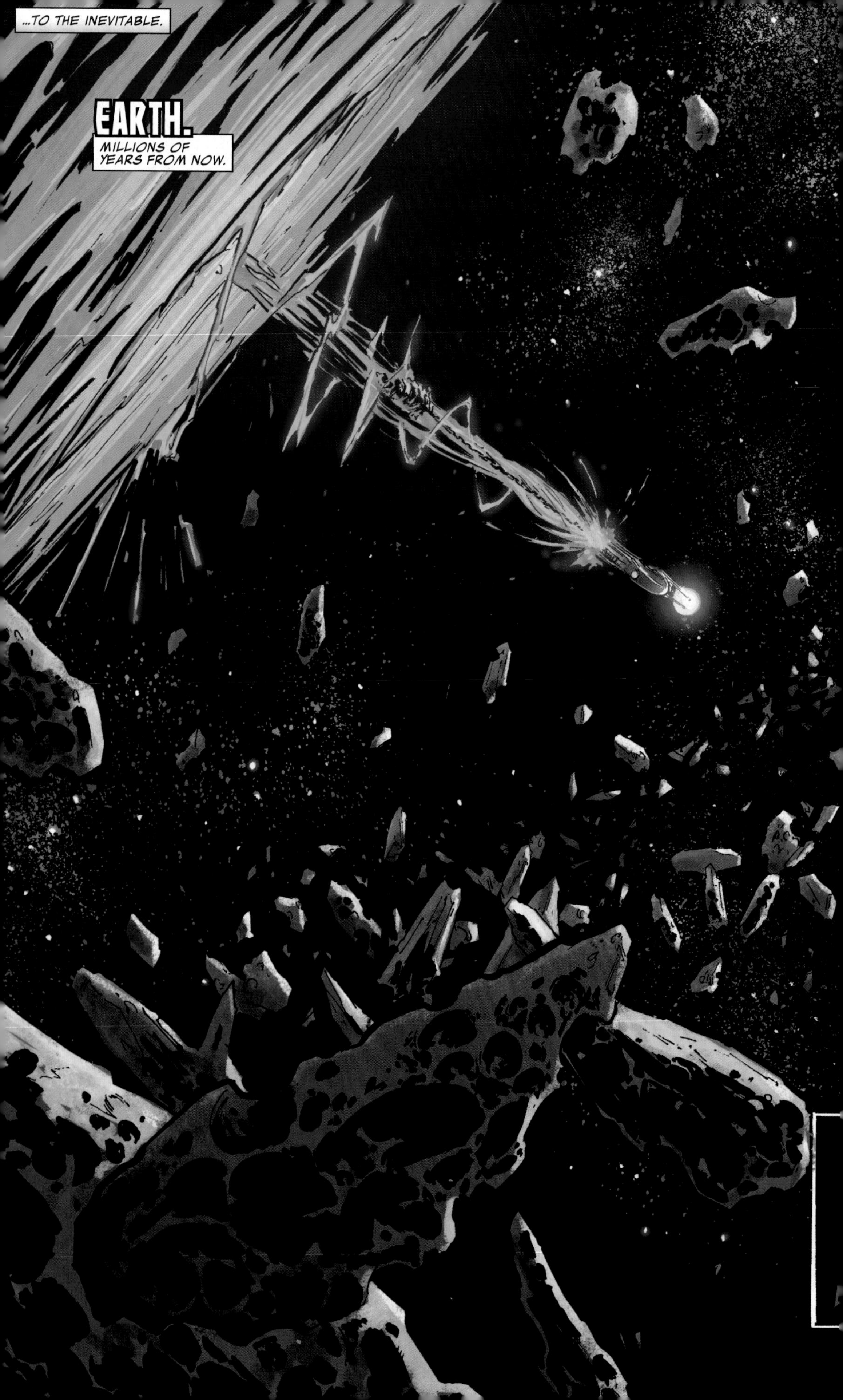
...TO THE INEVITABLE.
EARTH.
MILLIONS OF YEARS FROM NOW.

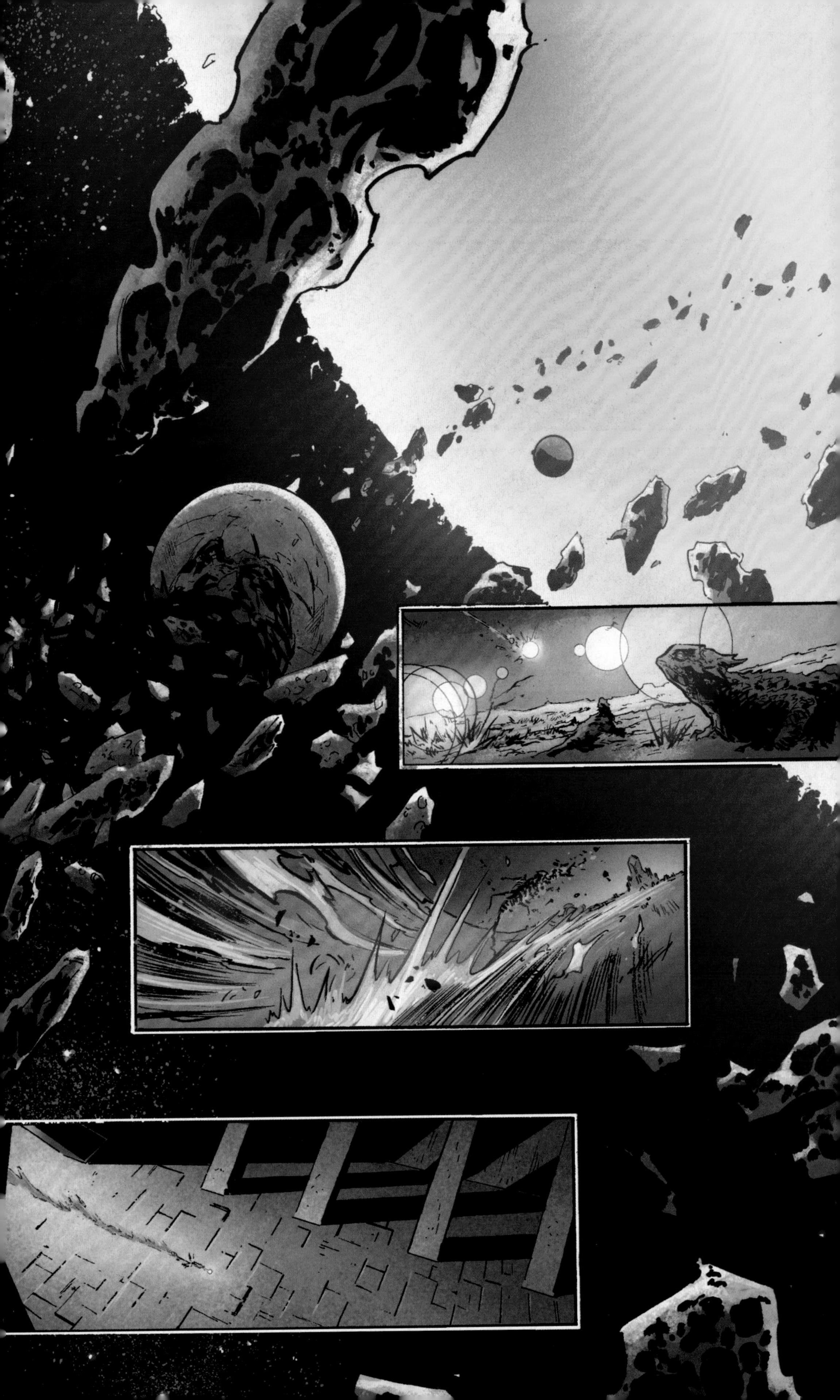

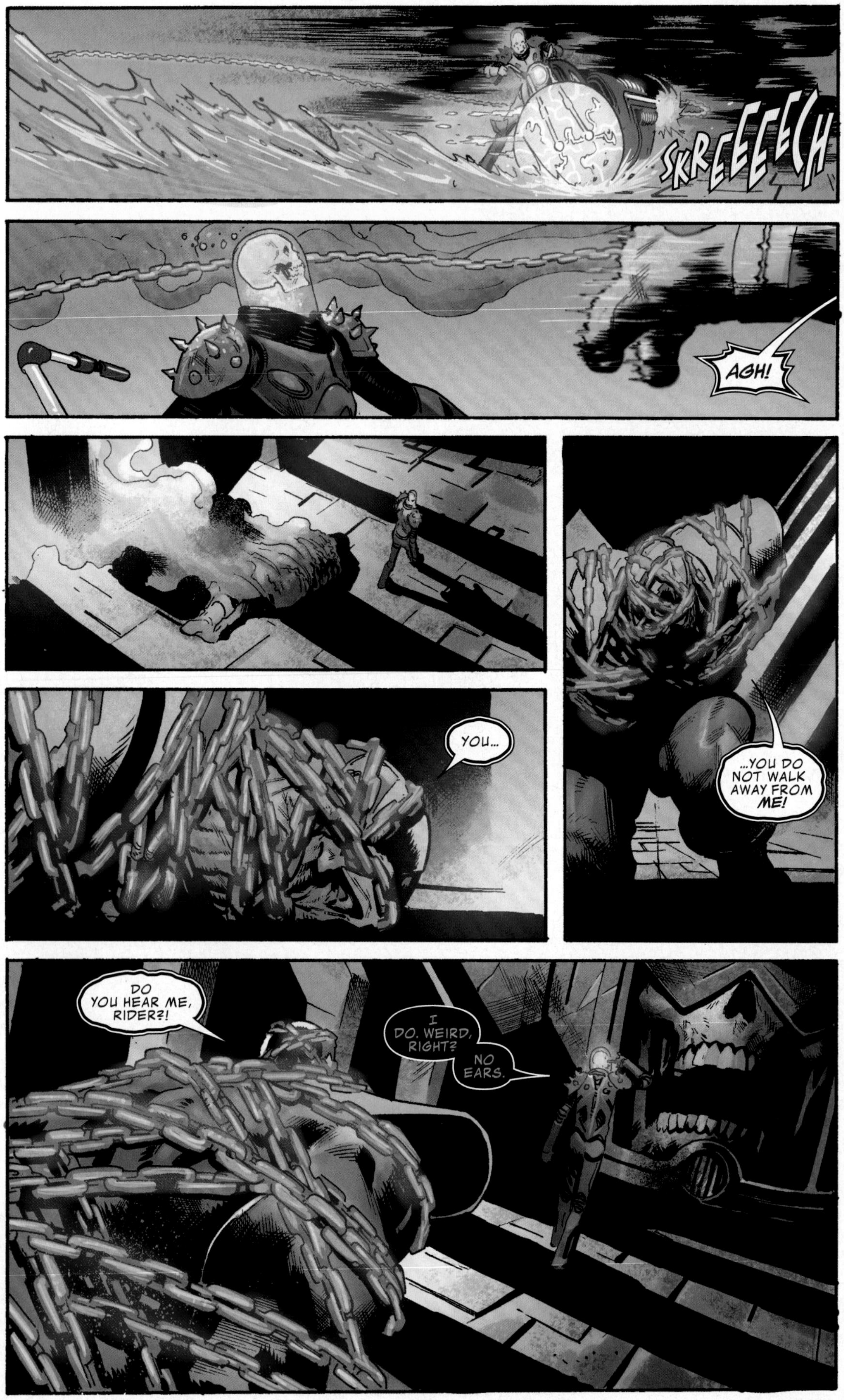
SKREEEECH
AGH!
YOU...
...YOU DO NOT WALK AWAY FROM ME!
DO YOU HEAR ME, RIDER?!
I DO. WEIRD, RIGHT?
NO EARS.

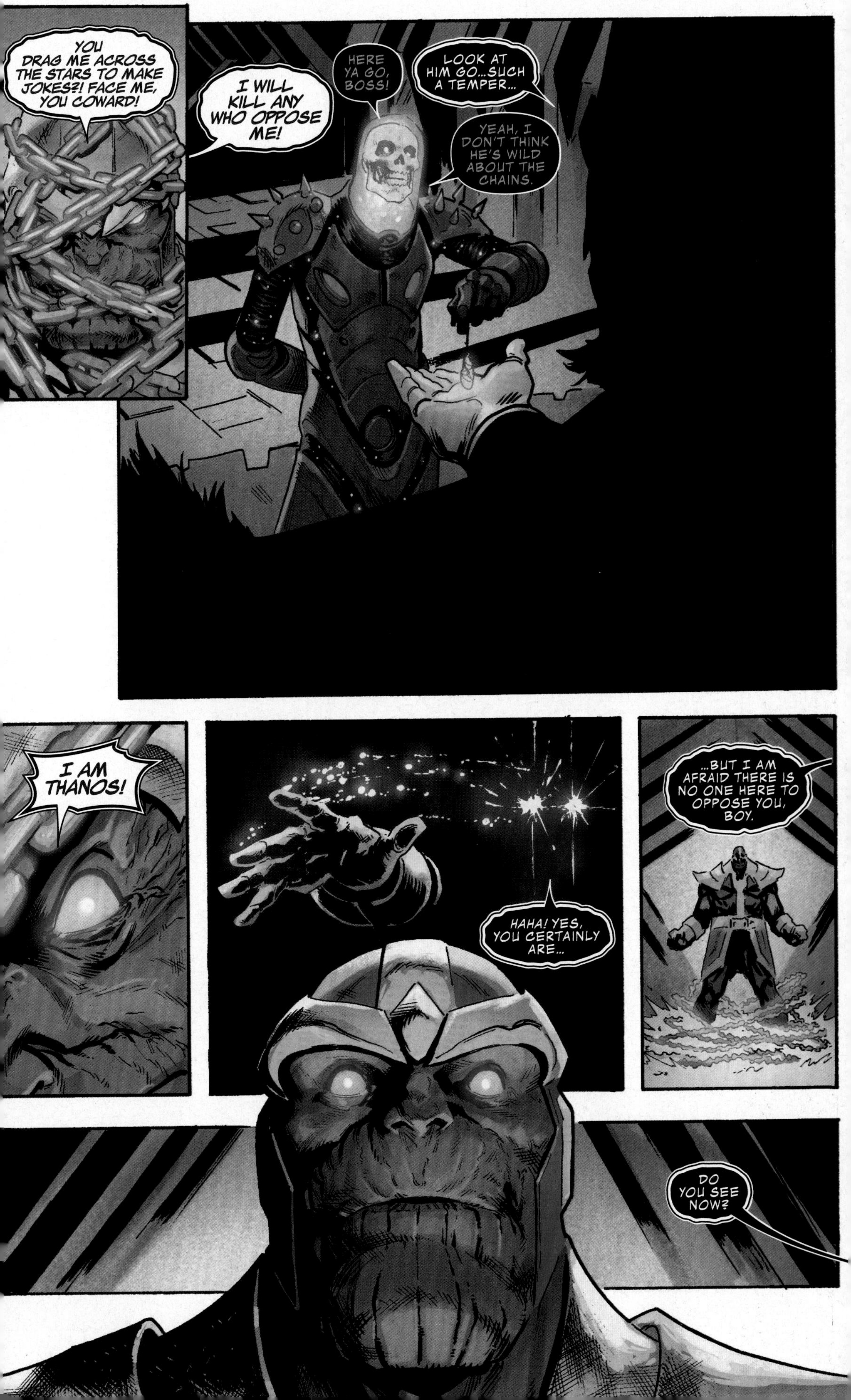
YOU DRAG ME ACROSS THE STARS TO MAKE JOKES?! FACE ME, YOU COWARD!
I WILL KILL ANY WHO OPPOSE ME!
HERE YA GO, BOSS!
LOOK AT HIM GO...SUCH A TEMPER...
YEAH, I DON'T THINK HE'S WILD ABOUT THE CHAINS.
I AM THANOS!
HAHA! YES, YOU CERTAINLY ARE...
...BUT I AM AFRAID THERE IS NO ONE HERE TO OPPOSE YOU, BOY.
DO YOU SEE NOW?

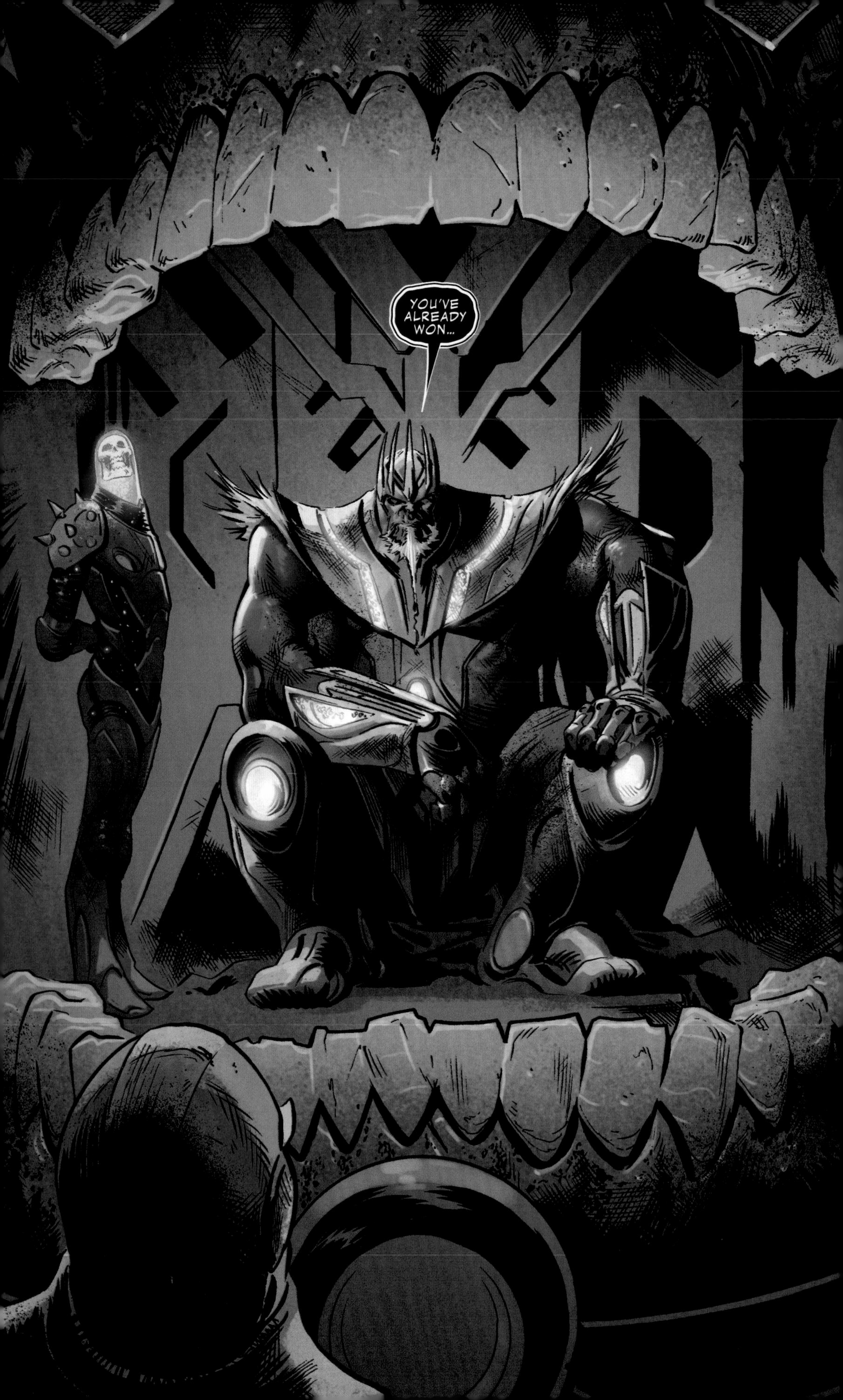
YOU'VE ALREADY WON...

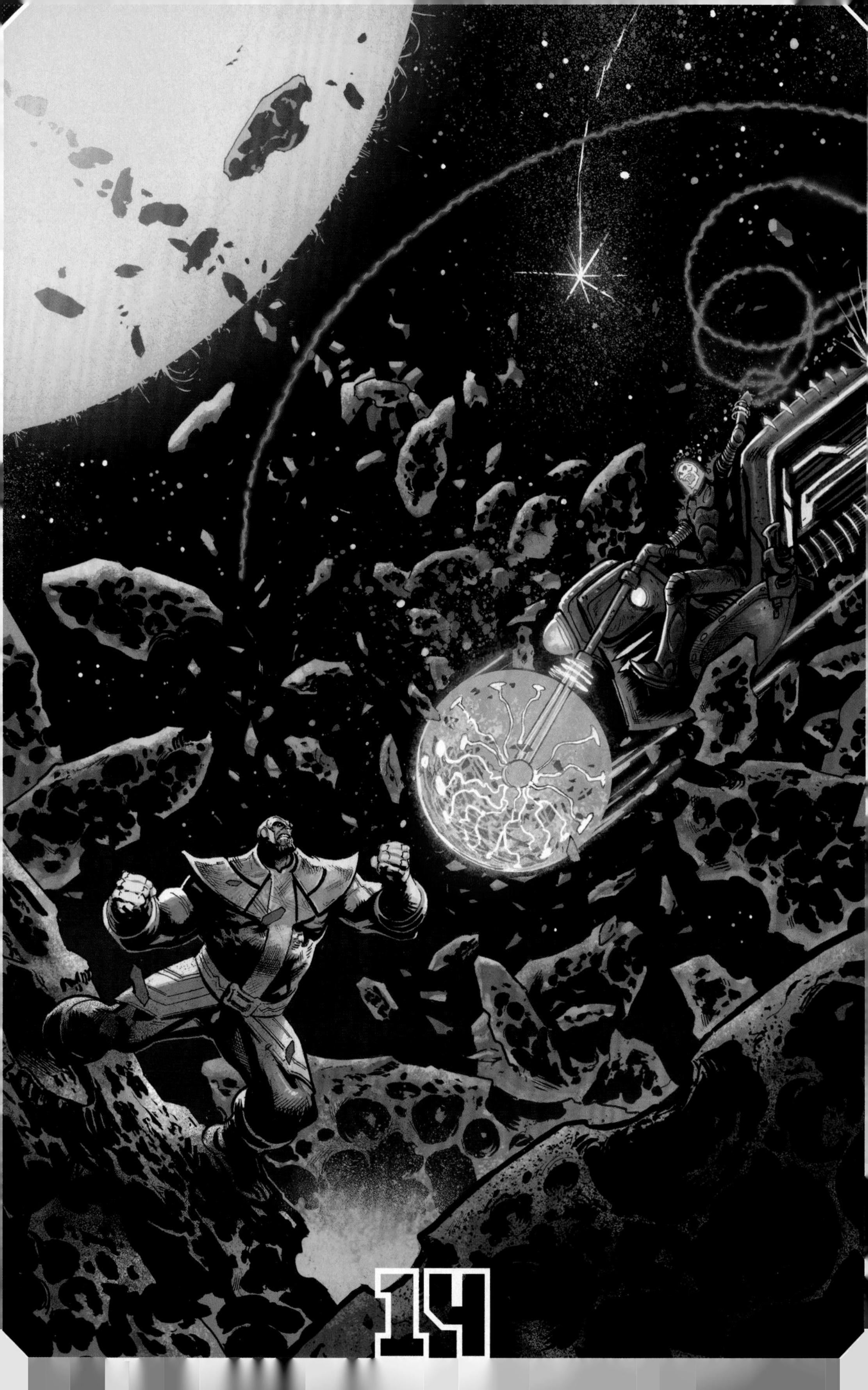
14

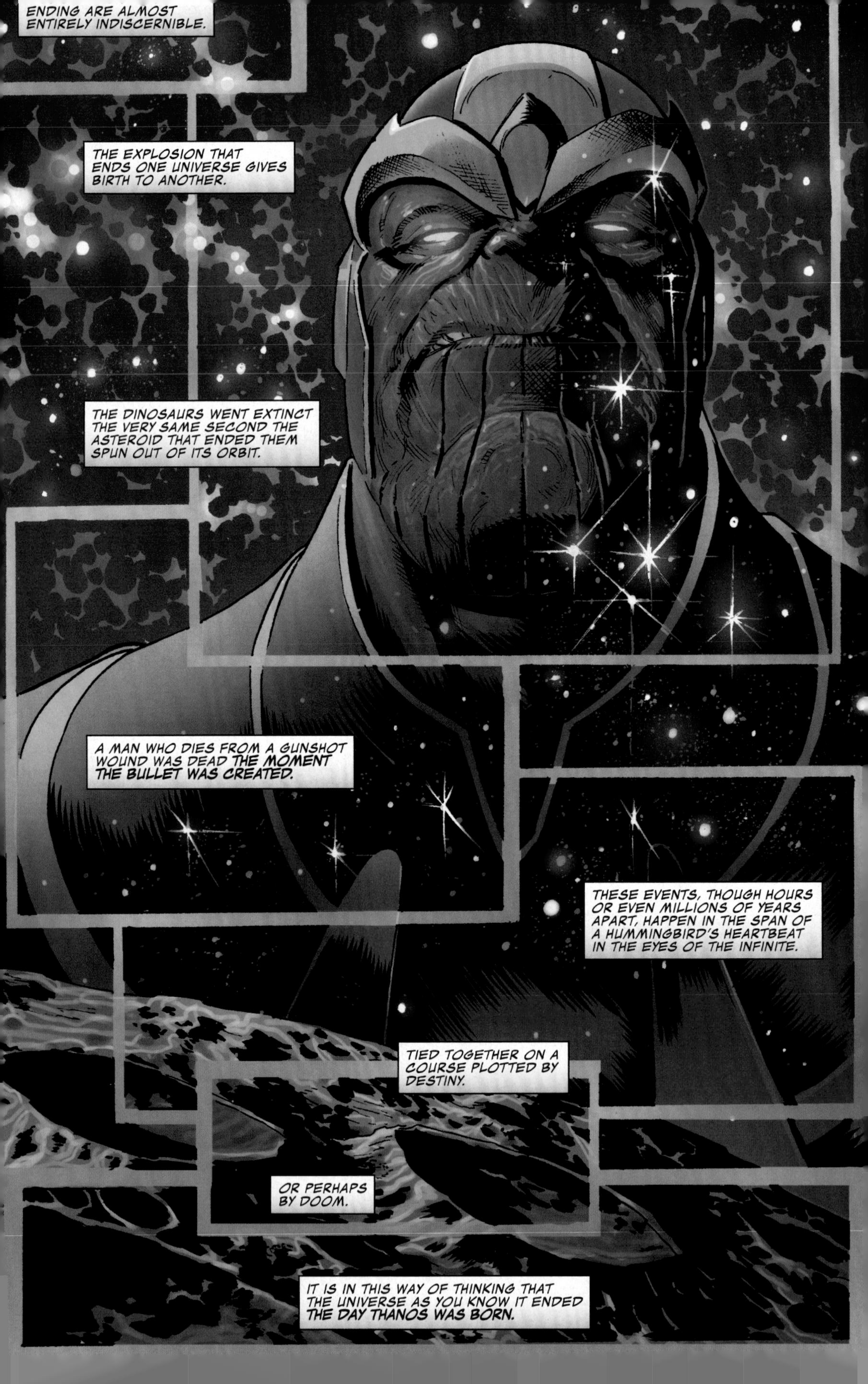

ENDING ARE ALMOST ENTIRELY INDISCERNIBLE.
THE EXPLOSION THAT ENDS ONE UNIVERSE GIVES BIRTH TO ANOTHER.
THE DINOSAURS WENT EXTINCT THE VERY SAME SECOND THE ASTEROID THAT ENDED THEM SPUN OUT OF ITS ORBIT.
A MAN WHO DIES FROM A GUNSHOT WOUND WAS DEAD THE MOMENT THE BULLET WAS CREATED.
THESE EVENTS, THOUGH HOURS OR EVEN MILLIONS OF YEARS APART, HAPPEN IN THE SPAN OF A HUMMINGBIRD'S HEARTBEAT IN THE EYES OF THE INFINITE.
TIED TOGETHER ON A COURSE PLOTTED BY DESTINY.
OR PERHAPS BY DOOM.
IT IS IN THIS WAY OF THINKING THAT THE UNIVERSE AS YOU KNOW IT ENDED THE DAY THANOS WAS BORN.

THE END OF ALL THINGS OCCURRED ON A WEDNESDAY SOME FORGOTTEN CENTURIES AGO ON A SMALL MOON OF SATURN CALLED TITAN.

AGGGHHH!

THANOS WAS BORN TO A RACE OF ETERNALS. BUT FOR SOME UNTOLD REASON, HE ARRIVED...DIFFERENT.

THEY CALLED HIM A MUTANT. A DEVIANT.

THEY SAY HIS MOTHER, SUI-SAN WAS HER NAME, WENT INSANE THE MOMENT SHE LAID HER EYES ON HIM...BUT THIS IS NOT ENTIRELY TRUE...

SHE LOST HER MIND WHEN SHE FIRST SPOKE HIS NAME.

...THANOS...

THANOS WAS NOT THE NAME SHE HAD PLANNED ON GIVING THE CHILD. YET WHEN SHE LOOKED INTO HIS PITCH-BLACK EYES...SHE SPOKE IT AT ONCE.

SHE HAD NEVER HEARD THE NAME BEFORE.

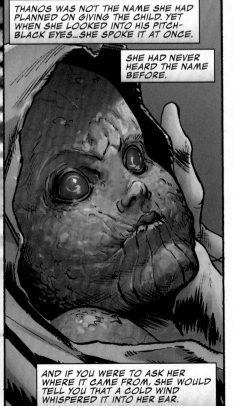

AND IF YOU WERE TO ASK HER WHERE IT CAME FROM, SHE WOULD TELL YOU THAT A COLD WIND WHISPERED IT INTO HER EAR.

SHE WOULD ALSO TELL YOU THAT GOING MAD IS A PERFECTLY REASONABLE REACTION TO STARING INTO THE EYES OF A UNIVERSAL CONSTANT.

YOU WOULD GO MAD TOO IF YOU GAVE BIRTH TO A GOD.

ANYWAY, THANOS KILLED HER WHEN HE WAS TWELVE.

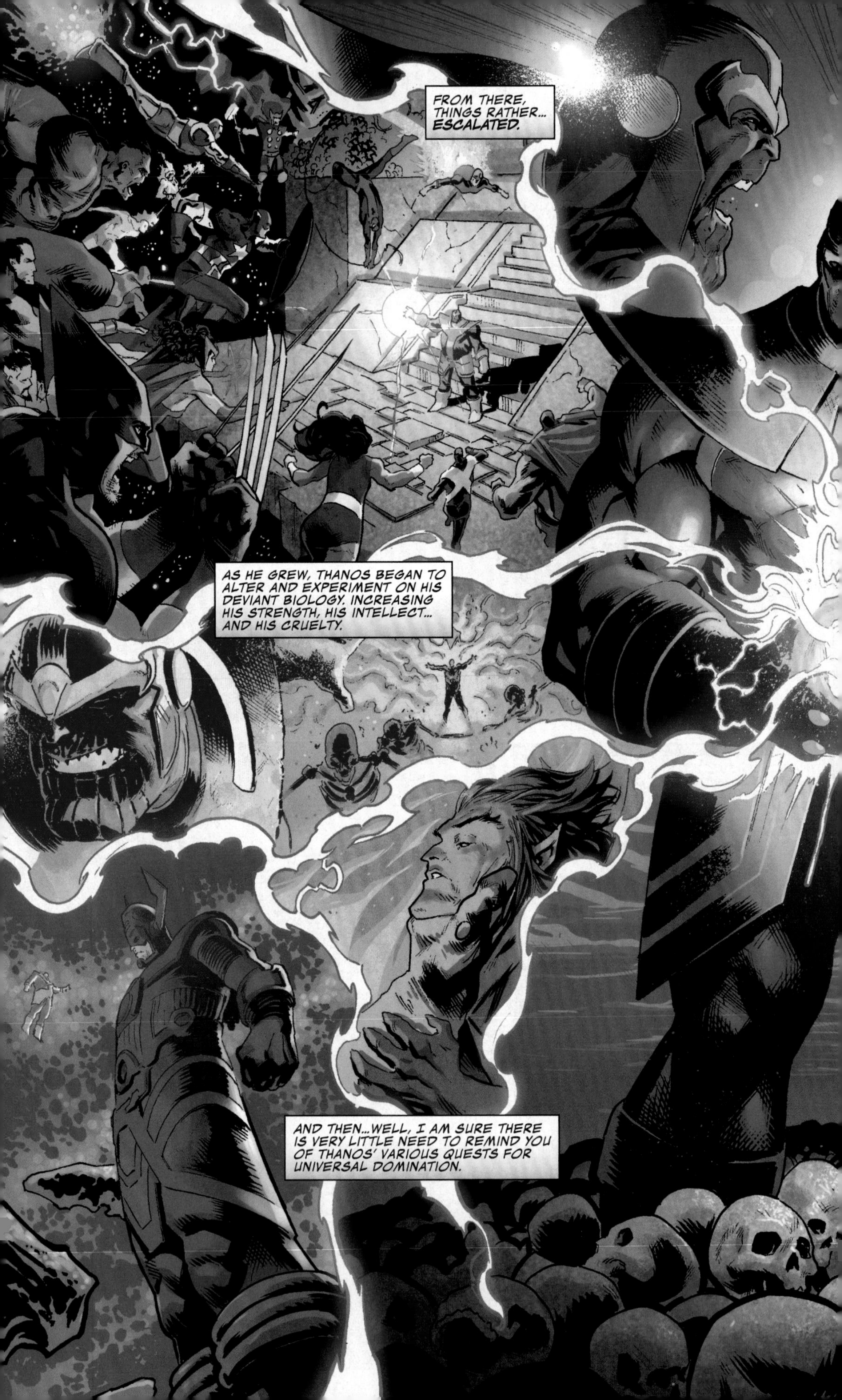
FROM THERE, THINGS RATHER... ESCALATED.
AS HE GREW, THANOS BEGAN TO ALTER AND EXPERIMENT ON HIS DEVIANT BIOLOGY, INCREASING HIS STRENGTH, HIS INTELLECT... AND HIS CRUELTY.
AND THEN...WELL, I AM SURE THERE IS VERY LITTLE NEED TO REMIND YOU OF THANOS' VARIOUS QUESTS FOR UNIVERSAL DOMINATION.

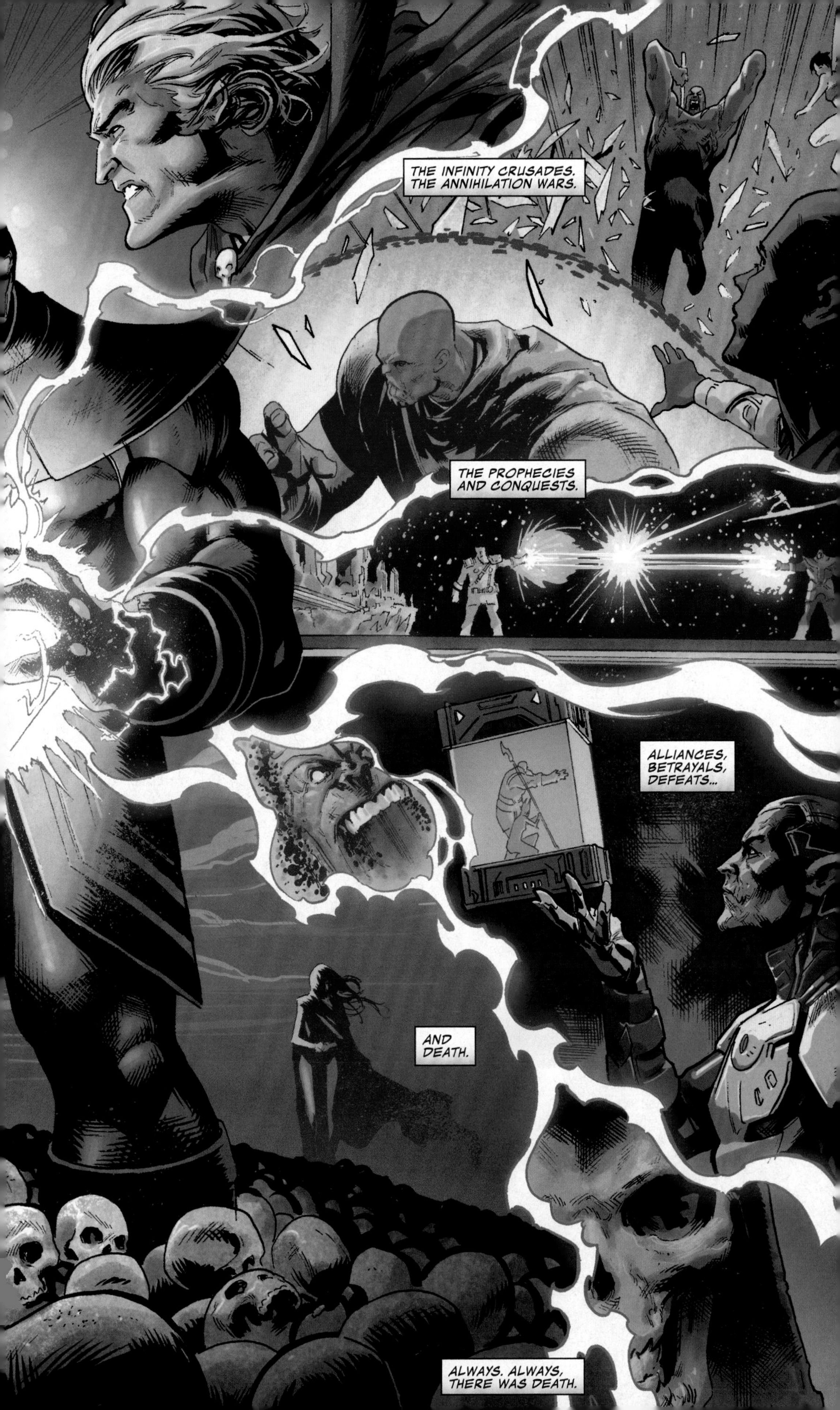
THE INFINITY CRUSADES. THE ANNIHILATION WARS.
THE PROPHECIES AND CONQUESTS.
ALLIANCES, BETRAYALS, DEFEATS...
AND DEATH.
ALWAYS. ALWAYS, THERE WAS DEATH.

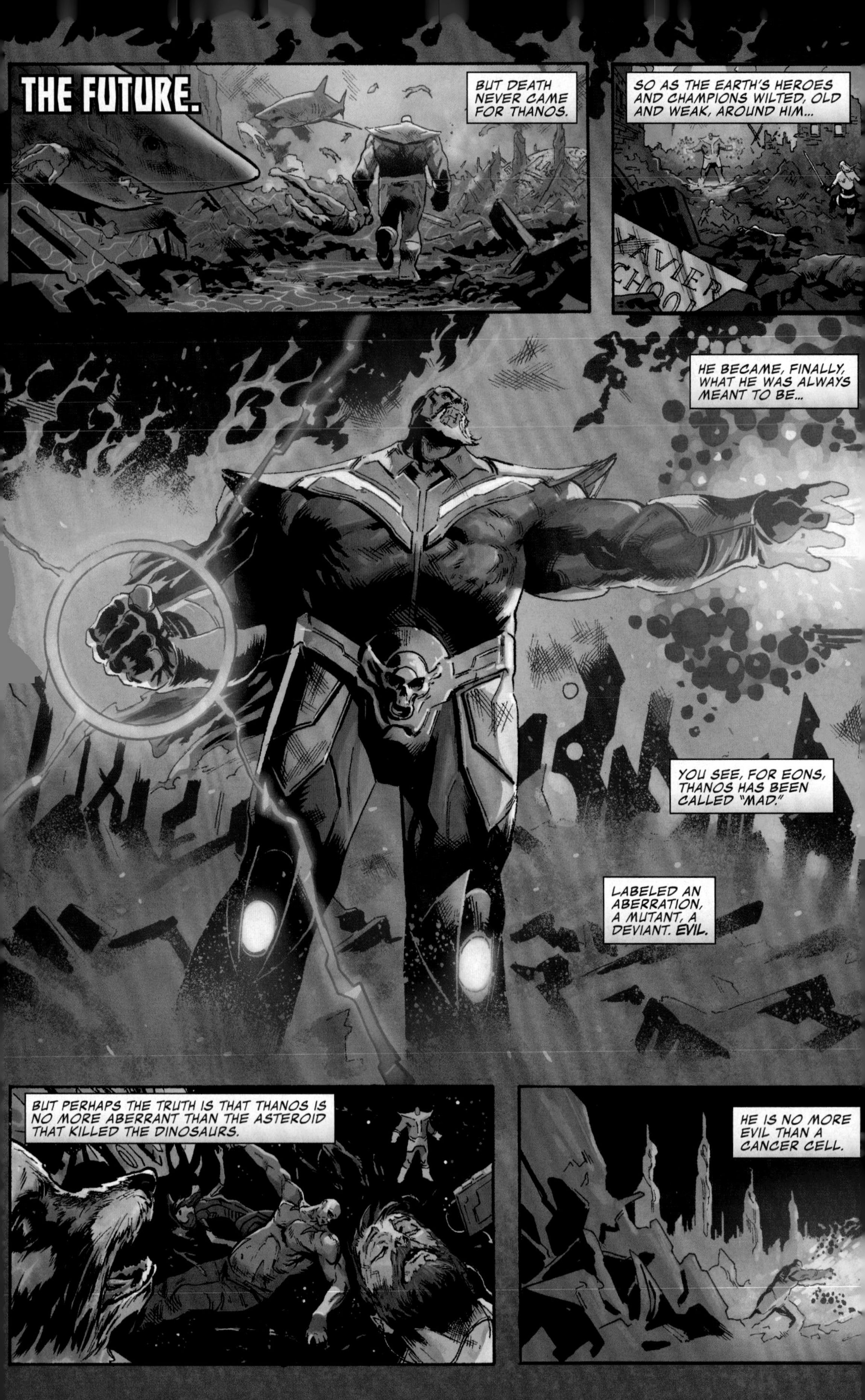
THE FUTURE.
BUT DEATH NEVER CAME FOR THANOS.
SO AS THE EARTH'S HEROES AND CHAMPIONS WILTED, OLD AND WEAK, AROUND HIM...
HE BECAME, FINALLY, WHAT HE WAS ALWAYS MEANT TO BE...
YOU SEE, FOR EONS, THANOS HAS BEEN CALLED "MAD."
LABELED AN ABERRATION, A MUTANT, A DEVIANT. EVIL.
BUT PERHAPS THE TRUTH IS THAT THANOS IS NO MORE ABERRANT THAN THE ASTEROID THAT KILLED THE DINOSAURS.
HE IS NO MORE EVIL THAN A CANCER CELL.

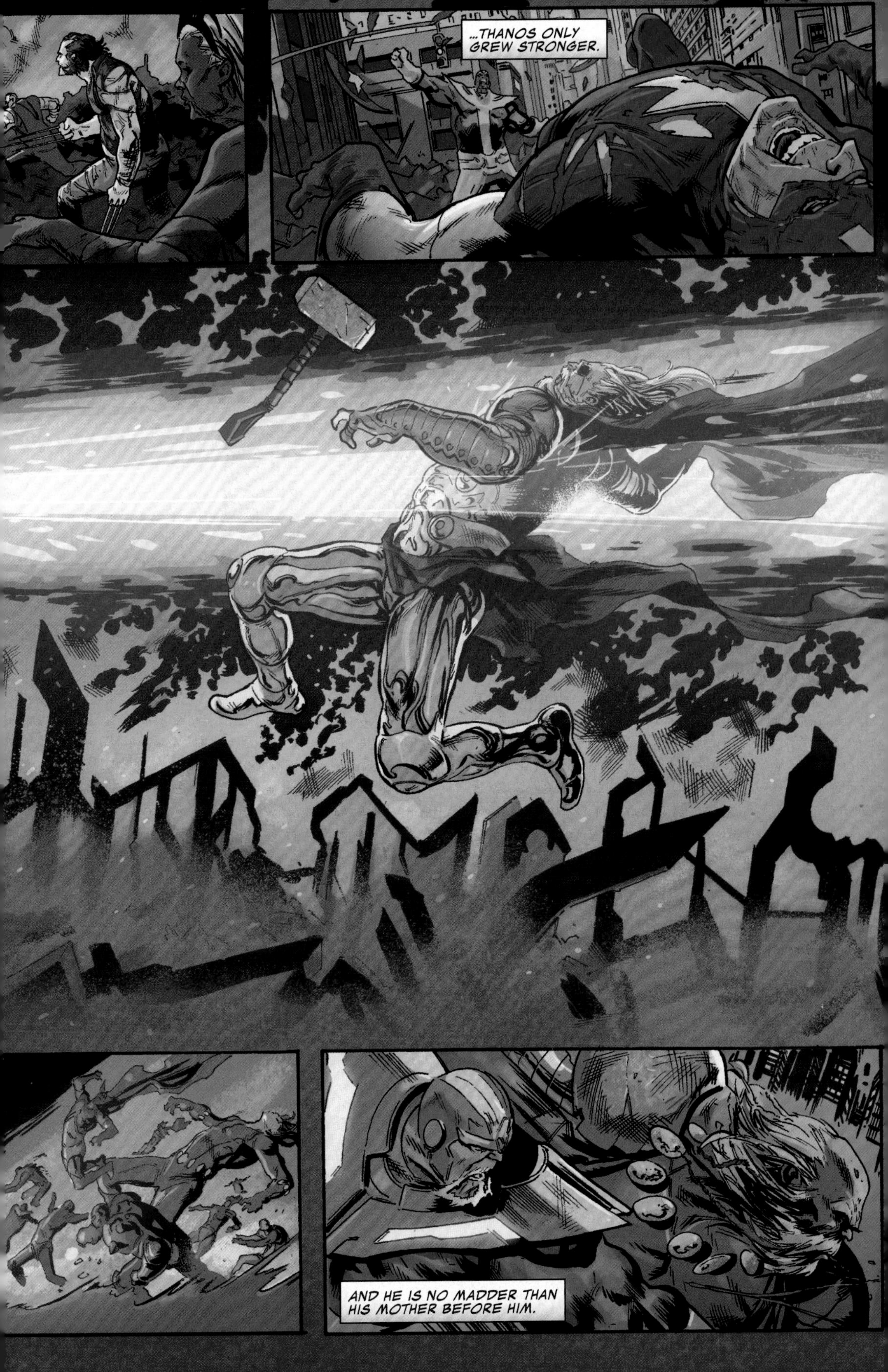
...THANOS ONLY GROW STRONGER.
AND HE IS NO MADDER THAN HIS MOTHER BEFORE HIM.

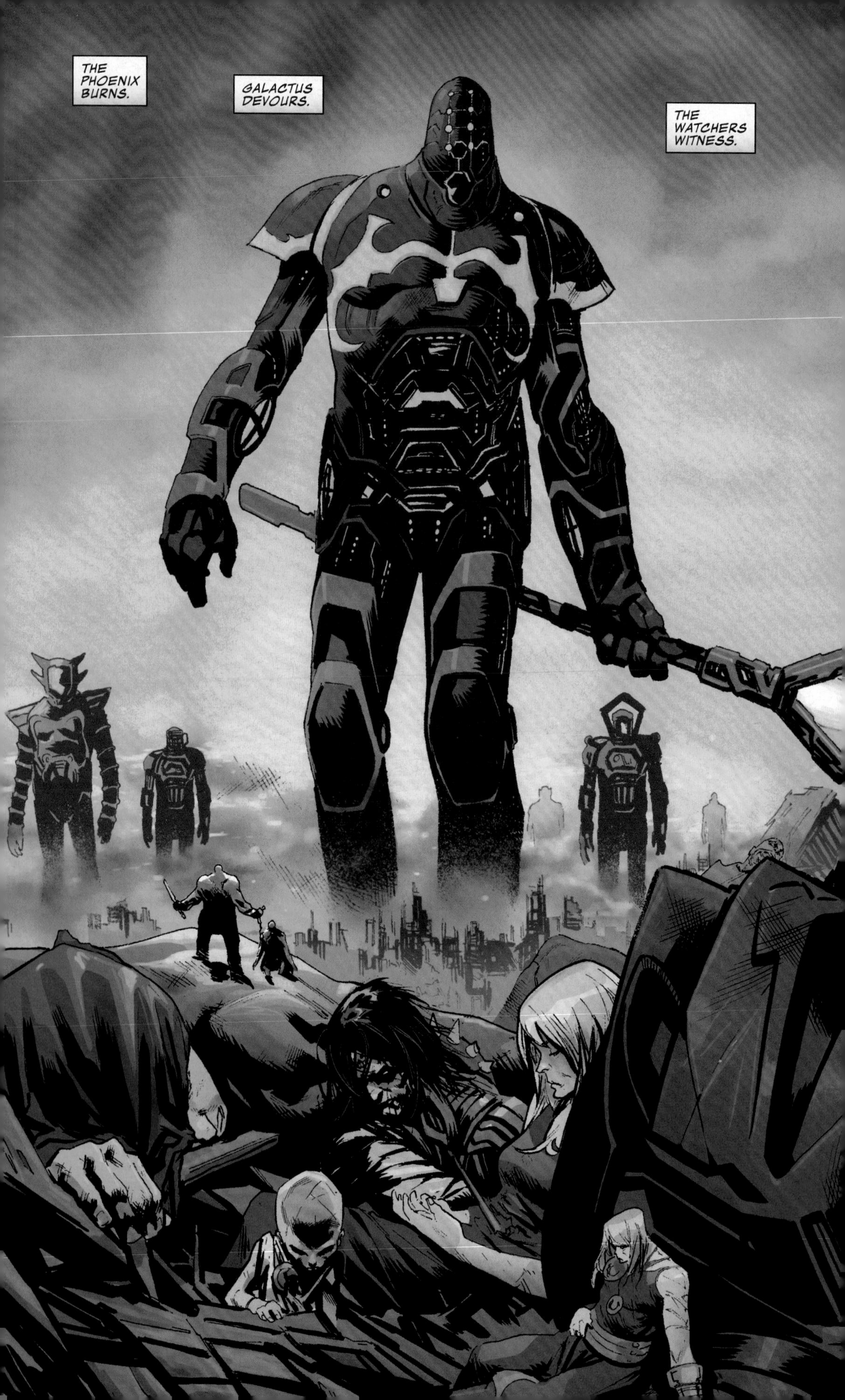
THE PHOENIX BURNS.
GALACTUS DEVOURS.
THE WATCHERS WITNESS.

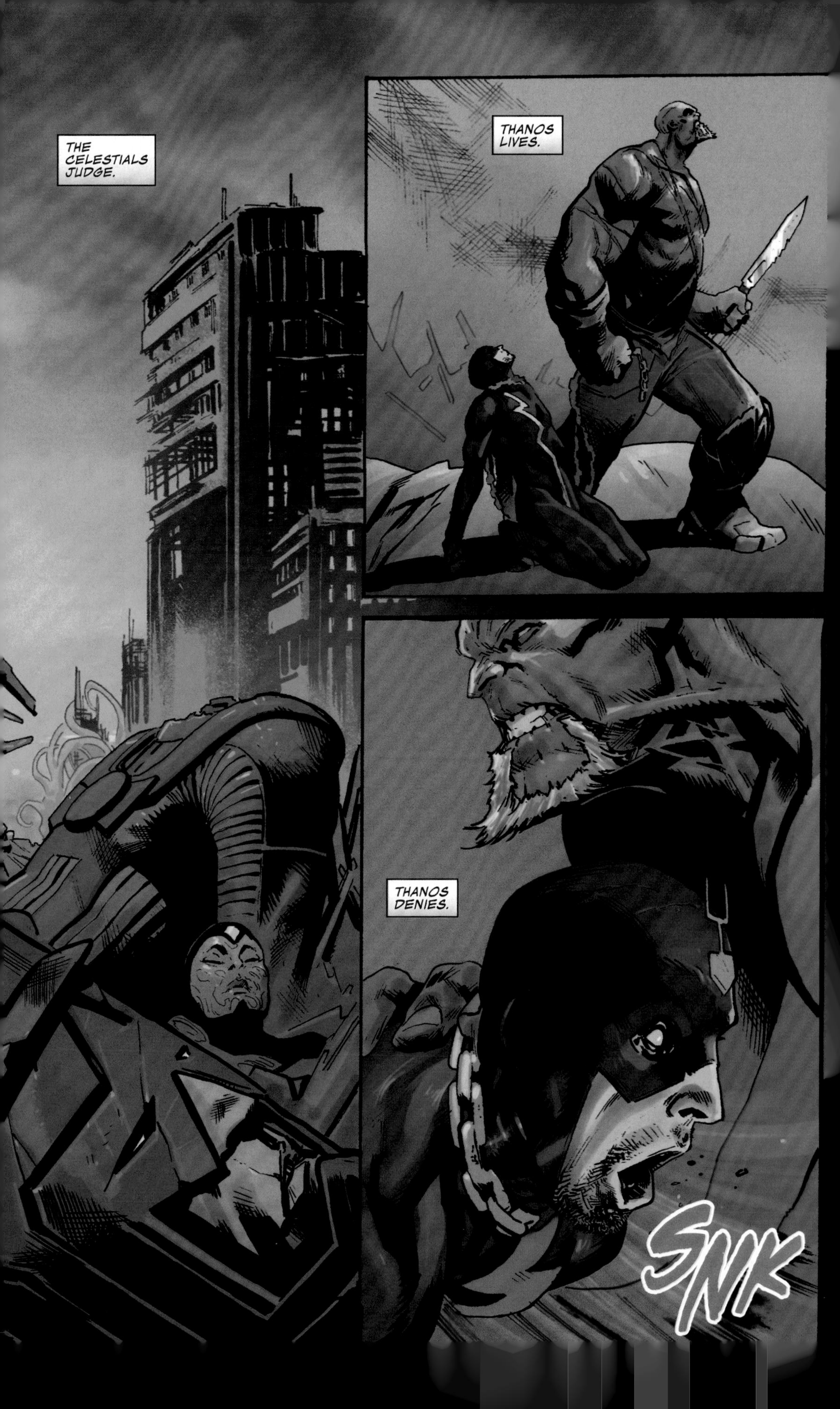
THE CELESTIALS JUDGE.
THANOS LIVES.
THANOS DENIES.
SNK

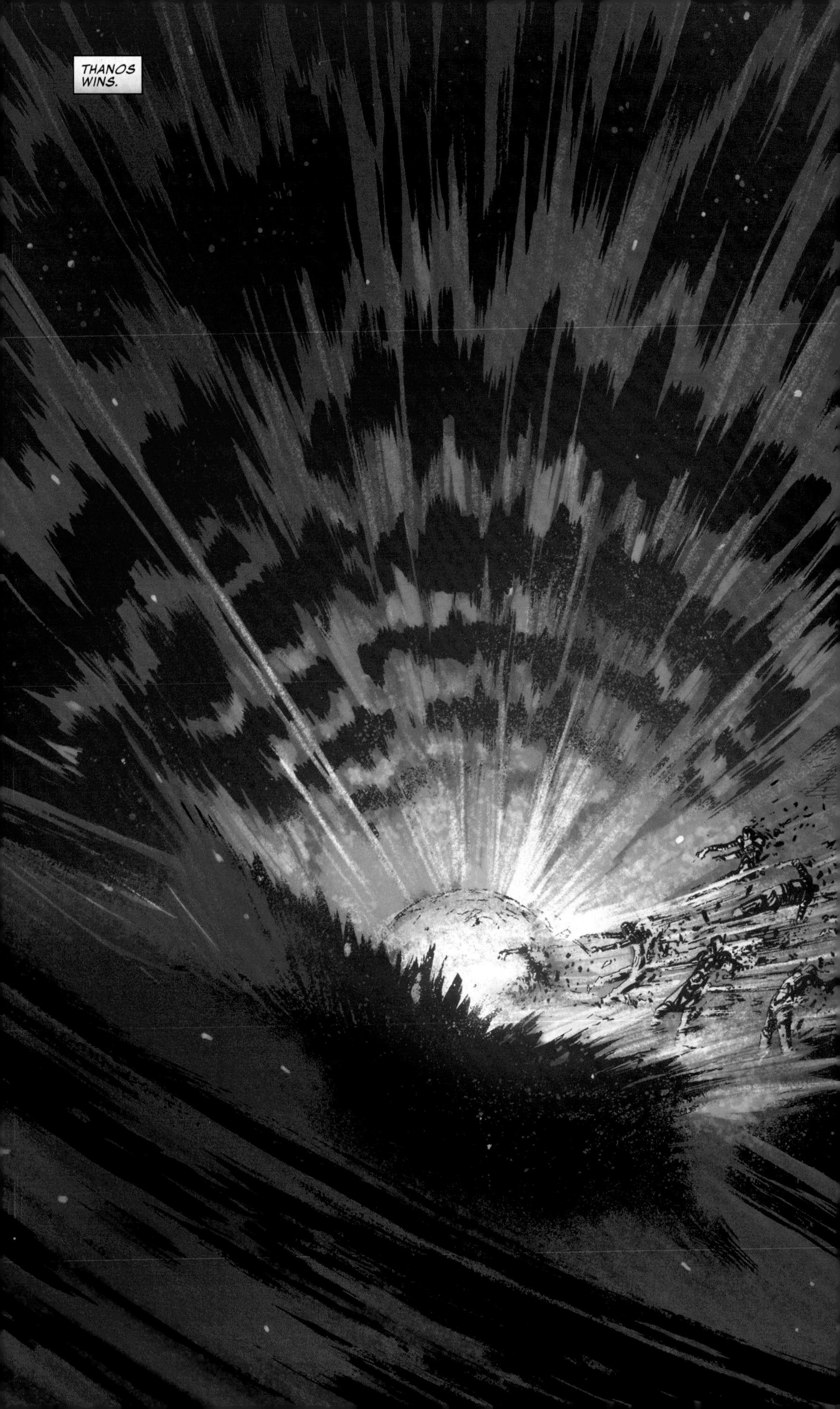
THANOS WINS.

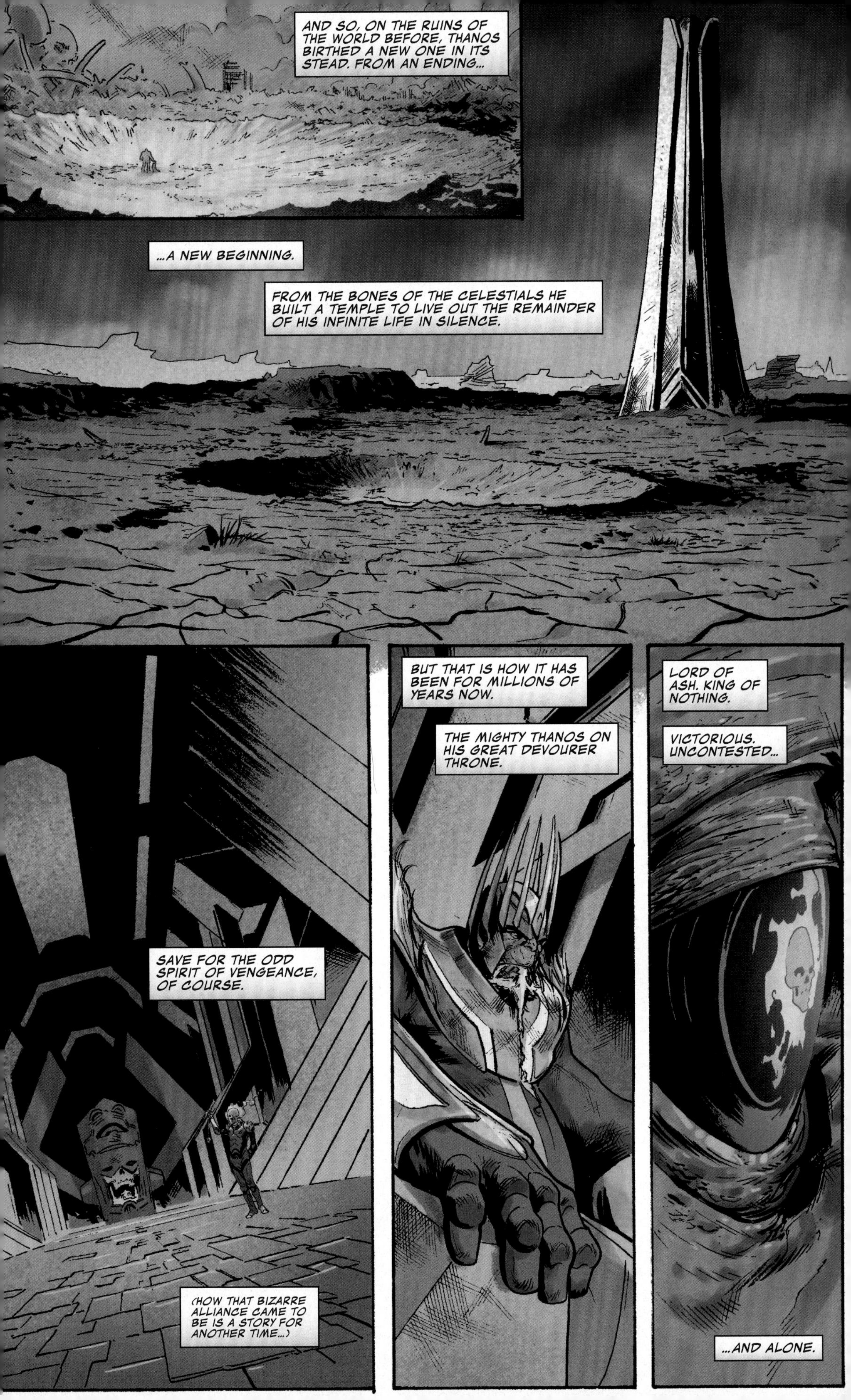
AND SO, ON THE RUINS OF THE WORLD BEFORE, THANOS BIRTHED A NEW ONE IN ITS STEAD. FROM AN ENDING...
...A NEW BEGINNING.
FROM THE BONES OF THE CELESTIALS HE BUILT A TEMPLE TO LIVE OUT THE REMAINDER OF HIS INFINITE LIFE IN SILENCE.
SAVE FOR THE ODD SPIRIT OF VENGEANCE, OF COURSE.
(HOW THAT BIZARRE ALLIANCE CAME TO BE IS A STORY FOR ANOTHER TIME...)
BUT THAT IS HOW IT HAS BEEN FOR MILLIONS OF YEARS NOW.
THE MIGHTY THANOS ON HIS GREAT DEVOURER THRONE.
LORD OF ASH. KING OF NOTHING.
VICTORIOUS. UNCONTESTED...
...AND ALONE.

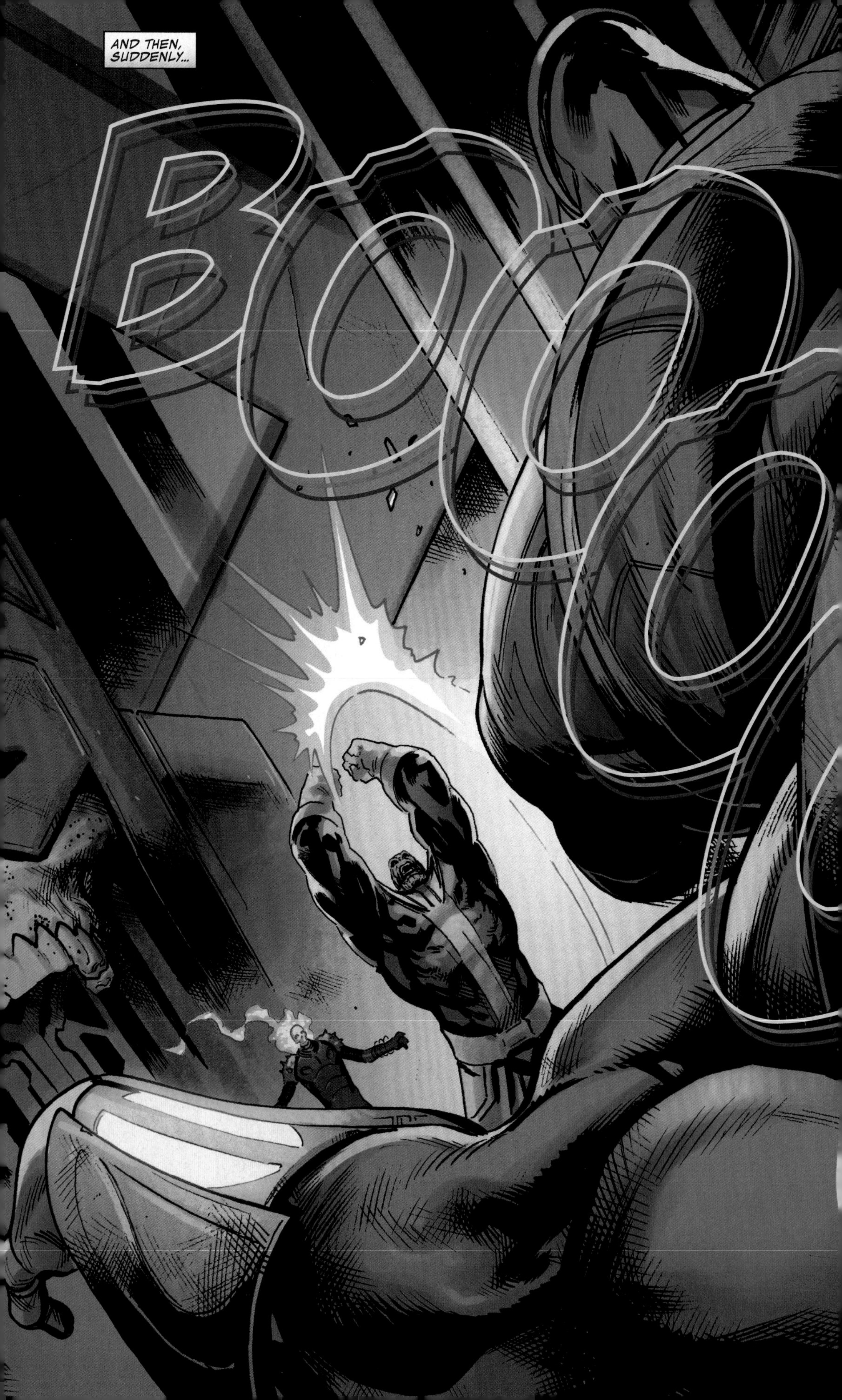
AND THEN, SUDDENLY...

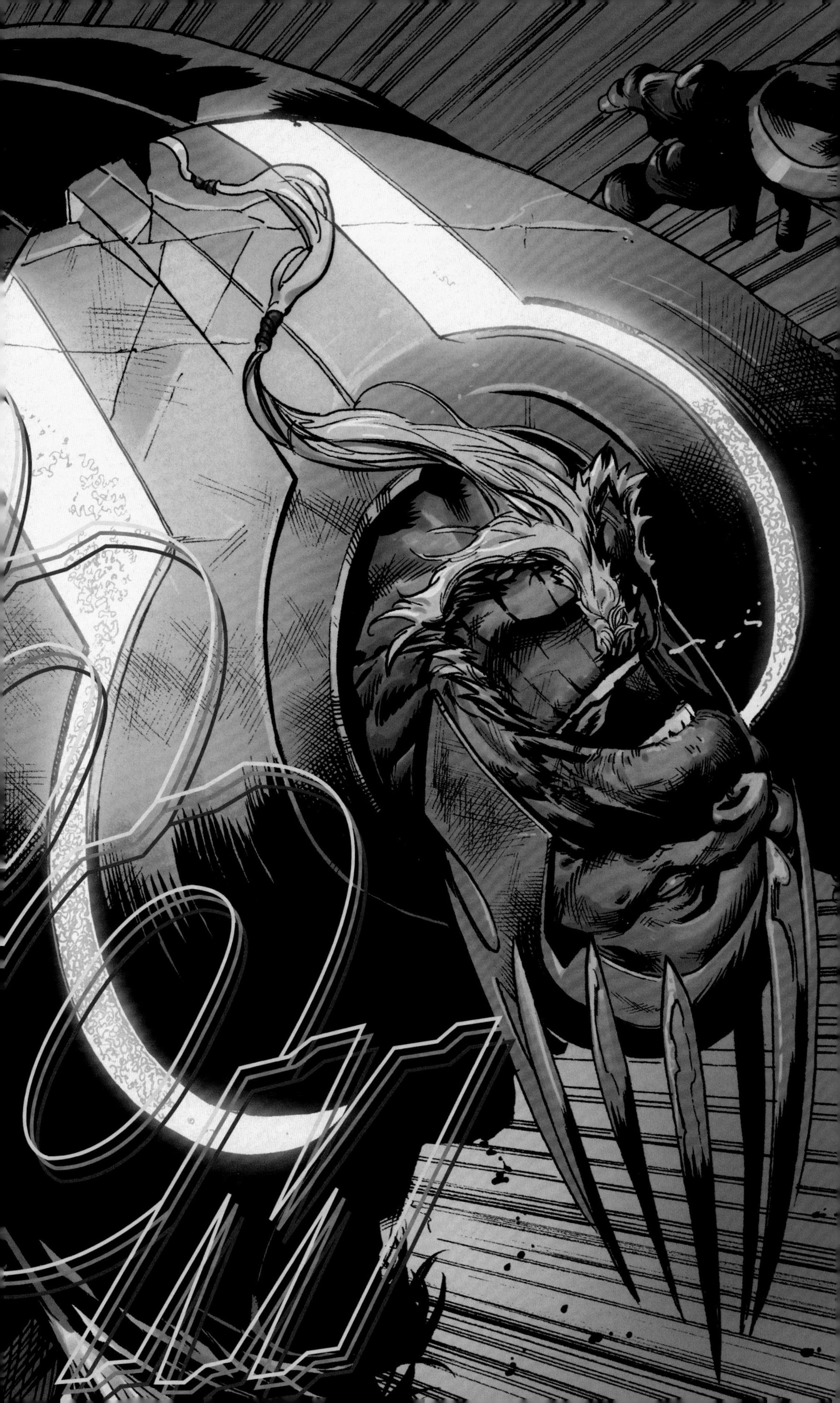

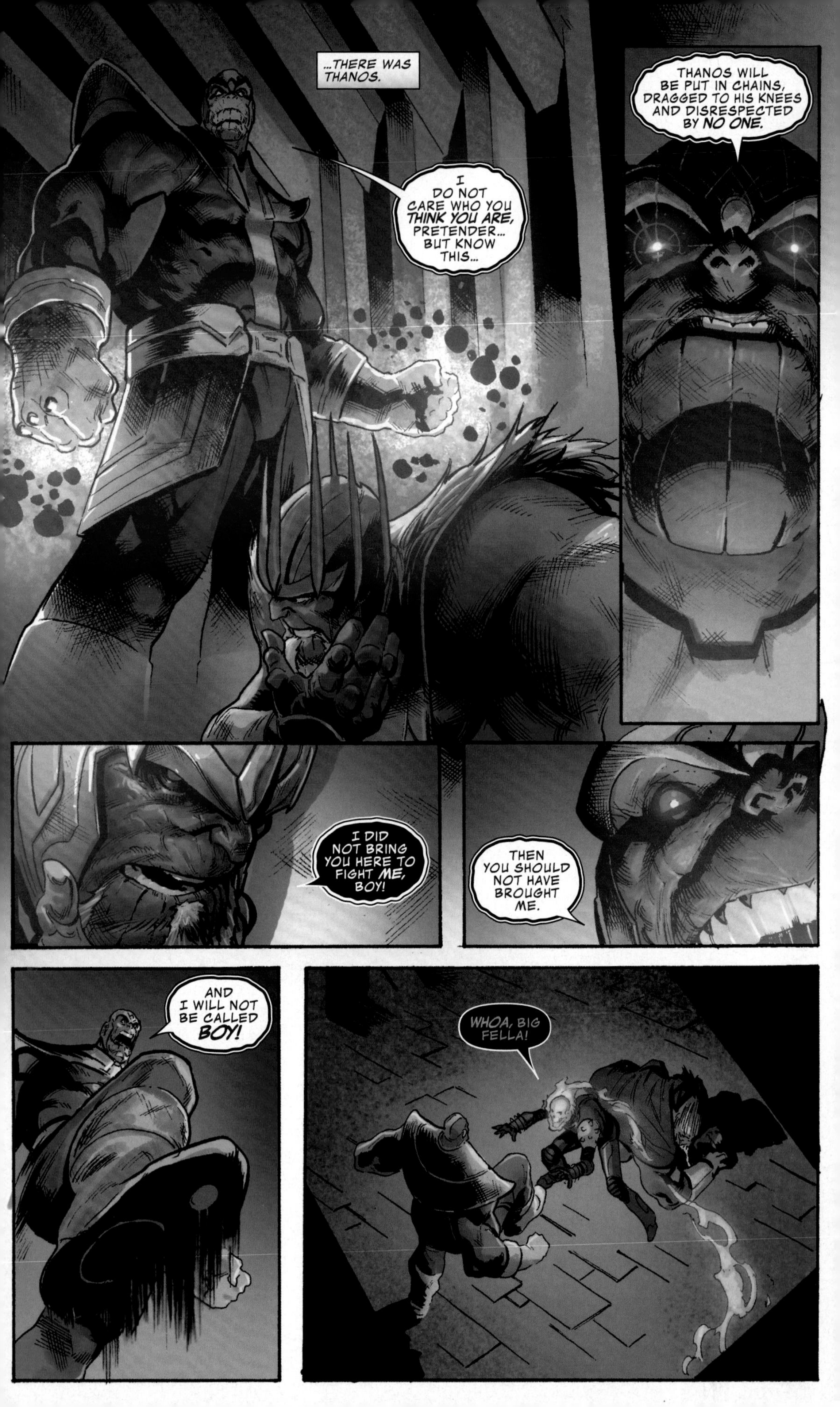
...THERE WAS THANOS.
I DO NOT CARE WHO YOU THINK YOU ARE, PRETENDER... BUT KNOW THIS...
THANOS WILL BE PUT IN CHAINS, DRAGGED TO HIS KNEES AND DISRESPECTED BY NO ONE.
I DID NOT BRING YOU HERE TO FIGHT ME, BOY!
THEN YOU SHOULD NOT HAVE BROUGHT ME.
AND I WILL NOT BE CALLED BOY!
WHOA, BIG FELLA!

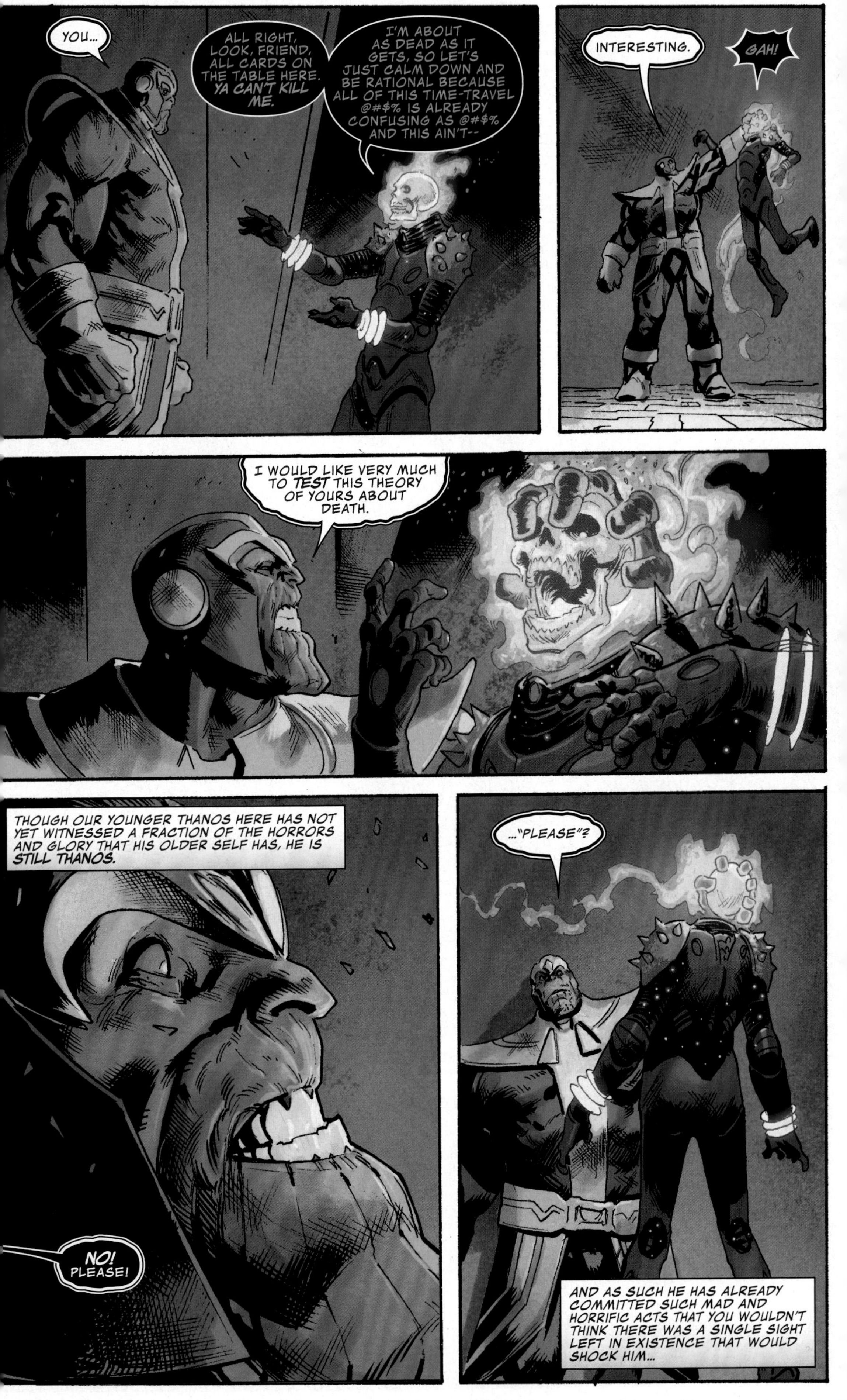

YOU...
ALL RIGHT, LOOK, FRIEND, ALL CARDS ON THE TABLE HERE. YA CAN'T KILL ME.
I'M ABOUT AS DEAD AS IT GETS, SO LET'S JUST CALM DOWN AND BE RATIONAL BECAUSE ALL OF THIS TIME-TRAVEL @#$% IS ALREADY CONFUSING AS @#$% AND THIS AIN'T--
INTERESTING.
GAH!
I WOULD LIKE VERY MUCH TO TEST THIS THEORY OF YOURS ABOUT DEATH.
THOUGH OUR YOUNGER THANOS HERE HAS NOT YET WITNESSED A FRACTION OF THE HORRORS AND GLORY THAT HIS OLDER SELF HAS, HE IS STILL THANOS.
NO! PLEASE!
..."PLEASE"?
AND AS SUCH HE HAS ALREADY COMMITTED SUCH MAD AND HORRIFIC ACTS THAT YOU WOULDN'T THINK THERE WAS A SINGLE SIGHT LEFT IN EXISTENCE THAT WOULD SHOCK HIM...

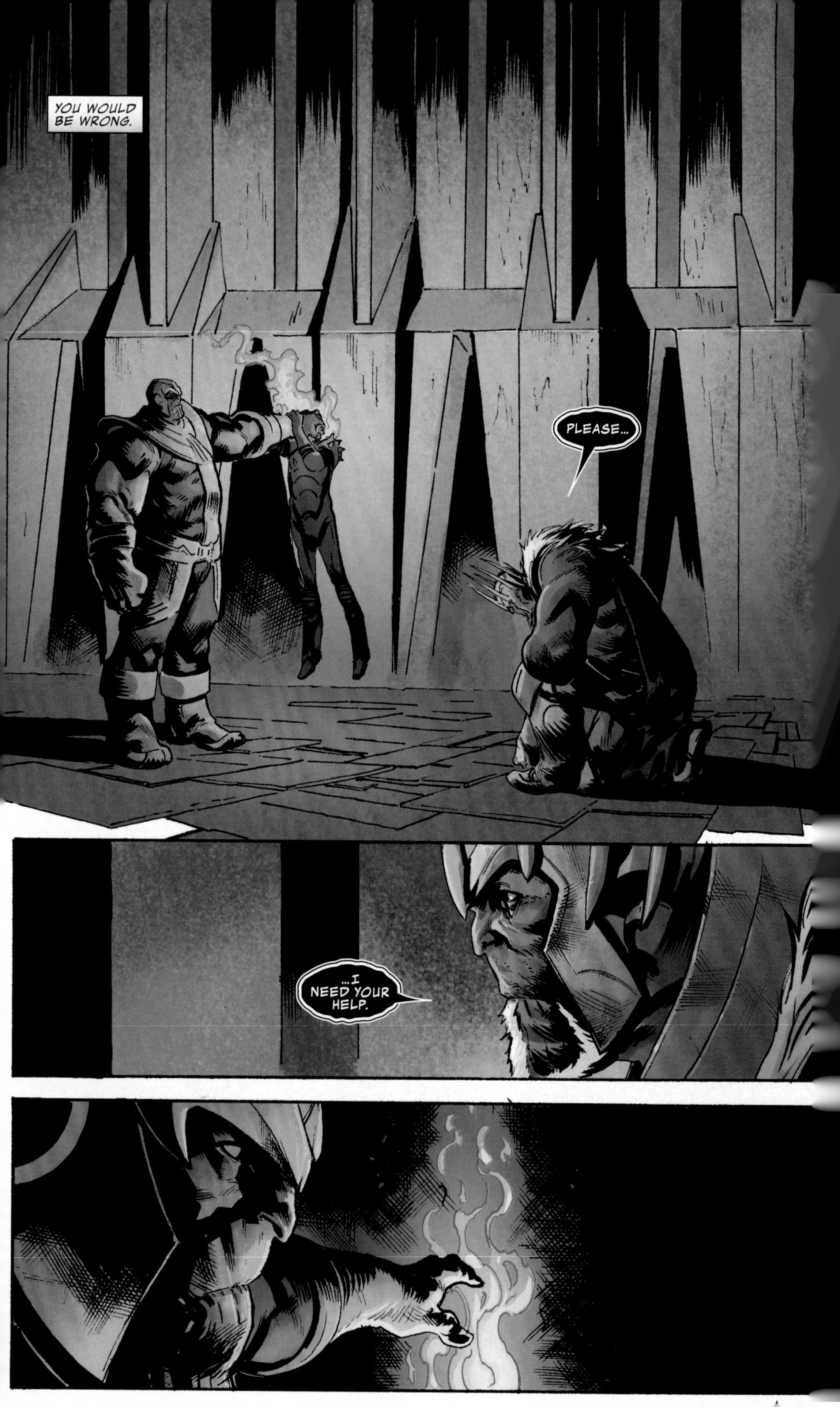
YOU WOULD BE WRONG.
PLEASE...
...I NEED YOUR HELP.

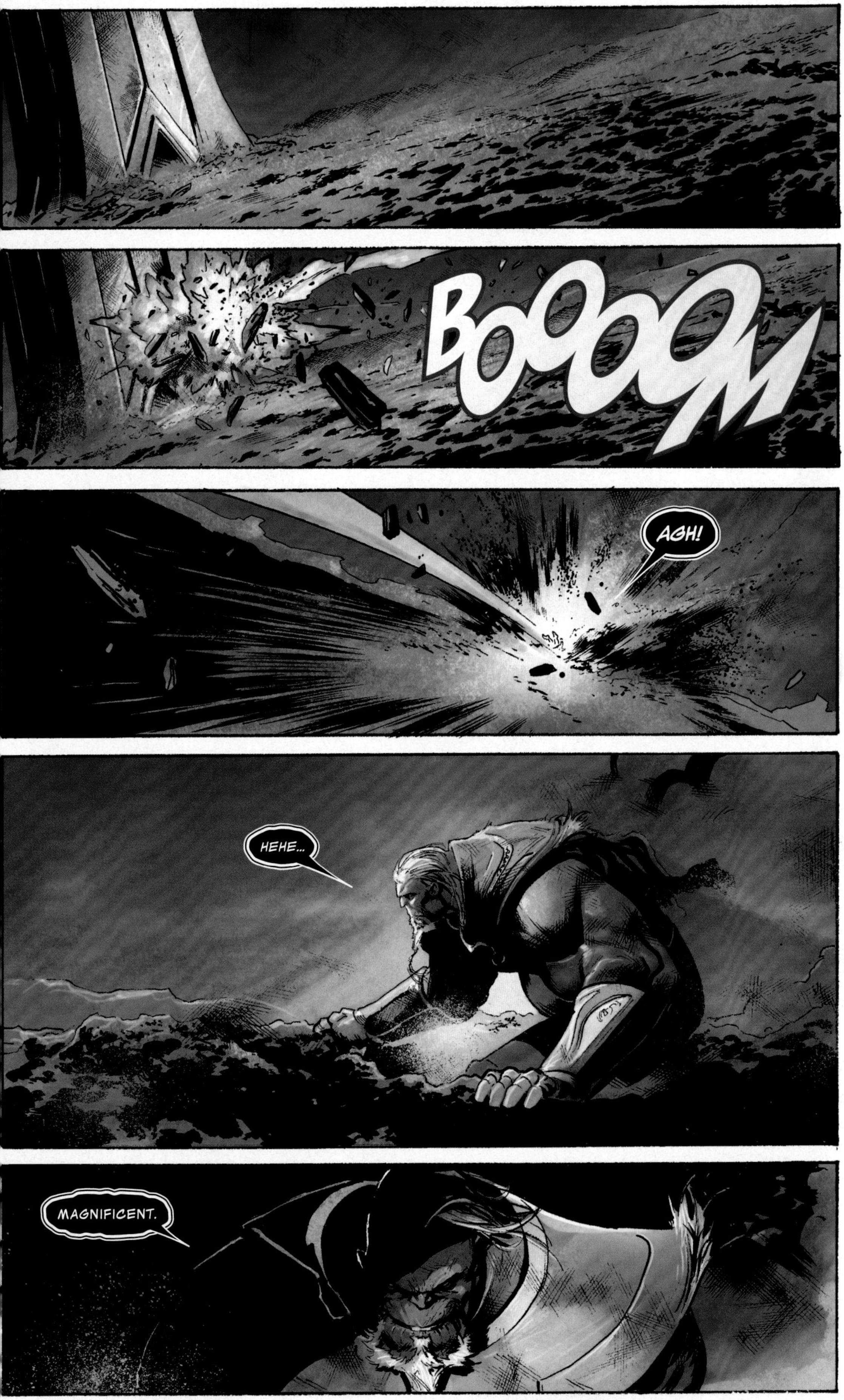
BOOOOM
AGH!
HEHE...
MAGNIFICENT.

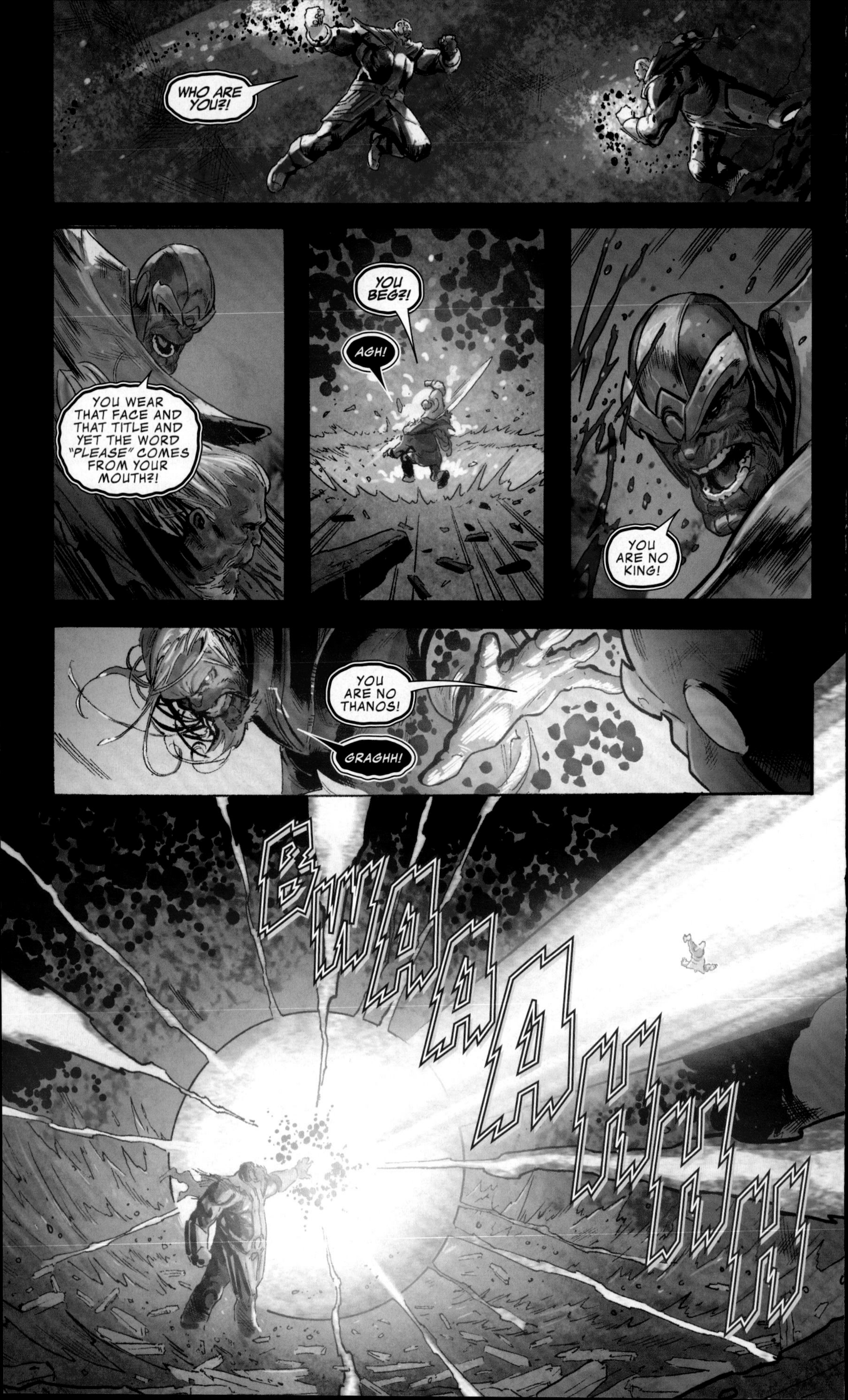
WHO ARE YOU?!
YOU WEAR THAT FACE AND THAT TITLE AND YET THE WORD "PLEASE" COMES FROM YOUR MOUTH?!
YOU BEG?!
AGH!
YOU ARE NO KING!
YOU ARE NO THANOS!
GRAGHH!
BWAAAWWWK

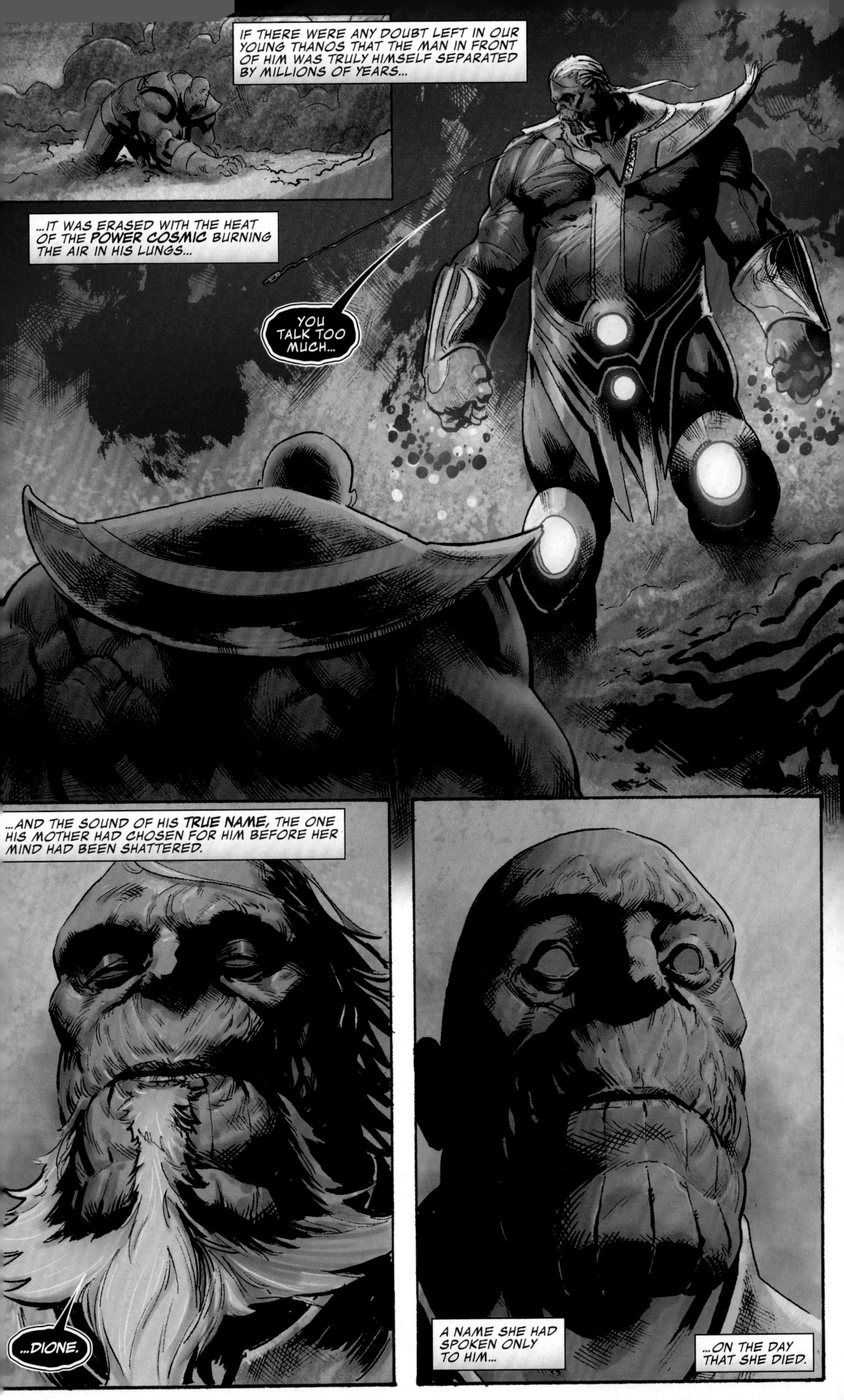
IF THERE WERE ANY DOUBT LEFT IN OUR YOUNG THANOS THAT THE MAN IN FRONT OF HIM WAS TRULY HIMSELF SEPARATED BY MILLIONS OF YEARS...
...IT WAS ERASED WITH THE HEAT OF THE POWER COSMIC BURNING THE AIR IN HIS LUNGS...
YOU TALK TOO MUCH...
...AND THE SOUND OF HIS TRUE NAME, THE ONE HIS MOTHER HAD CHOSEN FOR HIM BEFORE HER MIND HAD BEEN SHATTERED.
...DIONE.
A NAME SHE HAD SPOKEN ONLY TO HIM...
...ON THE DAY THAT SHE DIED.

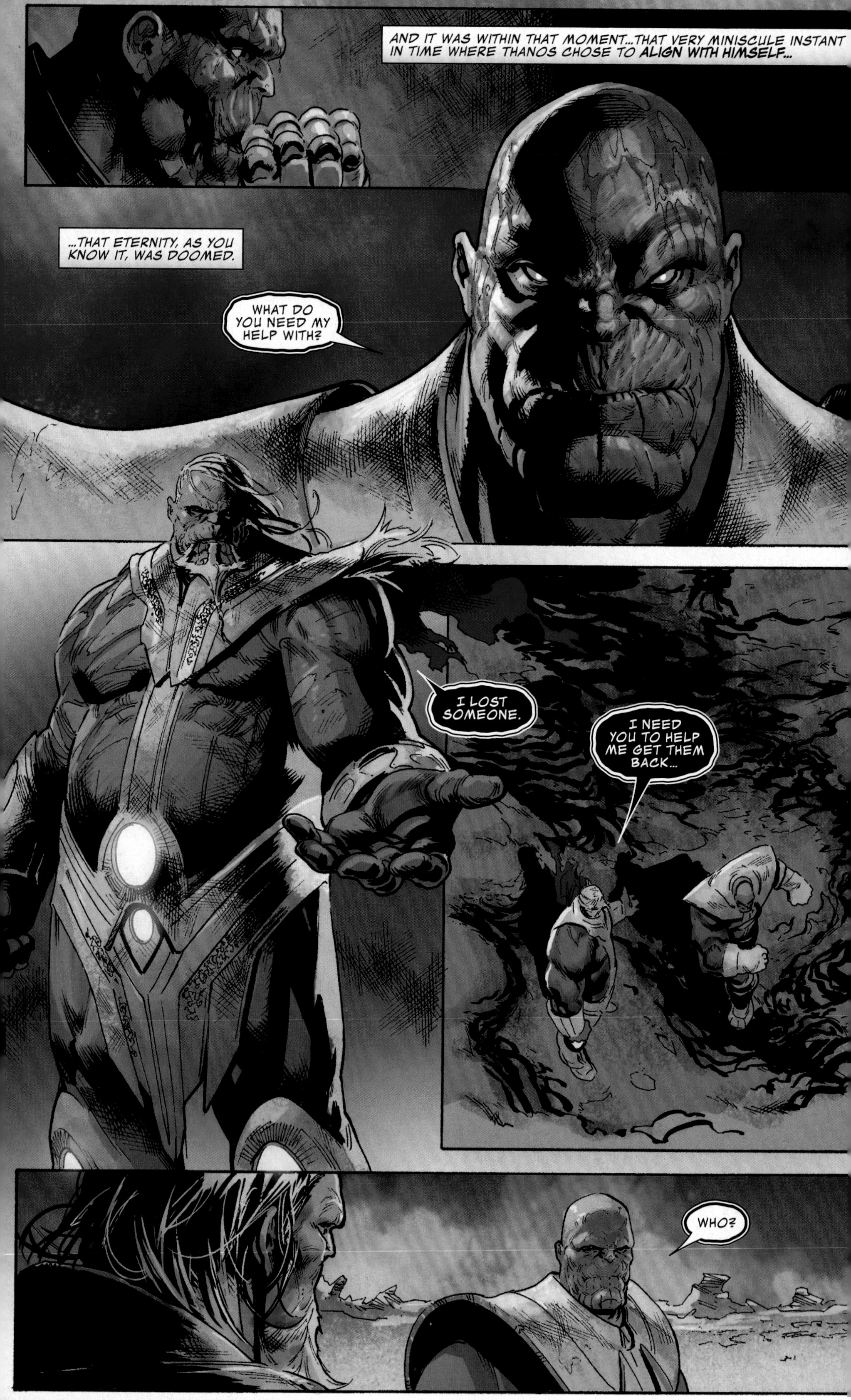
AND IT WAS WITHIN THAT MOMENT...THAT VERY MINISCULE INSTANT IN TIME WHERE THANOS CHOSE TO ALIGN WITH HIMSELF...
...THAT ETERNITY, AS YOU KNOW IT, WAS DOOMED.
WHAT DO YOU NEED MY HELP WITH?
I LOST SOMEONE.
I NEED YOU TO HELP ME GET THEM BACK...
WHO?

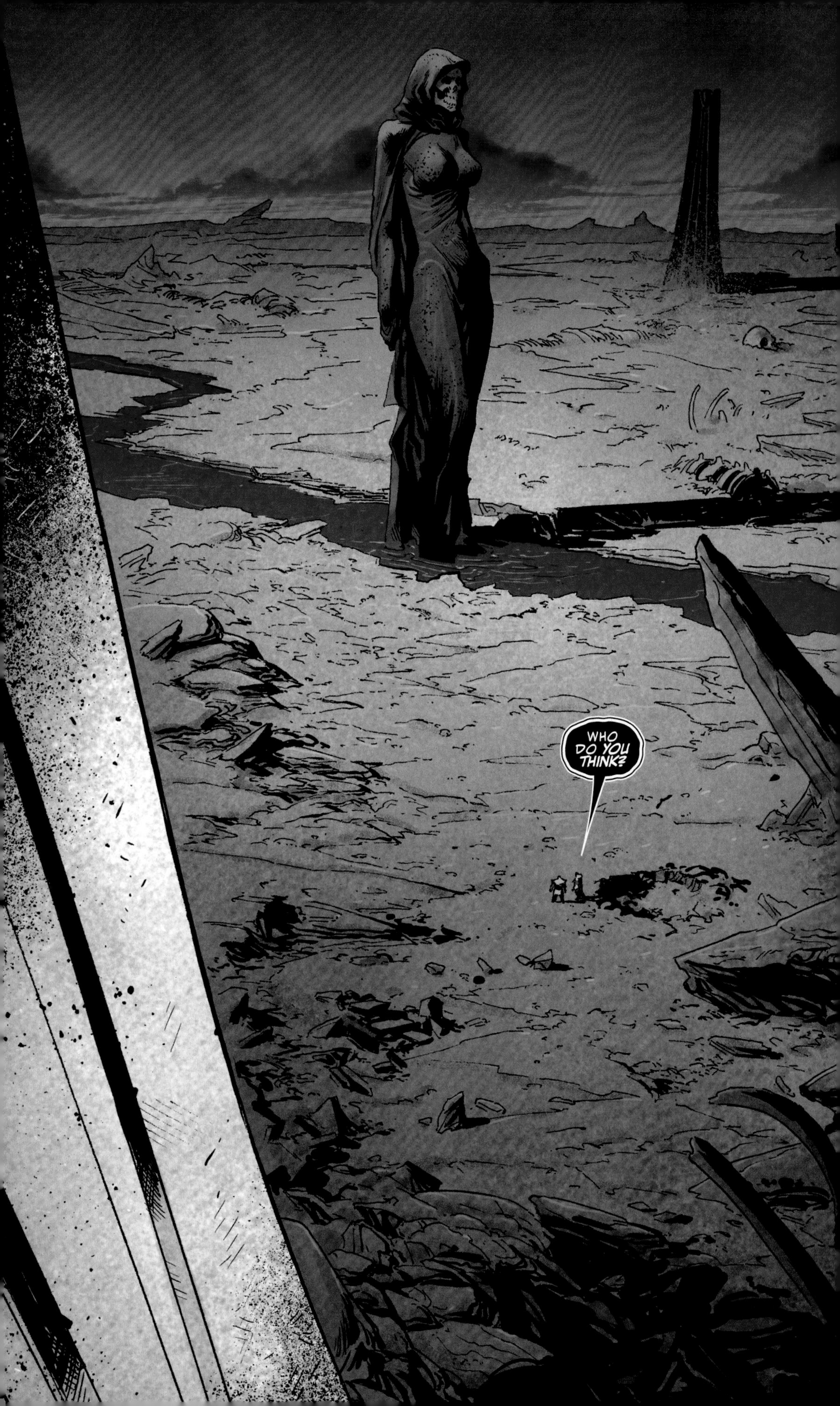
WHO DO YOU THINK?

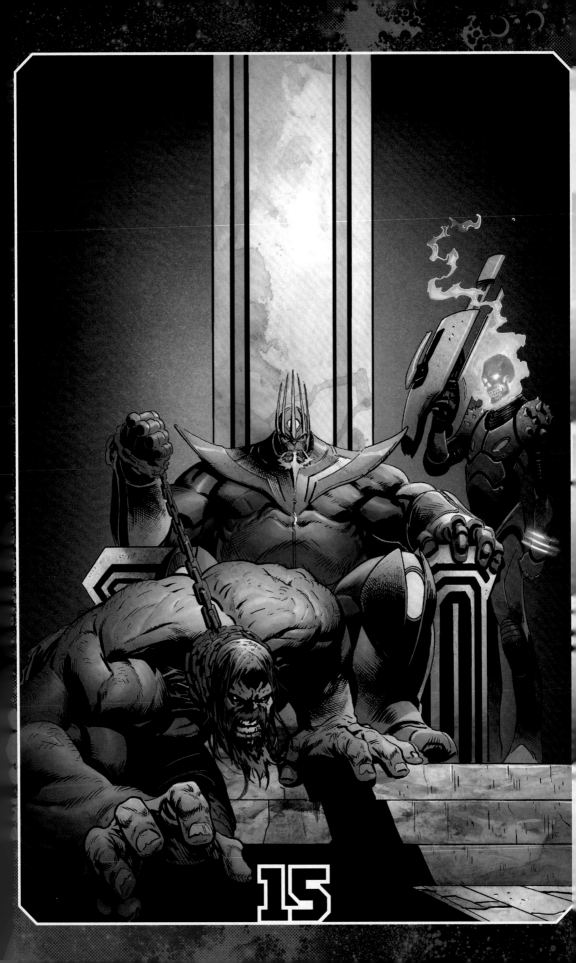

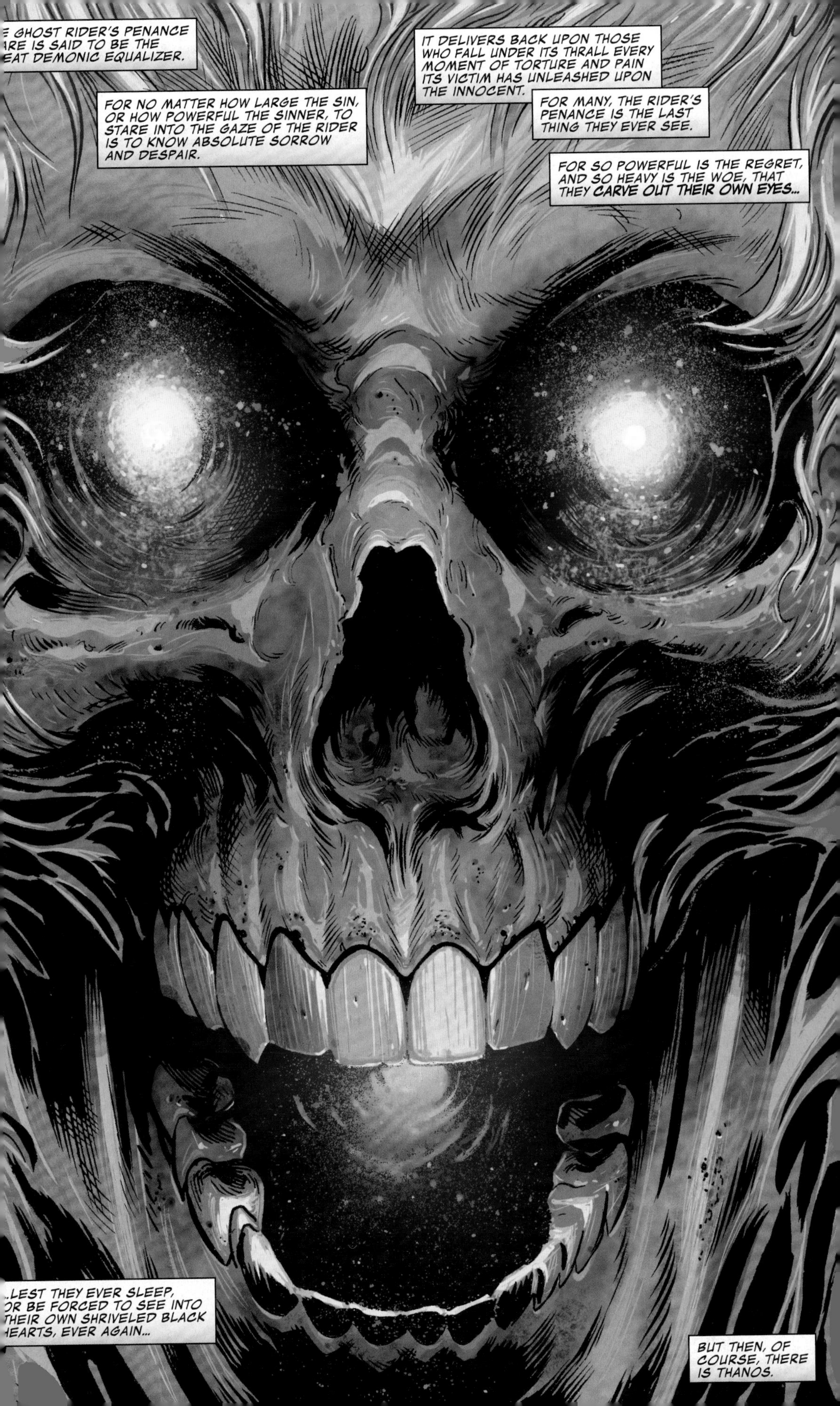

E GHOST RIDER'S PENANCE ARE IS SAID TO BE THE EAT DEMONIC EQUALIZER.
FOR NO MATTER HOW LARGE THE SIN, OR HOW POWERFUL THE SINNER, TO STARE INTO THE GAZE OF THE RIDER IS TO KNOW ABSOLUTE SORROW AND DESPAIR.
IT DELIVERS BACK UPON THOSE WHO FALL UNDER ITS THRALL EVERY MOMENT OF TORTURE AND PAIN ITS VICTIM HAS UNLEASHED UPON THE INNOCENT.
FOR MANY, THE RIDER'S PENANCE IS THE LAST THING THEY EVER SEE.
FOR SO POWERFUL IS THE REGRET, AND SO HEAVY IS THE WOE, THAT THEY **CARVE OUT THEIR OWN EYES...**
..LEST THEY EVER SLEEP, OR BE FORCED TO SEE INTO THEIR OWN SHRIVELED BLACK HEARTS, EVER AGAIN...
BUT THEN, OF COURSE, THERE IS THANOS.

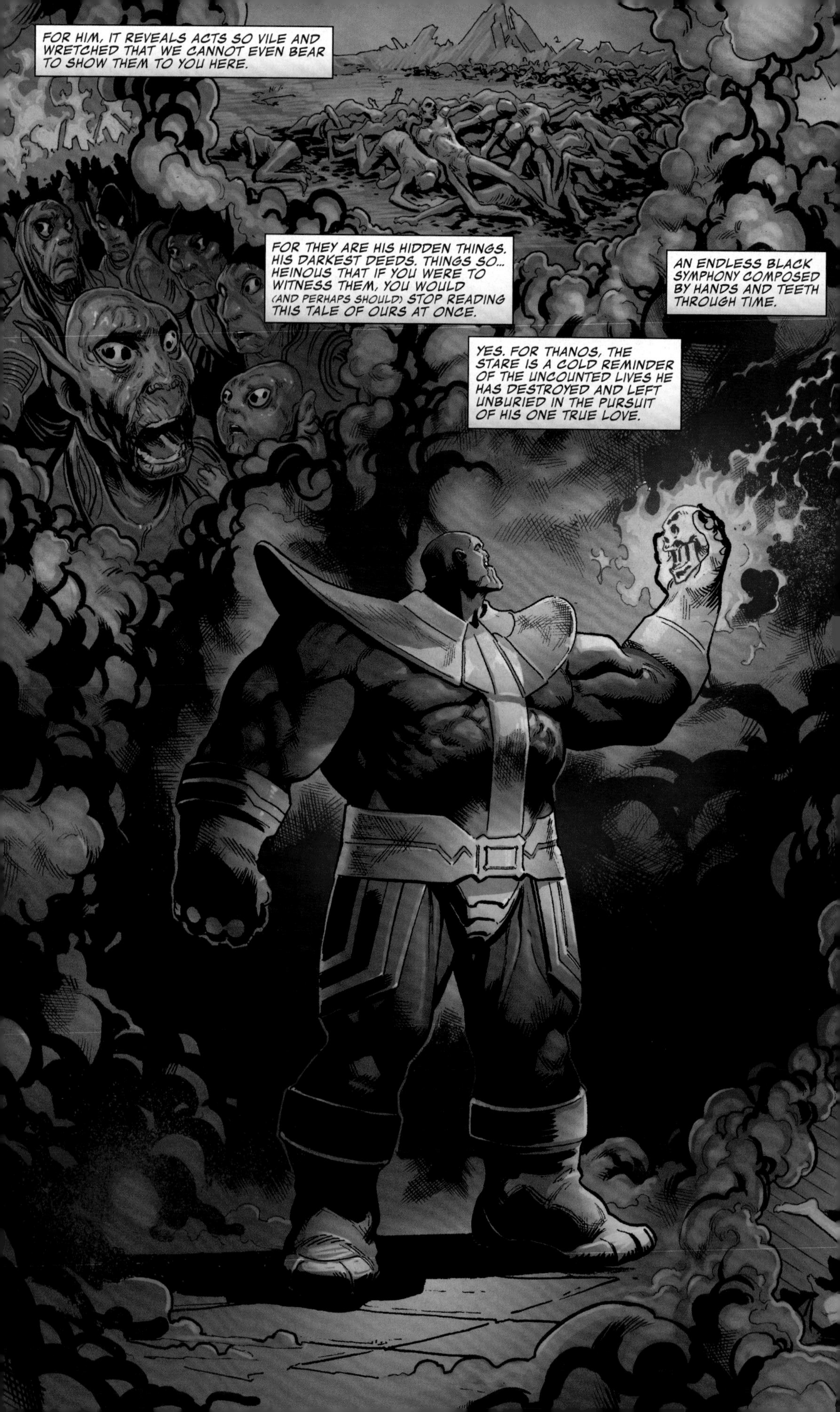
FOR HIM, IT REVEALS ACTS SO VILE AND WRETCHED THAT WE CANNOT EVEN BEAR TO SHOW THEM TO YOU HERE.
FOR THEY ARE HIS HIDDEN THINGS. HIS DARKEST DEEDS. THINGS SO... HEINOUS THAT IF YOU WERE TO WITNESS THEM, YOU WOULD (AND PERHAPS SHOULD) STOP READING THIS TALE OF OURS AT ONCE.
AN ENDLESS BLACK SYMPHONY COMPOSED BY HANDS AND TEETH THROUGH TIME.
YES. FOR THANOS, THE STARE IS A COLD REMINDER OF THE UNCOUNTED LIVES HE HAS DESTROYED AND LEFT UNBURIED IN THE PURSUIT OF HIS ONE TRUE LOVE.

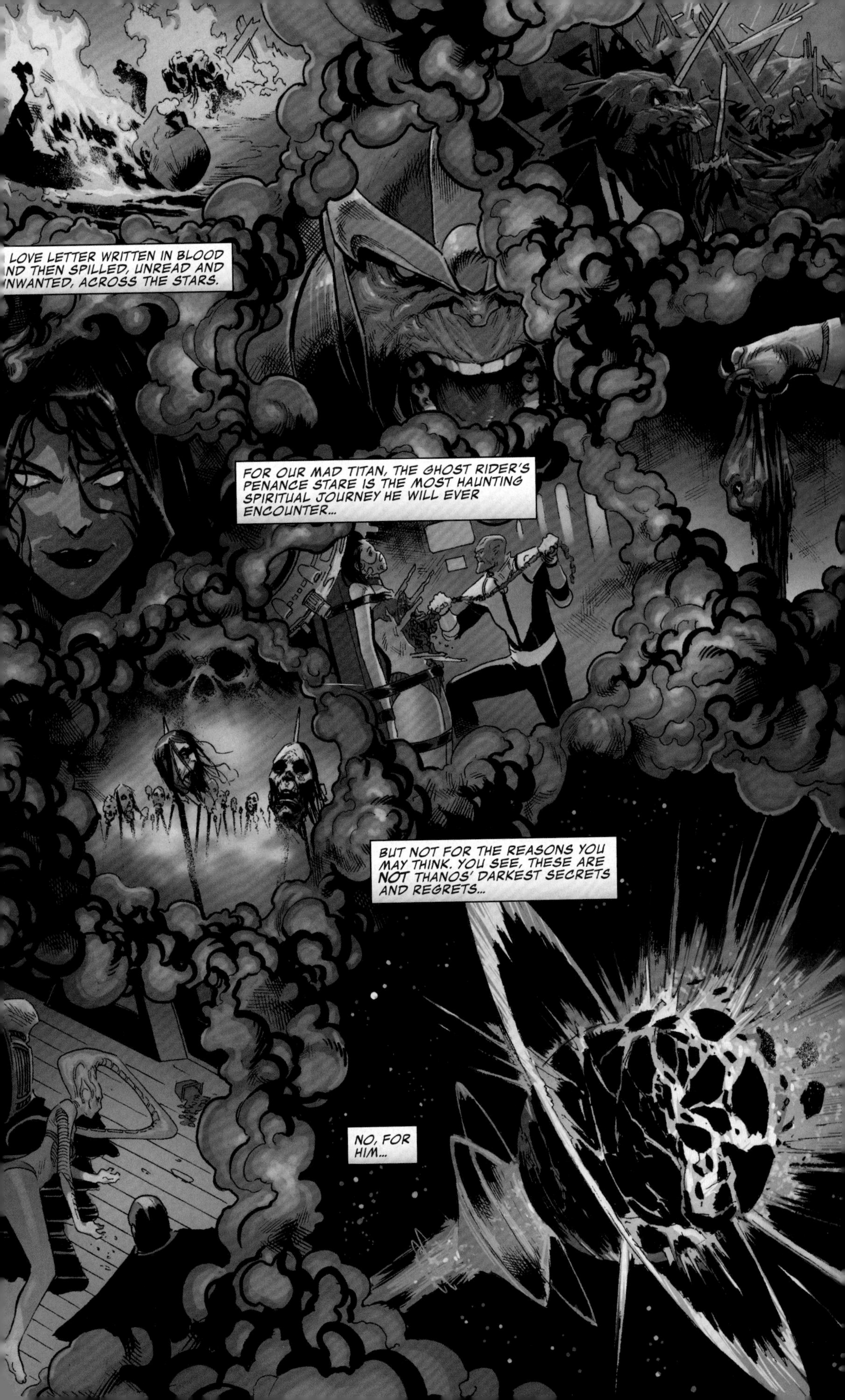
LOVE LETTER WRITTEN IN BLOOD
ND THEN SPILLED, UNREAD AND
NWANTED, ACROSS THE STARS.
FOR OUR MAD TITAN, THE GHOST RIDER'S PENANCE STARE IS THE MOST HAUNTING SPIRITUAL JOURNEY HE WILL EVER ENCOUNTER...
BUT NOT FOR THE REASONS YOU MAY THINK. YOU SEE, THESE ARE NOT THANOS' DARKEST SECRETS AND REGRETS...
NO, FOR HIM...

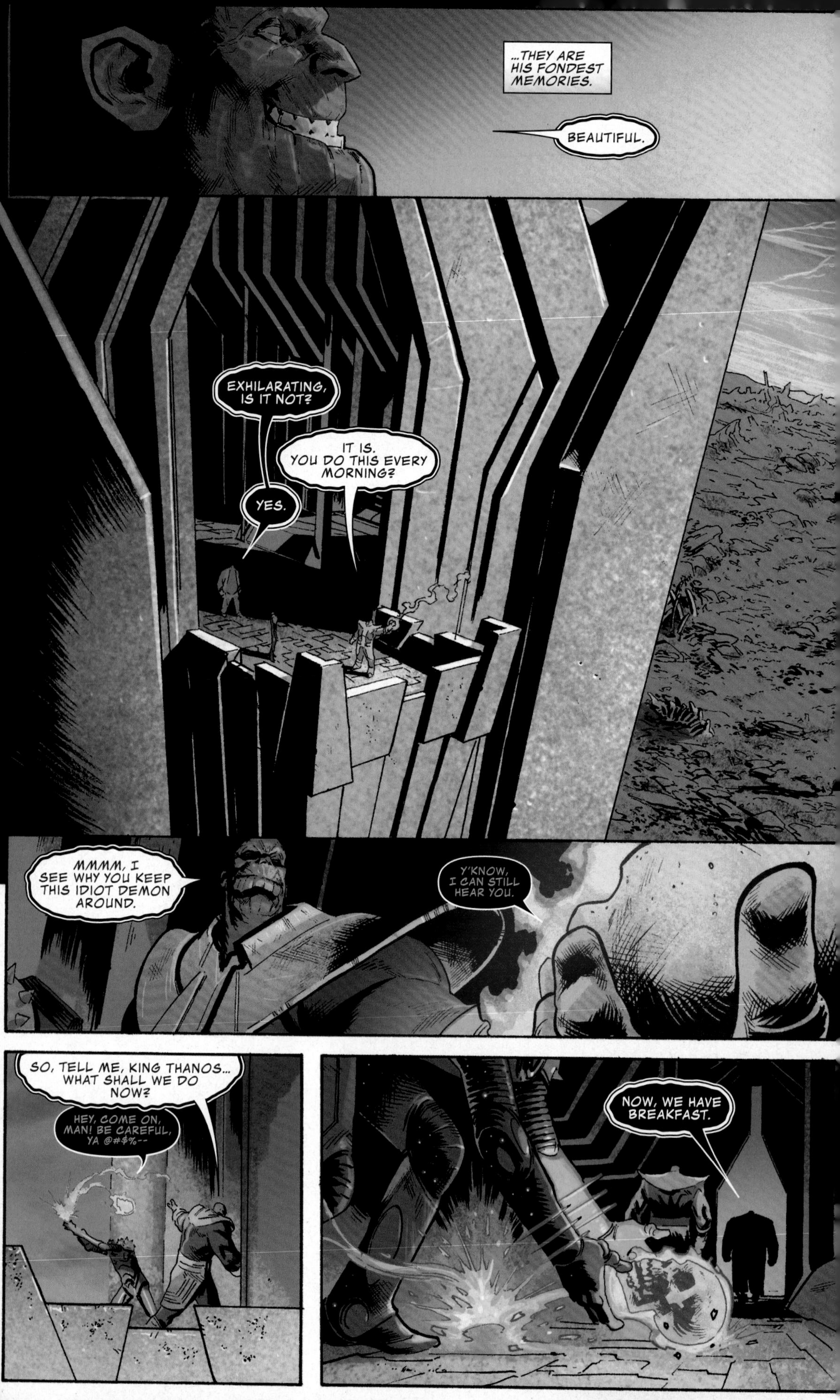

...THEY ARE HIS FONDEST MEMORIES.
BEAUTIFUL.
EXHILARATING, IS IT NOT?
IT IS. YOU DO THIS EVERY MORNING?
YES.
MMMM, I SEE WHY YOU KEEP THIS IDIOT DEMON AROUND.
Y'KNOW, I CAN STILL HEAR YOU.
SO, TELL ME, KING THANOS... WHAT SHALL WE DO NOW?
HEY, COME ON, MAN! BE CAREFUL, YA @#$%--
NOW, WE HAVE BREAKFAST.

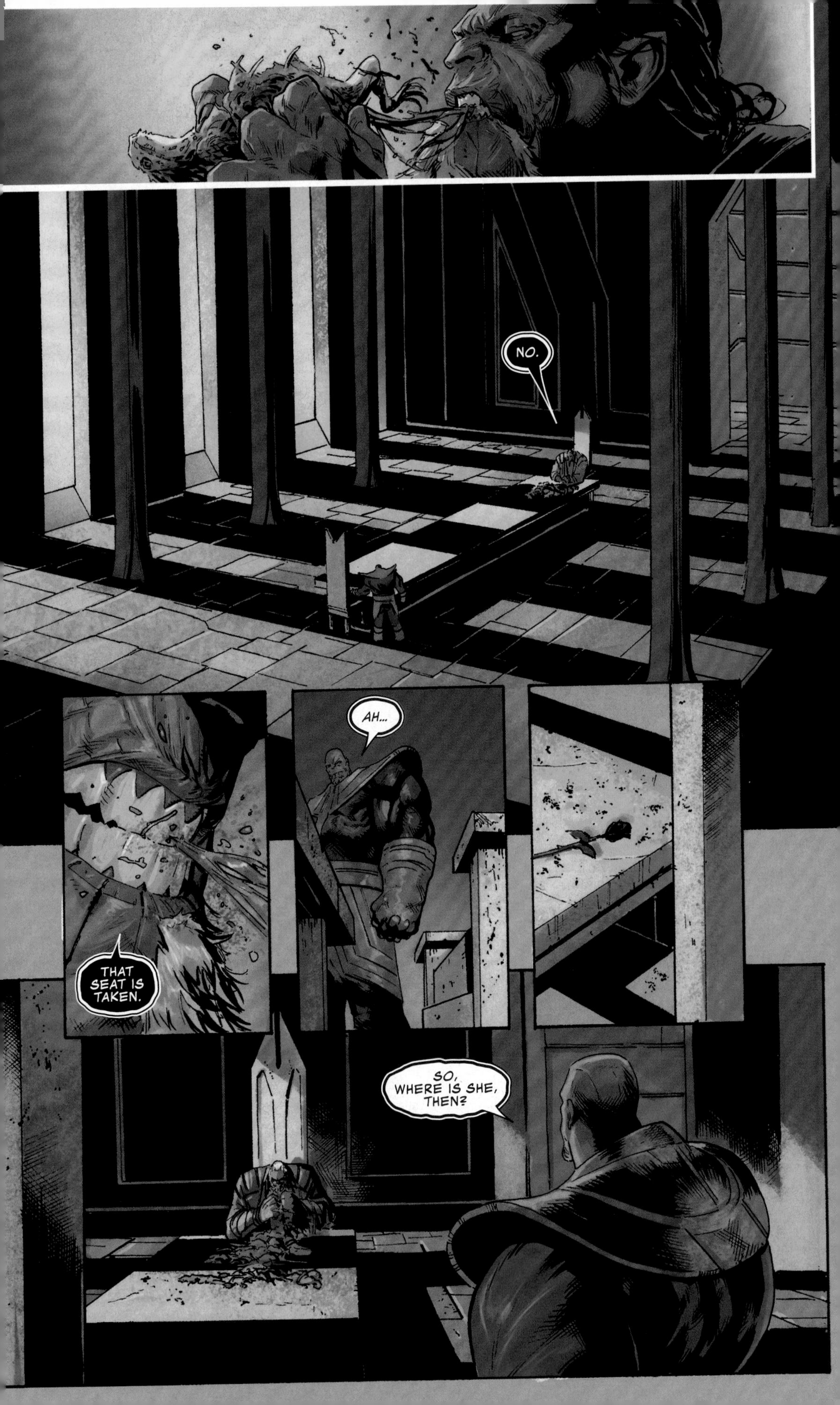

NO.
THAT SEAT IS TAKEN.
AH...
SO, WHERE IS SHE, THEN?

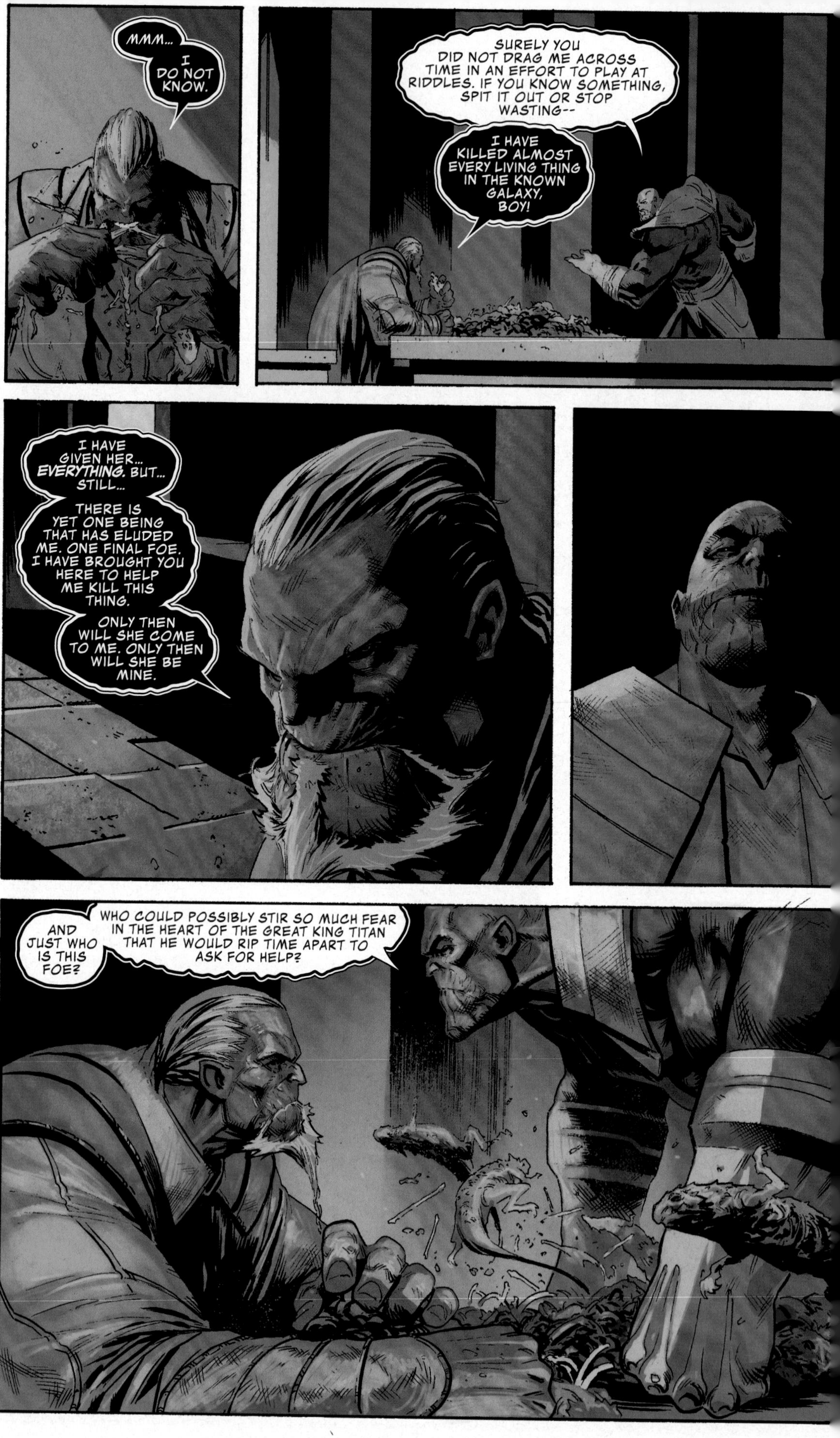
MMM... I DO NOT KNOW.
SURELY YOU DID NOT DRAG ME ACROSS TIME IN AN EFFORT TO PLAY AT RIDDLES. IF YOU KNOW SOMETHING, SPIT IT OUT OR STOP WASTING--
I HAVE KILLED ALMOST EVERY LIVING THING IN THE KNOWN GALAXY, BOY!
I HAVE GIVEN HER... EVERYTHING. BUT... STILL...
THERE IS YET ONE BEING THAT HAS ELUDED ME. ONE FINAL FOE. I HAVE BROUGHT YOU HERE TO HELP ME KILL THIS THING.
ONLY THEN WILL SHE COME TO ME. ONLY THEN WILL SHE BE MINE.
AND JUST WHO IS THIS FOE?
WHO COULD POSSIBLY STIR SO MUCH FEAR IN THE HEART OF THE GREAT KING TITAN THAT HE WOULD RIP TIME APART TO ASK FOR HELP?

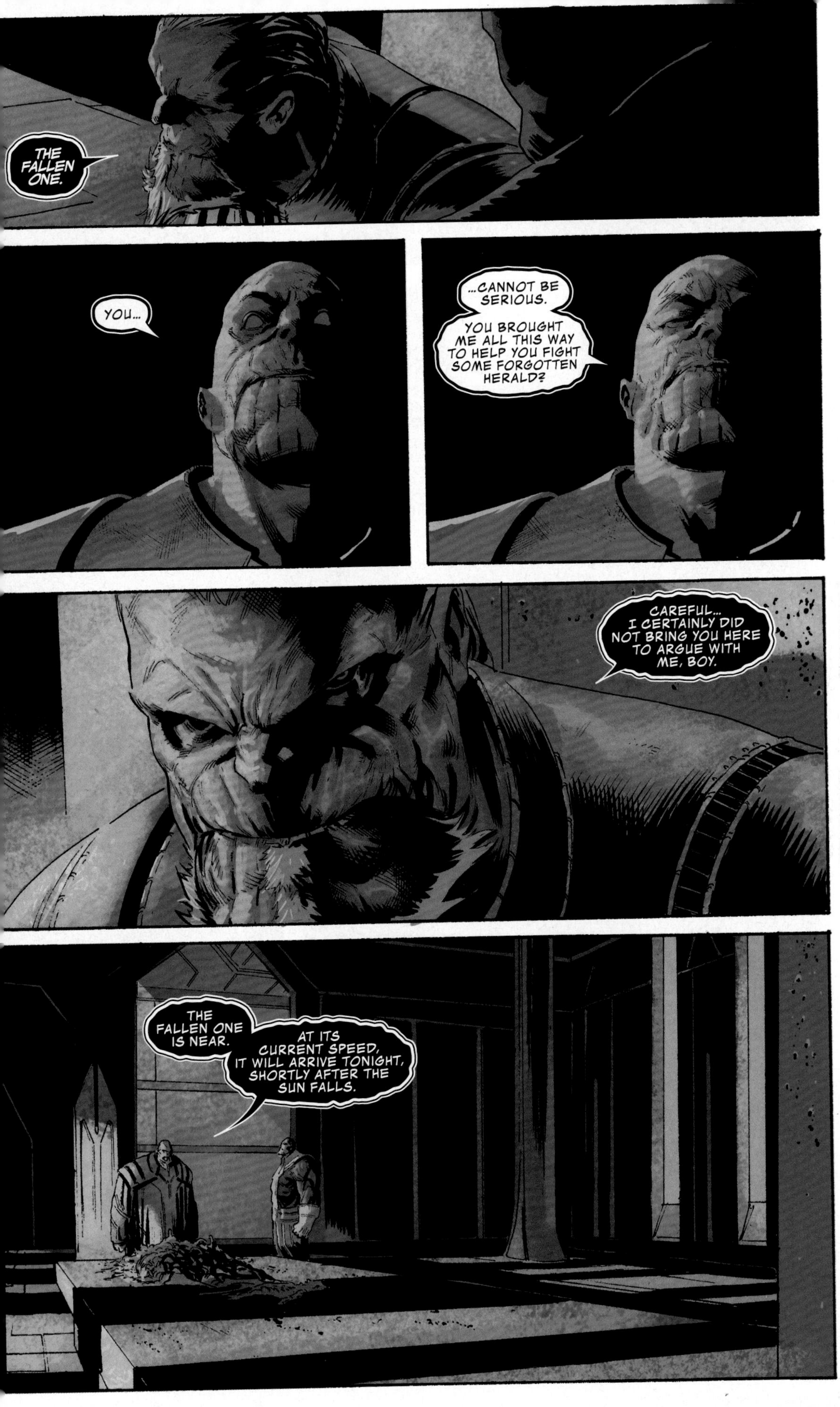
THE FALLEN ONE.
YOU...
...CANNOT BE SERIOUS.
YOU BROUGHT ME ALL THIS WAY TO HELP YOU FIGHT SOME FORGOTTEN HERALD?
CAREFUL... I CERTAINLY DID NOT BRING YOU HERE TO ARGUE WITH ME, BOY.
THE FALLEN ONE IS NEAR.
AT ITS CURRENT SPEED, IT WILL ARRIVE TONIGHT, SHORTLY AFTER THE SUN FALLS.

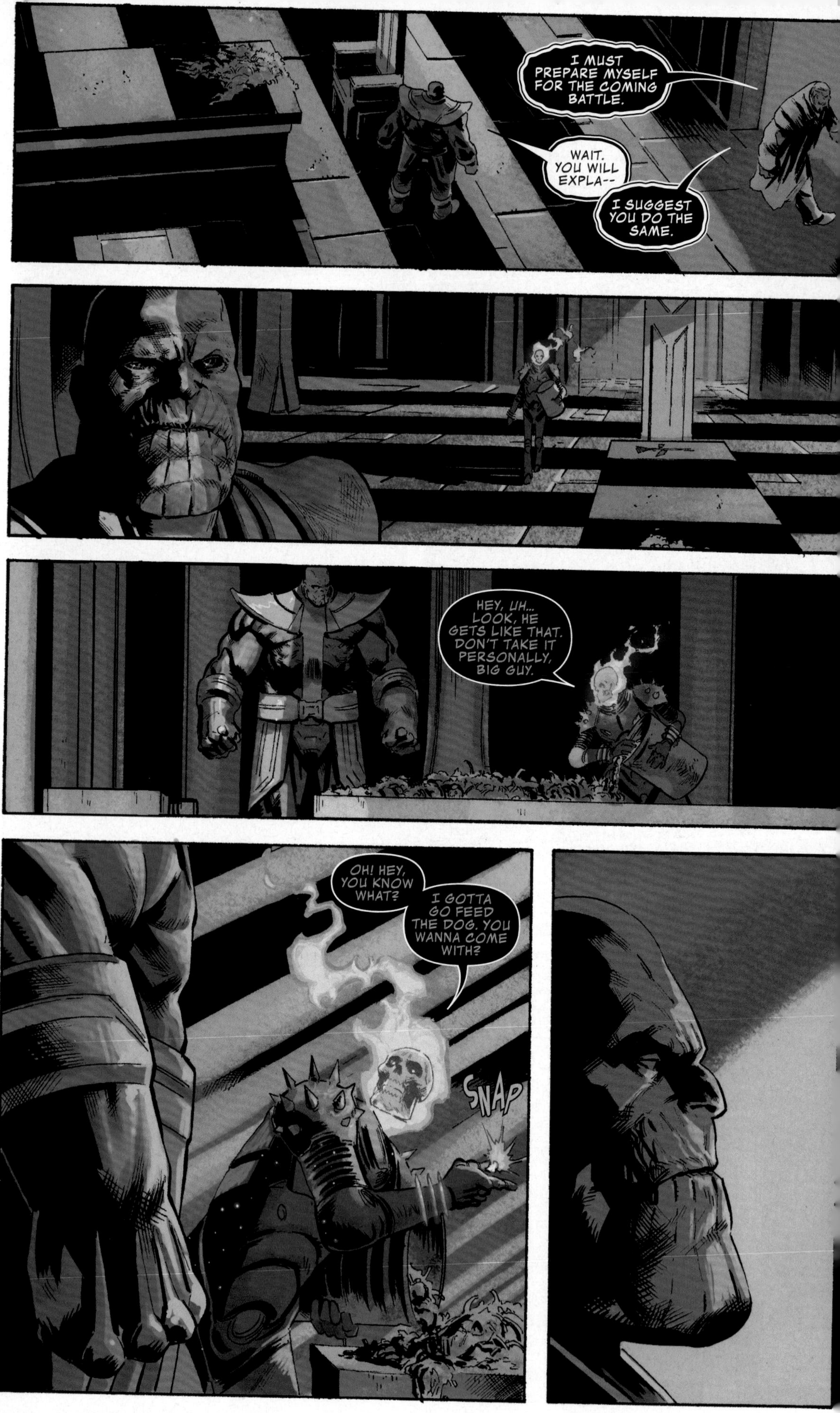
I MUST PREPARE MYSELF FOR THE COMING BATTLE.
WAIT. YOU WILL EXPLA--
I SUGGEST YOU DO THE SAME.
HEY, UH... LOOK, HE GETS LIKE THAT. DON'T TAKE IT PERSONALLY, BIG GUY.
OH! HEY, YOU KNOW WHAT?
I GOTTA GO FEED THE DOG. YOU WANNA COME WITH?
SNAP

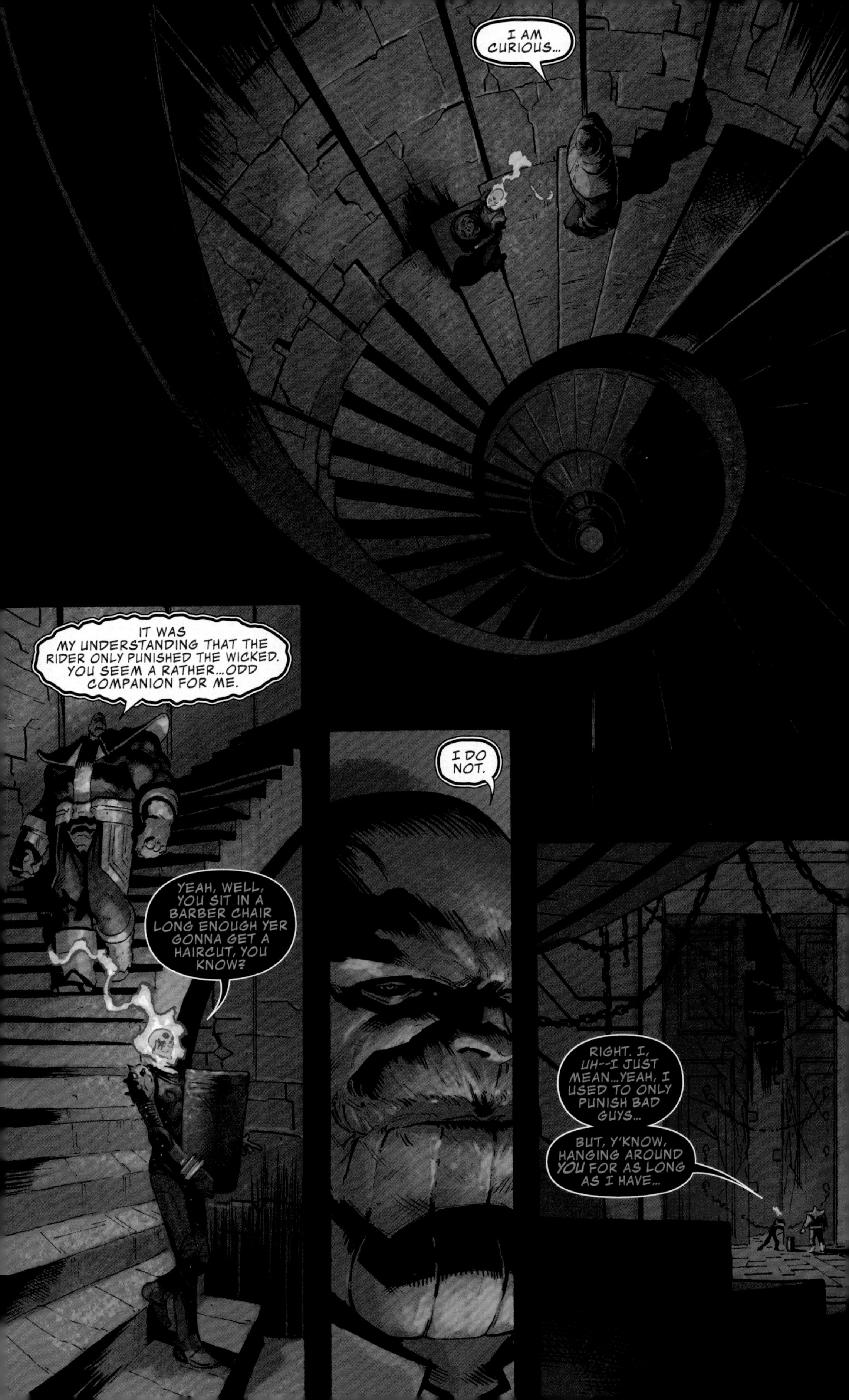
I AM CURIOUS...
IT WAS MY UNDERSTANDING THAT THE RIDER ONLY PUNISHED THE WICKED. YOU SEEM A RATHER...ODD COMPANION FOR ME.
YEAH, WELL, YOU SIT IN A BARBER CHAIR LONG ENOUGH YER GONNA GET A HAIRCUT, YOU KNOW?
I DO NOT.
RIGHT. I, UH--I JUST MEAN...YEAH, I USED TO ONLY PUNISH BAD GUYS...
BUT, Y'KNOW, HANGING AROUND YOU FOR AS LONG AS I HAVE...

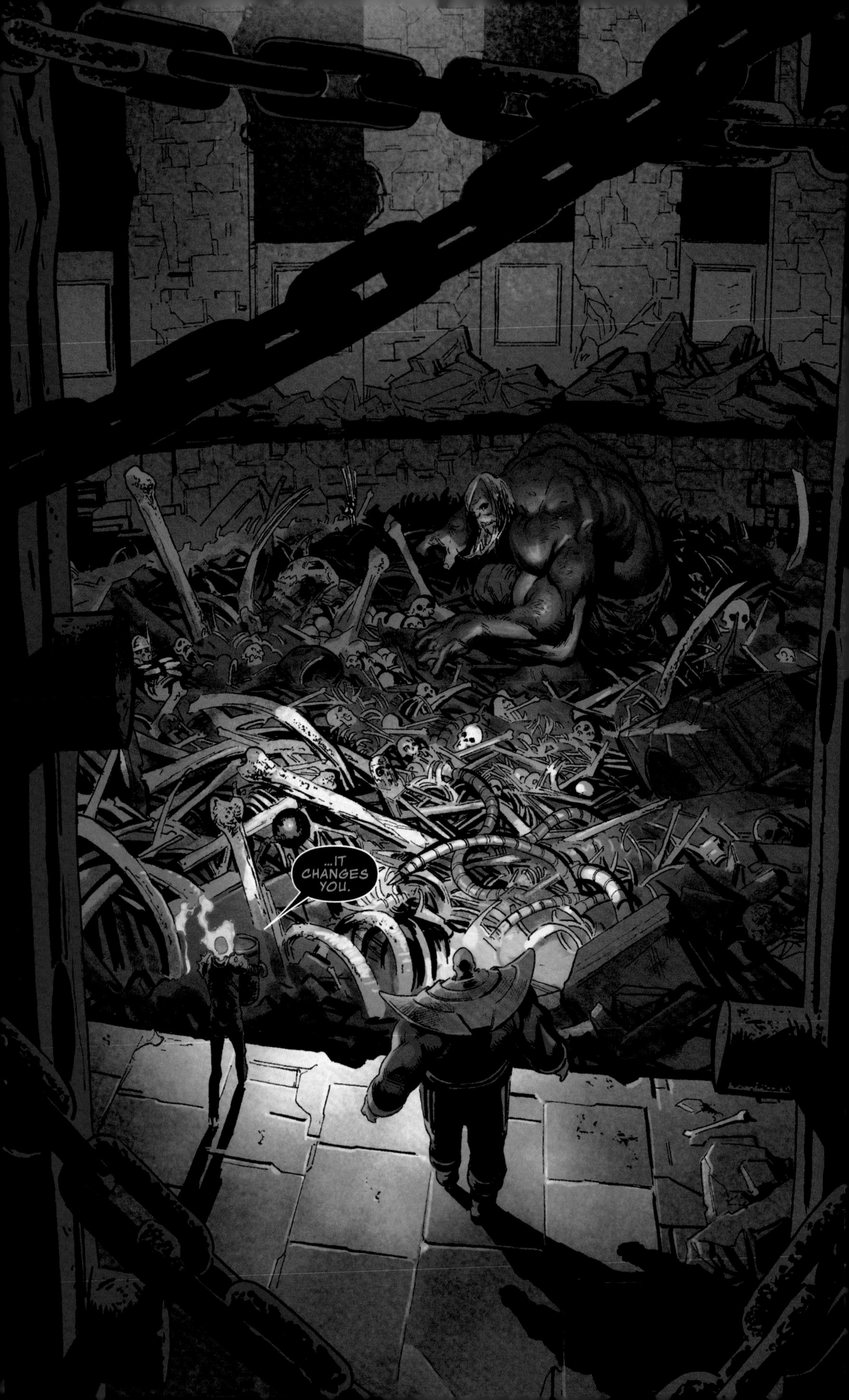
...IT CHANGES YOU.

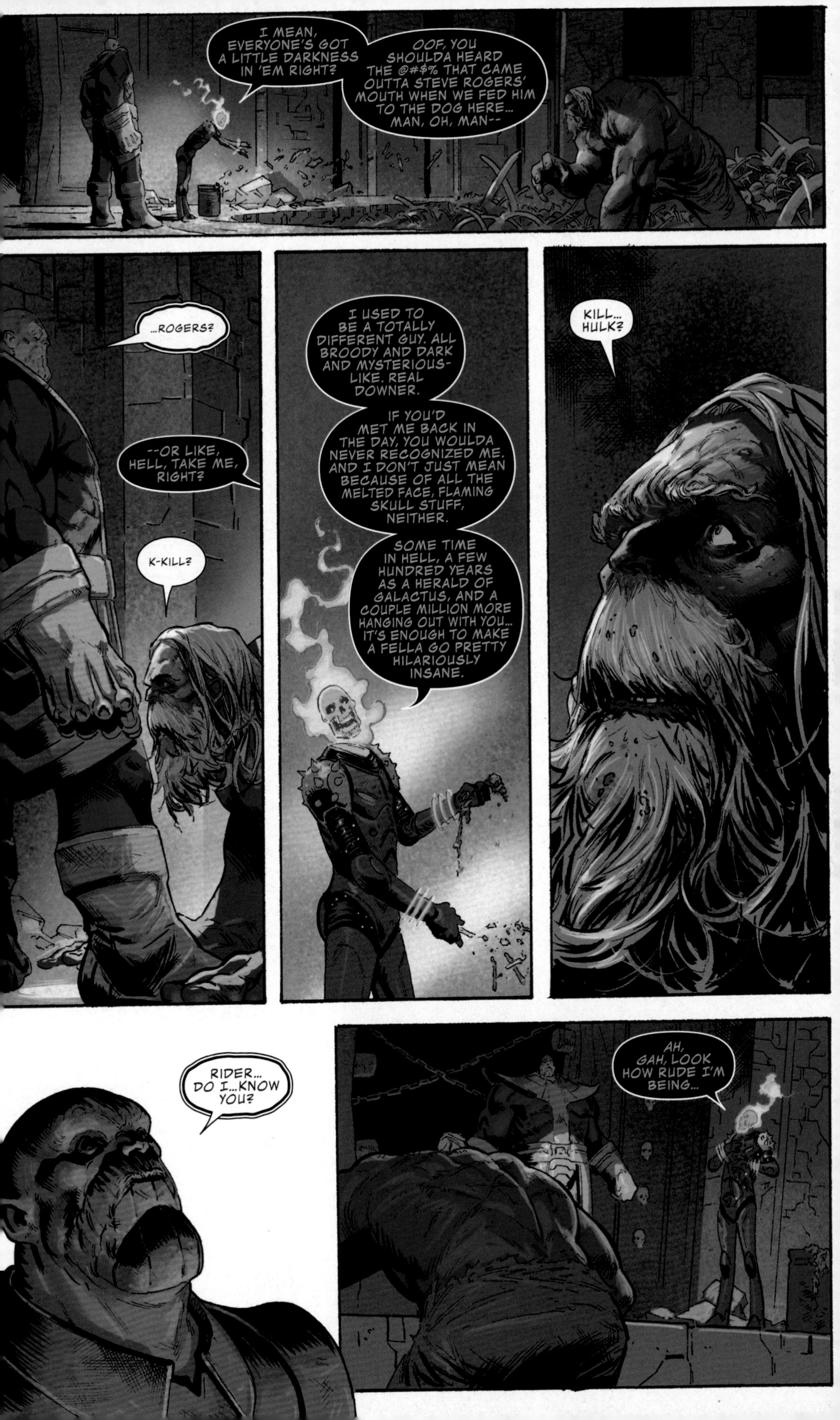
I MEAN, EVERYONE'S GOT A LITTLE DARKNESS IN 'EM RIGHT?
OOF, YOU SHOULDA HEARD THE @#$% THAT CAME OUTTA STEVE ROGERS' MOUTH WHEN WE FED HIM TO THE DOG HERE... MAN, OH, MAN--
...ROGERS?
--OR LIKE, HELL, TAKE ME, RIGHT?
K-KILL?
I USED TO BE A TOTALLY DIFFERENT GUY. ALL BROODY AND DARK AND MYSTERIOUS-LIKE. REAL DOWNER.
IF YOU'D MET ME BACK IN THE DAY, YOU WOULDA NEVER RECOGNIZED ME. AND I DON'T JUST MEAN BECAUSE OF ALL THE MELTED FACE, FLAMING SKULL STUFF, NEITHER.
SOME TIME IN HELL, A FEW HUNDRED YEARS AS A HERALD OF GALACTUS, AND A COUPLE MILLION MORE HANGING OUT WITH YOU... IT'S ENOUGH TO MAKE A FELLA GO PRETTY HILARIOUSLY INSANE.
KILL... HULK?
RIDER... DO I...KNOW YOU?
AH, GAH, LOOK HOW RUDE I'M BEING...

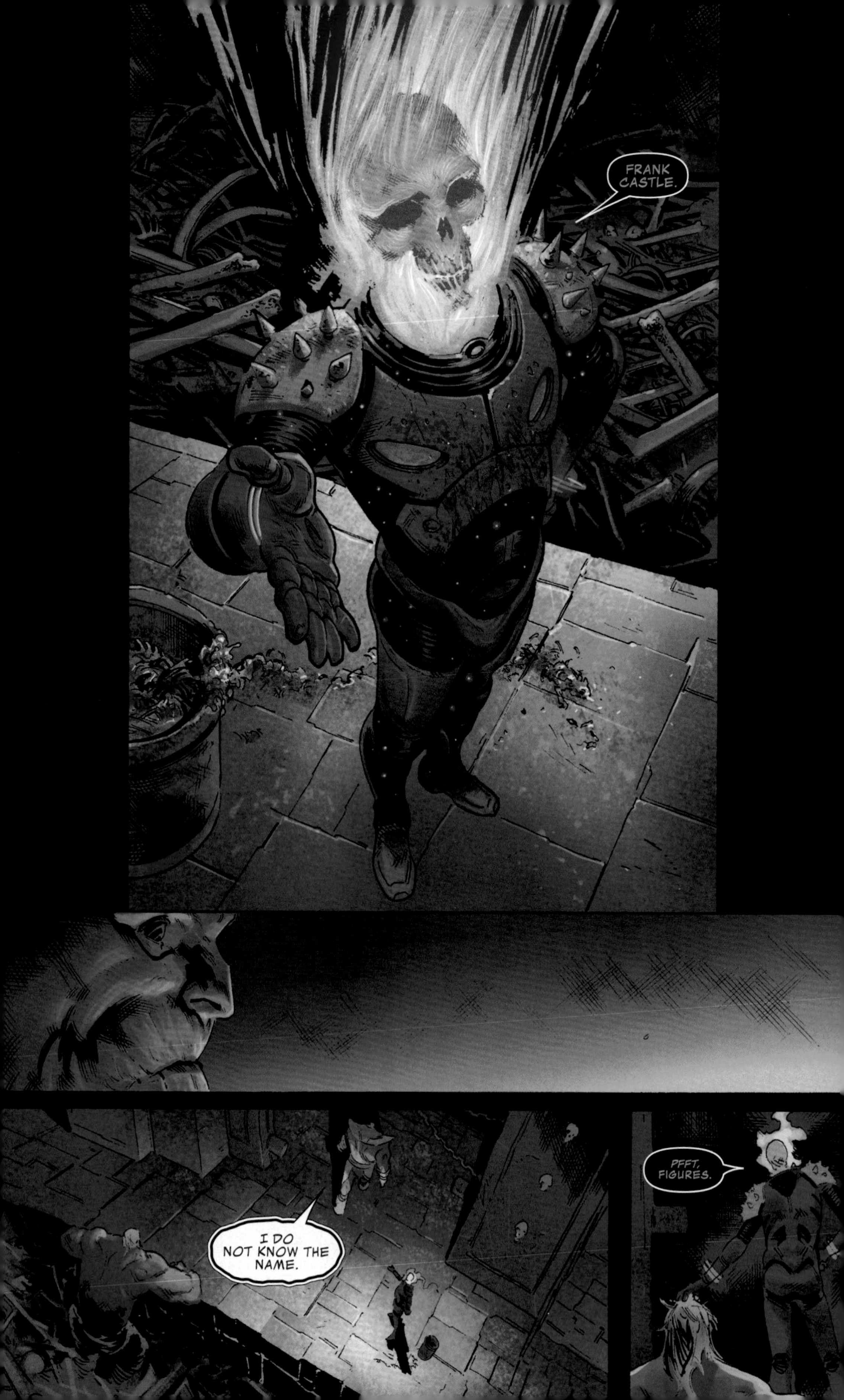
FRANK CASTLE.
I DO NOT KNOW THE NAME.
PFFT, FIGURES.

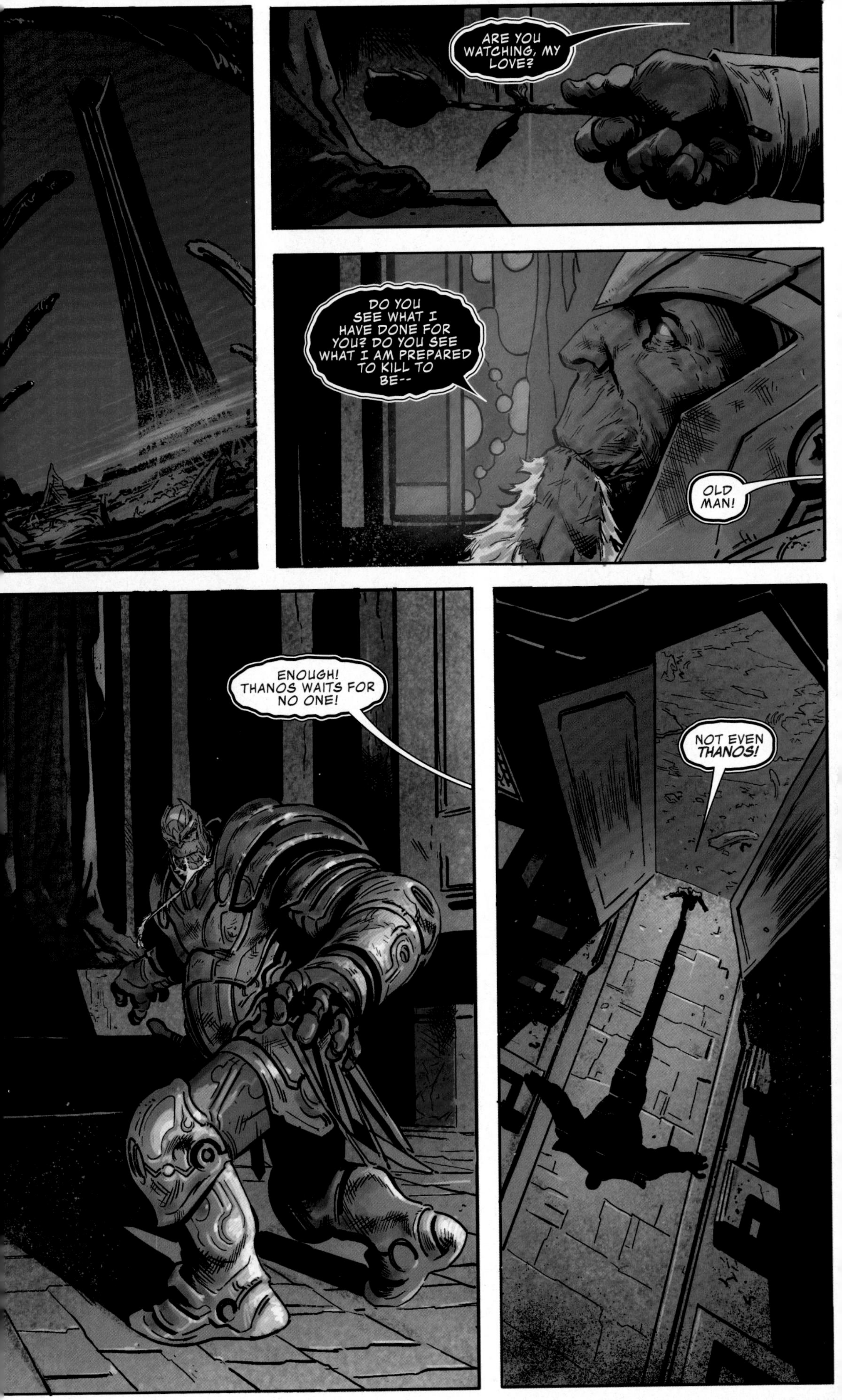
ARE YOU WATCHING, MY LOVE?
DO YOU SEE WHAT I HAVE DONE FOR YOU? DO YOU SEE WHAT I AM PREPARED TO KILL TO BE--
OLD MAN!
ENOUGH! THANOS WAITS FOR NO ONE!
NOT EVEN THANOS!

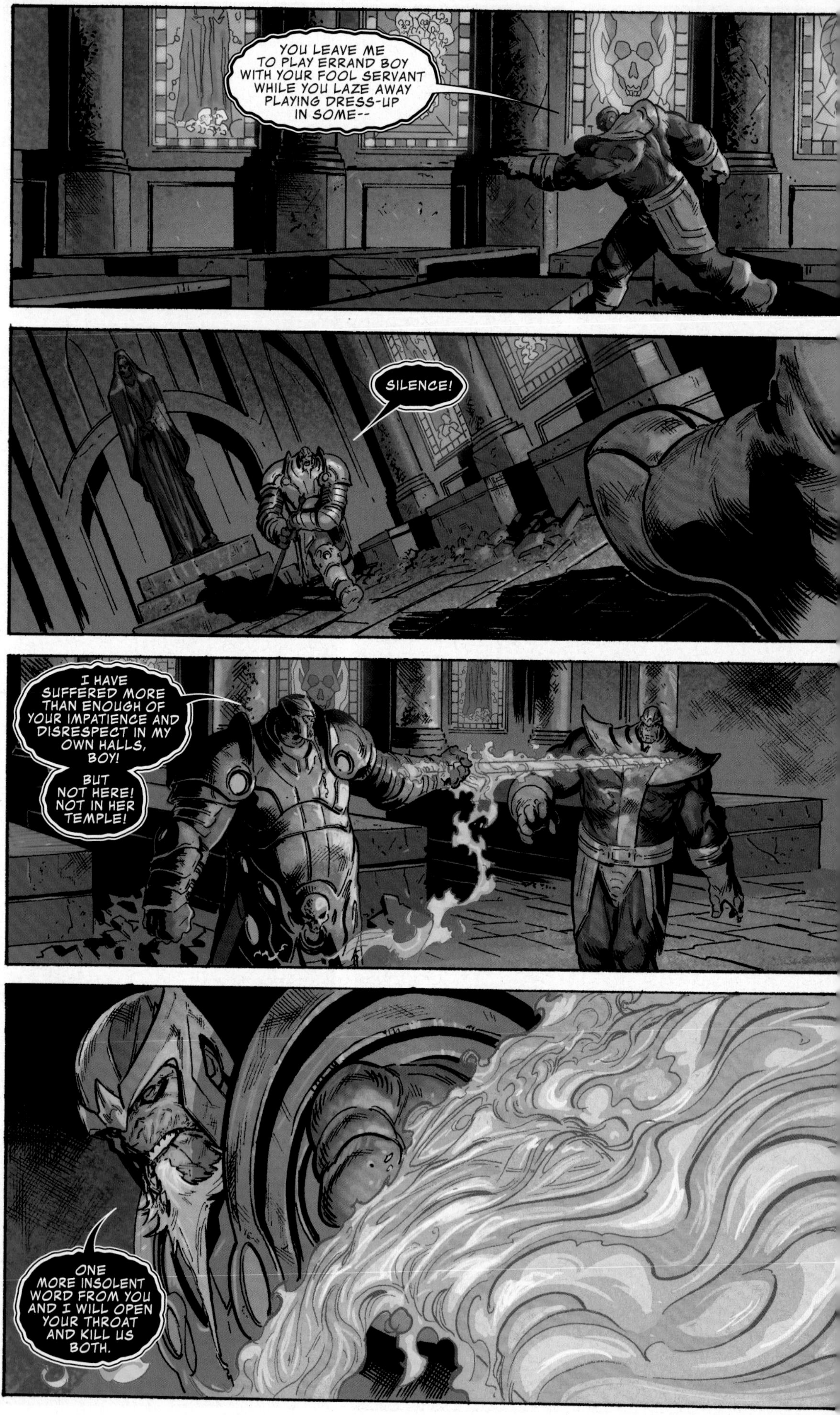
YOU LEAVE ME TO PLAY ERRAND BOY WITH YOUR FOOL SERVANT WHILE YOU LAZE AWAY PLAYING DRESS-UP IN SOME--
SILENCE!
I HAVE SUFFERED MORE THAN ENOUGH OF YOUR IMPATIENCE AND DISRESPECT IN MY OWN HALLS, BOY!
BUT NOT HERE! NOT IN HER TEMPLE!
ONE MORE INSOLENT WORD FROM YOU AND I WILL OPEN YOUR THROAT AND KILL US BOTH.

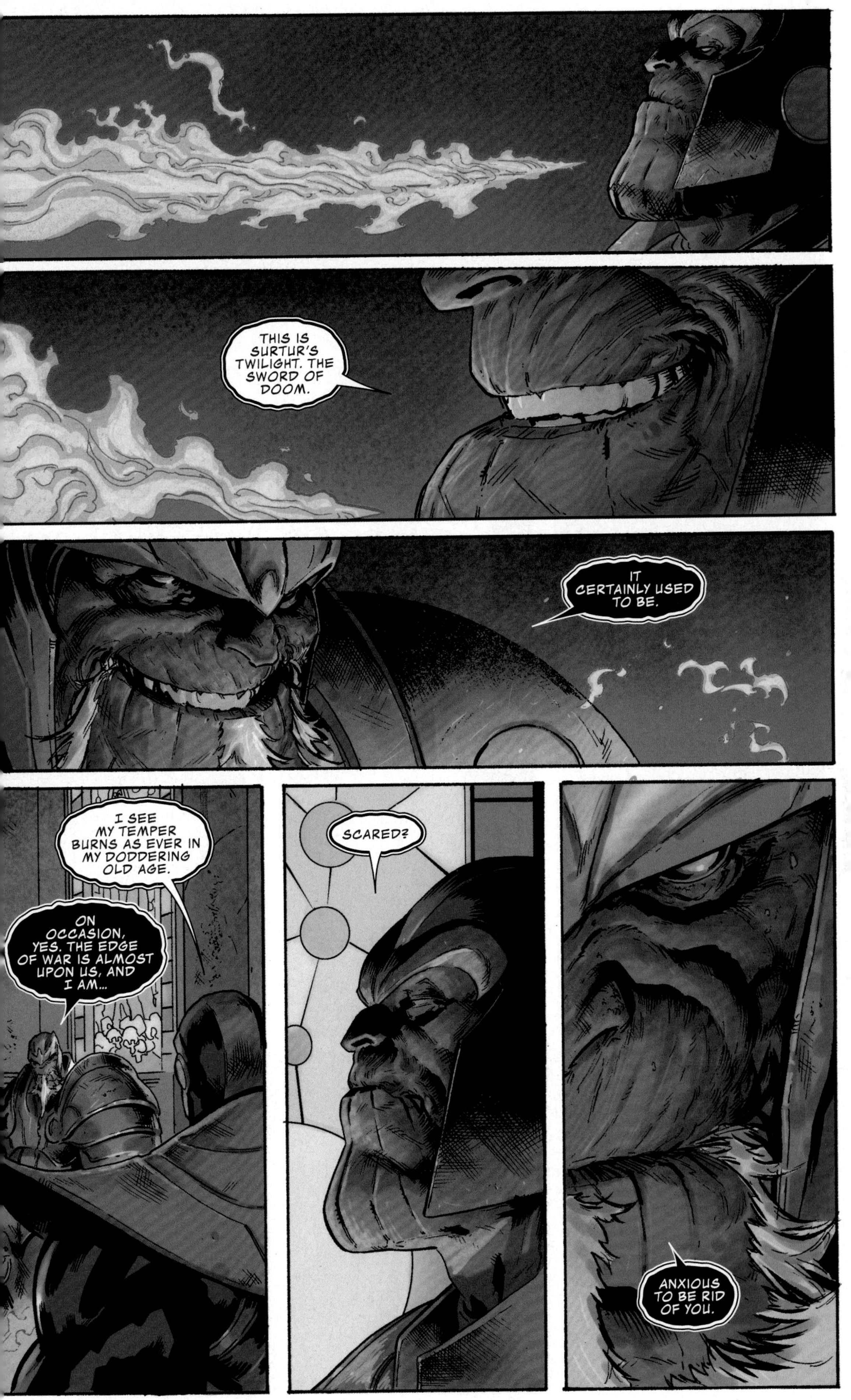
THIS IS SURTUR'S TWILIGHT. THE SWORD OF DOOM.
IT CERTAINLY USED TO BE.
I SEE MY TEMPER BURNS AS EVER IN MY DODDERING OLD AGE.
ON OCCASION, YES. THE EDGE OF WAR IS ALMOST UPON US, AND I AM...
SCARED?
ANXIOUS TO BE RID OF YOU.

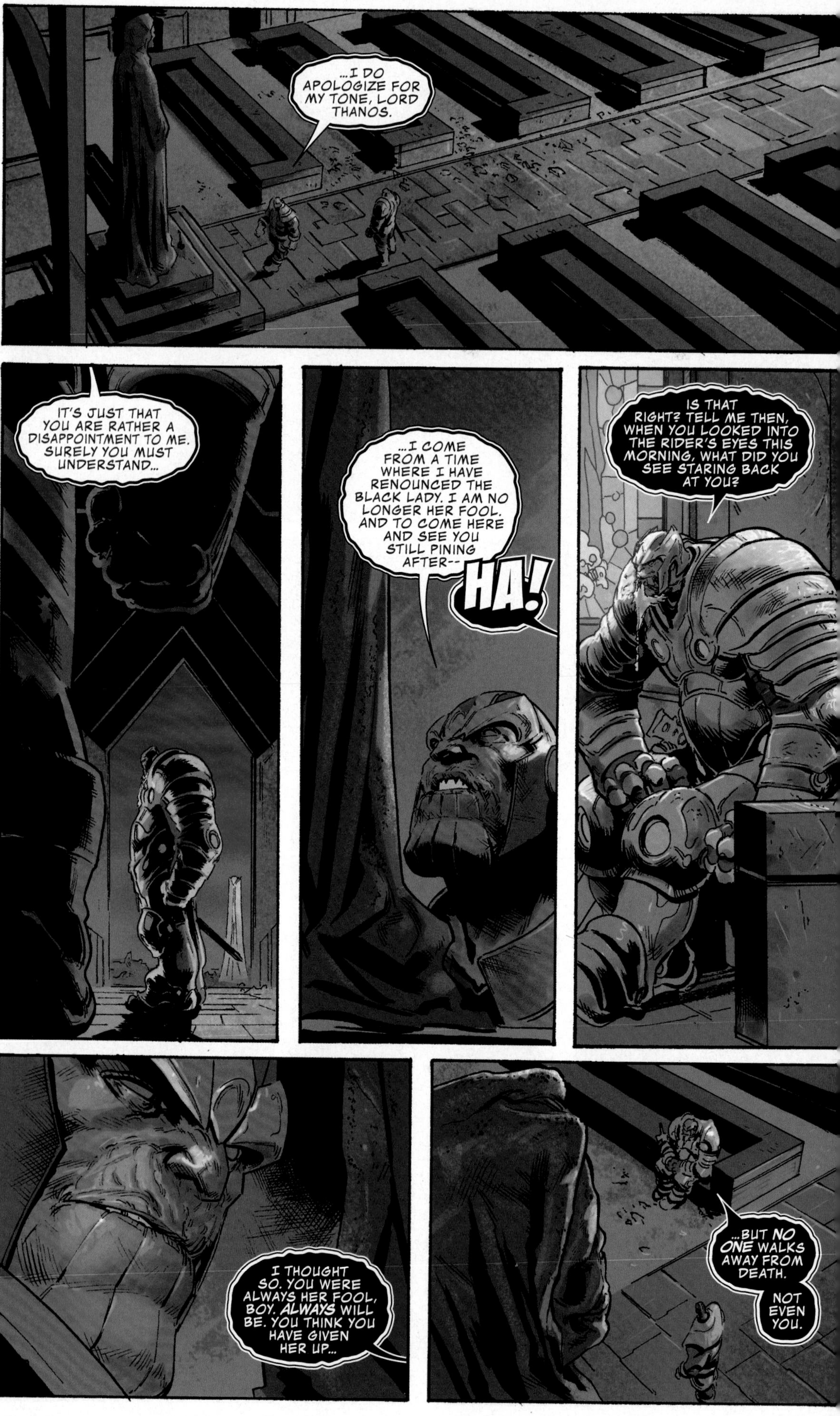

...I DO APOLOGIZE FOR MY TONE, LORD THANOS.
IT'S JUST THAT YOU ARE RATHER A DISAPPOINTMENT TO ME. SURELY YOU MUST UNDERSTAND...
...I COME FROM A TIME WHERE I HAVE RENOUNCED THE BLACK LADY. I AM NO LONGER HER FOOL. AND TO COME HERE AND SEE YOU STILL PINING AFTER--
HA!
IS THAT RIGHT? TELL ME THEN, WHEN YOU LOOKED INTO THE RIDER'S EYES THIS MORNING, WHAT DID YOU SEE STARING BACK AT YOU?
I THOUGHT SO. YOU WERE ALWAYS HER FOOL, BOY. ALWAYS WILL BE. YOU THINK YOU HAVE GIVEN HER UP...
...BUT NO ONE WALKS AWAY FROM DEATH.
NOT EVEN YOU.

AND WHEN EXACTLY WAS THE LAST TIME YOU SAW YOUR GREAT LOVE?

OH, HUNDREDS OF YEARS AGO? THOUSANDS? I DON'T RECALL TIME ANYMORE...

IT WAS...AFTER I KILLED THAT GOLD-SKINNED BOY... WHAT WAS HIS NAME? AARON SOMETHING?

...ADAM?

AH...YES, PERHAPS IT WAS.

SHE WAS... WAITING FOR ME AFTER THE BATTLE.

BUT, SHE... JUST STOOD THERE. NOT SAYING A WORD. AS IF SHE WERE WAITING FOR SOMETHING...

SOMETHING... MORE.

I DIDN'T KNOW WHAT IT WAS... IT TOOK ME SO LONG TO SEE IT.

I GAVE HER EVERYTHING... MY ENEMIES... MY ALLIES...MY CHILDREN...

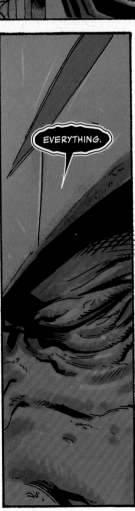

EVERYTHING.

AND YET...

WHRAAM-WHRAAM

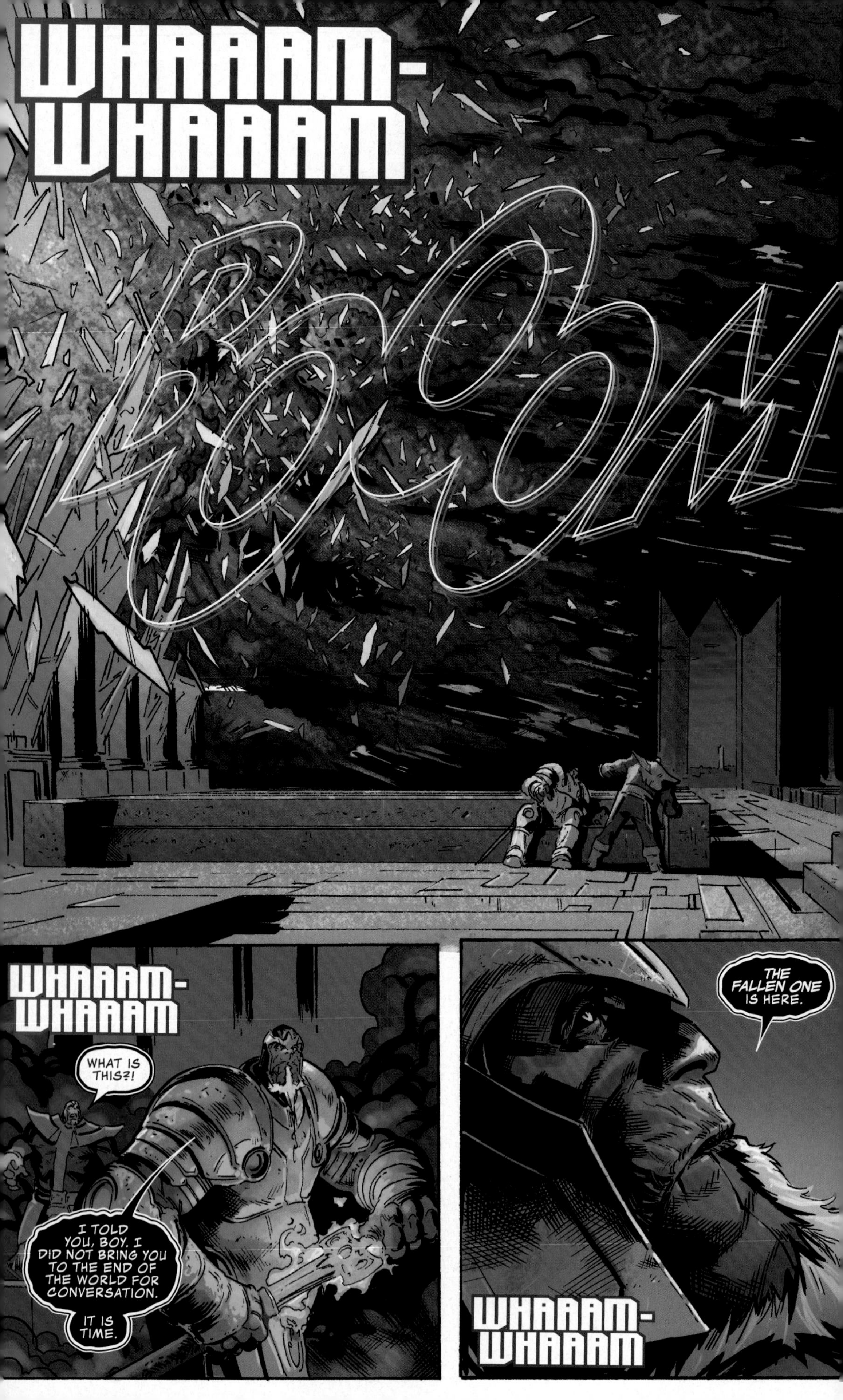
WHAAAM-
WHAAAM
BOOOM
WHAAAM-
WHAAAM
WHAT IS THIS?!
I TOLD YOU, BOY. I DID NOT BRING YOU TO THE END OF THE WORLD FOR CONVERSATION.
IT IS TIME.
THE FALLEN ONE IS HERE.
WHAAAM-
WHAAAM

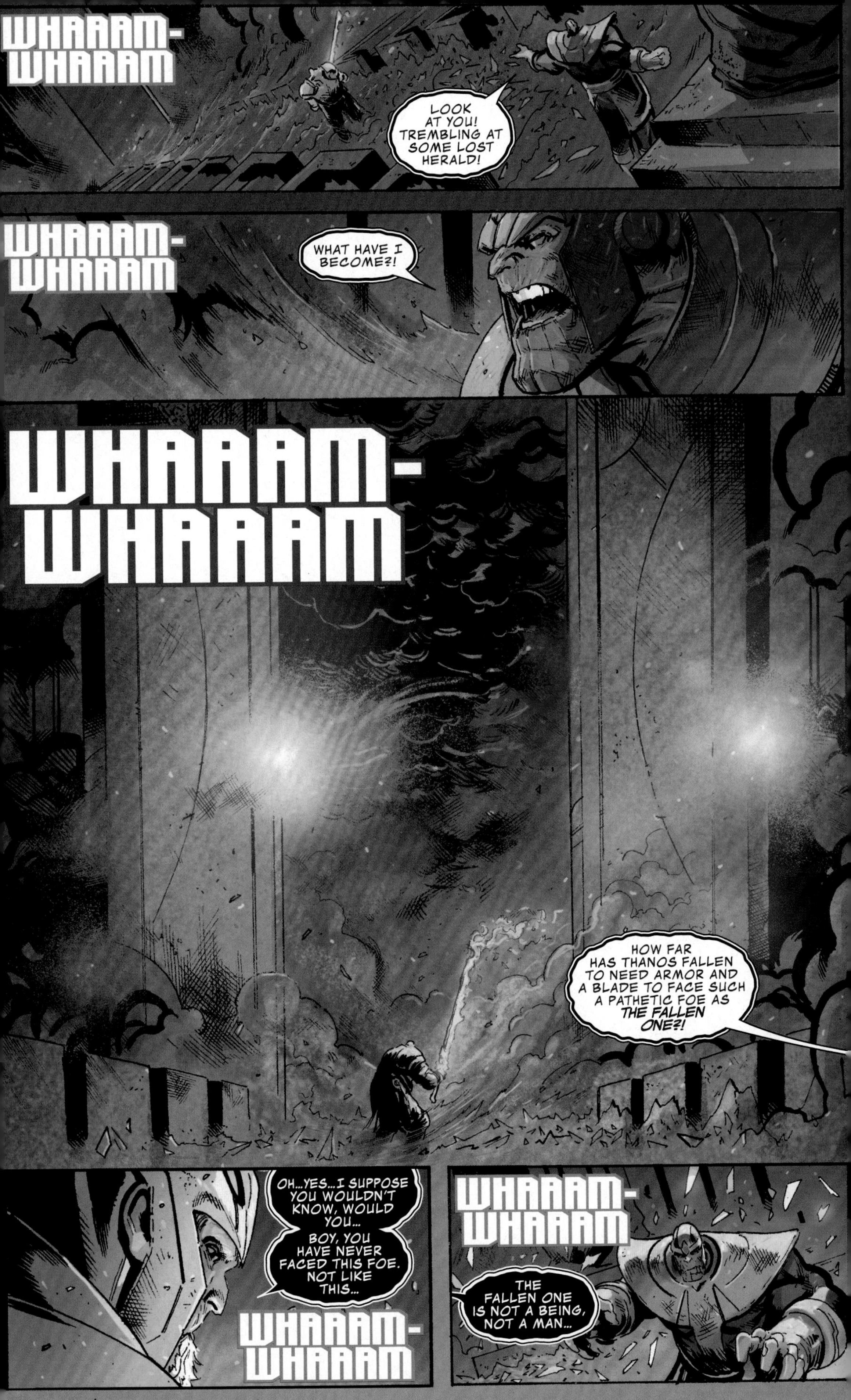
WHAAAM-WHAAAM
LOOK AT YOU! TREMBLING AT SOME LOST HERALD!
WHAAAM-WHAAAM
WHAT HAVE I BECOME?!
WHAAAM-WHAAAM
HOW FAR HAS THANOS FALLEN TO NEED ARMOR AND A BLADE TO FACE SUCH A PATHETIC FOE AS THE FALLEN ONE?!
OH...YES...I SUPPOSE YOU WOULDN'T KNOW, WOULD YOU...
BOY, YOU HAVE NEVER FACED THIS FOE. NOT LIKE THIS...
WHAAAM-WHAAAM
WHAAAM-WHAAAM
THE FALLEN ONE IS NOT A BEING, NOT A MAN...

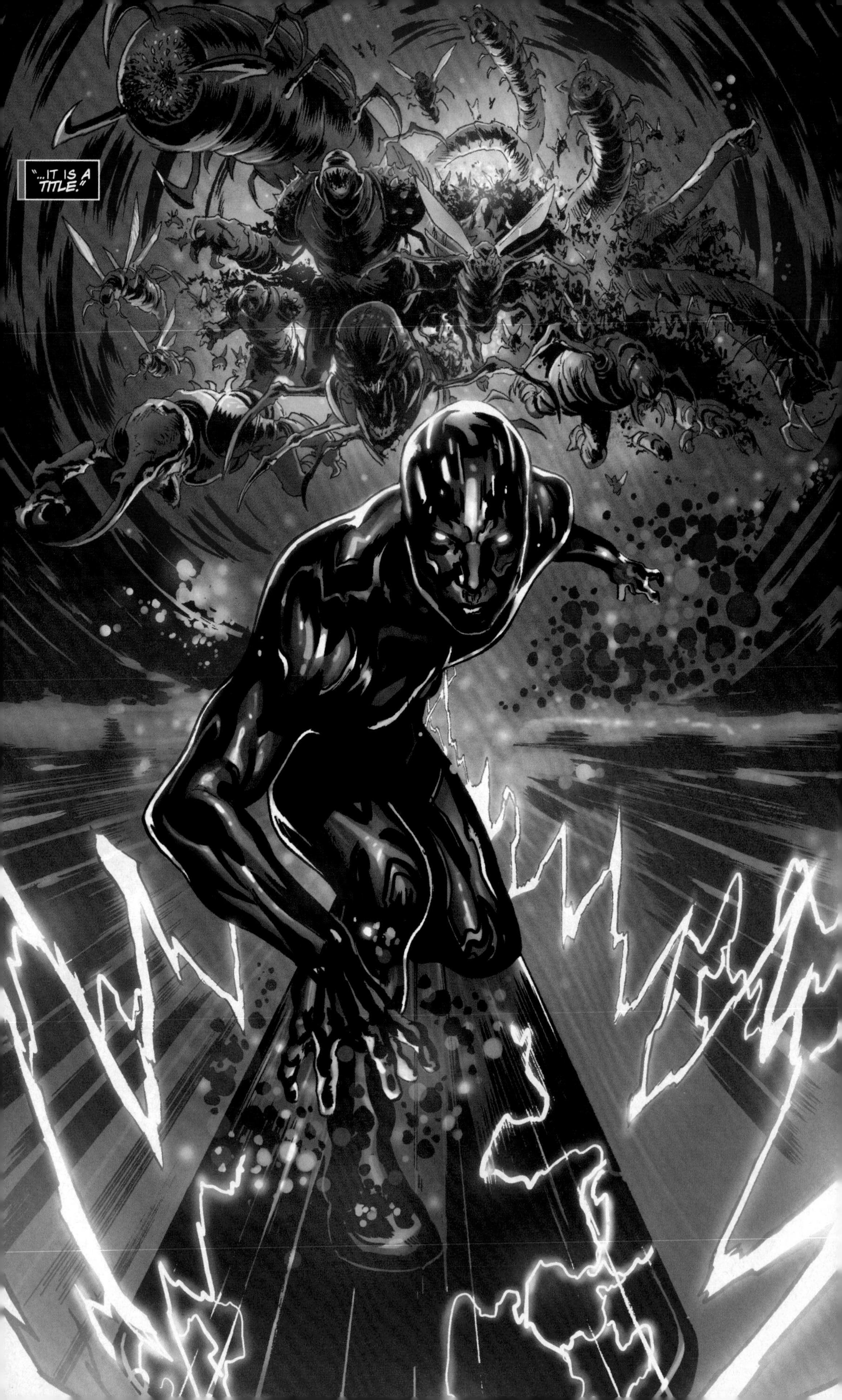
"...IT IS A TITLE."

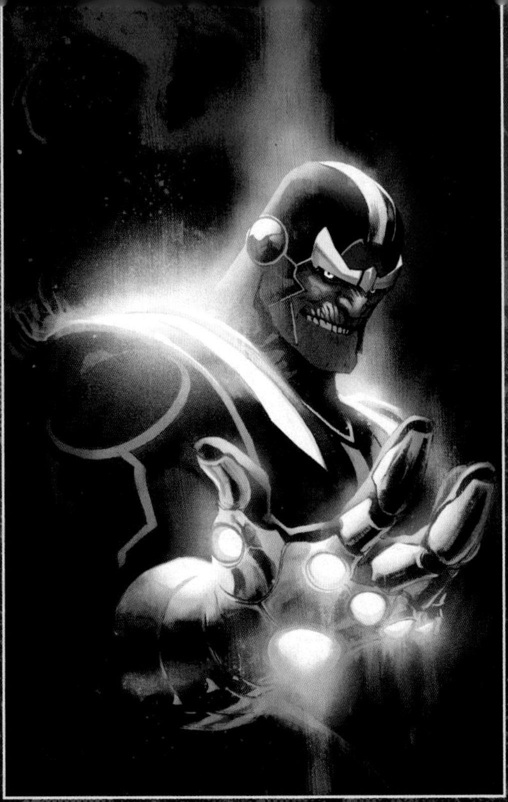

RAFAEL ALBUQUERQUE

NO. 13 VARIANT

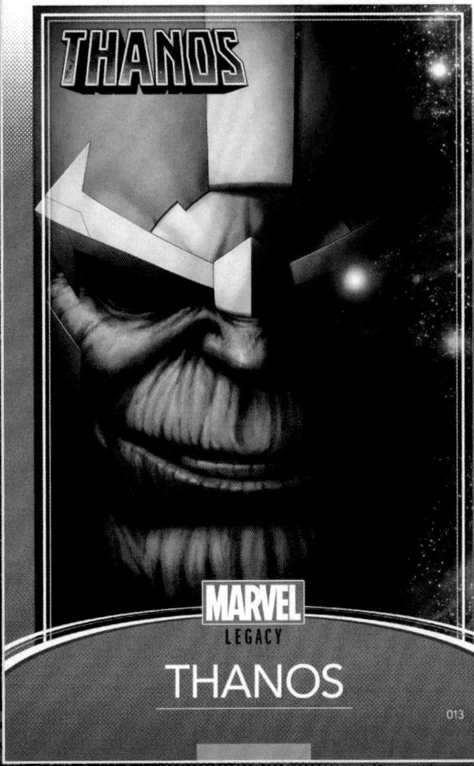
THANOS
MARVEL
LEGACY
THANOS
013

JOHN TYLER CHRISTOPHER

NO. 13 TRADING CARD VARIANT

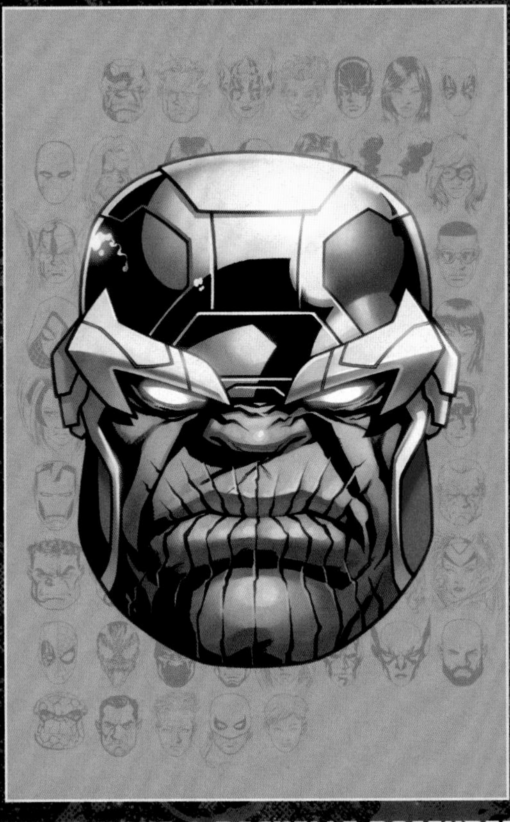

MIKE McKONE & RACHELLE ROSENBERG

NO. 13 LEGACY HEADSHOT VARIANT

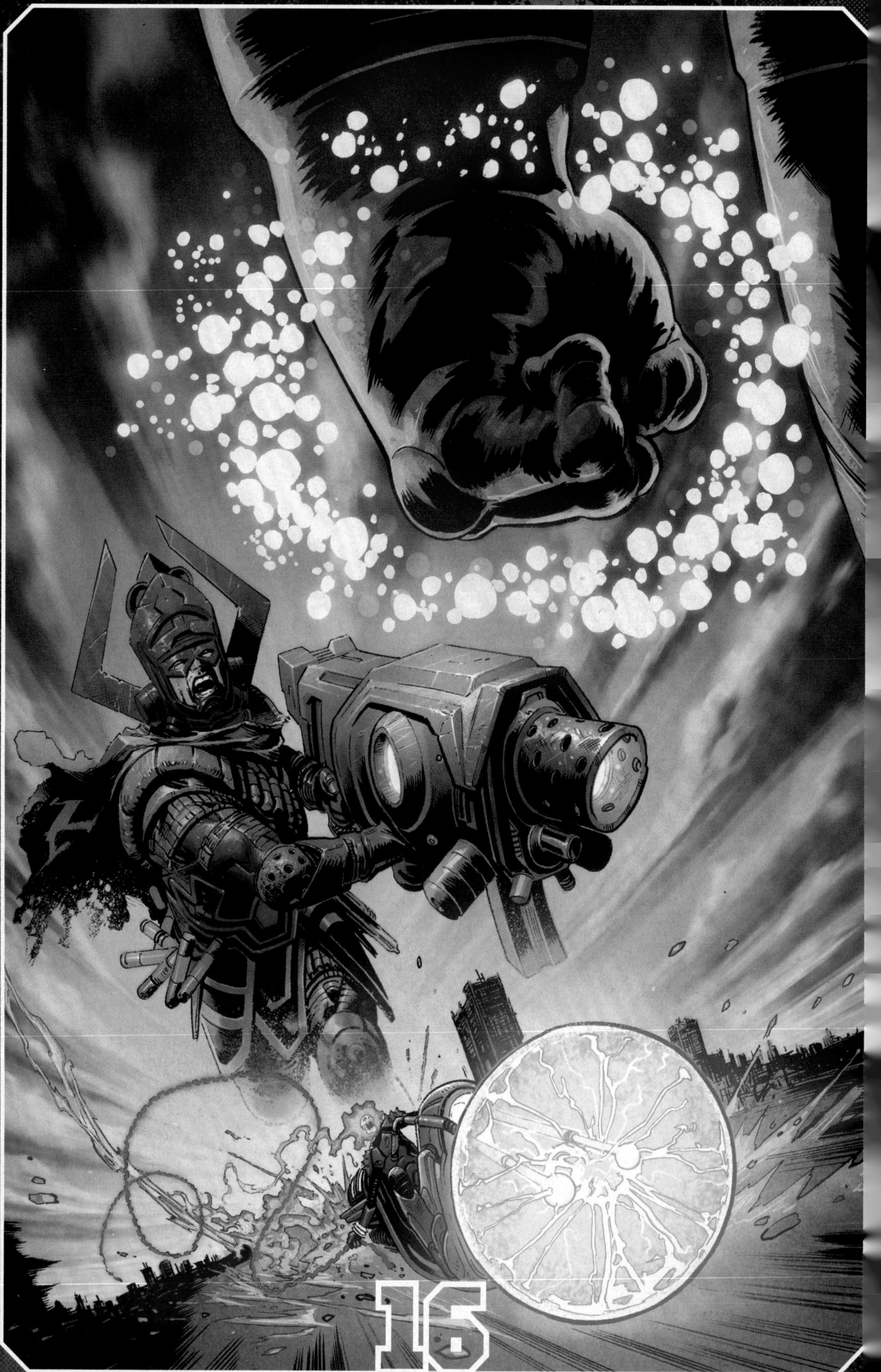
16

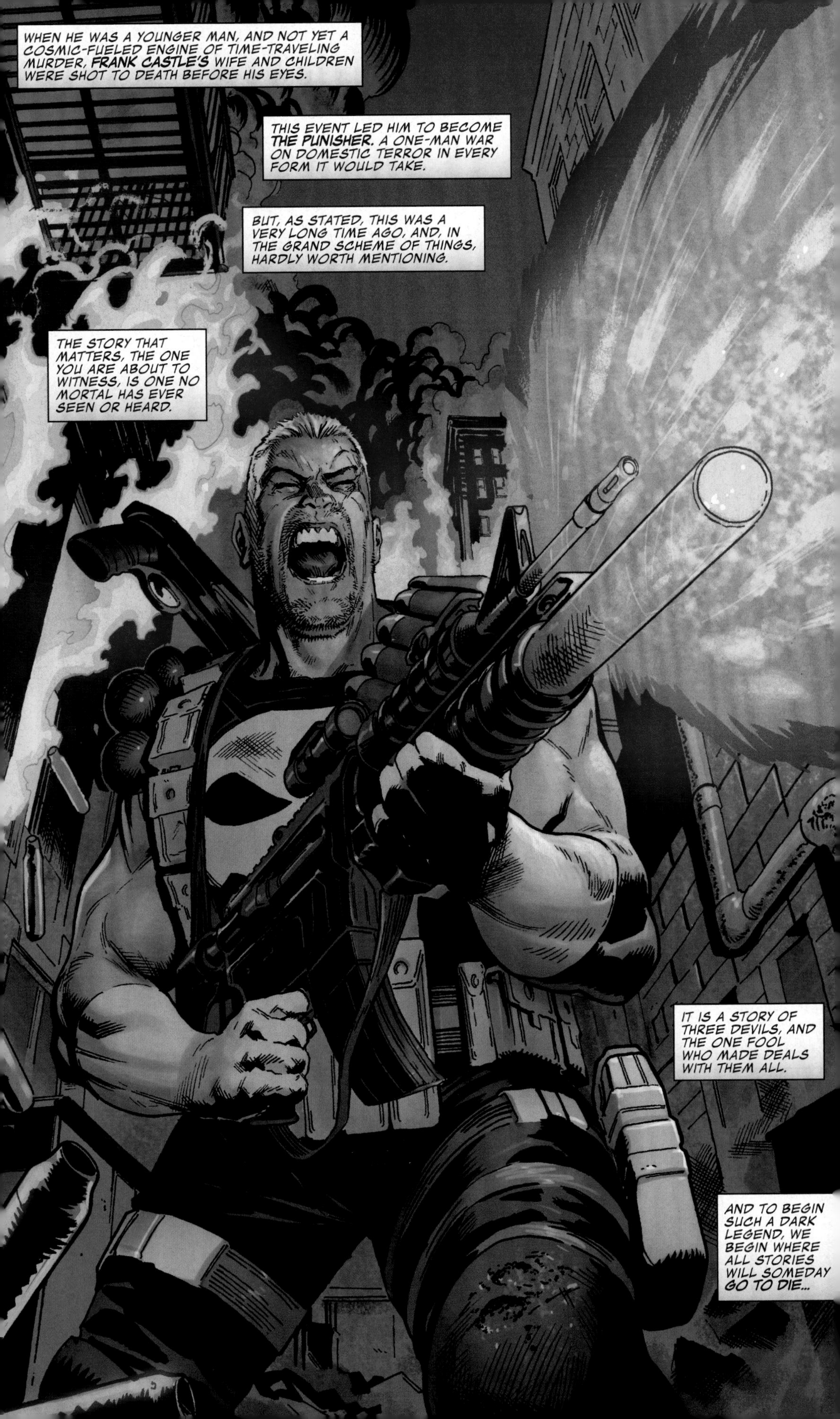
WHEN HE WAS A YOUNGER MAN, AND NOT YET A COSMIC-FUELED ENGINE OF TIME-TRAVELING MURDER, FRANK CASTLE'S WIFE AND CHILDREN WERE SHOT TO DEATH BEFORE HIS EYES.
THIS EVENT LED HIM TO BECOME THE PUNISHER. A ONE-MAN WAR ON DOMESTIC TERROR IN EVERY FORM IT WOULD TAKE.
BUT, AS STATED, THIS WAS A VERY LONG TIME AGO, AND, IN THE GRAND SCHEME OF THINGS, HARDLY WORTH MENTIONING.
THE STORY THAT MATTERS, THE ONE YOU ARE ABOUT TO WITNESS, IS ONE NO MORTAL HAS EVER SEEN OR HEARD.
IT IS A STORY OF THREE DEVILS, AND THE ONE FOOL WHO MADE DEALS WITH THEM ALL.
AND TO BEGIN SUCH A DARK LEGEND, WE BEGIN WHERE ALL STORIES WILL SOMEDAY GO TO DIE...

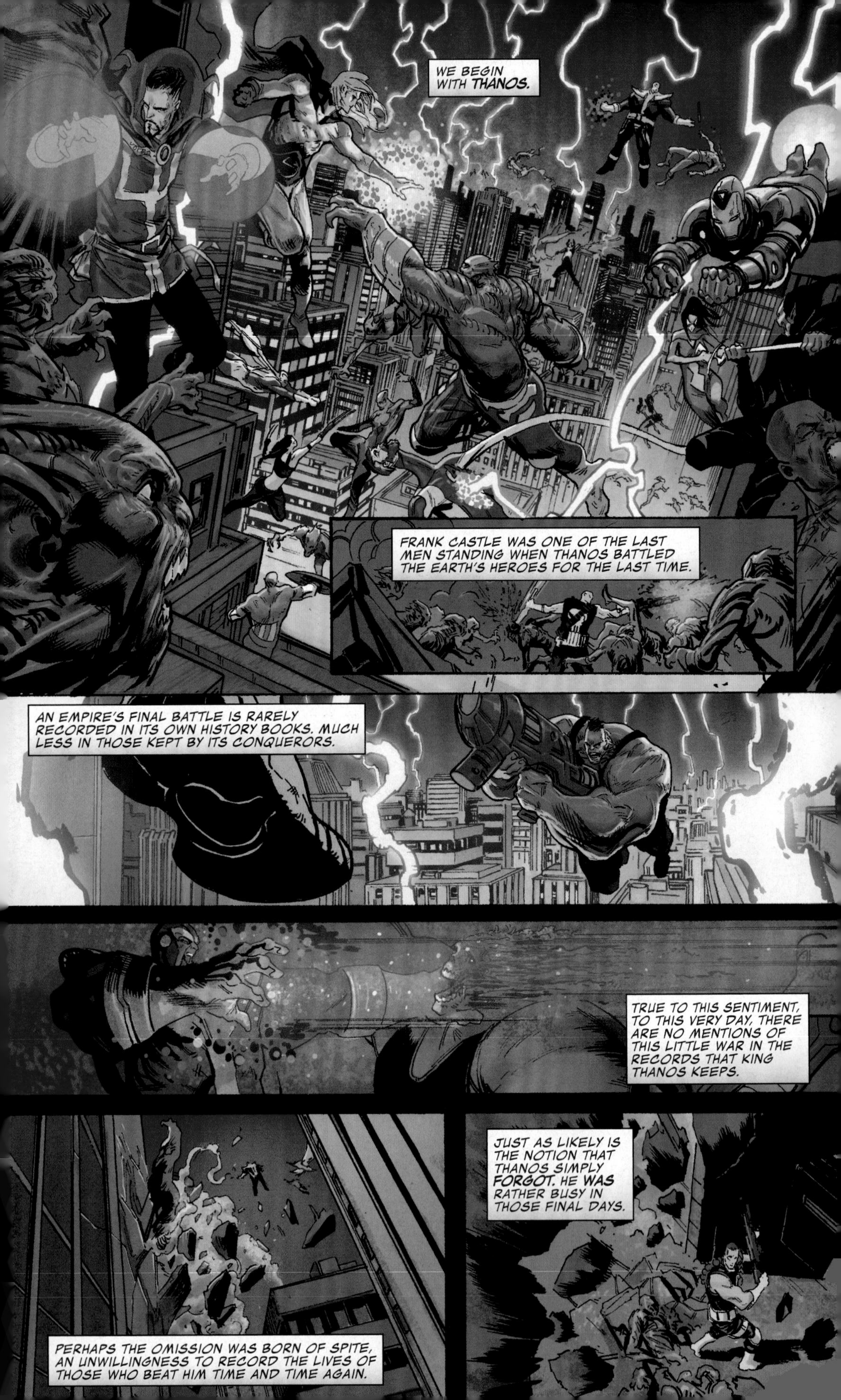
WE BEGIN WITH THANOS.
FRANK CASTLE WAS ONE OF THE LAST MEN STANDING WHEN THANOS BATTLED THE EARTH'S HEROES FOR THE LAST TIME.
AN EMPIRE'S FINAL BATTLE IS RARELY RECORDED IN ITS OWN HISTORY BOOKS. MUCH LESS IN THOSE KEPT BY ITS CONQUERORS.
TRUE TO THIS SENTIMENT, TO THIS VERY DAY, THERE ARE NO MENTIONS OF THIS LITTLE WAR IN THE RECORDS THAT KING THANOS KEEPS.
PERHAPS THE OMISSION WAS BORN OF SPITE, AN UNWILLINGNESS TO RECORD THE LIVES OF THOSE WHO BEAT HIM TIME AND TIME AGAIN.
JUST AS LIKELY IS THE NOTION THAT THANOS SIMPLY FORGOT. HE WAS RATHER BUSY IN THOSE FINAL DAYS.

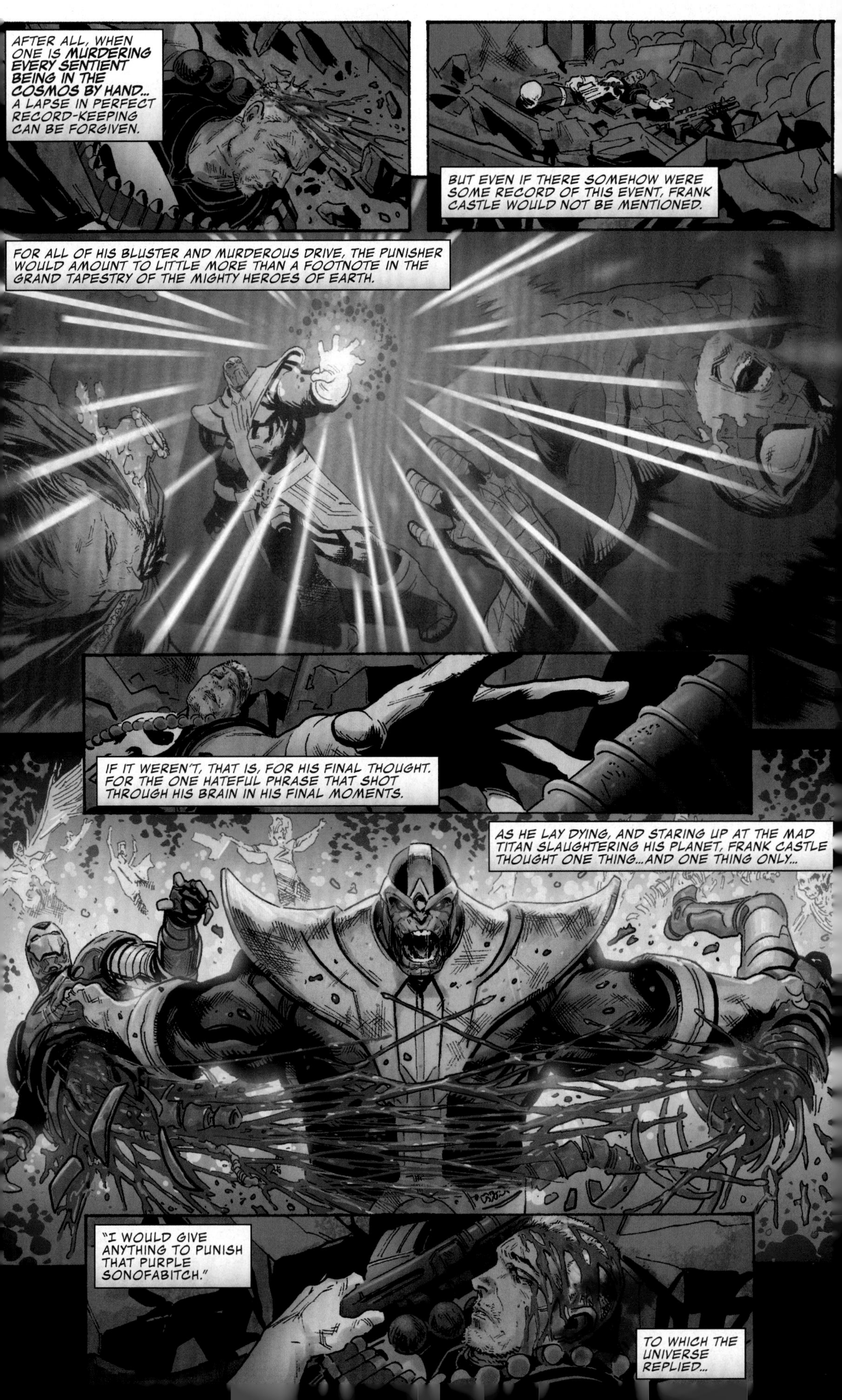
AFTER ALL, WHEN ONE IS MURDERING EVERY SENTIENT BEING IN THE COSMOS BY HAND... A LAPSE IN PERFECT RECORD-KEEPING CAN BE FORGIVEN.
BUT EVEN IF THERE SOMEHOW WERE SOME RECORD OF THIS EVENT, FRANK CASTLE WOULD NOT BE MENTIONED.
FOR ALL OF HIS BLUSTER AND MURDEROUS DRIVE, THE PUNISHER WOULD AMOUNT TO LITTLE MORE THAN A FOOTNOTE IN THE GRAND TAPESTRY OF THE MIGHTY HEROES OF EARTH.
IF IT WEREN'T, THAT IS, FOR HIS FINAL THOUGHT. FOR THE ONE HATEFUL PHRASE THAT SHOT THROUGH HIS BRAIN IN HIS FINAL MOMENTS.
AS HE LAY DYING, AND STARING UP AT THE MAD TITAN SLAUGHTERING HIS PLANET, FRANK CASTLE THOUGHT ONE THING...AND ONE THING ONLY...
"I WOULD GIVE ANYTHING TO PUNISH THAT PURPLE SONOFABITCH."
TO WHICH THE UNIVERSE REPLIED...

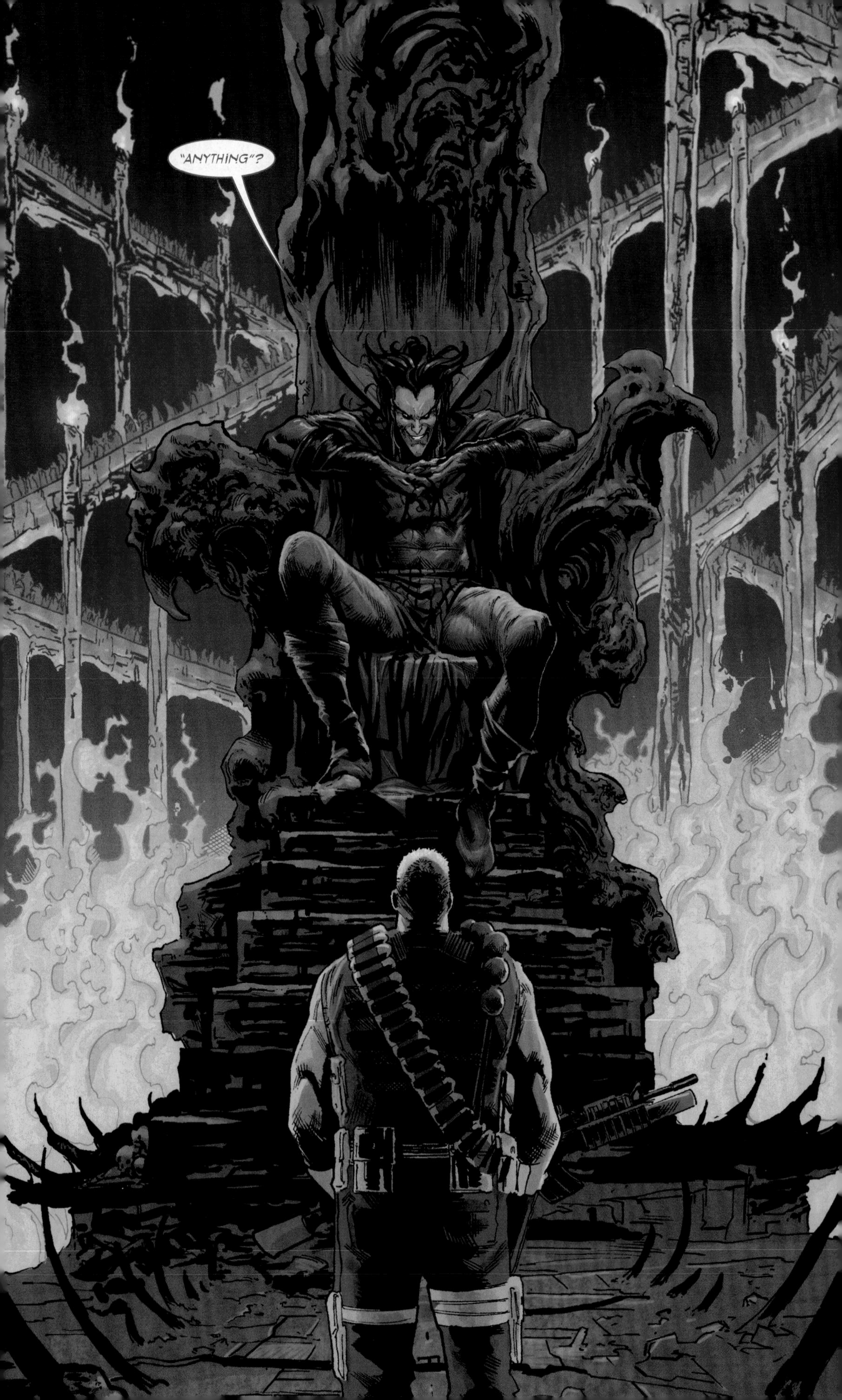
"ANYTHING"?

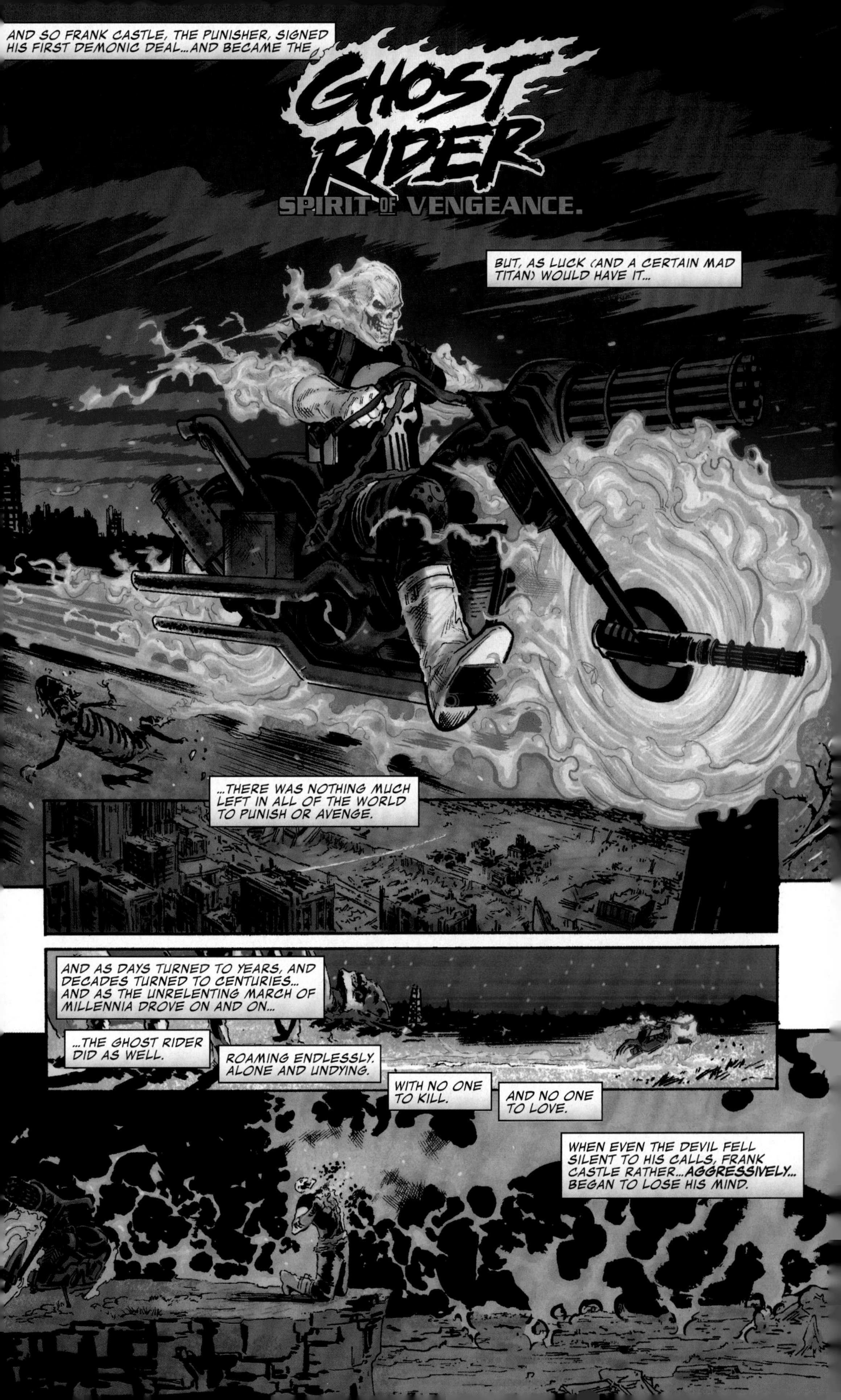
AND SO FRANK CASTLE, THE PUNISHER, SIGNED HIS FIRST DEMONIC DEAL...AND BECAME THE
GHOST RIDER
SPIRIT OF VENGEANCE.
BUT, AS LUCK (AND A CERTAIN MAD TITAN) WOULD HAVE IT...
...THERE WAS NOTHING MUCH LEFT IN ALL OF THE WORLD TO PUNISH OR AVENGE.
AND AS DAYS TURNED TO YEARS, AND DECADES TURNED TO CENTURIES... AND AS THE UNRELENTING MARCH OF MILLENNIA DROVE ON AND ON...
...THE GHOST RIDER DID AS WELL.
ROAMING ENDLESSLY. ALONE AND UNDYING.
WITH NO ONE TO KILL.
AND NO ONE TO LOVE.
WHEN EVEN THE DEVIL FELL SILENT TO HIS CALLS, FRANK CASTLE RATHER...AGGRESSIVELY... BEGAN TO LOSE HIS MIND.

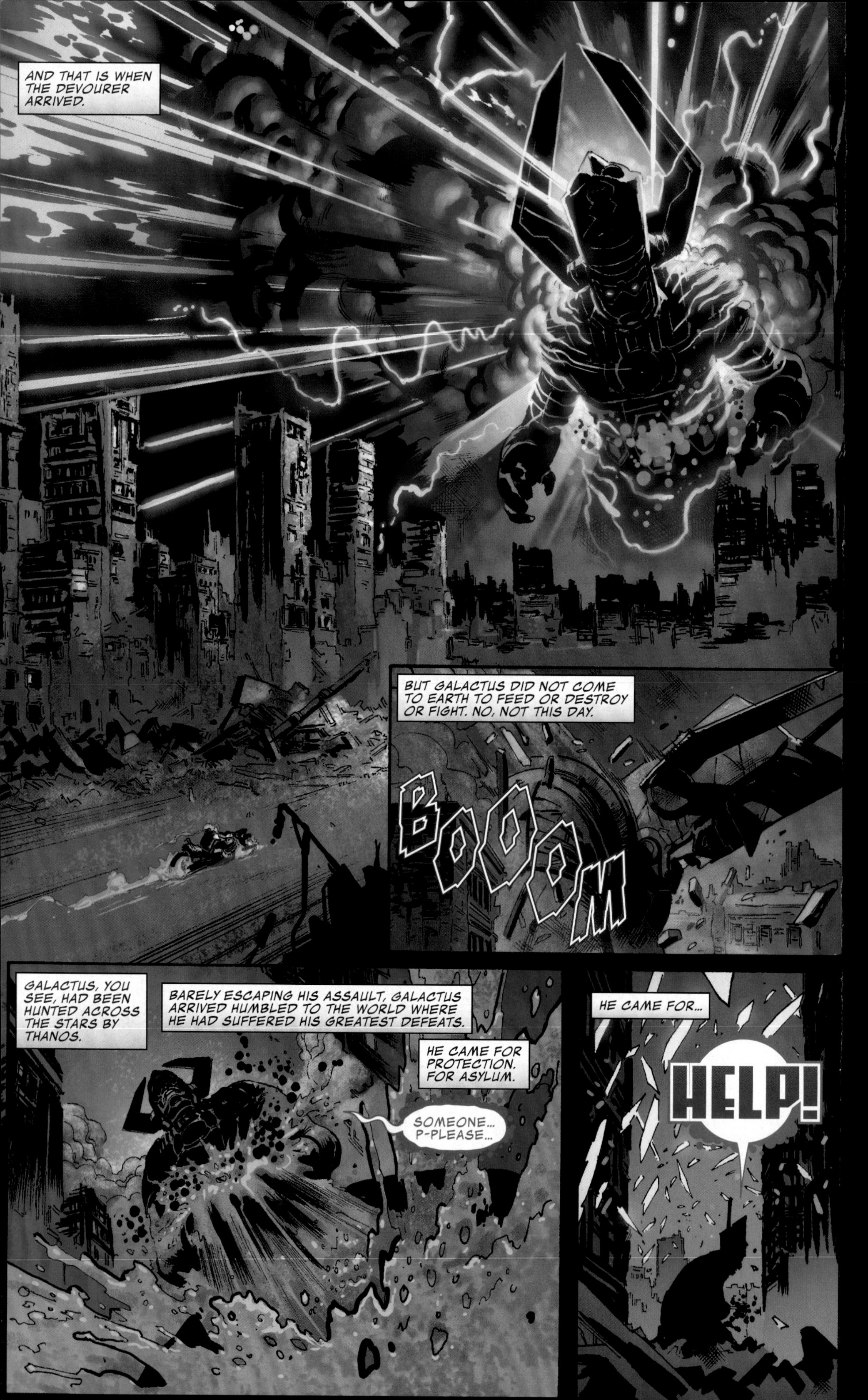
AND THAT IS WHEN THE DEVOURER ARRIVED.
BUT GALACTUS DID NOT COME TO EARTH TO FEED OR DESTROY OR FIGHT. NO, NOT THIS DAY.
BOOOOM
GALACTUS, YOU SEE, HAD BEEN HUNTED ACROSS THE STARS BY THANOS.
BARELY ESCAPING HIS ASSAULT, GALACTUS ARRIVED HUMBLED TO THE WORLD WHERE HE HAD SUFFERED HIS GREATEST DEFEATS.
HE CAME FOR PROTECTION. FOR ASYLUM.
SOMEONE... P-PLEASE...
HE CAME FOR...
HELP!

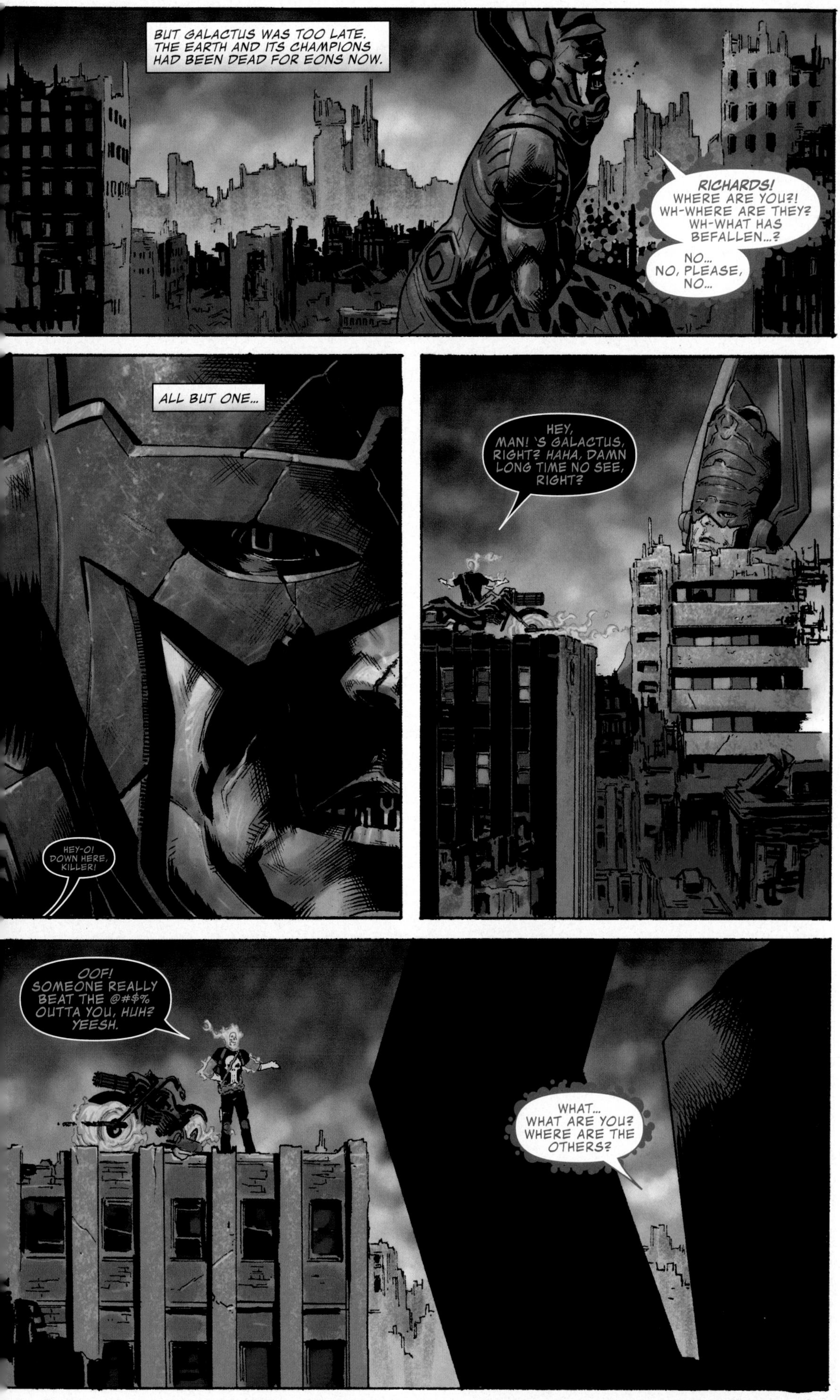

BUT GALACTUS WAS TOO LATE. THE EARTH AND ITS CHAMPIONS HAD BEEN DEAD FOR EONS NOW.
RICHARDS! WHERE ARE YOU?! WH-WHERE ARE THEY? WH-WHAT HAS BEFALLEN...?
NO... NO, PLEASE, NO...
ALL BUT ONE...
HEY-O! DOWN HERE, KILLER!
HEY, MAN! 'S GALACTUS, RIGHT? HAHA, DAMN LONG TIME NO SEE, RIGHT?
OOF! SOMEONE REALLY BEAT THE @#$% OUTTA YOU, HUH? YEESH.
WHAT... WHAT ARE YOU? WHERE ARE THE OTHERS?

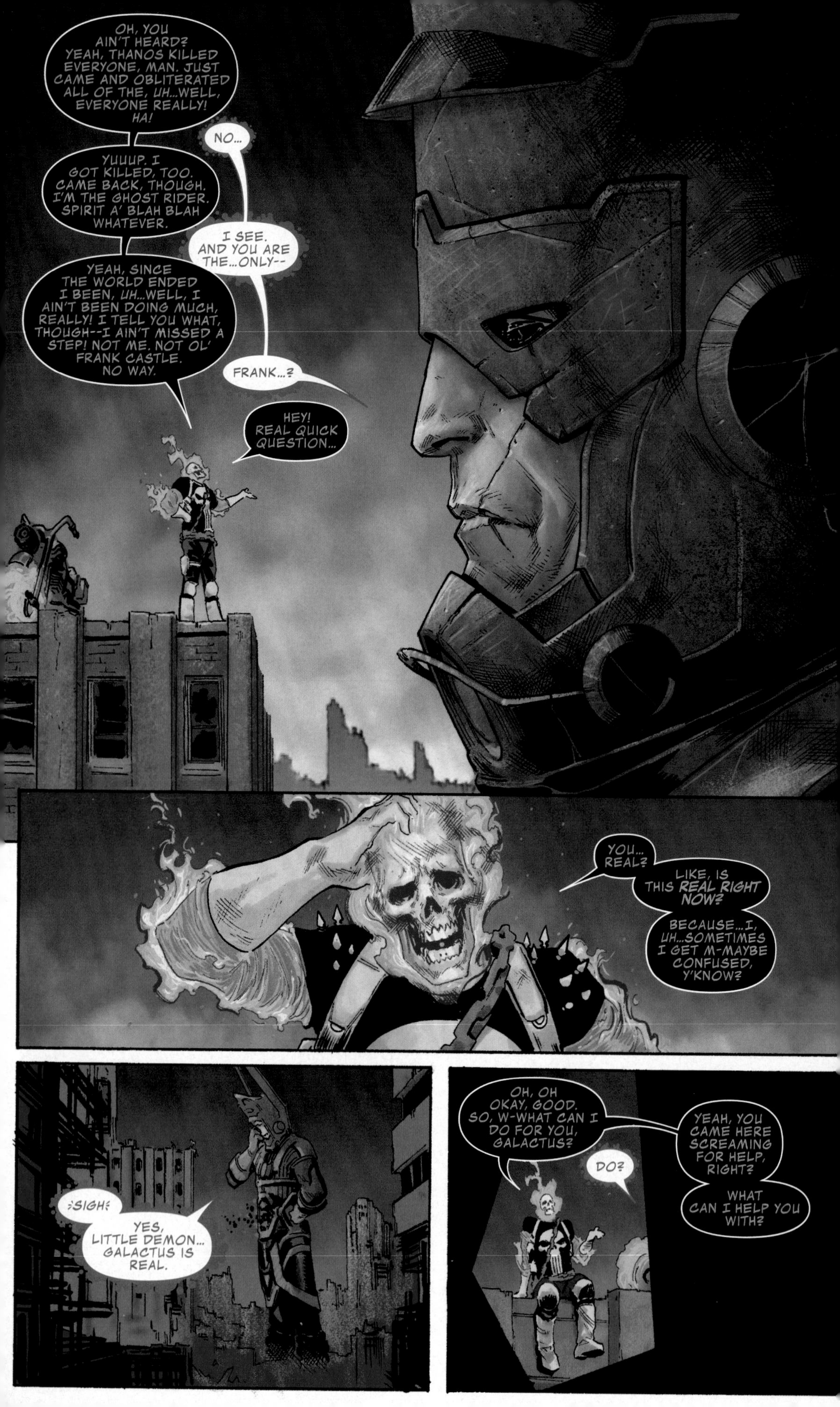

OH, YOU AIN'T HEARD? YEAH, THANOS KILLED EVERYONE, MAN. JUST CAME AND OBLITERATED ALL OF THE, UH...WELL, EVERYONE REALLY! HA!
NO...
YUUUP. I GOT KILLED, TOO. CAME BACK, THOUGH. I'M THE GHOST RIDER. SPIRIT A' BLAH BLAH WHATEVER.
I SEE. AND YOU ARE THE...ONLY--
YEAH, SINCE THE WORLD ENDED I BEEN, UH...WELL, I AIN'T BEEN DOING MUCH, REALLY! I TELL YOU WHAT, THOUGH--I AIN'T MISSED A STEP! NOT ME. NOT OL' FRANK CASTLE. NO WAY.
FRANK...?
HEY! REAL QUICK QUESTION...
YOU... REAL?
LIKE, IS THIS REAL RIGHT NOW?
BECAUSE...I, UH...SOMETIMES I GET M-MAYBE CONFUSED, Y'KNOW?
:SIGH:
YES, LITTLE DEMON... GALACTUS IS REAL.
OH, OH OKAY, GOOD. SO, W-WHAT CAN I DO FOR YOU, GALACTUS?
DO?
YEAH, YOU CAME HERE SCREAMING FOR HELP, RIGHT?
WHAT CAN I HELP YOU WITH?

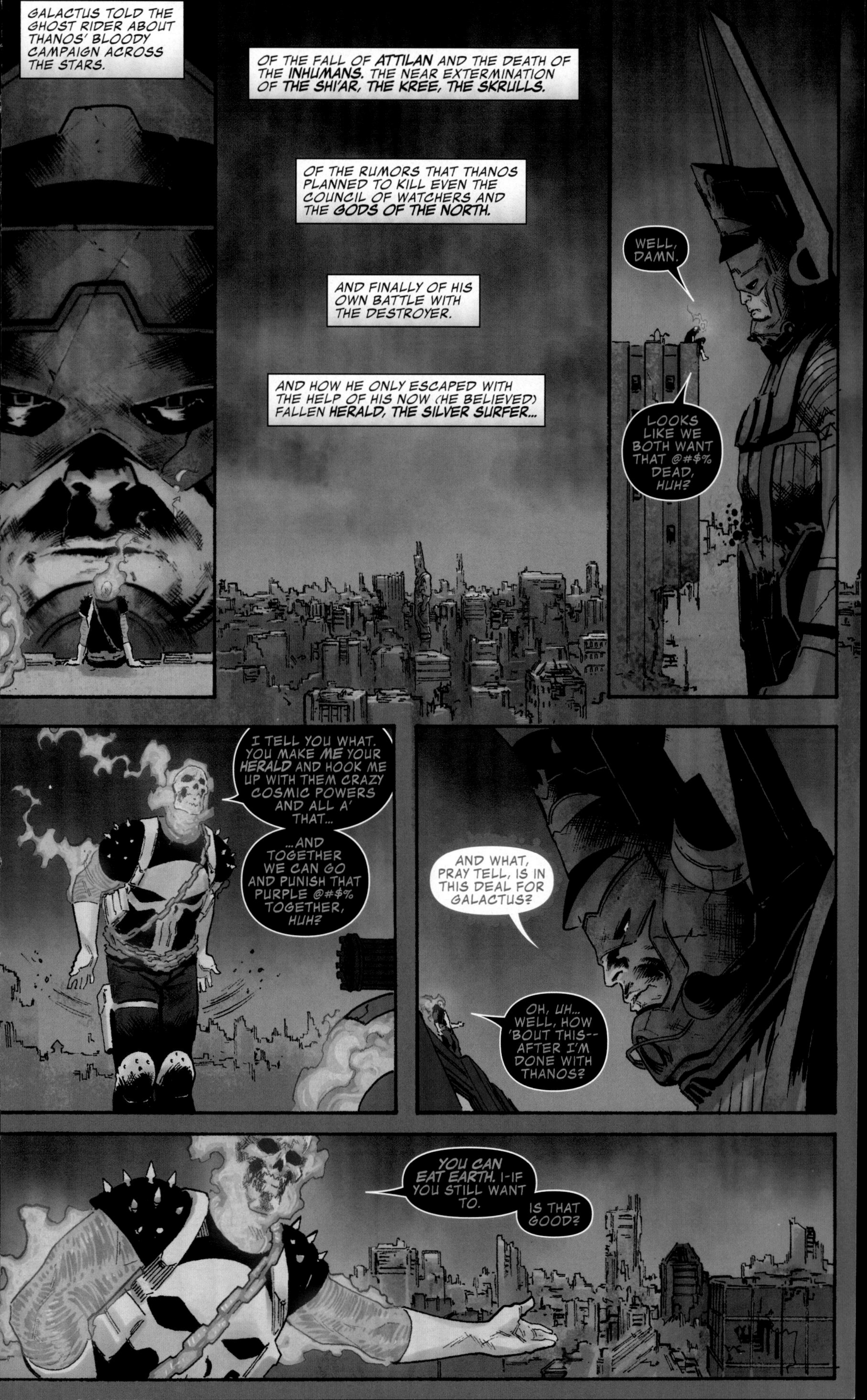
GALACTUS TOLD THE GHOST RIDER ABOUT THANOS' BLOODY CAMPAIGN ACROSS THE STARS.
OF THE FALL OF ATTILAN AND THE DEATH OF THE INHUMANS. THE NEAR EXTERMINATION OF THE SHI'AR, THE KREE, THE SKRULLS.
OF THE RUMORS THAT THANOS PLANNED TO KILL EVEN THE COUNCIL OF WATCHERS AND THE GODS OF THE NORTH.
AND FINALLY OF HIS OWN BATTLE WITH THE DESTROYER.
AND HOW HE ONLY ESCAPED WITH THE HELP OF HIS NOW (HE BELIEVED) FALLEN HERALD, THE SILVER SURFER...
WELL, DAMN.
LOOKS LIKE WE BOTH WANT THAT @#$% DEAD, HUH?
I TELL YOU WHAT. YOU MAKE ME YOUR HERALD AND HOOK ME UP WITH THEM CRAZY COSMIC POWERS AND ALL A' THAT...
...AND TOGETHER WE CAN GO AND PUNISH THAT PURPLE @#$% TOGETHER, HUH?
AND WHAT, PRAY TELL, IS IN THIS DEAL FOR GALACTUS?
OH, UH... WELL, HOW 'BOUT THIS-- AFTER I'M DONE WITH THANOS?
YOU CAN EAT EARTH. I-IF YOU STILL WANT TO.
IS THAT GOOD?

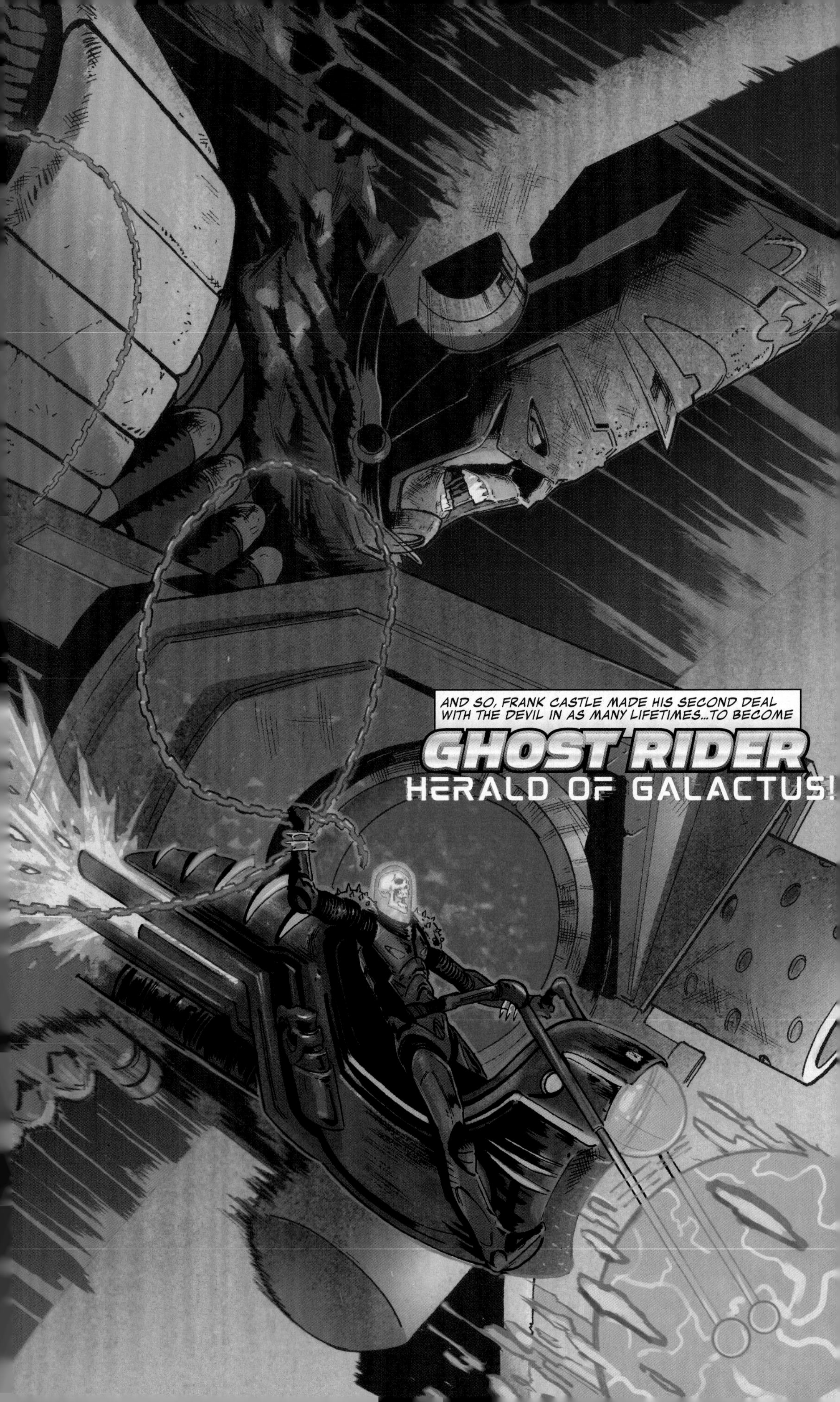
AND SO, FRANK CASTLE MADE HIS SECOND DEAL WITH THE DEVIL IN AS MANY LIFETIMES...TO BECOME
GHOST RIDER
HERALD OF GALACTUS!

TOGETHER THEY ROARED ACROSS THE COSMOS ON A QUEST TO HALT THANOS' SYSTEMATIC ANNIHILATION OF EVERY SENTIENT BEING IN EXISTENCE.

THEIR INCREDIBLE STORY LASTED CENTURIES.

THE HERCULEAN DEEDS THEY ACCOMPLISHED, AND THE FOES THEY VANQUISHED IN THEIR SEARCH FOR THE MAD TITAN KING, BECAME LEGEND.

THE ROAR OF THE RIDER'S ENGINES (AUDIBLE EVEN IN THE VACUUM OF SPACE) BECAME A BEACON OF HOPE TO THOSE STILL ALIVE TO HEAR THEM.

A FAINT, DISTANT PROMISE THAT... PERHAPS NOT ALL WAS LOST IN THE STARS.

THAT EVEN IN THESE DARKEST OF DAYS...THE HEART OF A HERO STILL BEAT INSIDE OF THE CHEST OF A DEAD MAN.

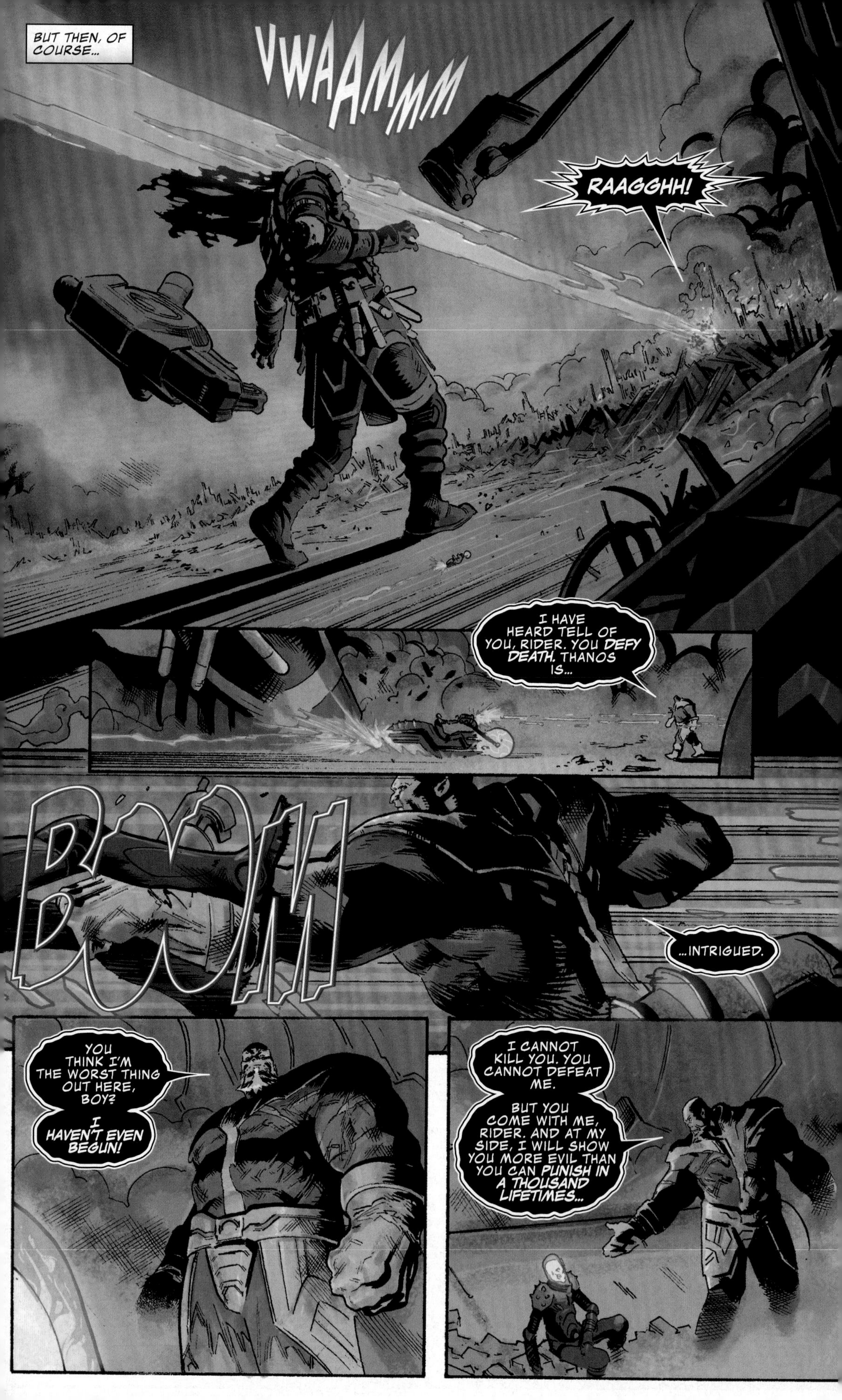
BUT THEN, OF COURSE...
VWAAMMM
RAAGGHH!
I HAVE HEARD TELL OF YOU, RIDER. YOU DEFY DEATH. THANOS IS...
BOOM
...INTRIGUED.
YOU THINK I'M THE WORST THING OUT HERE, BOY?
I HAVEN'T EVEN BEGUN!
I CANNOT KILL YOU. YOU CANNOT DEFEAT ME.
BUT YOU COME WITH ME, RIDER. AND AT MY SIDE, I WILL SHOW YOU MORE EVIL THAN YOU CAN PUNISH IN A THOUSAND LIFETIMES...

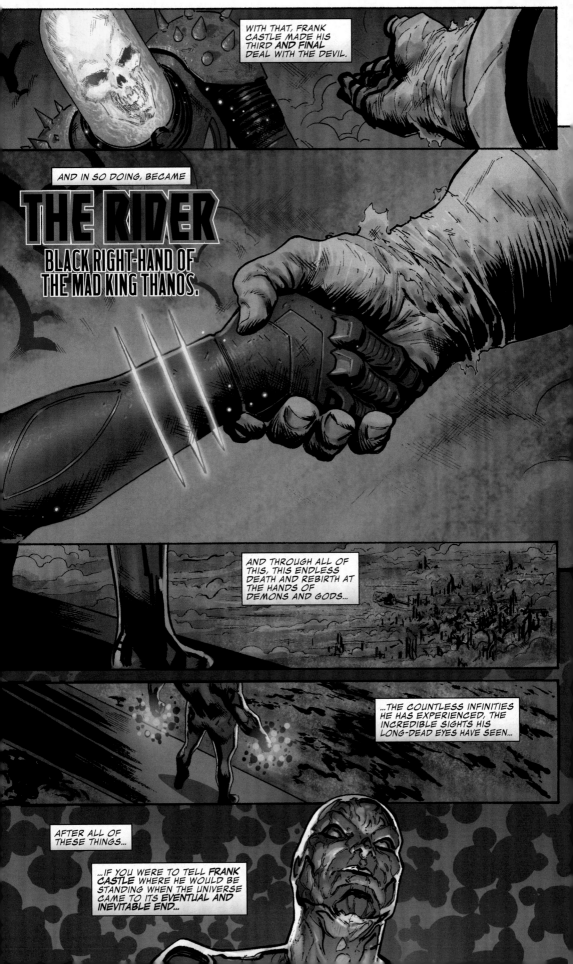

WITH THAT, FRANK CASTLE MADE HIS THIRD **AND FINAL** DEAL WITH THE DEVIL.

AND IN SO DOING, BECAME

THE RIDER
BLACK RIGHT-HAND OF THE MAD KING THANOS.

AND THROUGH ALL OF THIS, THIS ENDLESS DEATH AND REBIRTH AT THE HANDS OF DEMONS AND GODS...

...THE COUNTLESS INFINITIES HE HAS EXPERIENCED, THE INCREDIBLE SIGHTS HIS LONG-DEAD EYES HAVE SEEN...

AFTER ALL OF THESE THINGS...

...IF YOU WERE TO TELL **FRANK CASTLE** WHERE HE WOULD BE STANDING WHEN THE UNIVERSE CAME TO ITS EVENTUAL AND INEVITABLE END...

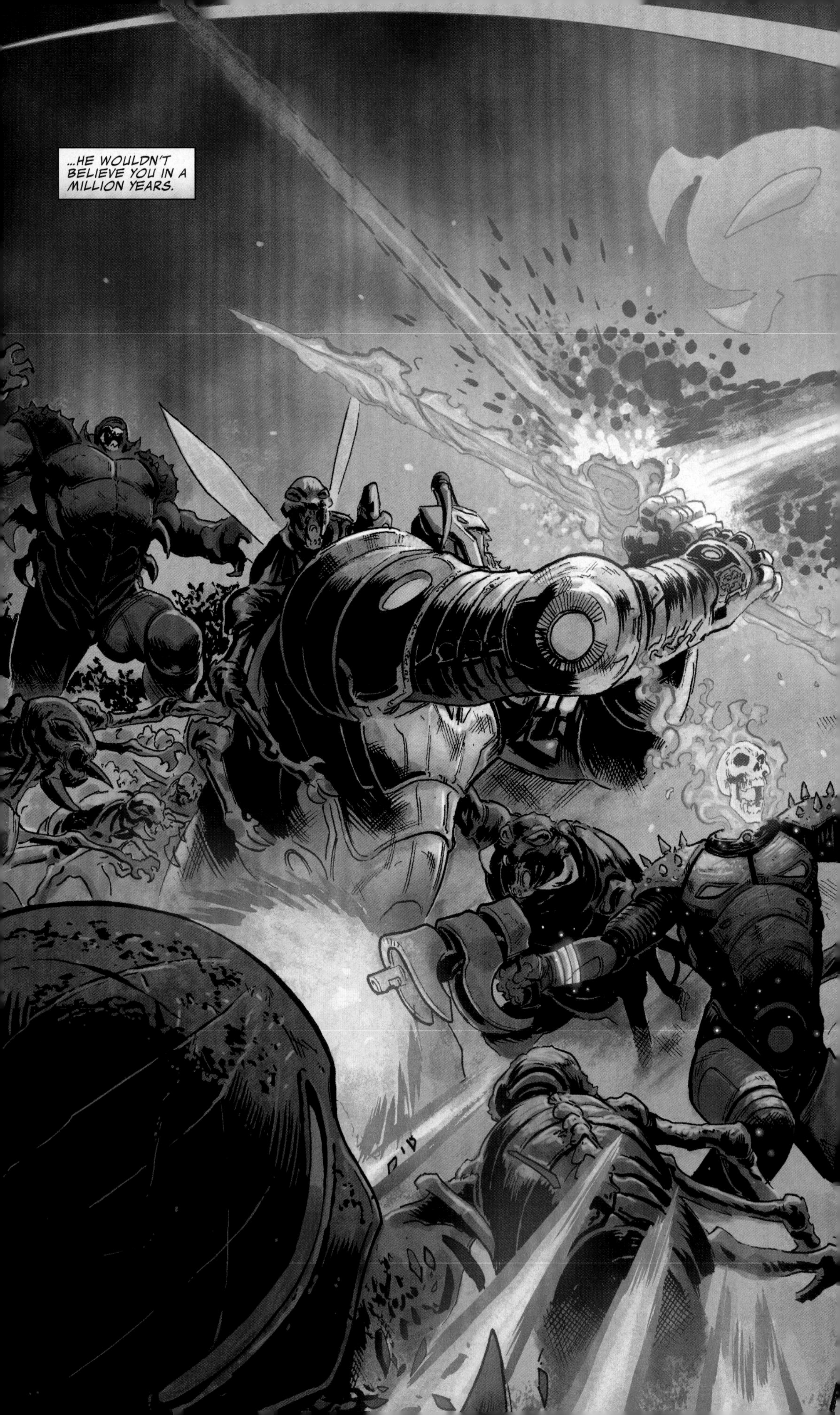
...HE WOULDN'T BELIEVE YOU IN A MILLION YEARS.

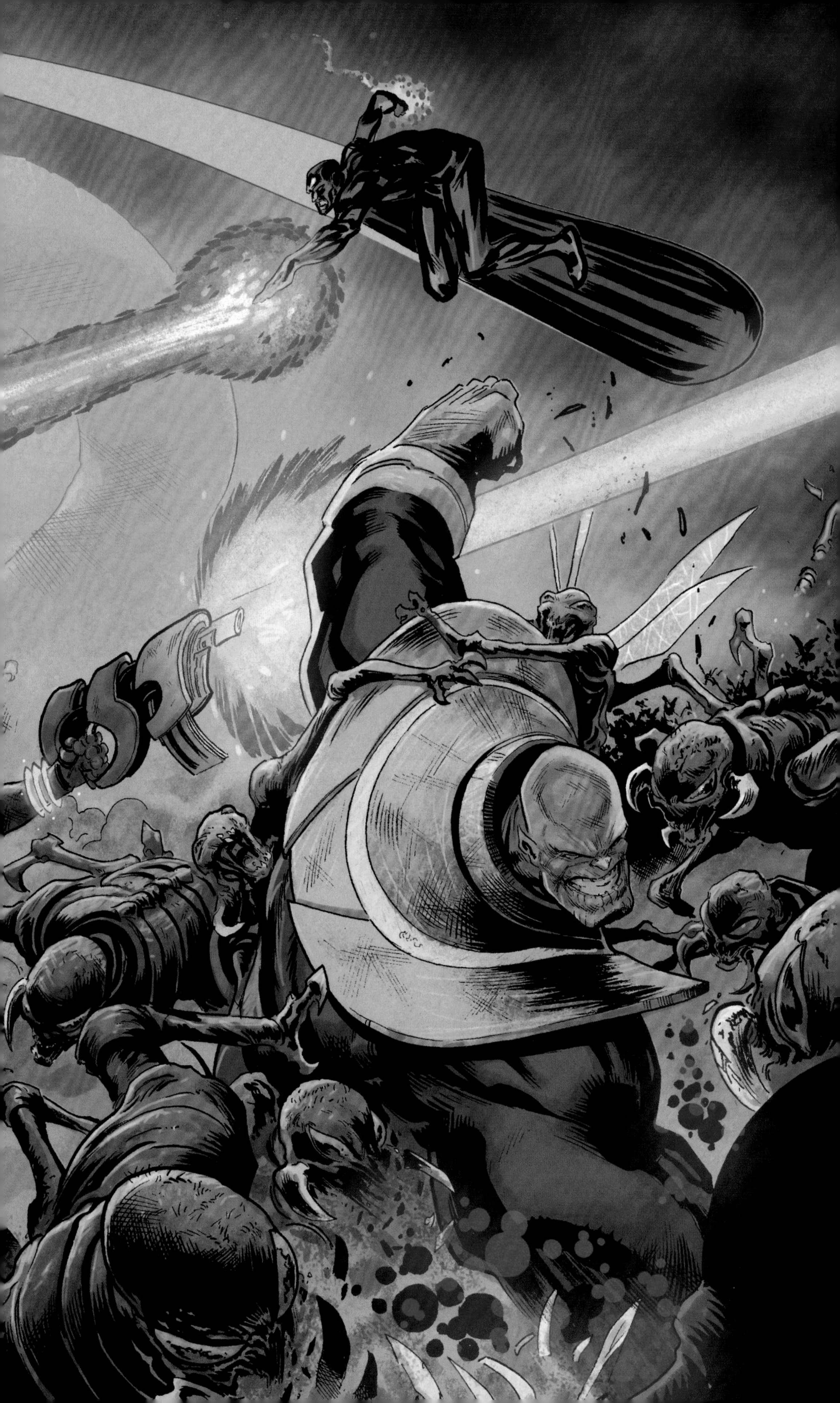

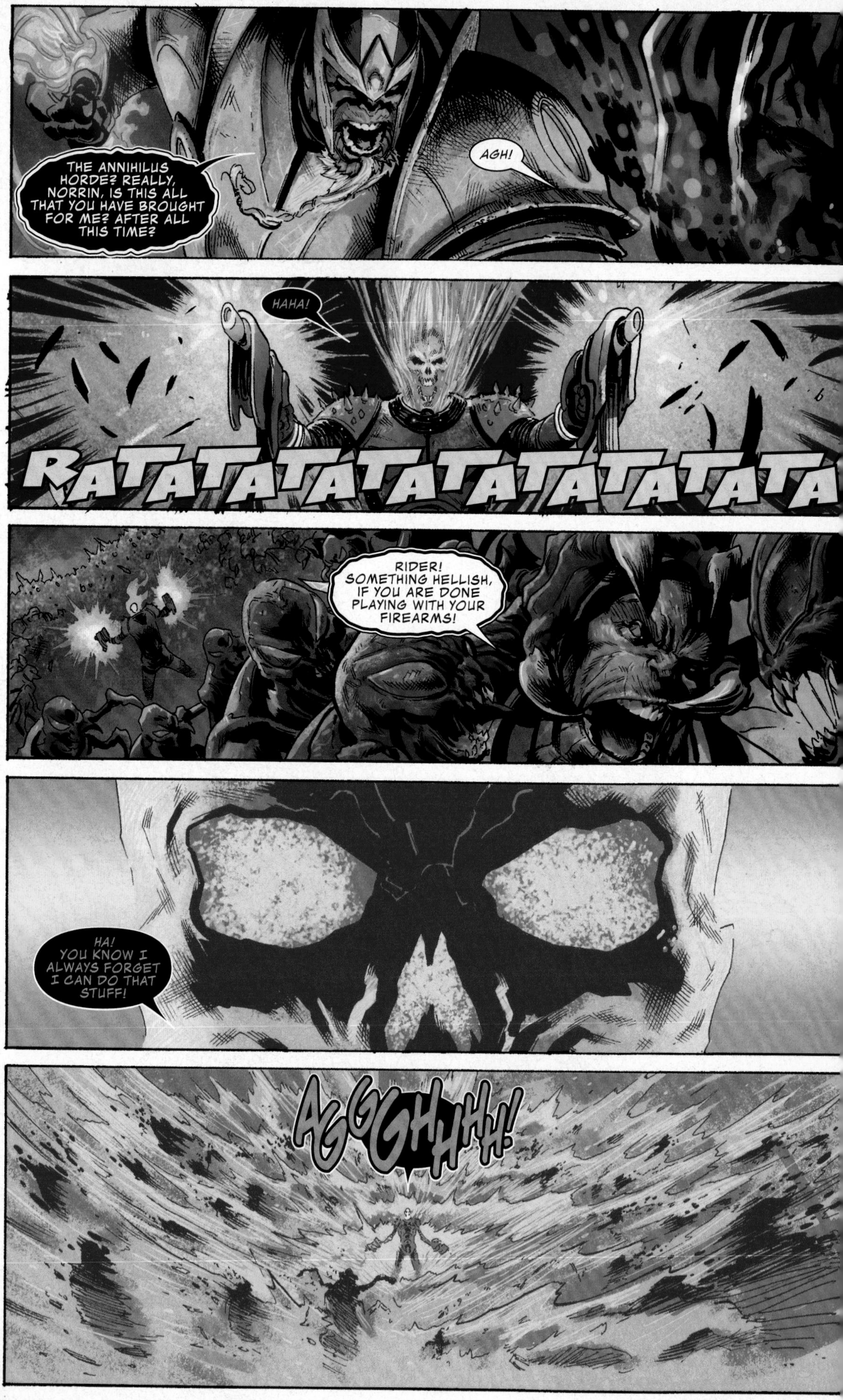

THE ANNIHILUS HORDE? REALLY, NORRIN, IS THIS ALL THAT YOU HAVE BROUGHT FOR ME? AFTER ALL THIS TIME?
AGH!
HAHA!
RATATATATATATATATATATA
RIDER! SOMETHING HELLISH, IF YOU ARE DONE PLAYING WITH YOUR FIREARMS!
HA! YOU KNOW I ALWAYS FORGET I CAN DO THAT STUFF!
AGGGHHHH!

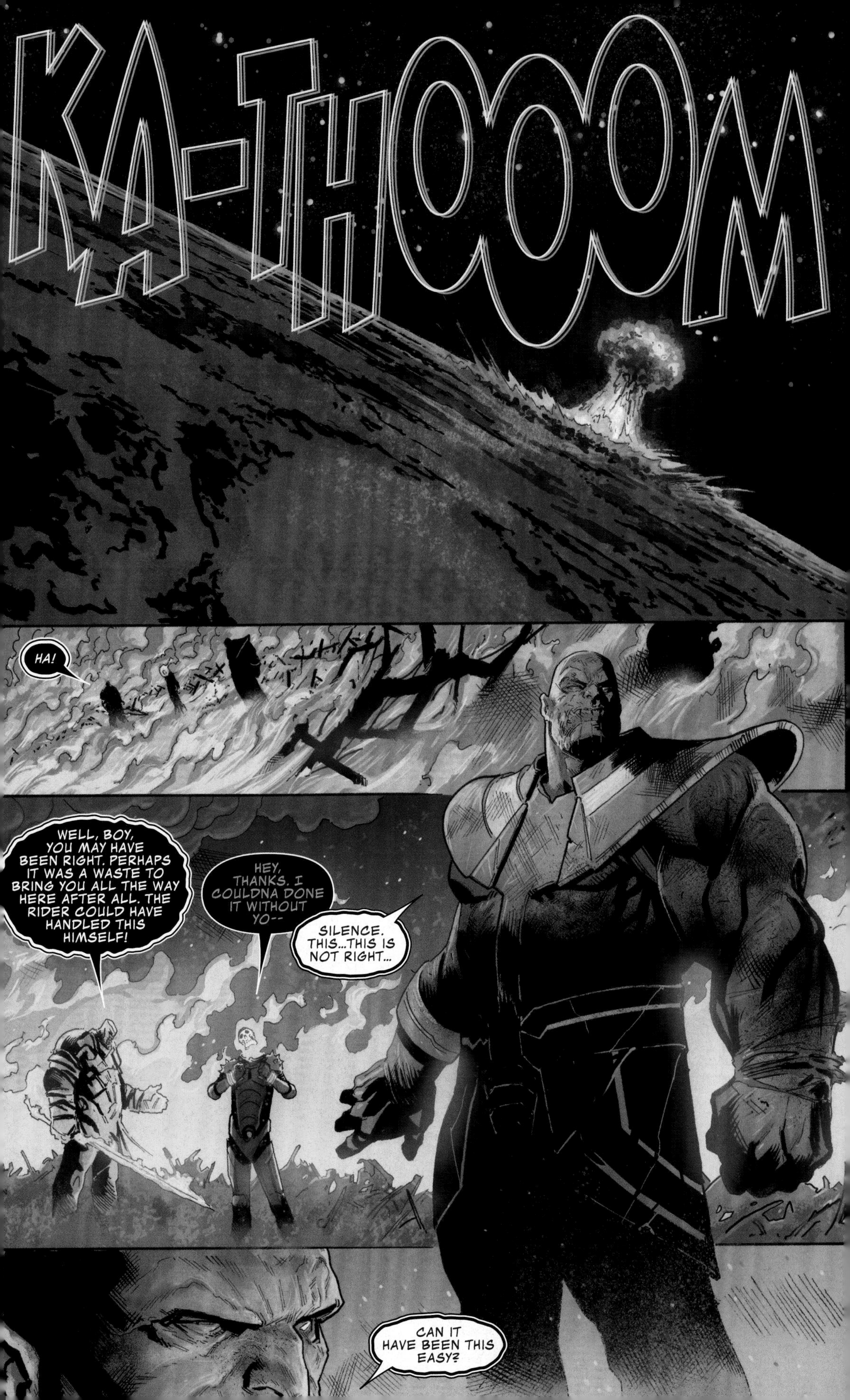
KA-THOOOM
HA!
WELL, BOY, YOU MAY HAVE BEEN RIGHT. PERHAPS IT WAS A WASTE TO BRING YOU ALL THE WAY HERE AFTER ALL. THE RIDER COULD HAVE HANDLED THIS HIMSELF!
HEY, THANKS. I COULDNA DONE IT WITHOUT YO--
SILENCE. THIS...THIS IS NOT RIGHT...
CAN IT HAVE BEEN THIS EASY?

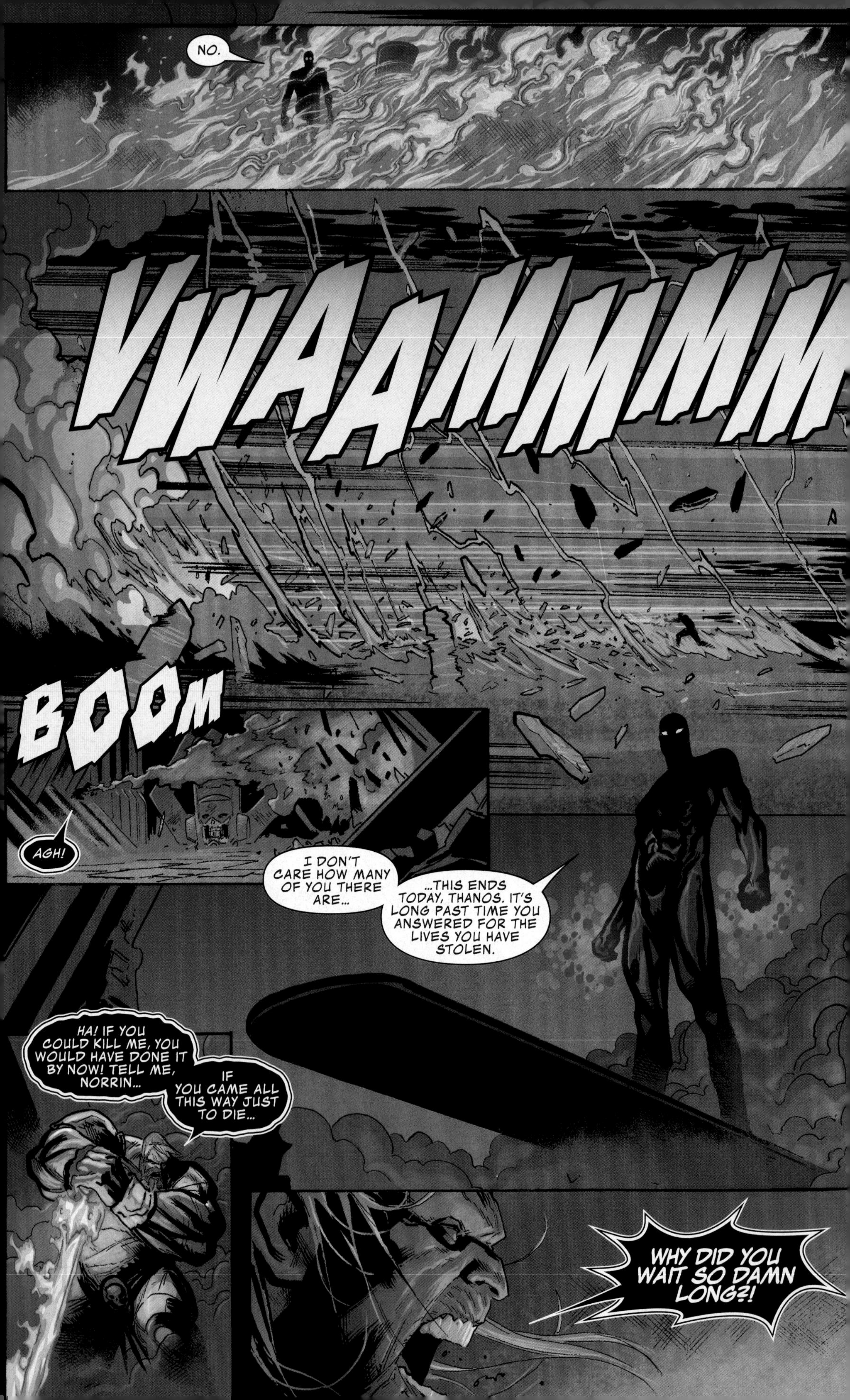
NO.
VWAAMMMMM
BOOM
AGH!
I DON'T CARE HOW MANY OF YOU THERE ARE...
...THIS ENDS TODAY, THANOS. IT'S LONG PAST TIME YOU ANSWERED FOR THE LIVES YOU HAVE STOLEN.
HA! IF YOU COULD KILL ME, YOU WOULD HAVE DONE IT BY NOW! TELL ME, NORRIN...
IF YOU CAME ALL THIS WAY JUST TO DIE...
WHY DID YOU WAIT SO DAMN LONG?!

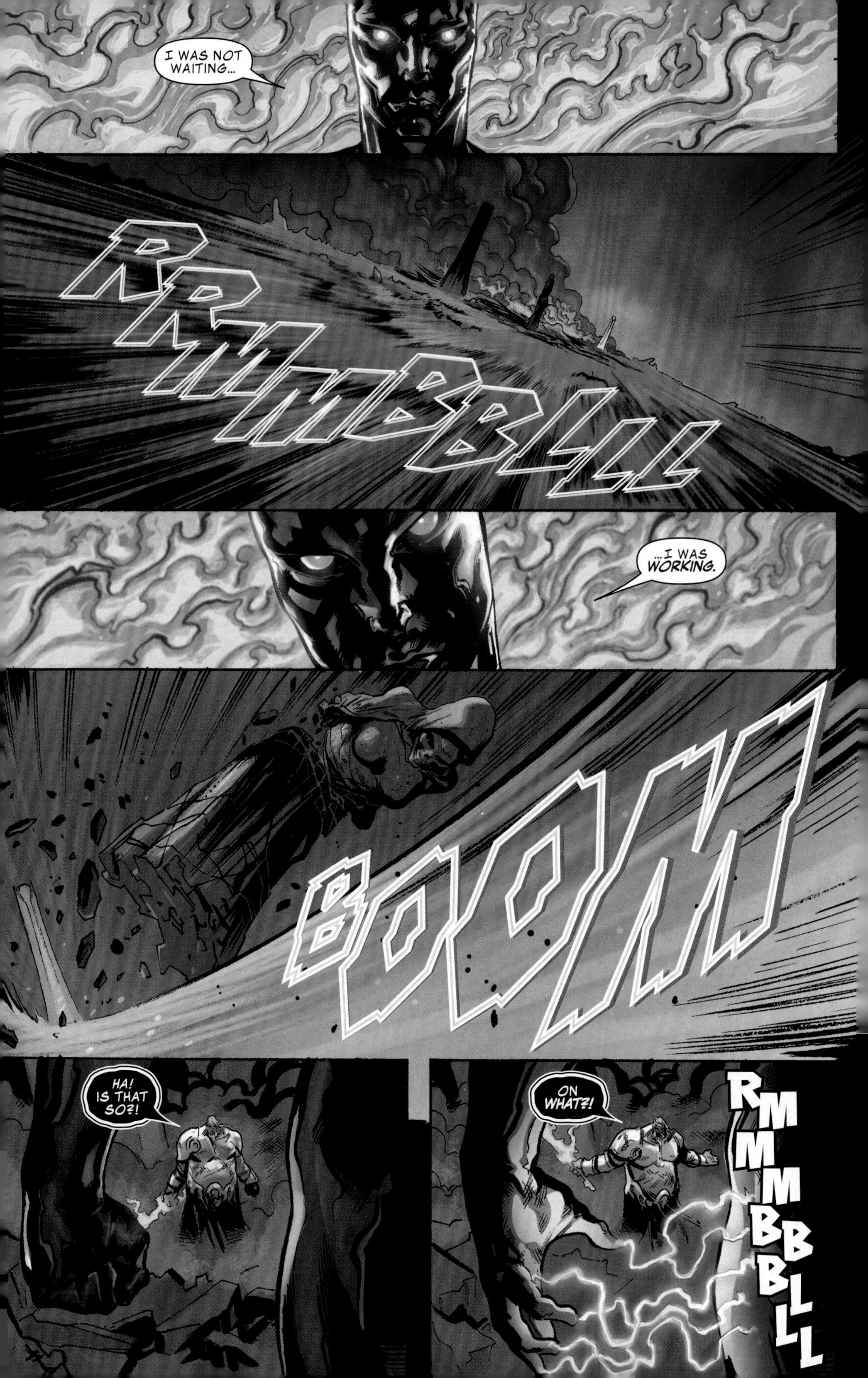
I WAS NOT WAITING...
RRUMBLL
...I WAS WORKING.
BOOM
HA! IS THAT SO?!
ON WHAT?!
RMMMBBLLL

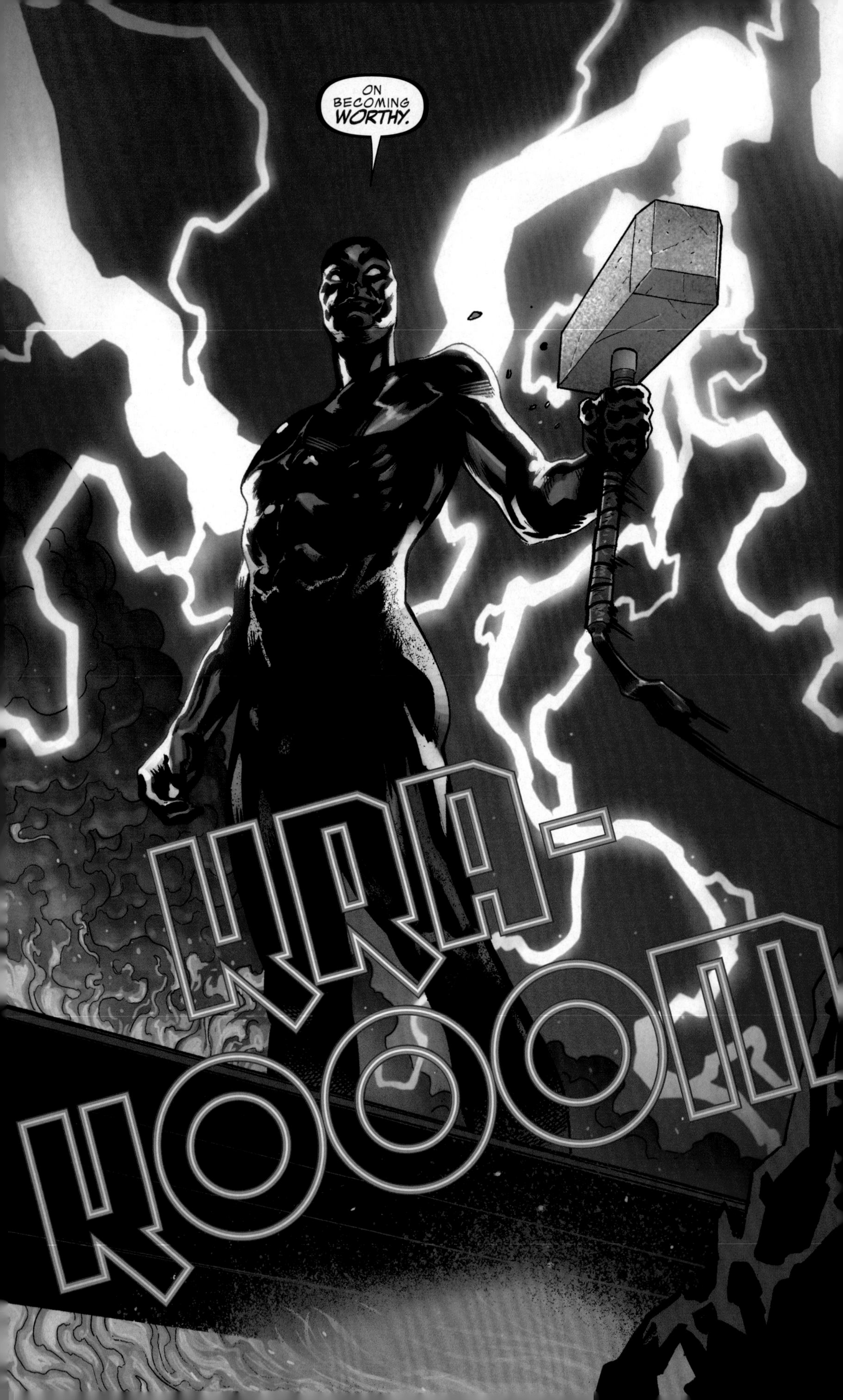
ON BECOMING WORTHY.
KRA-KOOOM

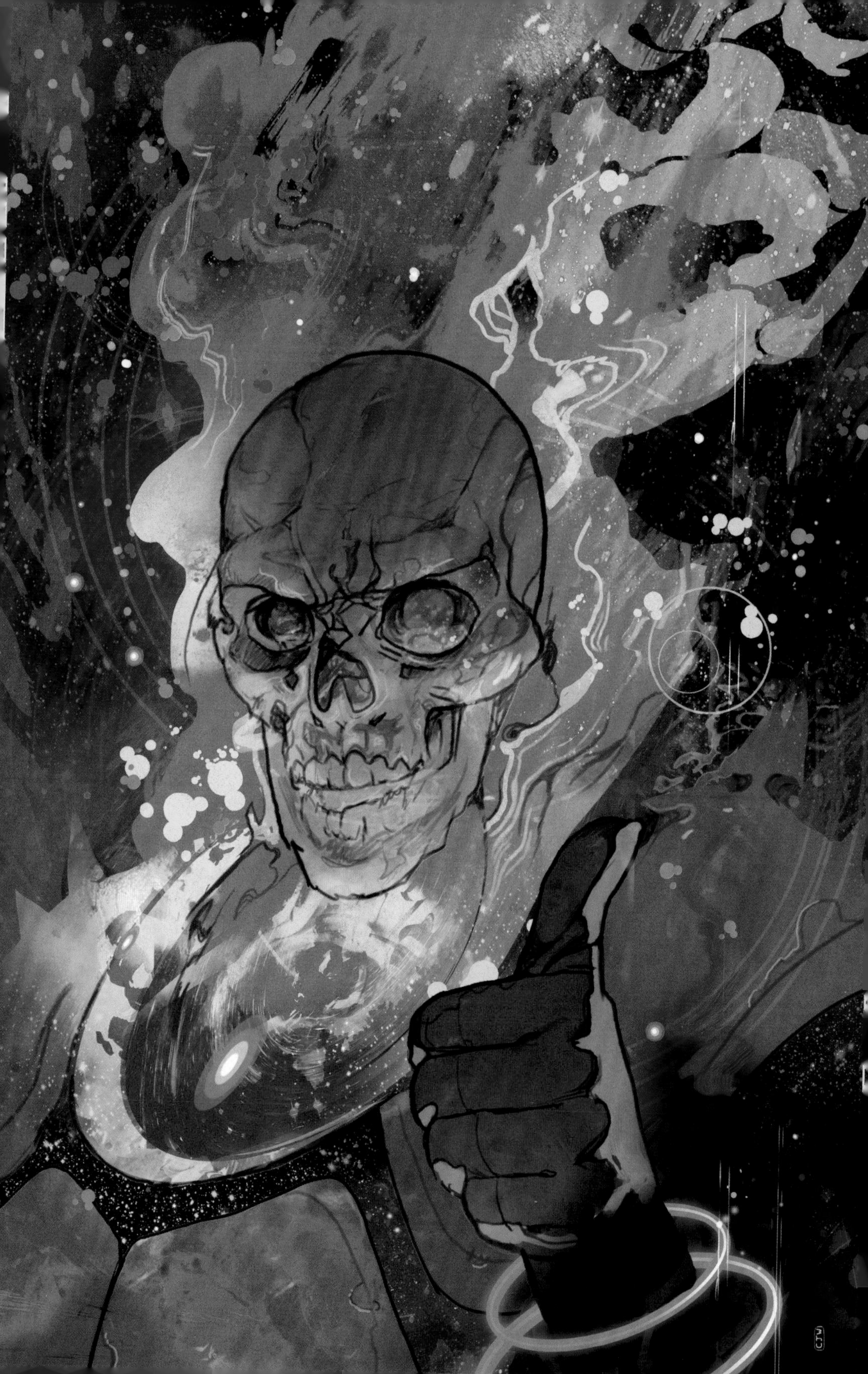

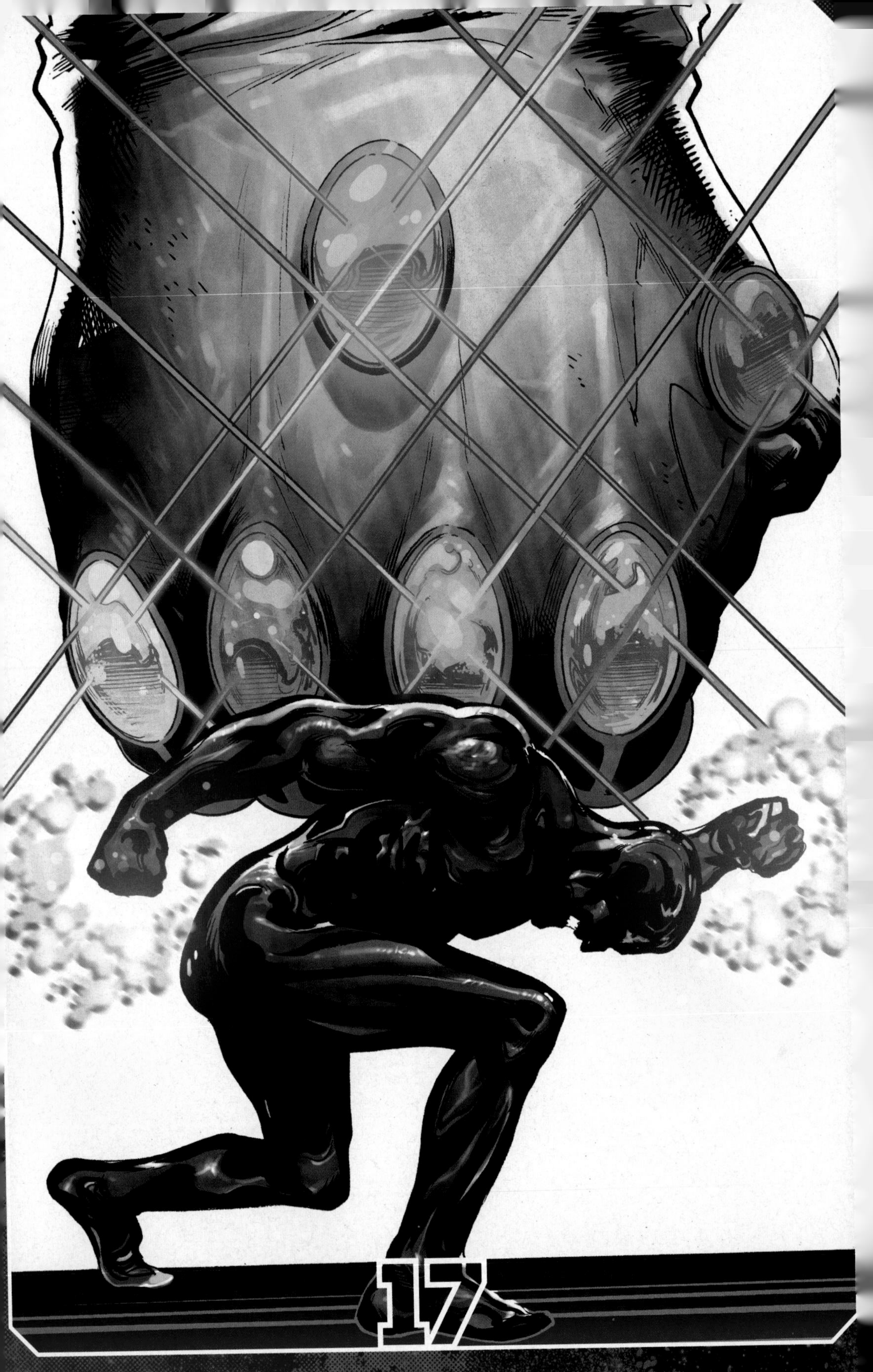
17

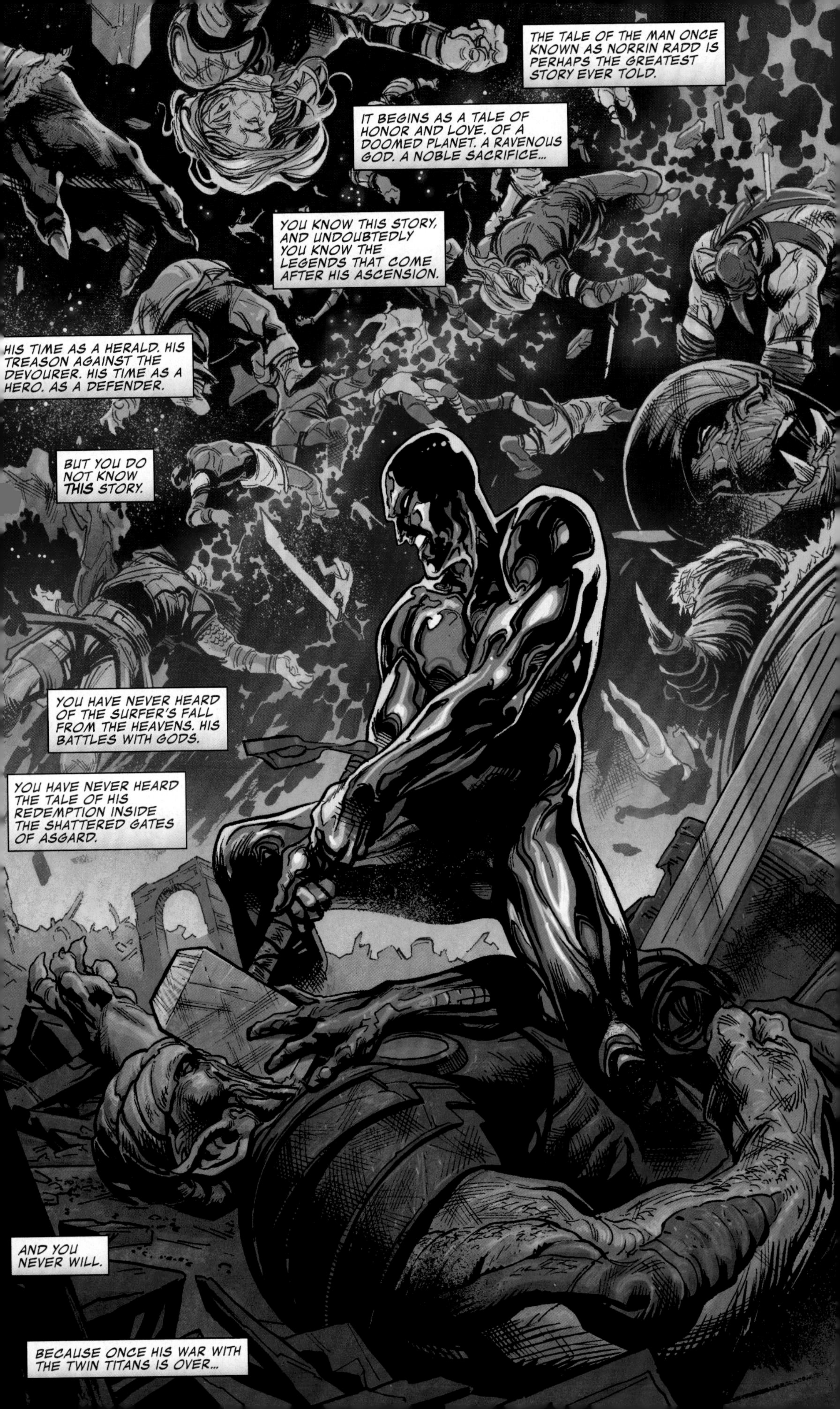

THE TALE OF THE MAN ONCE KNOWN AS NORRIN RADD IS PERHAPS THE GREATEST STORY EVER TOLD.
IT BEGINS AS A TALE OF HONOR AND LOVE. OF A DOOMED PLANET. A RAVENOUS GOD. A NOBLE SACRIFICE...
YOU KNOW THIS STORY, AND UNDOUBTEDLY YOU KNOW THE LEGENDS THAT COME AFTER HIS ASCENSION.
HIS TIME AS A HERALD. HIS TREASON AGAINST THE DEVOURER. HIS TIME AS A HERO. AS A DEFENDER.
BUT YOU DO NOT KNOW THIS STORY.
YOU HAVE NEVER HEARD OF THE SURFER'S FALL FROM THE HEAVENS. HIS BATTLES WITH GODS.
YOU HAVE NEVER HEARD THE TALE OF HIS REDEMPTION INSIDE THE SHATTERED GATES OF ASGARD.
AND YOU NEVER WILL.
BECAUSE ONCE HIS WAR WITH THE TWIN TITANS IS OVER...

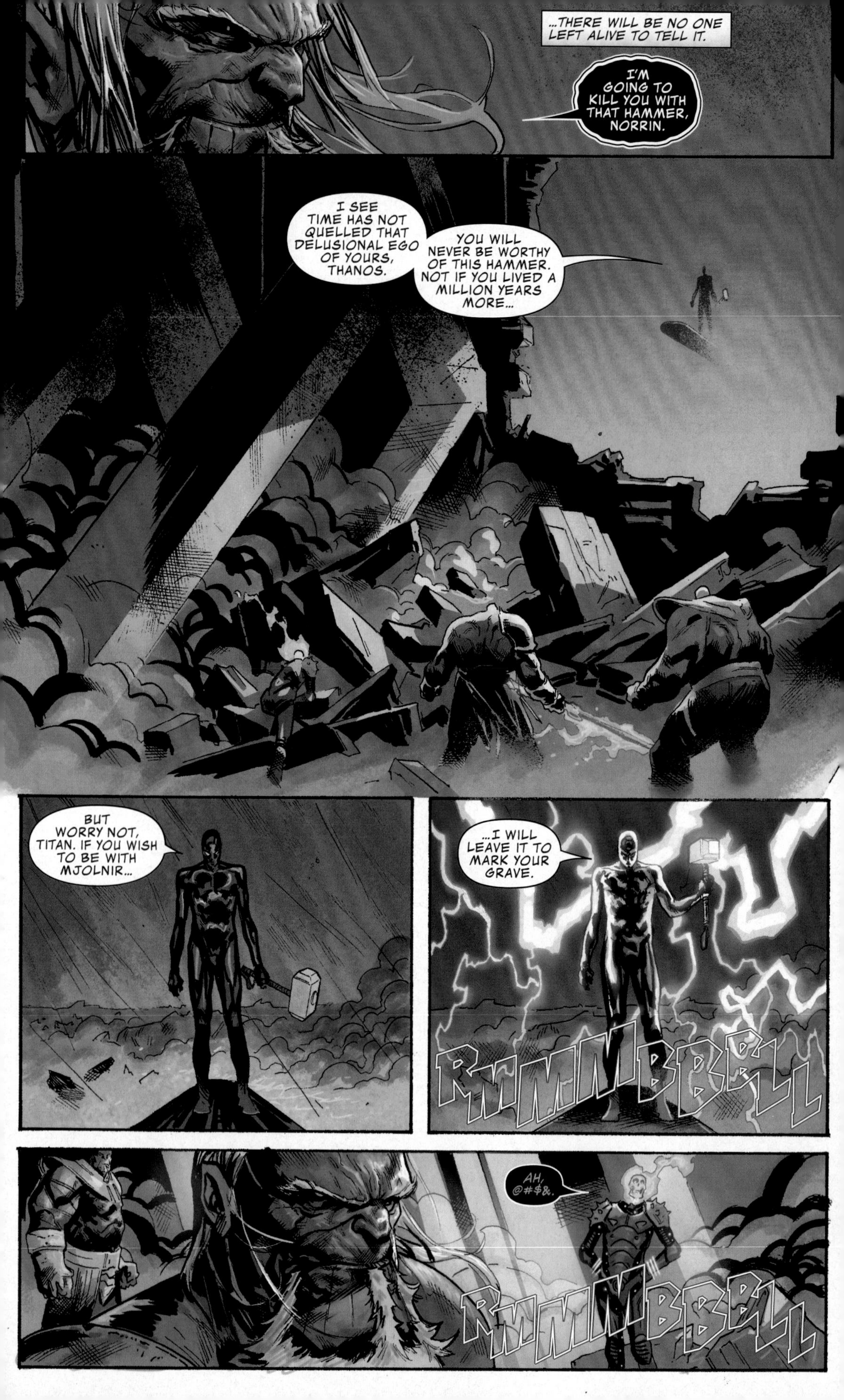
...THERE WILL BE NO ONE LEFT ALIVE TO TELL IT.
I'M GOING TO KILL YOU WITH THAT HAMMER, NORRIN.
I SEE TIME HAS NOT QUELLED THAT DELUSIONAL EGO OF YOURS, THANOS.
YOU WILL NEVER BE WORTHY OF THIS HAMMER. NOT IF YOU LIVED A MILLION YEARS MORE...
BUT WORRY NOT, TITAN. IF YOU WISH TO BE WITH MJOLNIR...
...I WILL LEAVE IT TO MARK YOUR GRAVE.
RMMMBBRLL
AH, @#$&.
RMMMMBBRLL

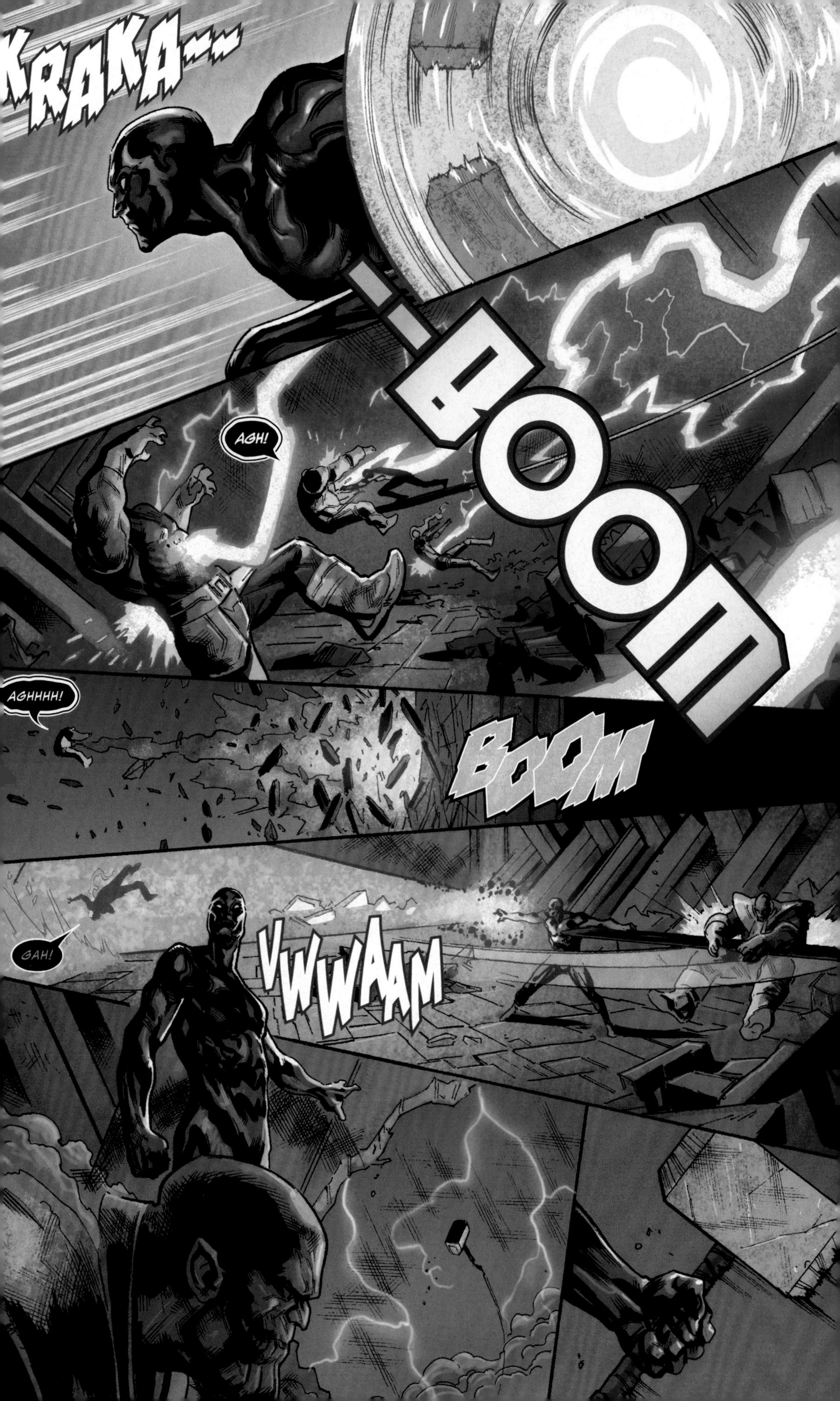
KRAKA--
--BOOM
AGH!
AGHHHH!
BOOM
GAH!
VWWAAM

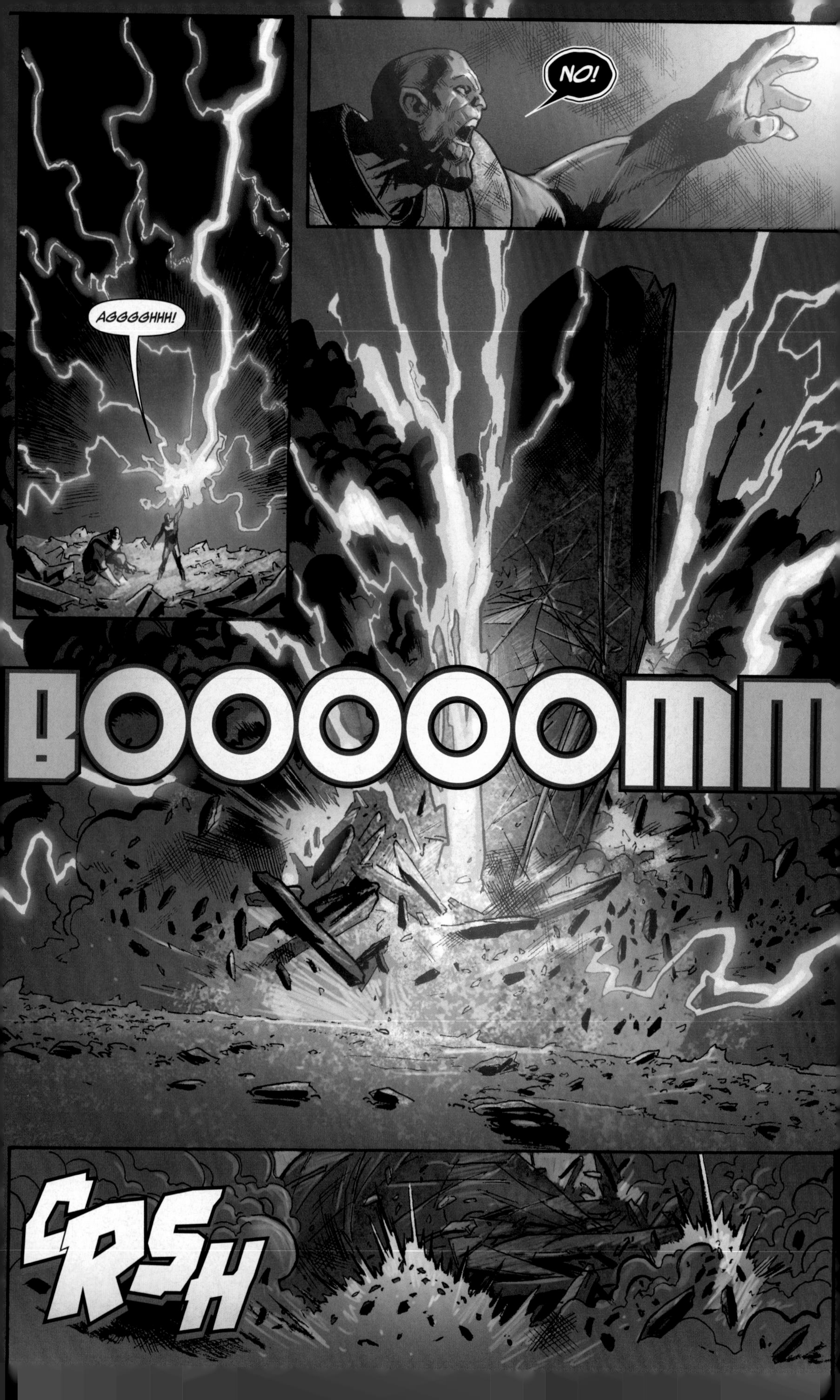

AGGGGHHH!
NO!
BOOOOOOMM
CRSH

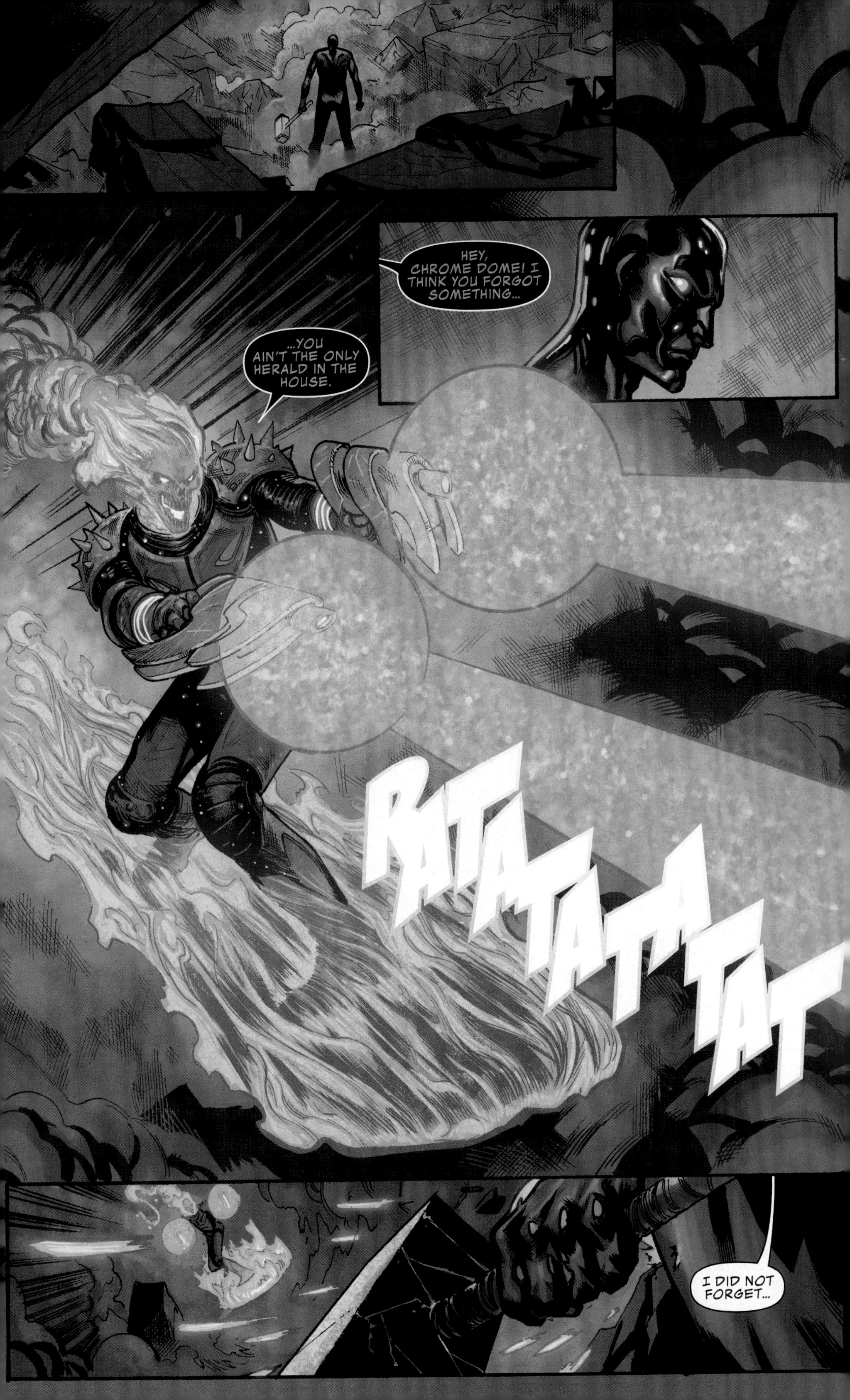

HEY, CHROME DOME! I THINK YOU FORGOT SOMETHING...
...YOU AIN'T THE ONLY HERALD IN THE HOUSE.
RATATATATATAT
I DID NOT FORGET...

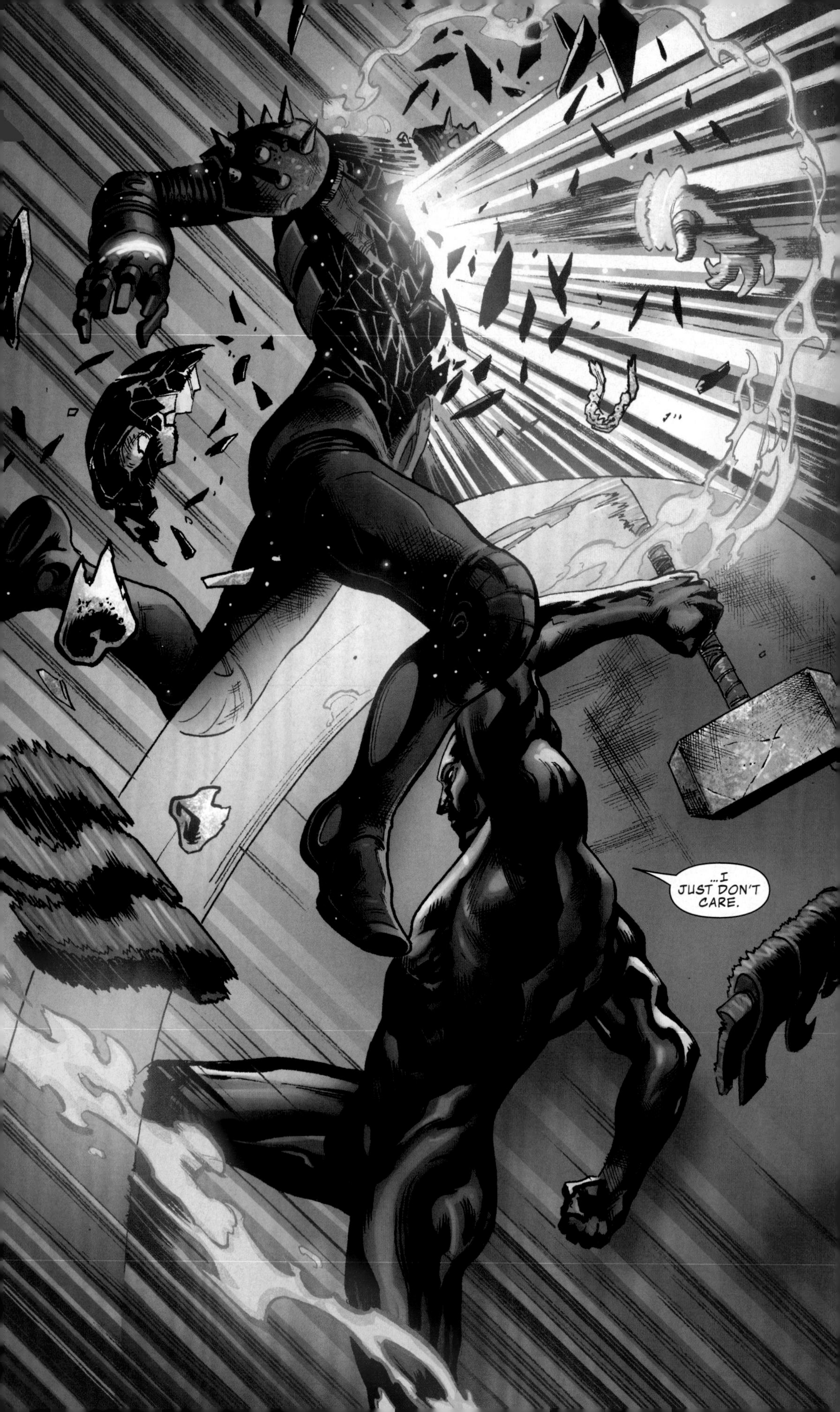
...I JUST DON'T CARE.

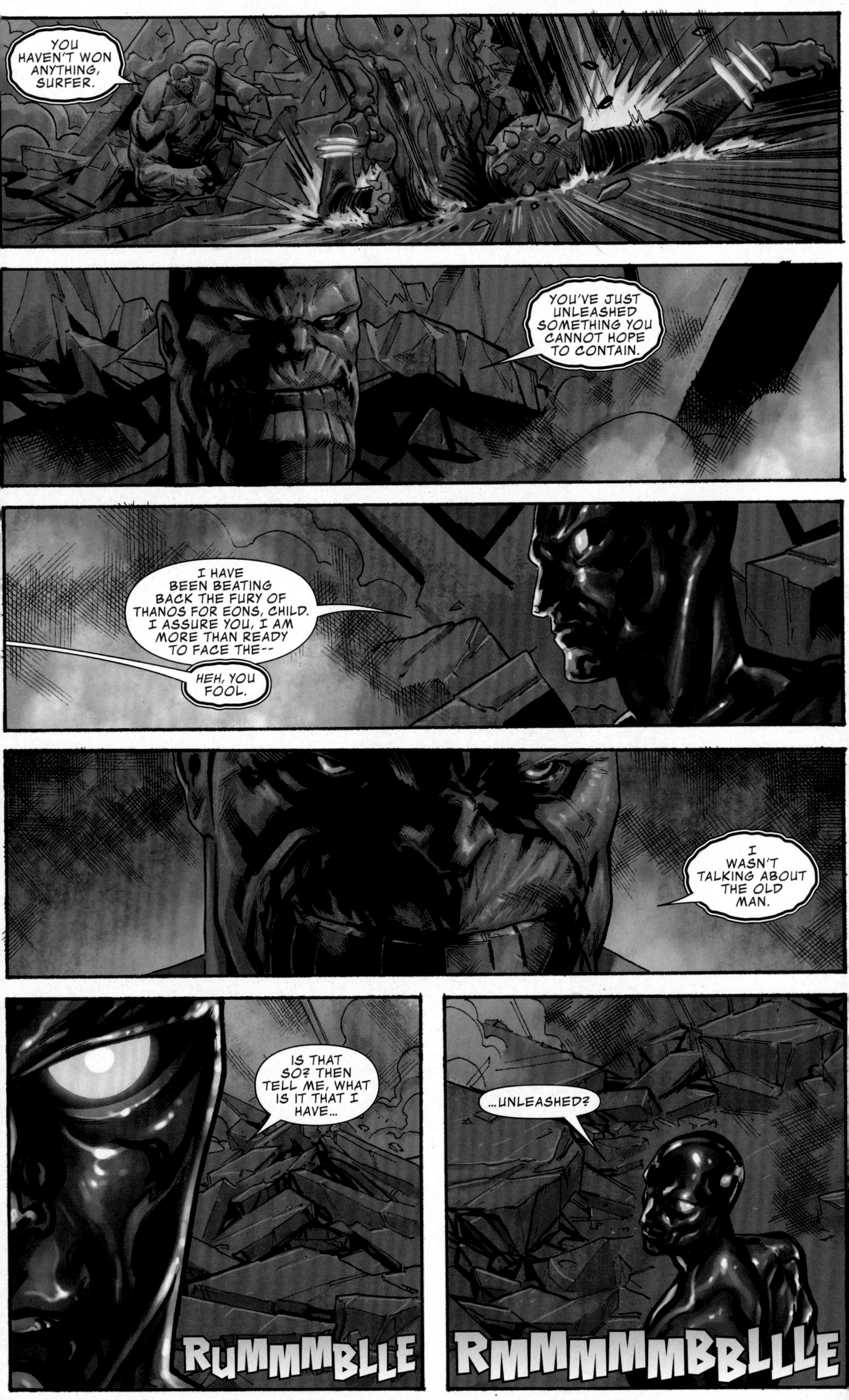
YOU HAVEN'T WON ANYTHING, SURFER.
YOU'VE JUST UNLEASHED SOMETHING YOU CANNOT HOPE TO CONTAIN.
I HAVE BEEN BEATING BACK THE FURY OF THANOS FOR EONS, CHILD. I ASSURE YOU, I AM MORE THAN READY TO FACE THE--
HEH, YOU FOOL.
I WASN'T TALKING ABOUT THE OLD MAN.
IS THAT SO? THEN TELL ME, WHAT IS IT THAT I HAVE...
RUMMMBLLE
...UNLEASHED?
RMMMMMMBBLLLE

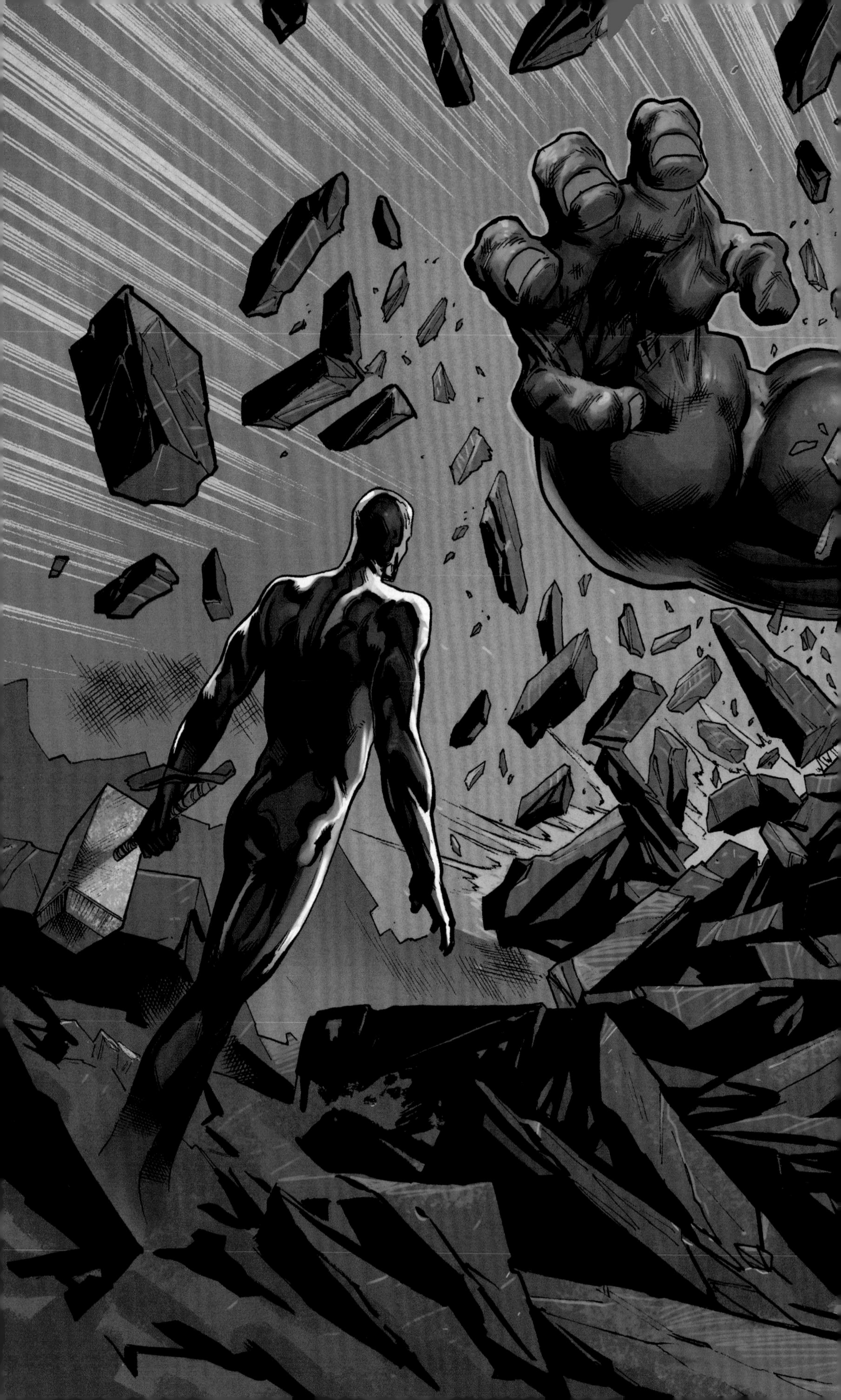

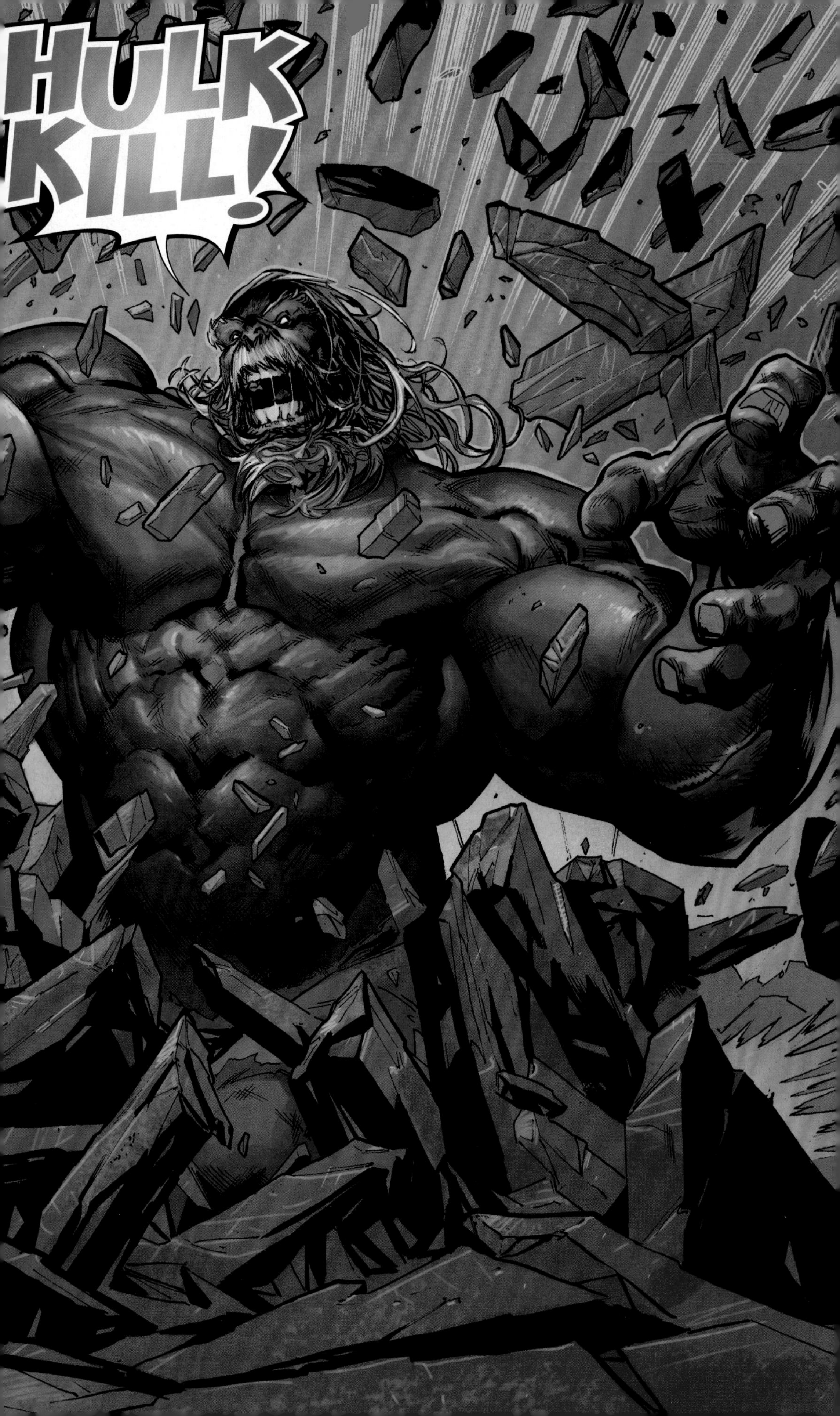
HULK KILL!

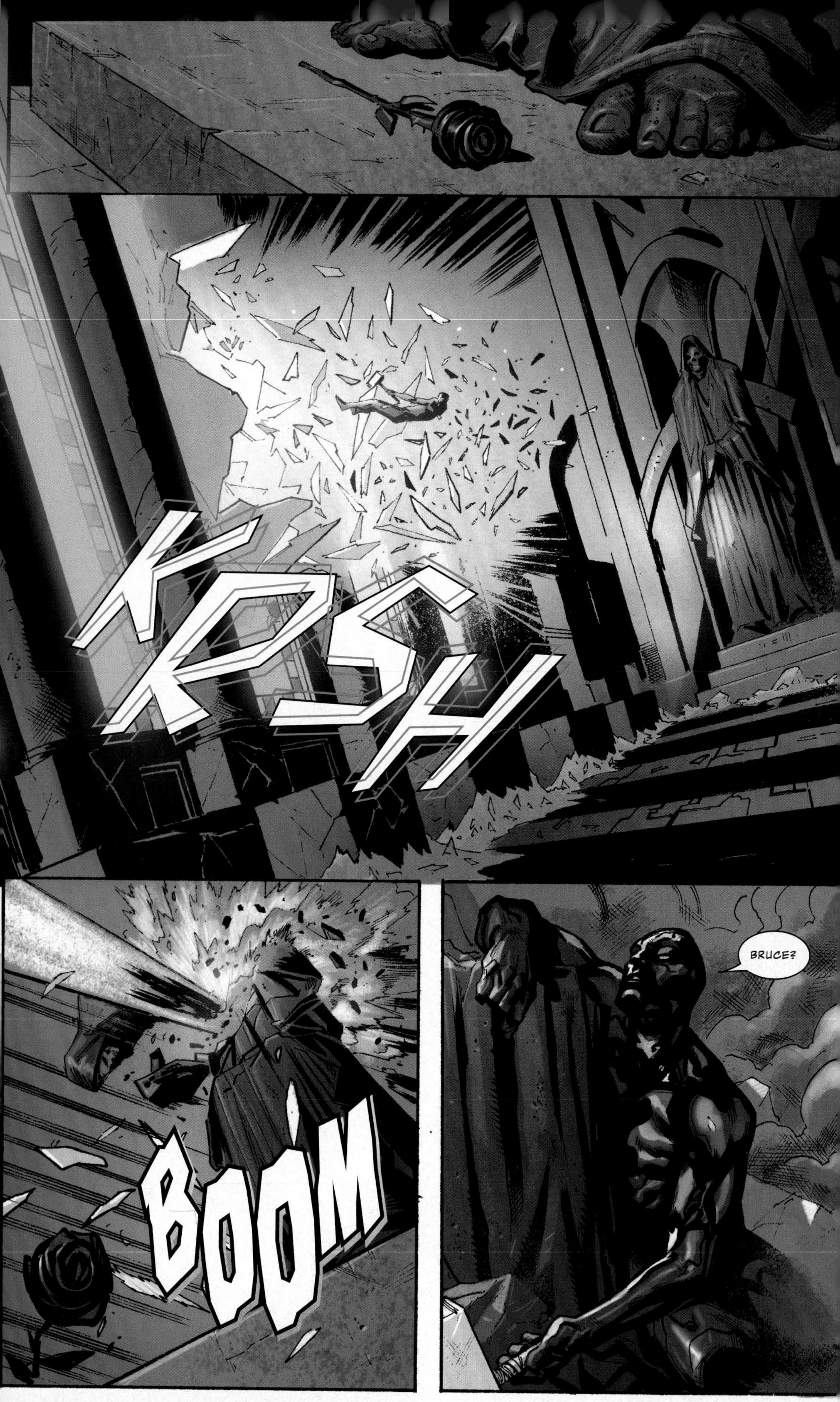
KRSH
BOOM
BRUCE?

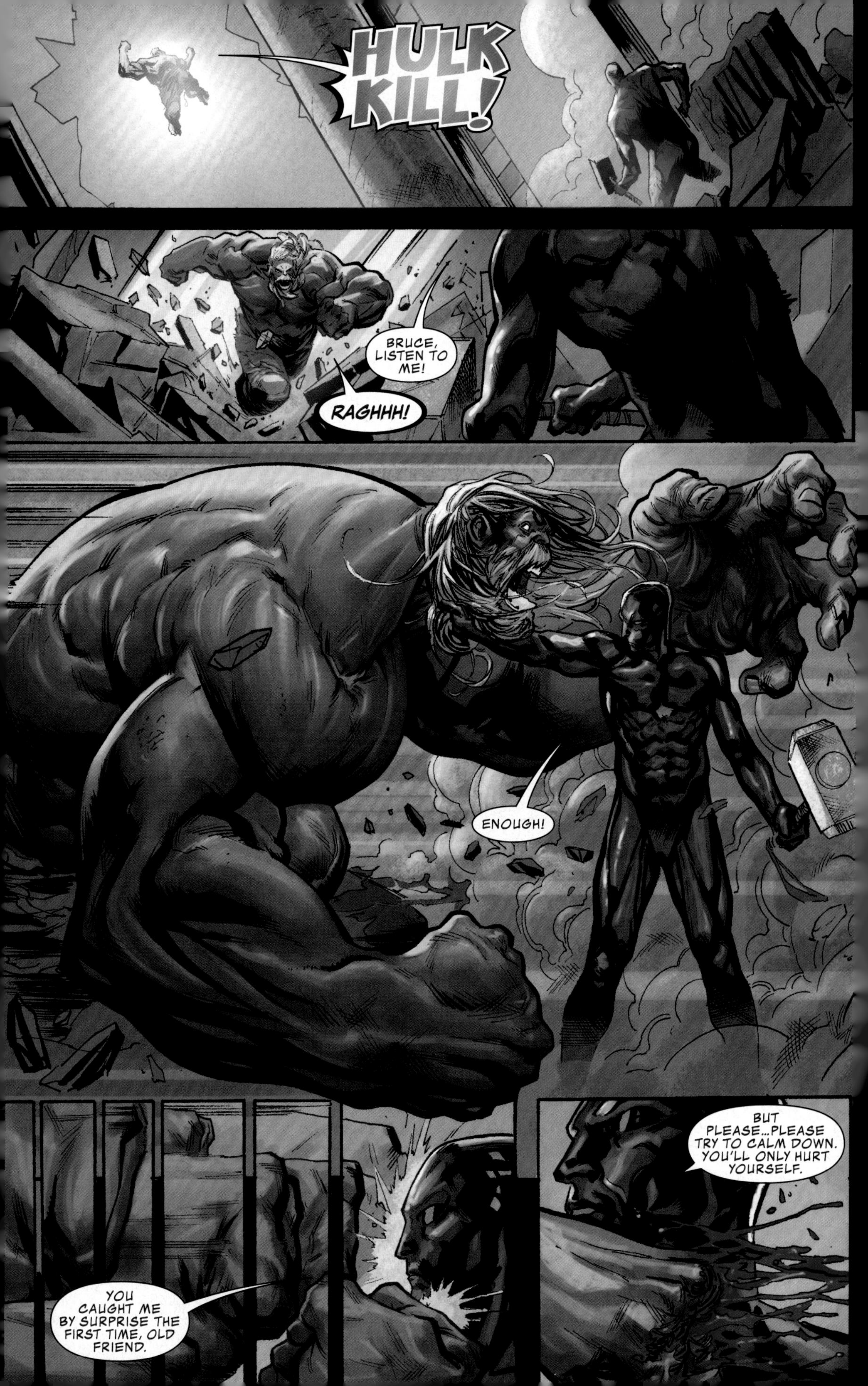
HULK KILL!
BRUCE, LISTEN TO ME!
RAGHHH!
ENOUGH!
YOU CAUGHT ME BY SURPRISE THE FIRST TIME, OLD FRIEND.
BUT PLEASE...PLEASE TRY TO CALM DOWN. YOU'LL ONLY HURT YOURSELF.

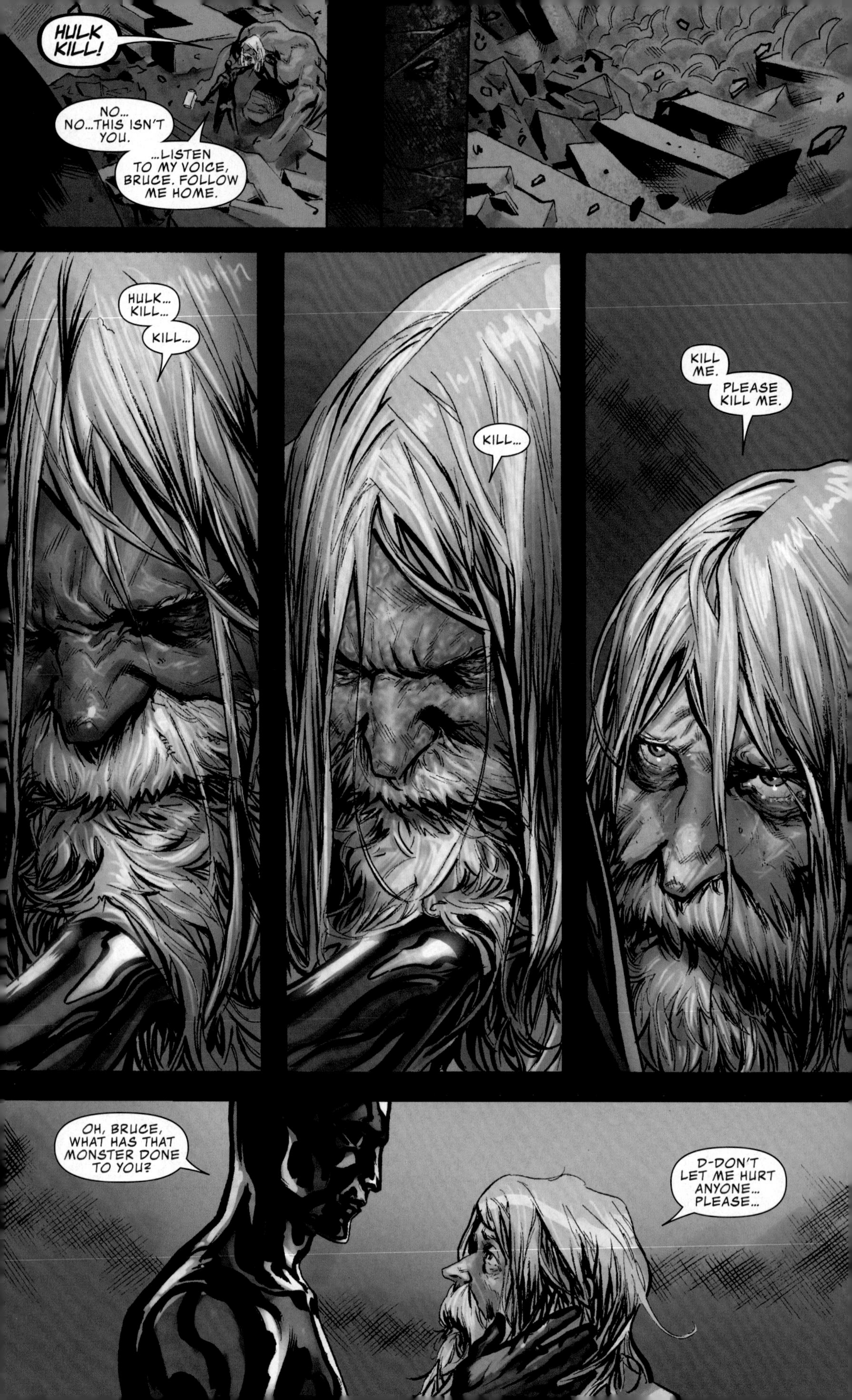
HULK KILL!
NO... NO...THIS ISN'T YOU.
...LISTEN TO MY VOICE, BRUCE. FOLLOW ME HOME.
HULK... KILL...
KILL...
KILL...
KILL ME.
PLEASE KILL ME.
OH, BRUCE, WHAT HAS THAT MONSTER DONE TO YOU?
D-DON'T LET ME HURT ANYONE... PLEASE...

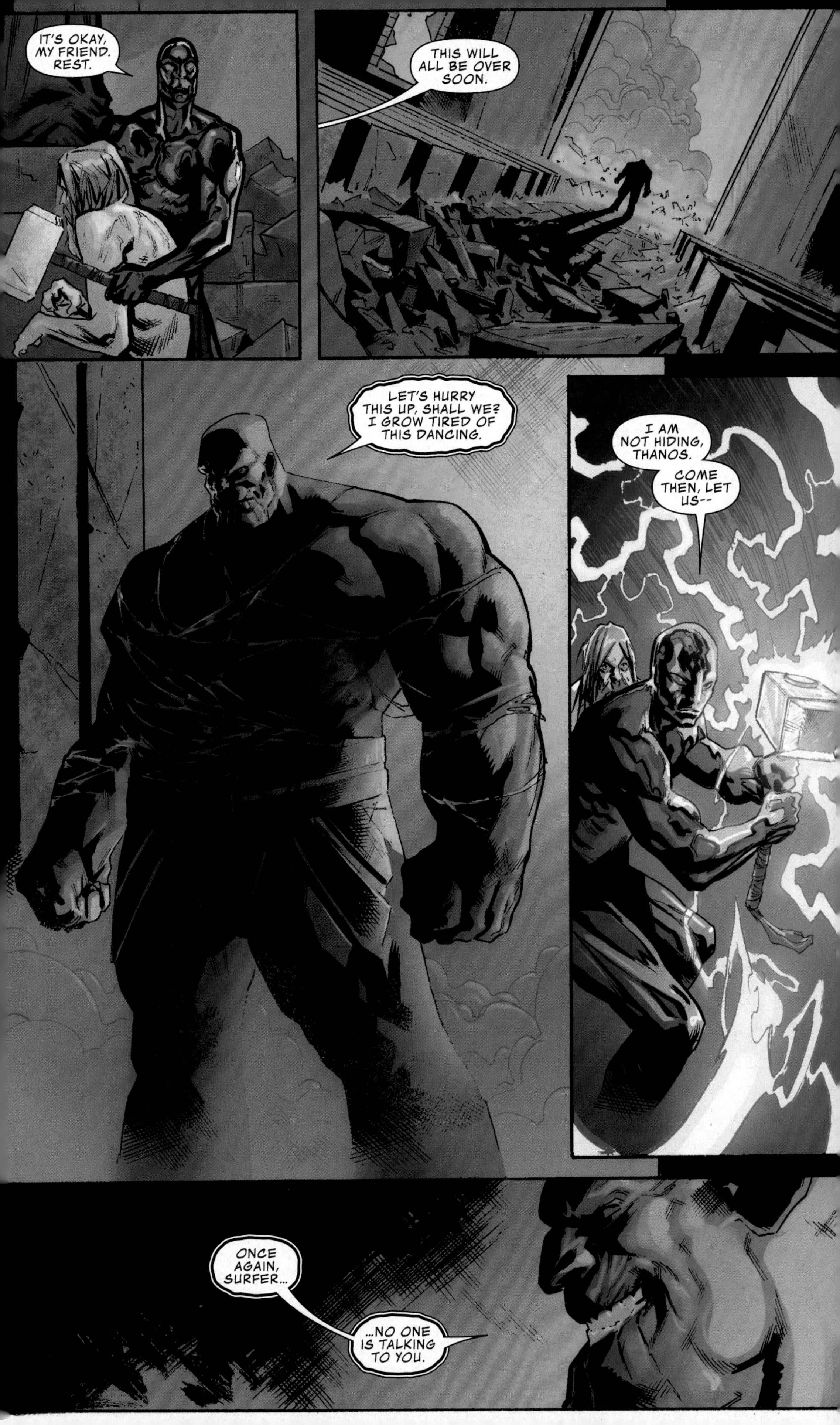
IT'S OKAY, MY FRIEND. REST.
THIS WILL ALL BE OVER SOON.
LET'S HURRY THIS UP, SHALL WE? I GROW TIRED OF THIS DANCING.
I AM NOT HIDING, THANOS.
COME THEN, LET US--
ONCE AGAIN, SURFER...
...NO ONE IS TALKING TO YOU.

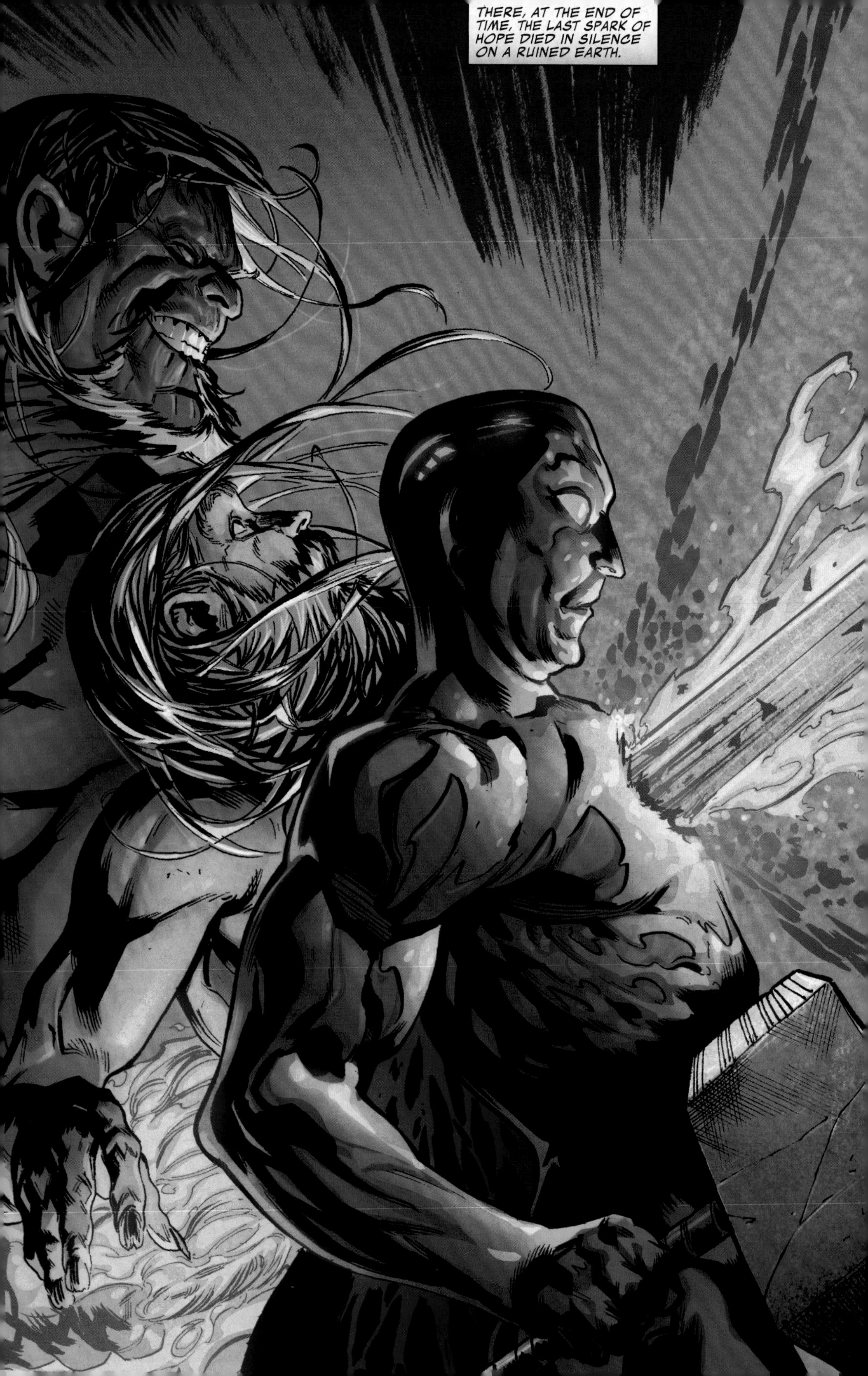
THERE, AT THE END OF TIME, THE LAST SPARK OF HOPE DIED IN SILENCE ON A RUINED EARTH.

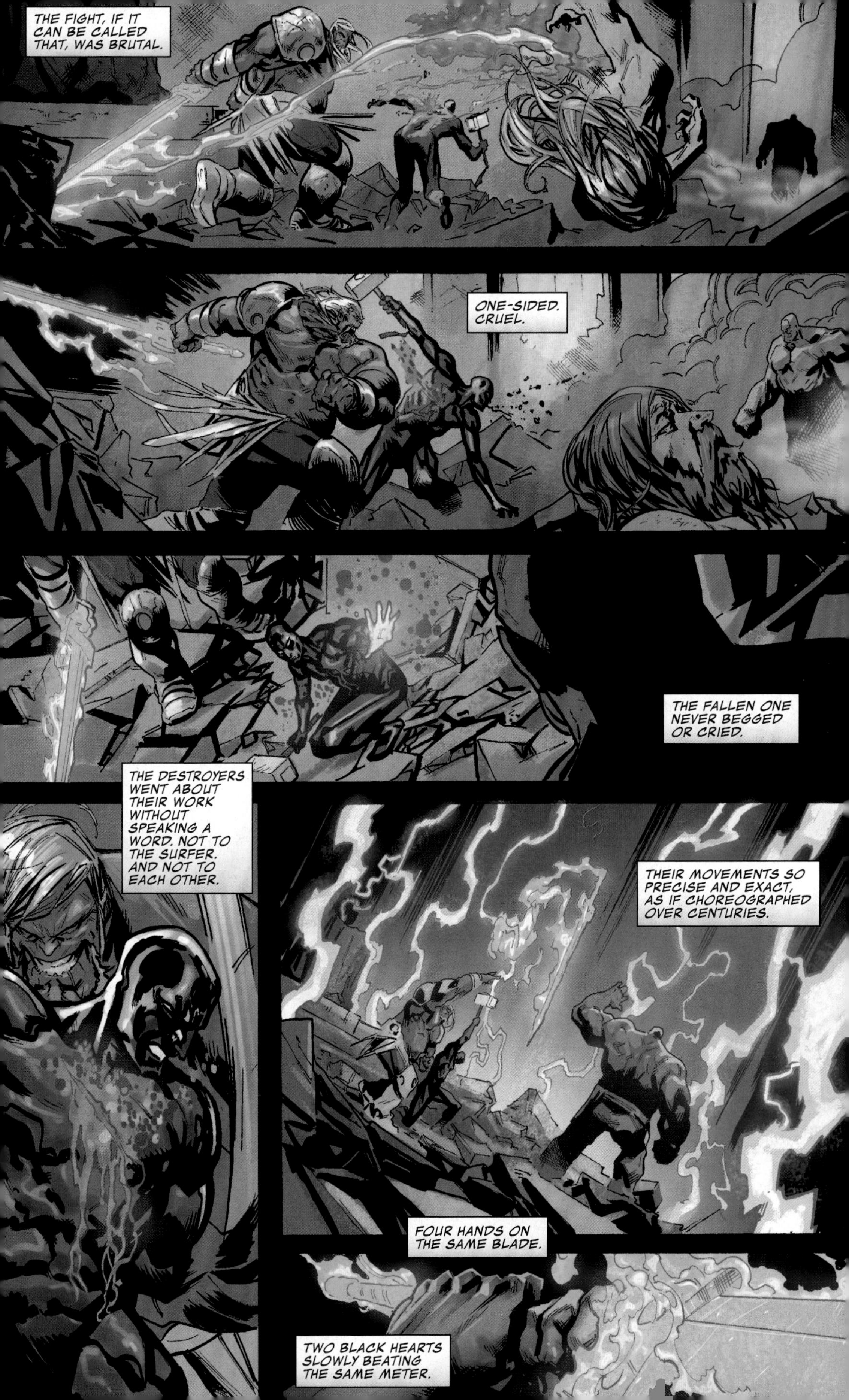
THE FIGHT, IF IT CAN BE CALLED THAT, WAS BRUTAL.
ONE-SIDED. CRUEL.
THE FALLEN ONE NEVER BEGGED OR CRIED.
THE DESTROYERS WENT ABOUT THEIR WORK WITHOUT SPEAKING A WORD. NOT TO THE SURFER. AND NOT TO EACH OTHER.
THEIR MOVEMENTS SO PRECISE AND EXACT, AS IF CHOREOGRAPHED OVER CENTURIES.
FOUR HANDS ON THE SAME BLADE.
TWO BLACK HEARTS SLOWLY BEATING THE SAME METER.

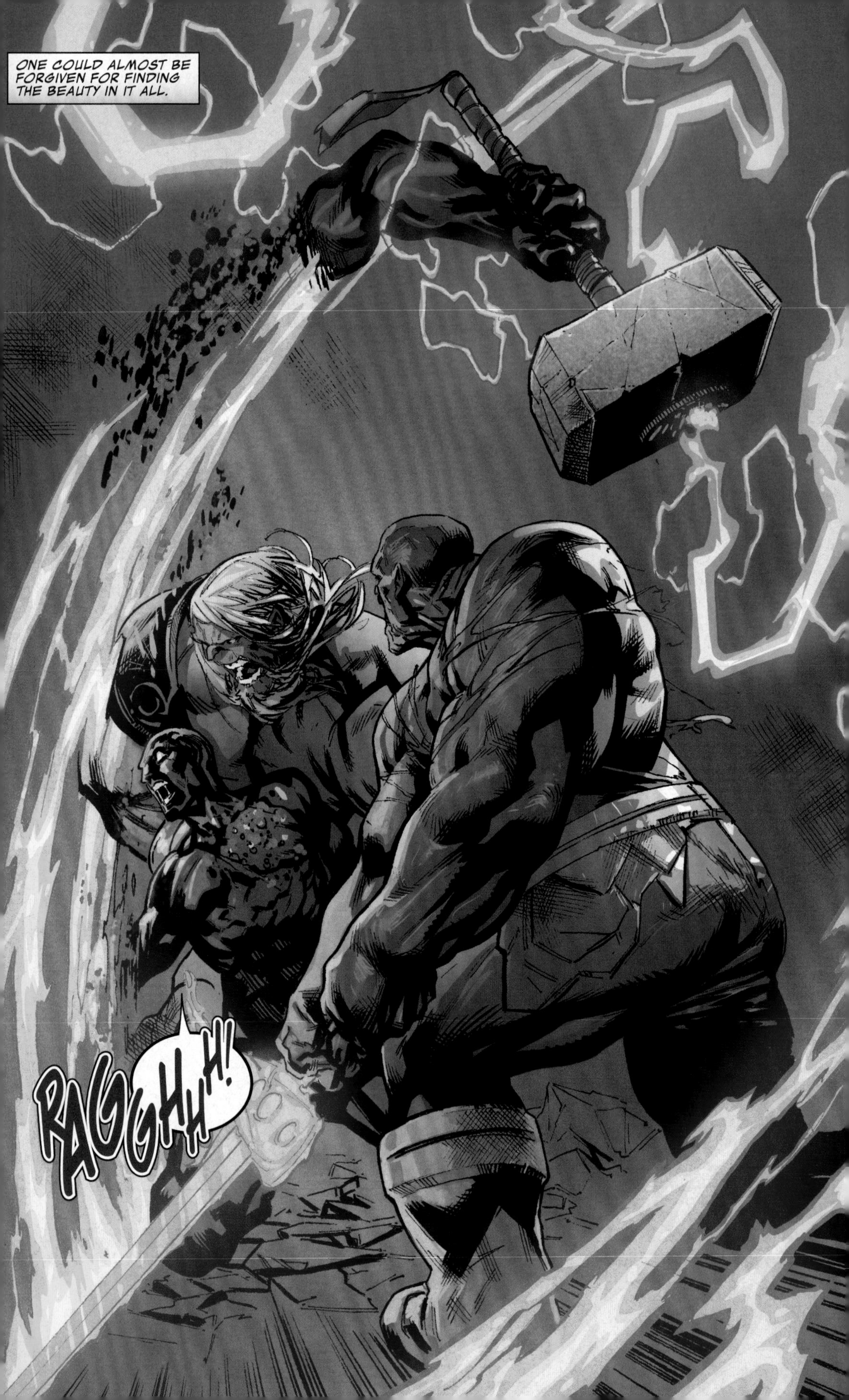
ONE COULD ALMOST BE FORGIVEN FOR FINDING THE BEAUTY IN IT ALL.
RAGGHHH!

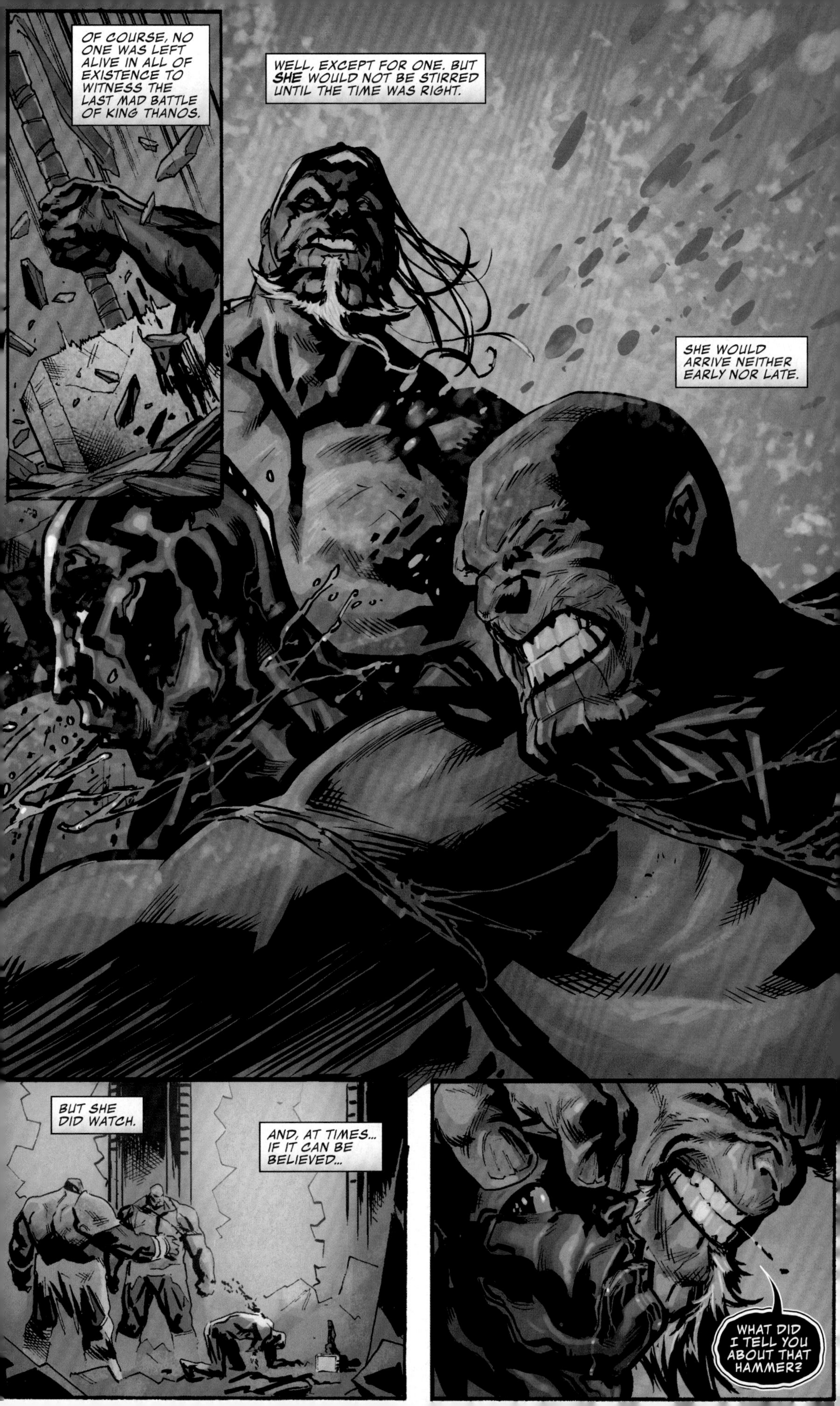
OF COURSE, NO ONE WAS LEFT ALIVE IN ALL OF EXISTENCE TO WITNESS THE LAST MAD BATTLE OF KING THANOS.
WELL, EXCEPT FOR ONE. BUT SHE WOULD NOT BE STIRRED UNTIL THE TIME WAS RIGHT.
SHE WOULD ARRIVE NEITHER EARLY NOR LATE.
BUT SHE DID WATCH.
AND, AT TIMES... IF IT CAN BE BELIEVED...
WHAT DID I TELL YOU ABOUT THAT HAMMER?

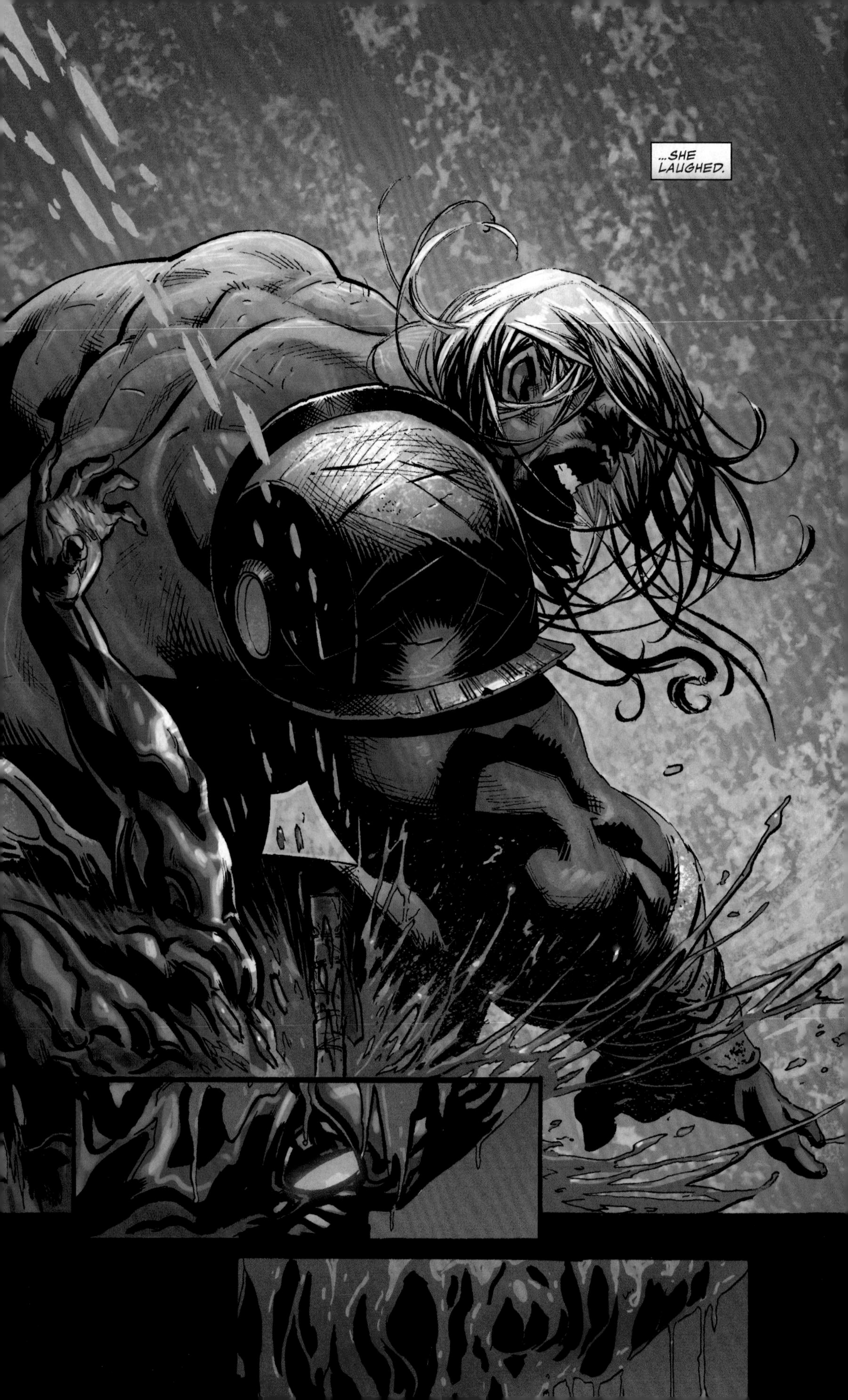
...SHE LAUGHED.

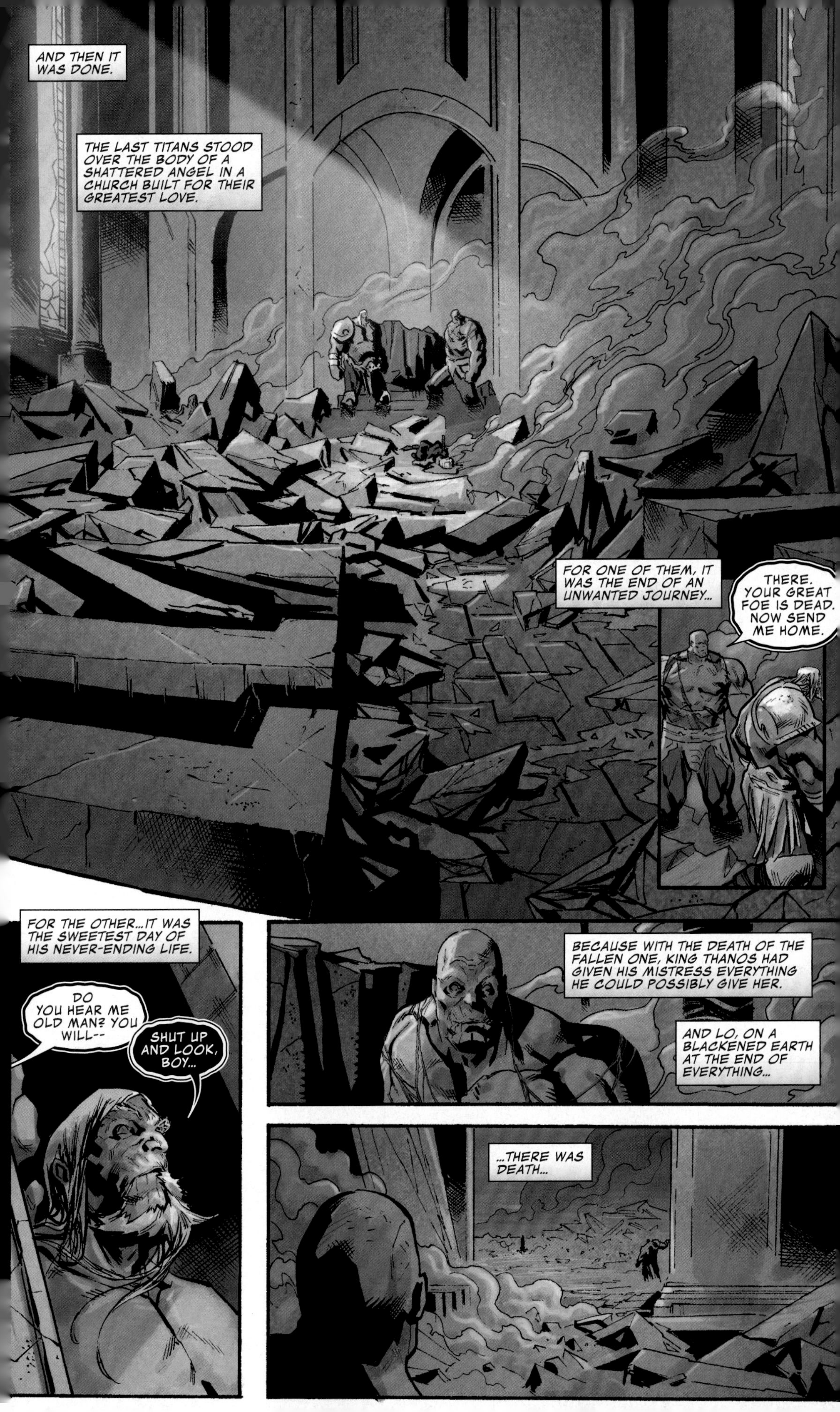
AND THEN IT WAS DONE.
THE LAST TITANS STOOD OVER THE BODY OF A SHATTERED ANGEL IN A CHURCH BUILT FOR THEIR GREATEST LOVE.
FOR ONE OF THEM, IT WAS THE END OF AN UNWANTED JOURNEY...
THERE. YOUR GREAT FOE IS DEAD. NOW SEND ME HOME.
FOR THE OTHER...IT WAS THE SWEETEST DAY OF HIS NEVER-ENDING LIFE.
DO YOU HEAR ME OLD MAN? YOU WILL--
SHUT UP AND LOOK, BOY...
BECAUSE WITH THE DEATH OF THE FALLEN ONE, KING THANOS HAD GIVEN HIS MISTRESS EVERYTHING HE COULD POSSIBLY GIVE HER.
AND LO, ON A BLACKENED EARTH AT THE END OF EVERYTHING...
...THERE WAS DEATH...

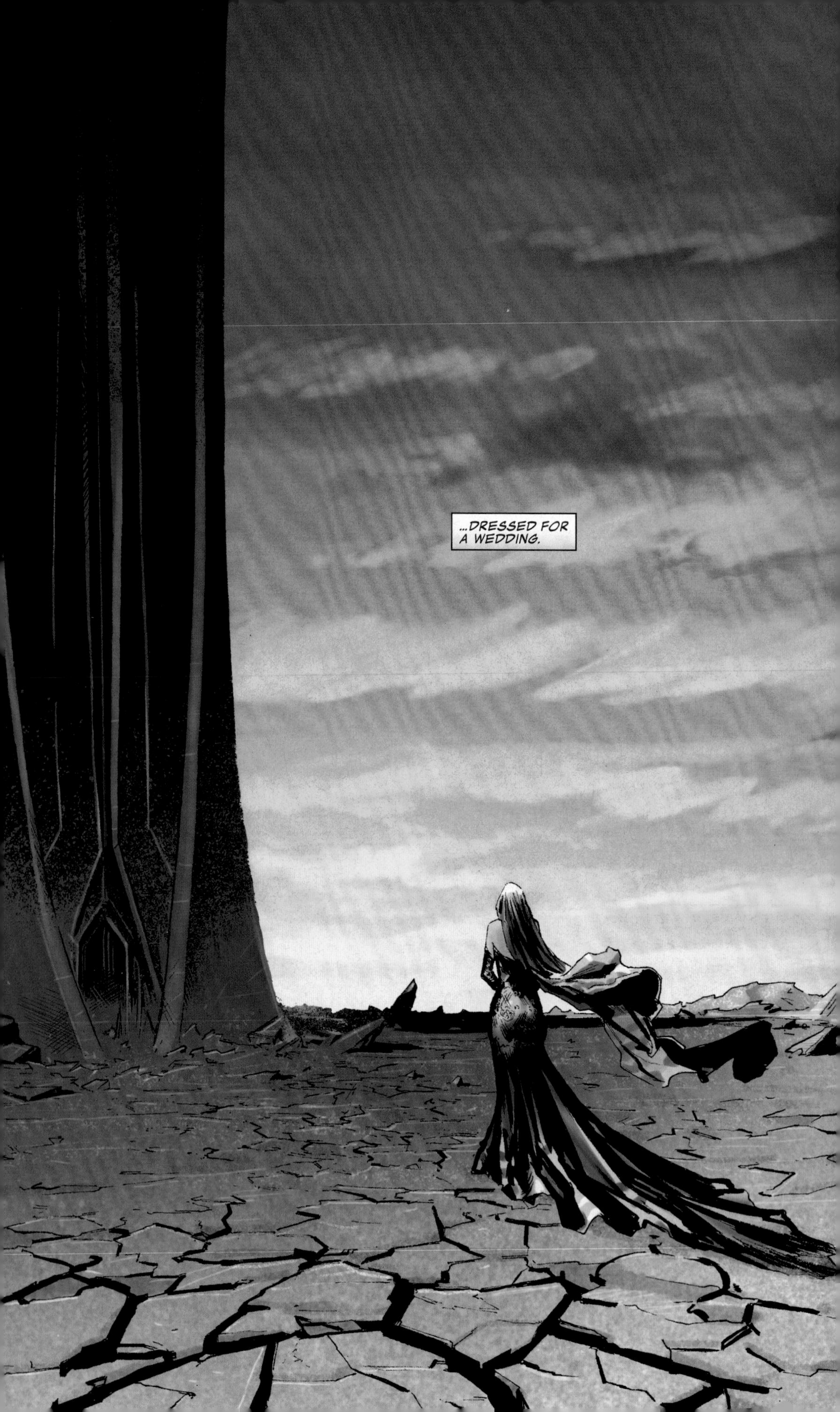
...DRESSED FOR A WEDDING.

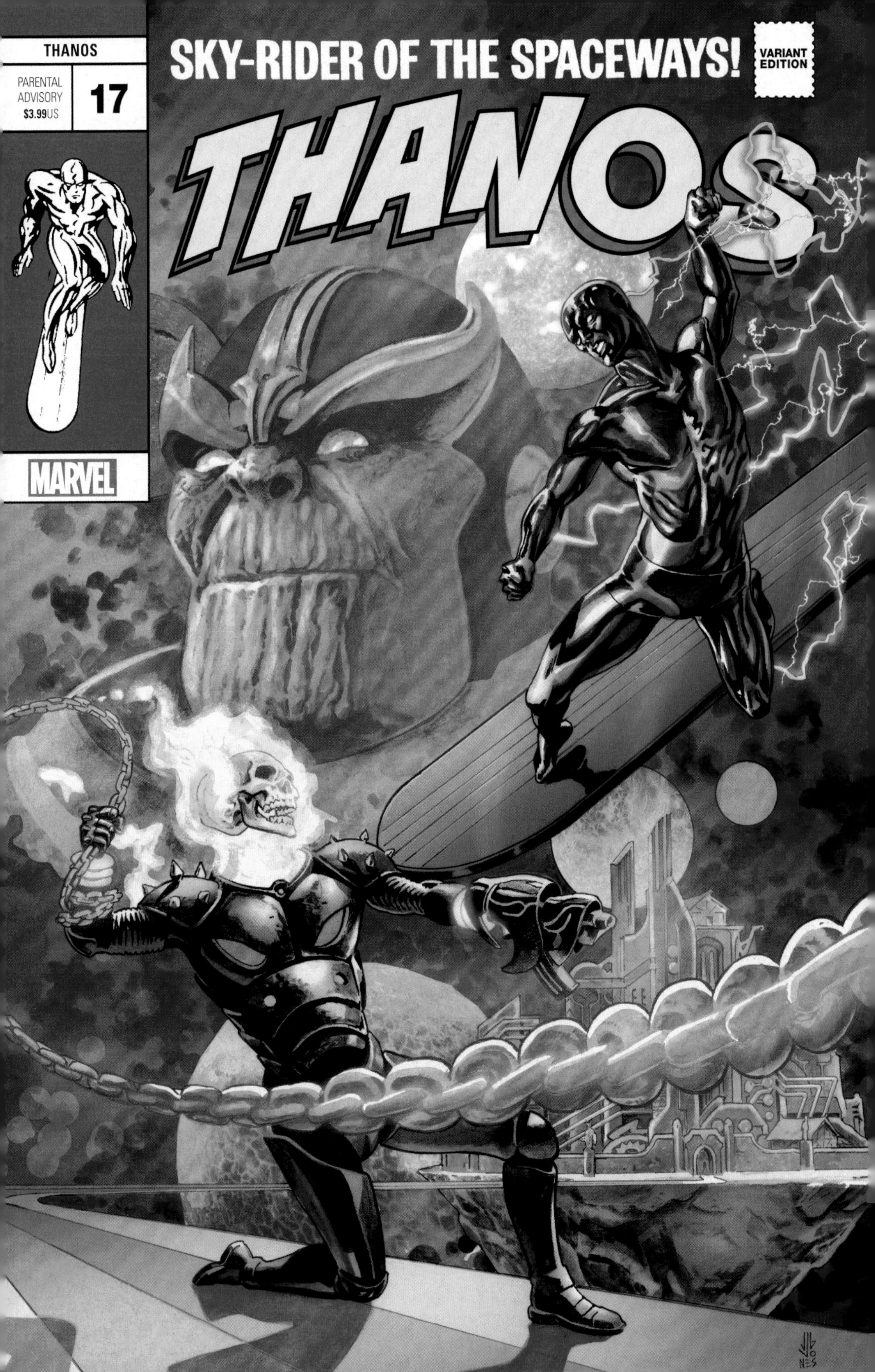
THANOS
PARENTAL ADVISORY
$3.99US
17
MARVEL
SKY-RIDER OF THE SPACEWAYS!
VARIANT EDITION
THANOS

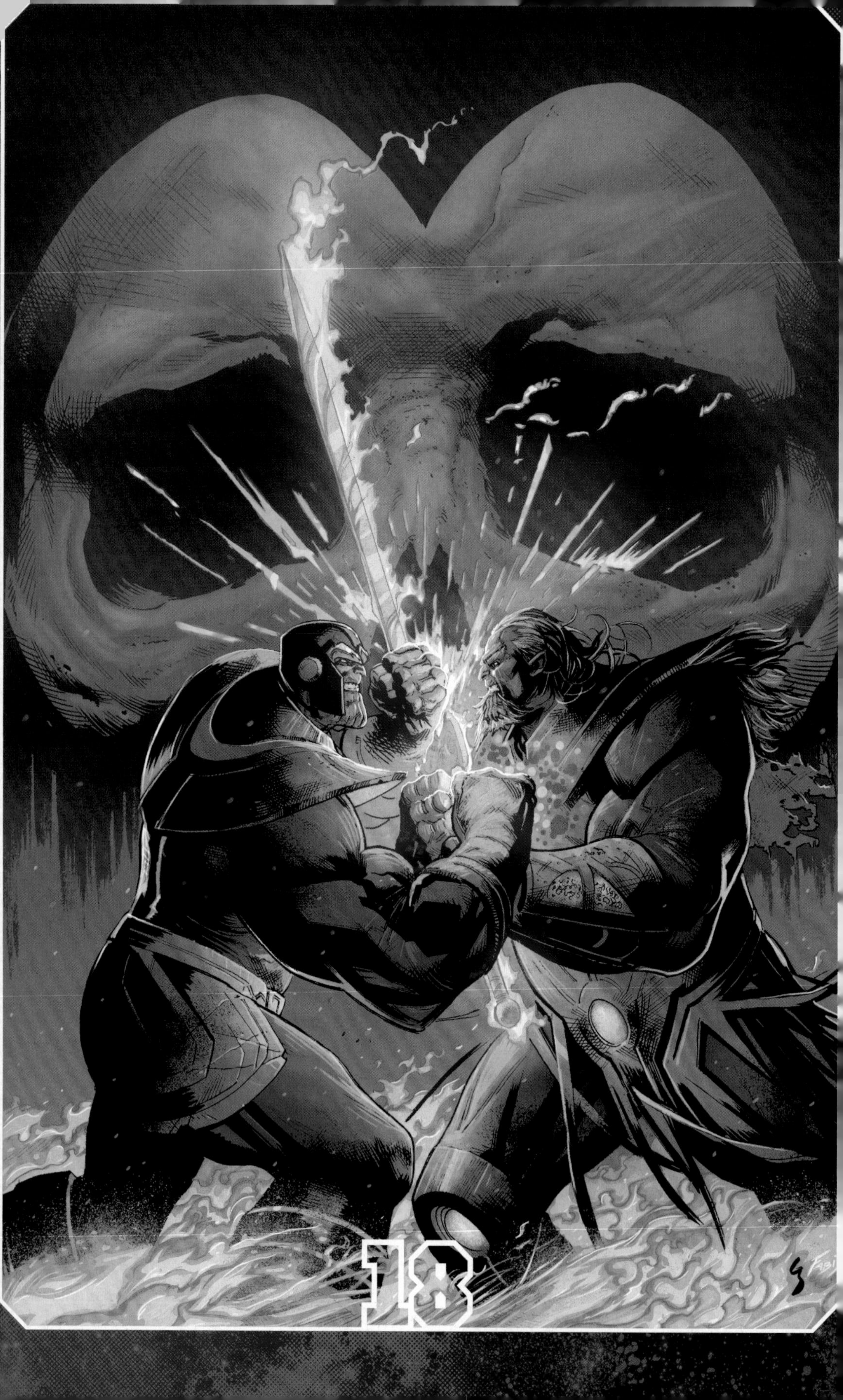

18

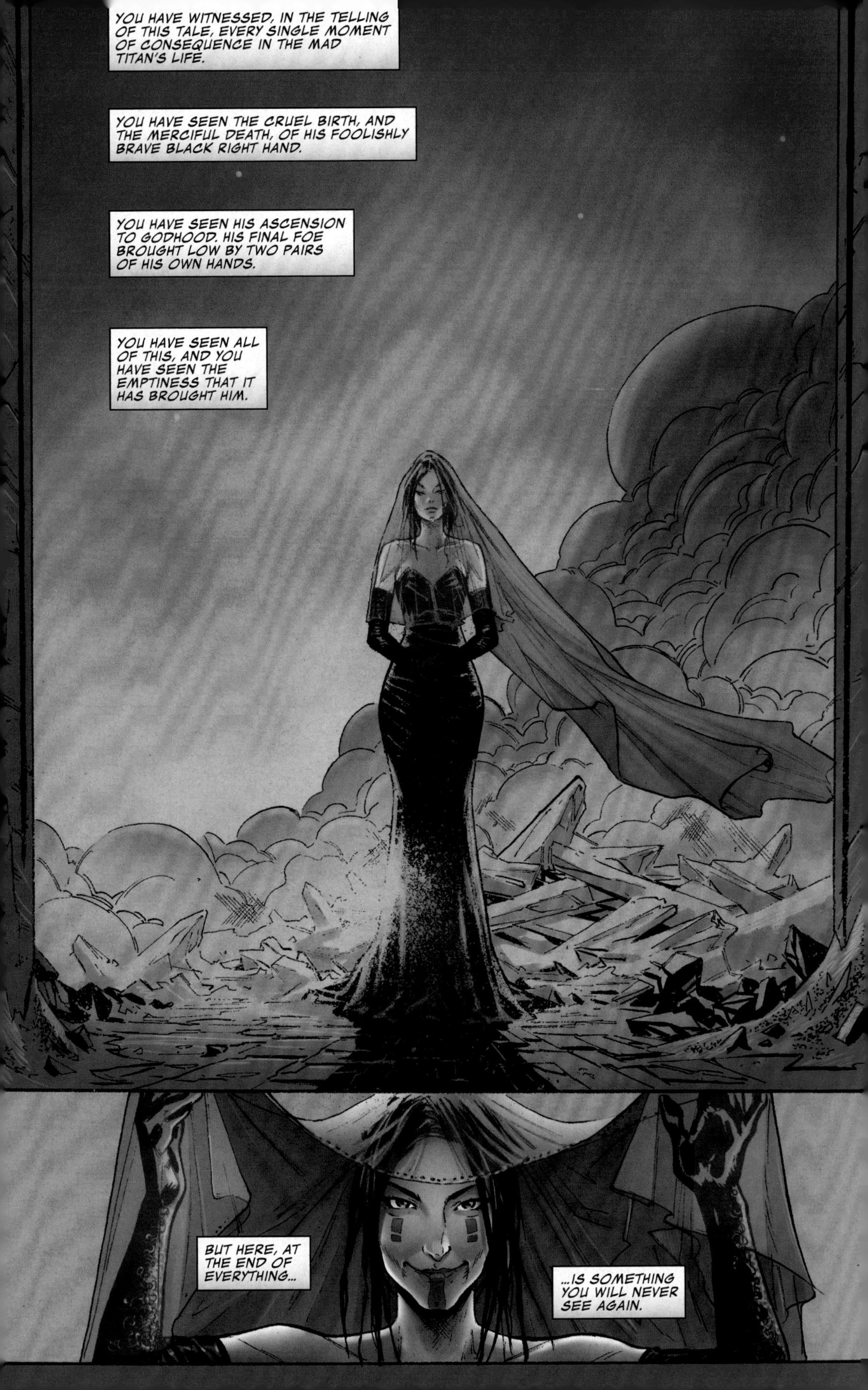
YOU HAVE WITNESSED, IN THE TELLING OF THIS TALE, EVERY SINGLE MOMENT OF CONSEQUENCE IN THE MAD TITAN'S LIFE.
YOU HAVE SEEN THE CRUEL BIRTH, AND THE MERCIFUL DEATH, OF HIS FOOLISHLY BRAVE BLACK RIGHT HAND.
YOU HAVE SEEN HIS ASCENSION TO GODHOOD. HIS FINAL FOE BROUGHT LOW BY TWO PAIRS OF HIS OWN HANDS.
YOU HAVE SEEN ALL OF THIS, AND YOU HAVE SEEN THE EMPTINESS THAT IT HAS BROUGHT HIM.
BUT HERE, AT THE END OF EVERYTHING...
...IS SOMETHING YOU WILL NEVER SEE AGAIN.

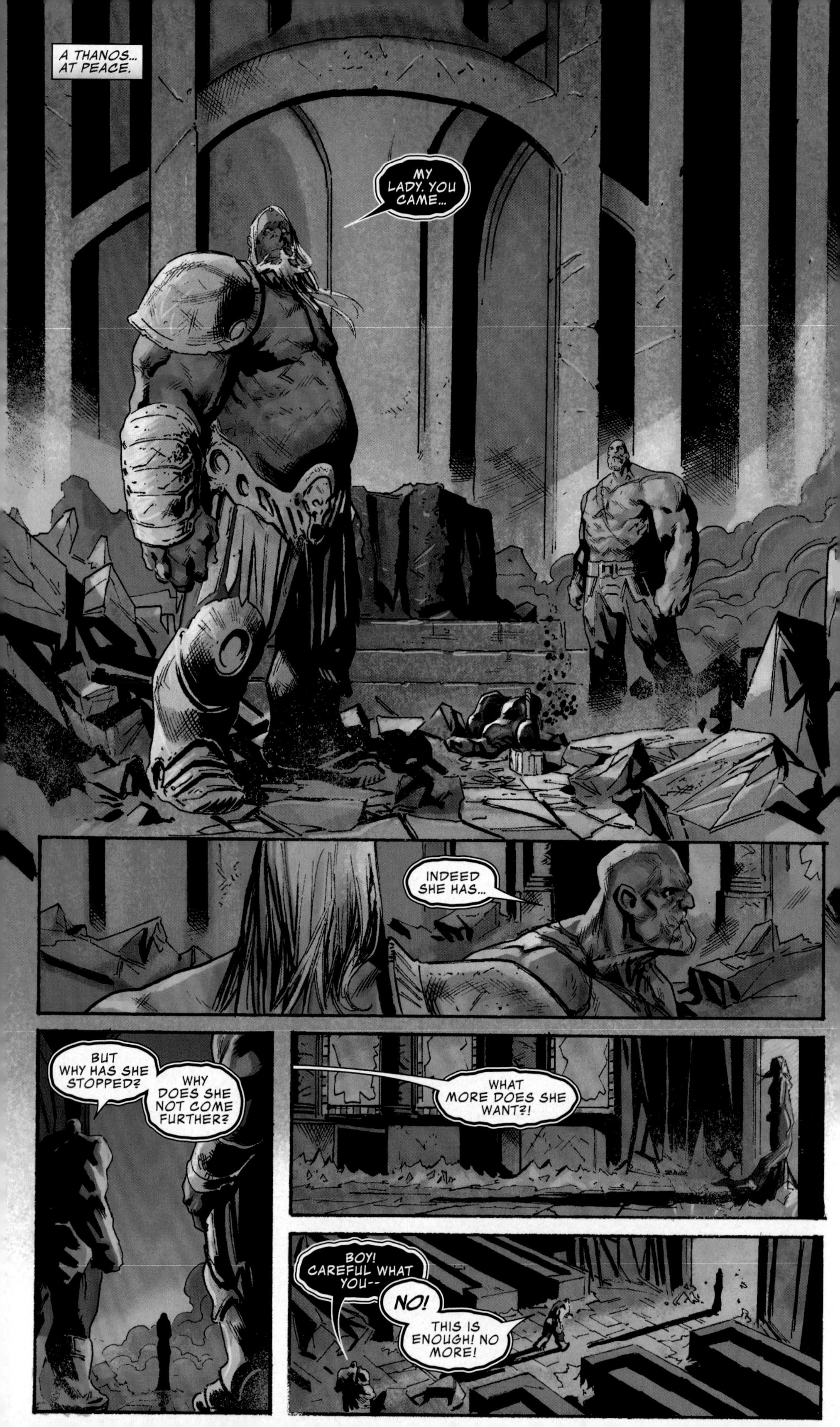
A THANOS... AT PEACE.
MY LADY. YOU CAME...
INDEED SHE HAS...
BUT WHY HAS SHE STOPPED?
WHY DOES SHE NOT COME FURTHER?
WHAT MORE DOES SHE WANT?!
BOY! CAREFUL WHAT YOU--
NO!
THIS IS ENOUGH! NO MORE!

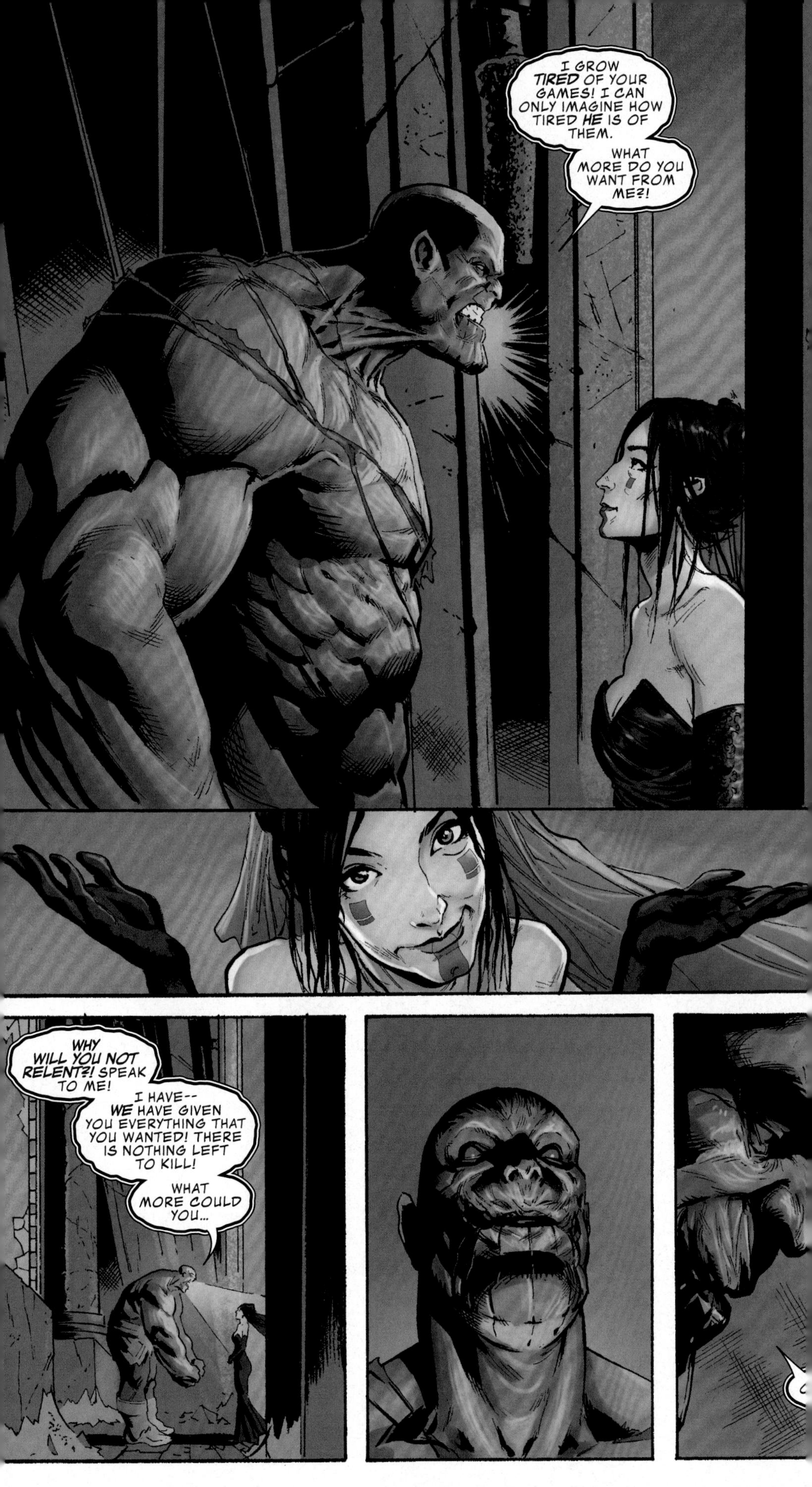
I GROW TIRED OF YOUR GAMES! I CAN ONLY IMAGINE HOW TIRED HE IS OF THEM.
WHAT MORE DO YOU WANT FROM ME?!
WHY WILL YOU NOT RELENT?! SPEAK TO ME!
I HAVE-- WE HAVE GIVEN YOU EVERYTHING THAT YOU WANTED! THERE IS NOTHING LEFT TO KILL!
WHAT MORE COULD YOU...

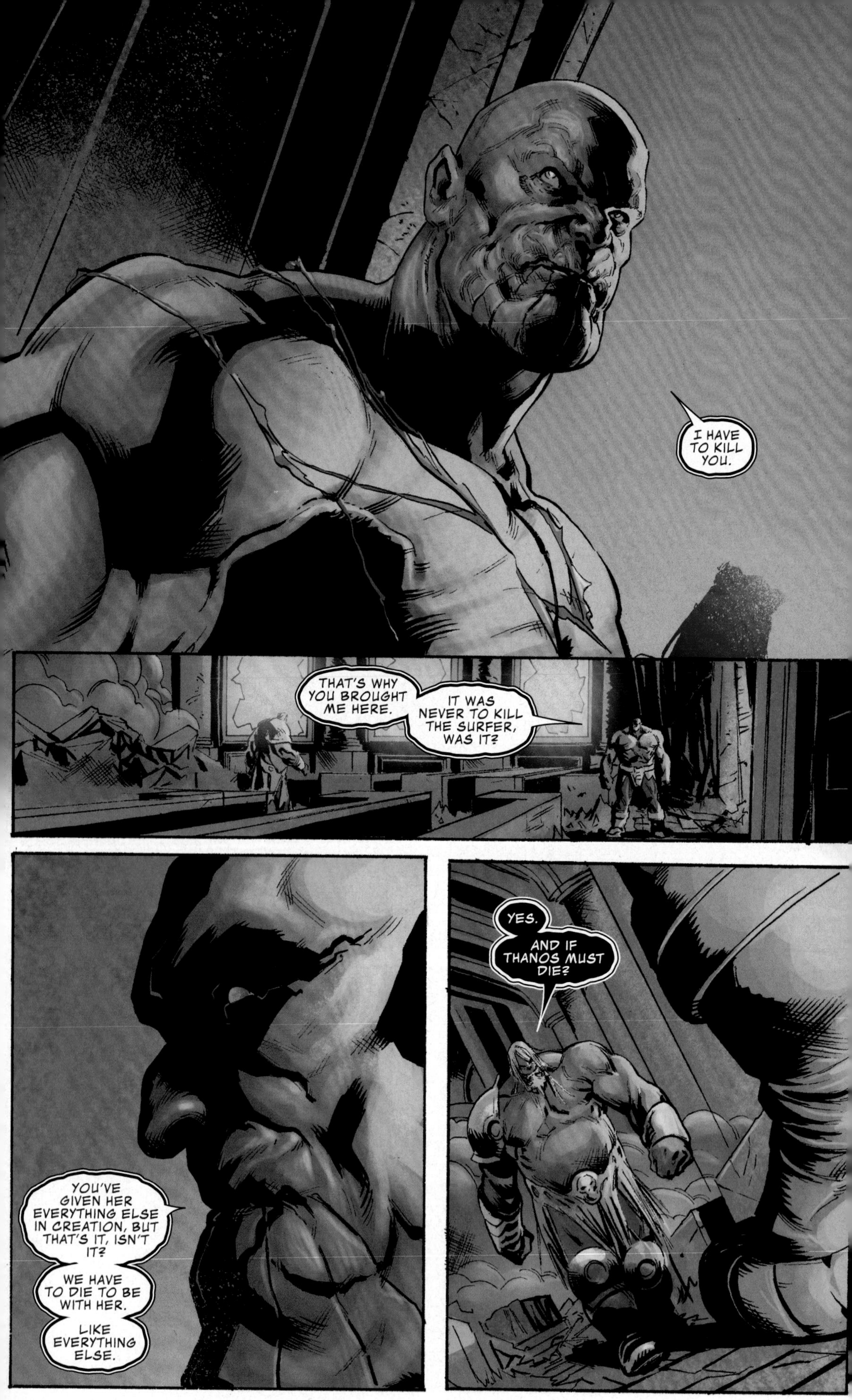
I HAVE TO KILL YOU.
THAT'S WHY YOU BROUGHT ME HERE.
IT WAS NEVER TO KILL THE SURFER, WAS IT?
YOU'VE GIVEN HER EVERYTHING ELSE IN CREATION, BUT THAT'S IT, ISN'T IT?
WE HAVE TO DIE TO BE WITH HER.
LIKE EVERYTHING ELSE.
YES.
AND IF THANOS MUST DIE?

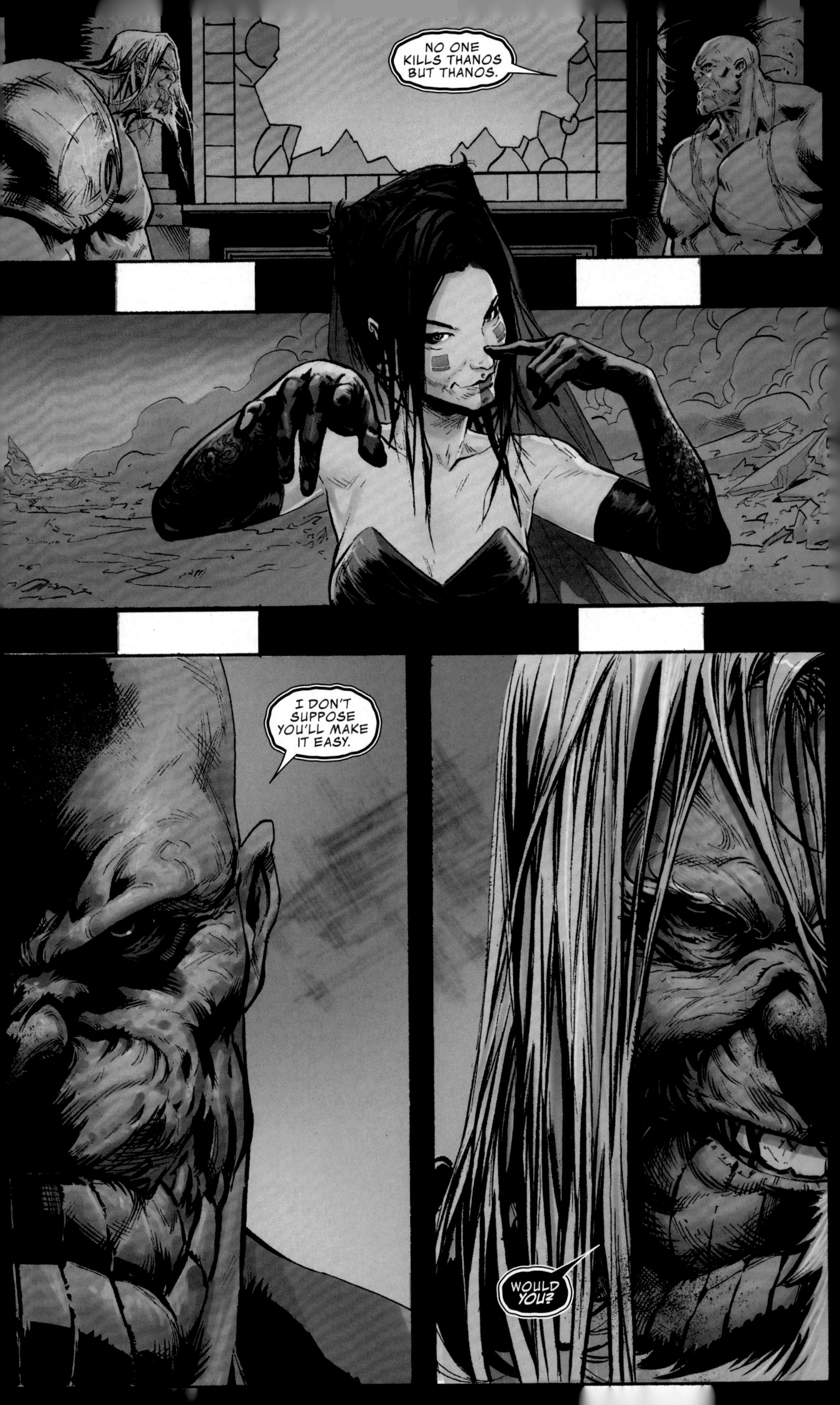
NO ONE KILLS THANOS BUT THANOS.
I DON'T SUPPOSE YOU'LL MAKE IT EASY.
WOULD YOU?

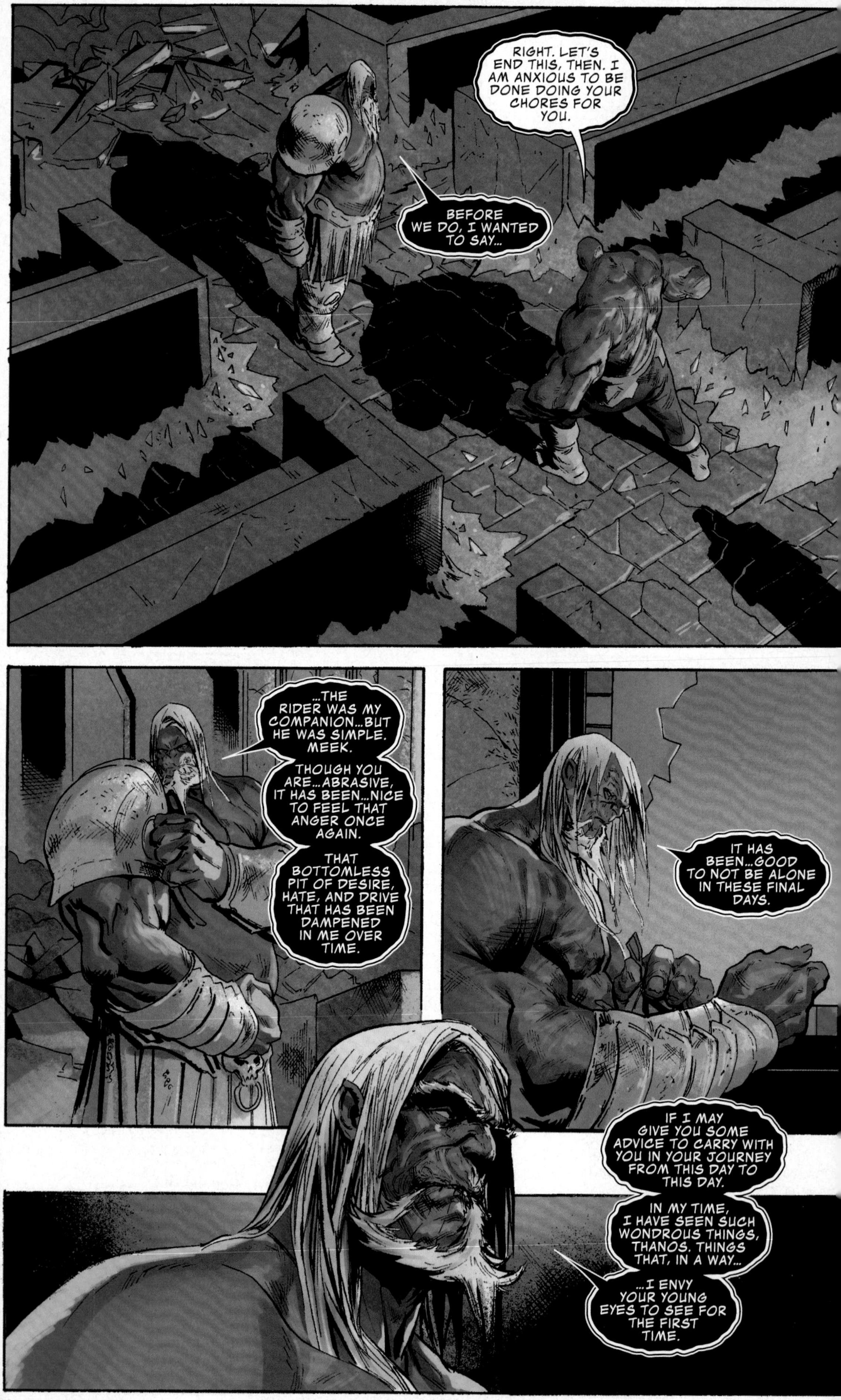

RIGHT. LET'S END THIS, THEN. I AM ANXIOUS TO BE DONE DOING YOUR CHORES FOR YOU.
BEFORE WE DO, I WANTED TO SAY...
...THE RIDER WAS MY COMPANION...BUT HE WAS SIMPLE. MEEK.
THOUGH YOU ARE...ABRASIVE, IT HAS BEEN...NICE TO FEEL THAT ANGER ONCE AGAIN.
THAT BOTTOMLESS PIT OF DESIRE, HATE, AND DRIVE THAT HAS BEEN DAMPENED IN ME OVER TIME.
IT HAS BEEN...GOOD TO NOT BE ALONE IN THESE FINAL DAYS.
IF I MAY GIVE YOU SOME ADVICE TO CARRY WITH YOU IN YOUR JOURNEY FROM THIS DAY TO THIS DAY.
IN MY TIME, I HAVE SEEN SUCH WONDROUS THINGS, THANOS. THINGS THAT, IN A WAY...
...I ENVY YOUR YOUNG EYES TO SEE FOR THE FIRST TIME.

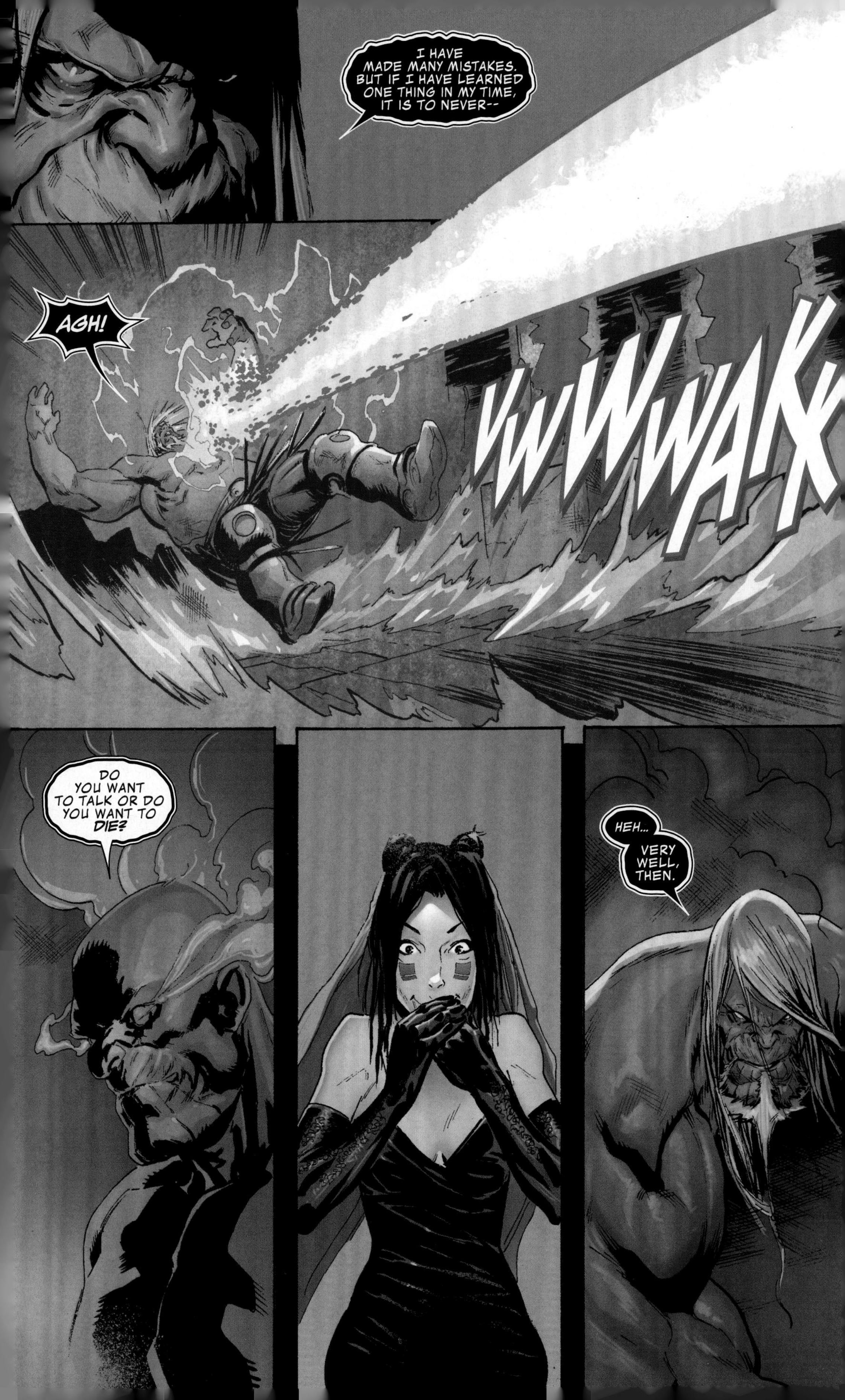
I HAVE MADE MANY MISTAKES. BUT IF I HAVE LEARNED ONE THING IN MY TIME, IT IS TO NEVER--
AGH!
VWWWAK
DO YOU WANT TO TALK OR DO YOU WANT TO DIE?
HEH...
VERY WELL, THEN.

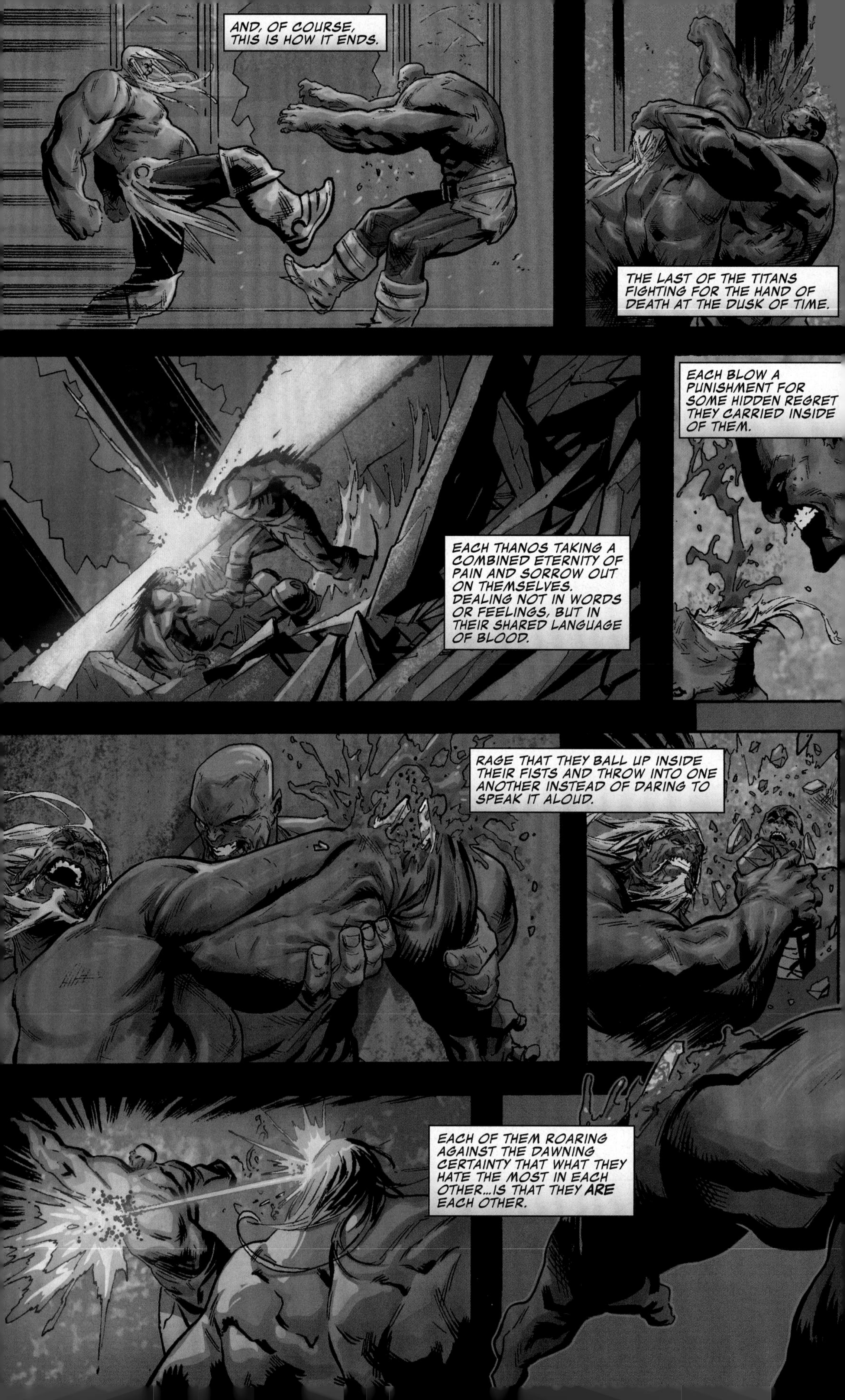
AND, OF COURSE, THIS IS HOW IT ENDS.
THE LAST OF THE TITANS FIGHTING FOR THE HAND OF DEATH AT THE DUSK OF TIME.
EACH THANOS TAKING A COMBINED ETERNITY OF PAIN AND SORROW OUT ON THEMSELVES. DEALING NOT IN WORDS OR FEELINGS, BUT IN THEIR SHARED LANGUAGE OF BLOOD.
EACH BLOW A PUNISHMENT FOR SOME HIDDEN REGRET THEY CARRIED INSIDE OF THEM.
RAGE THAT THEY BALL UP INSIDE THEIR FISTS AND THROW INTO ONE ANOTHER INSTEAD OF DARING TO SPEAK IT ALOUD.
EACH OF THEM ROARING AGAINST THE DAWNING CERTAINTY THAT WHAT THEY HATE THE MOST IN EACH OTHER...IS THAT THEY **ARE** EACH OTHER.

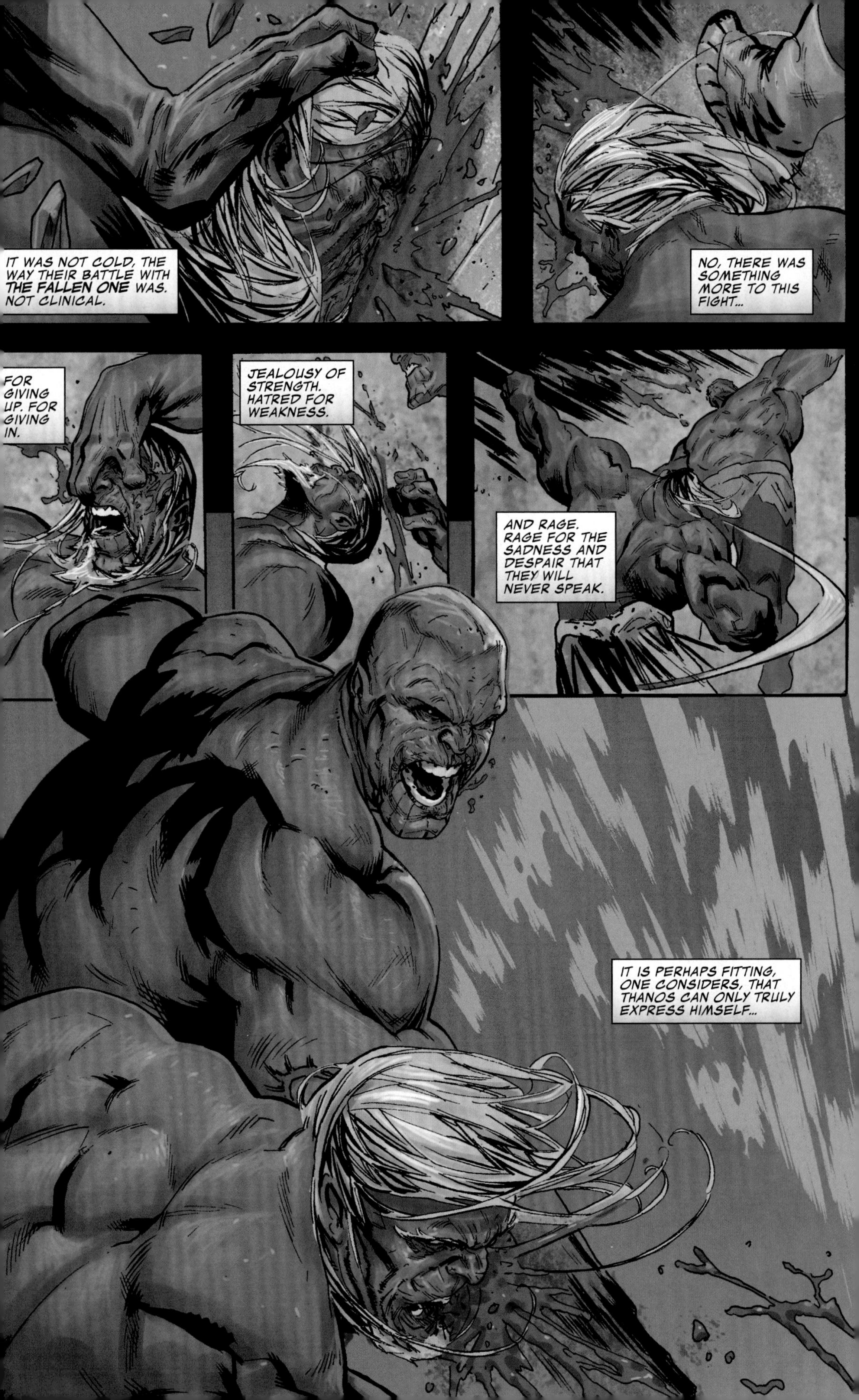
IT WAS NOT COLD, THE WAY THEIR BATTLE WITH THE FALLEN ONE WAS. NOT CLINICAL.
NO, THERE WAS SOMETHING MORE TO THIS FIGHT...
FOR GIVING UP. FOR GIVING IN.
JEALOUSY OF STRENGTH. HATRED FOR WEAKNESS.
AND RAGE. RAGE FOR THE SADNESS AND DESPAIR THAT THEY WILL NEVER SPEAK.
IT IS PERHAPS FITTING, ONE CONSIDERS, THAT THANOS CAN ONLY TRULY EXPRESS HIMSELF...

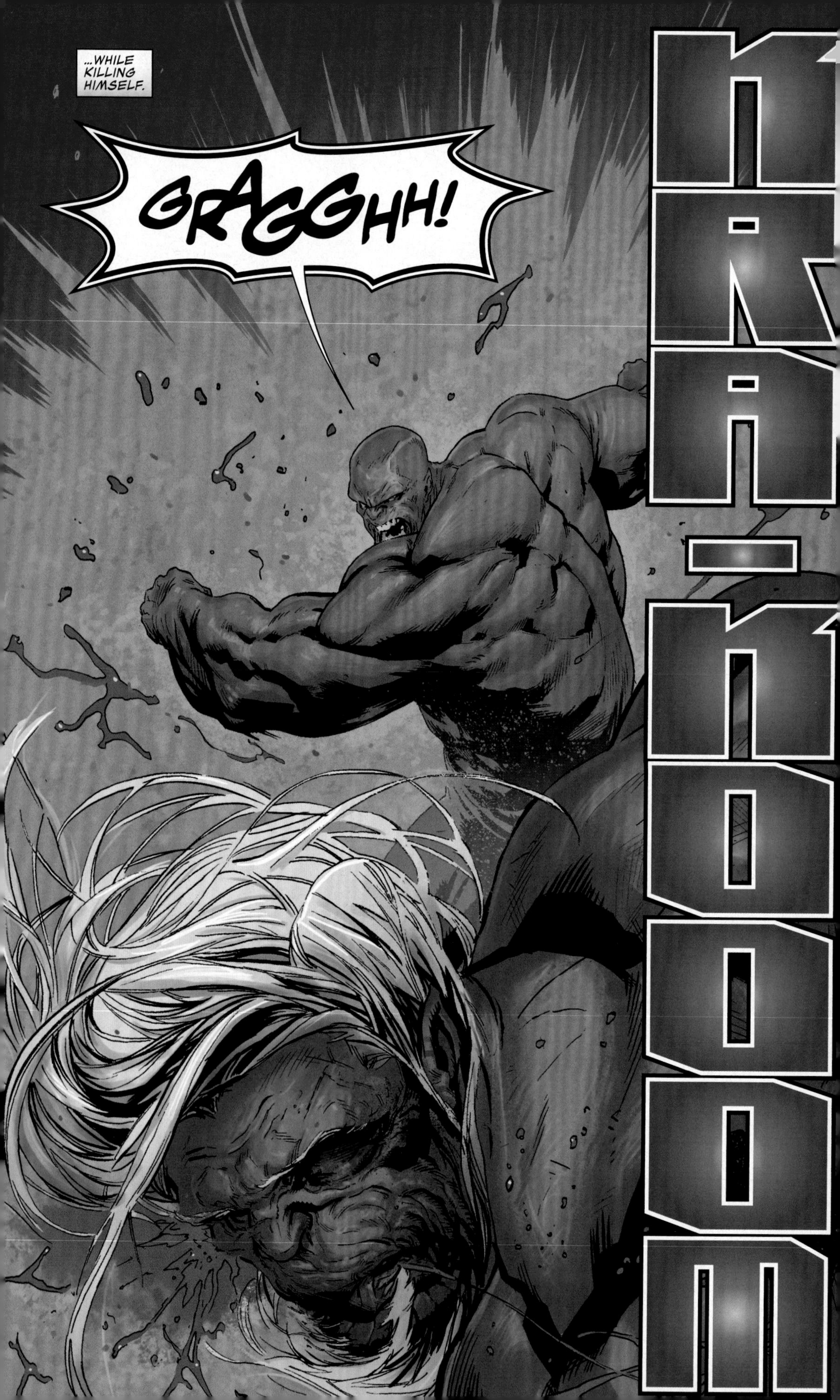
...WHILE KILLING HIMSELF.
GRAGGHH!
KRA-KOOOM

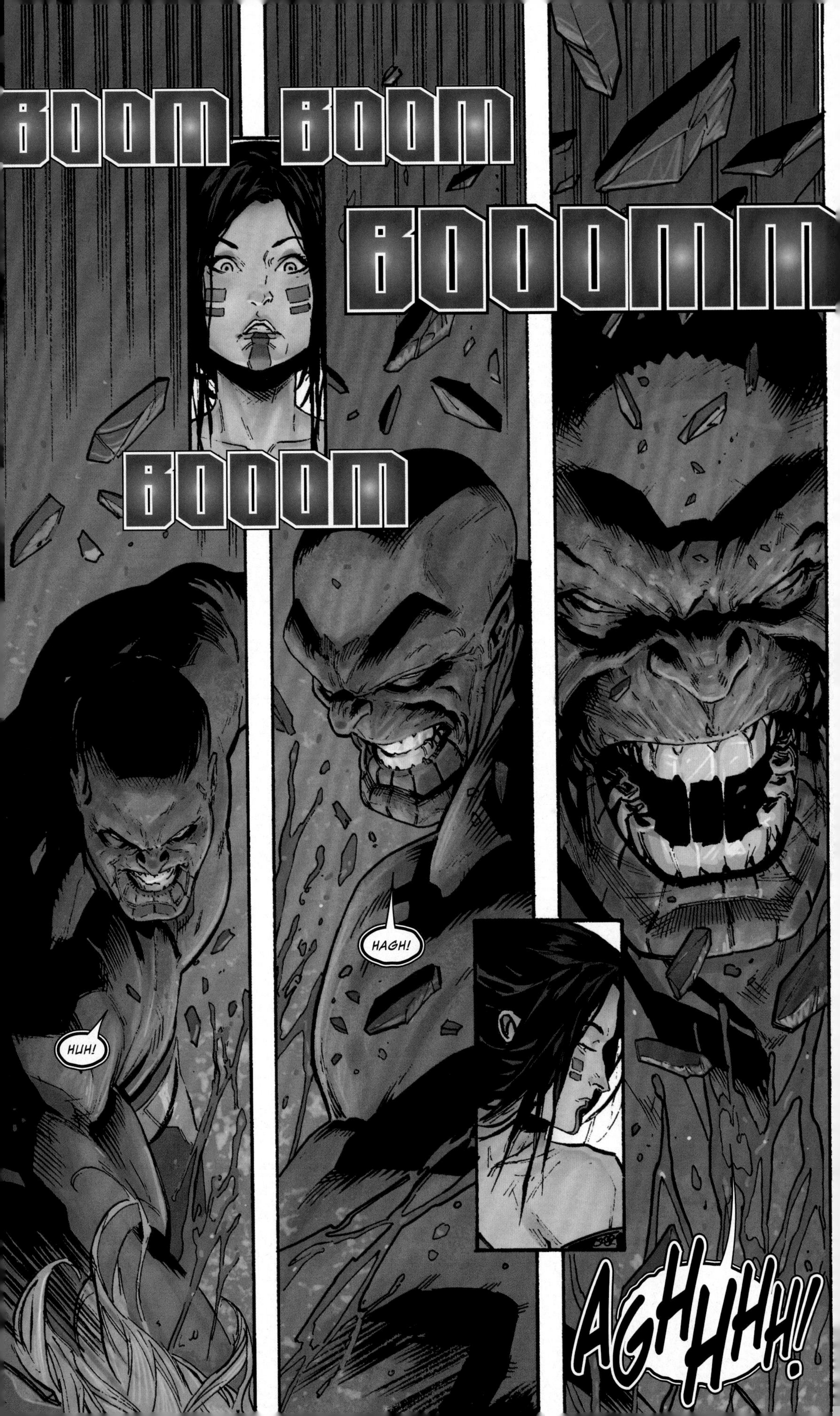
BOOM BOOM
BOOOM
BOOOMM
HUH!
HAGH!
AGHHHH!!

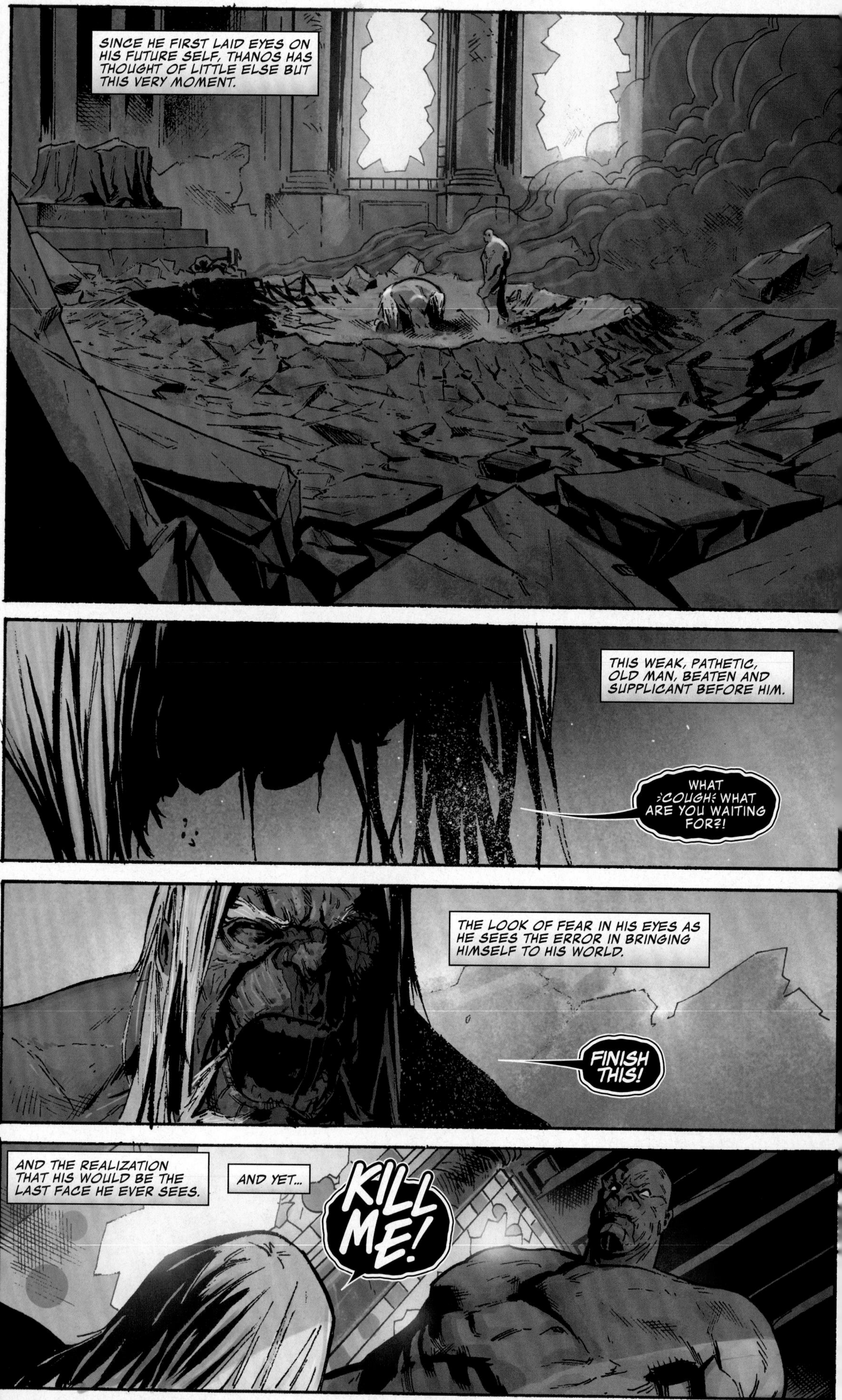
SINCE HE FIRST LAID EYES ON HIS FUTURE SELF, THANOS HAS THOUGHT OF LITTLE ELSE BUT THIS VERY MOMENT.
THIS WEAK, PATHETIC, OLD MAN, BEATEN AND SUPPLICANT BEFORE HIM.
WHAT *COUGH* WHAT ARE YOU WAITING FOR?!
THE LOOK OF FEAR IN HIS EYES AS HE SEES THE ERROR IN BRINGING HIMSELF TO HIS WORLD.
FINISH THIS!
AND THE REALIZATION THAT HIS WOULD BE THE LAST FACE HE EVER SEES.
AND YET...
KILL ME!

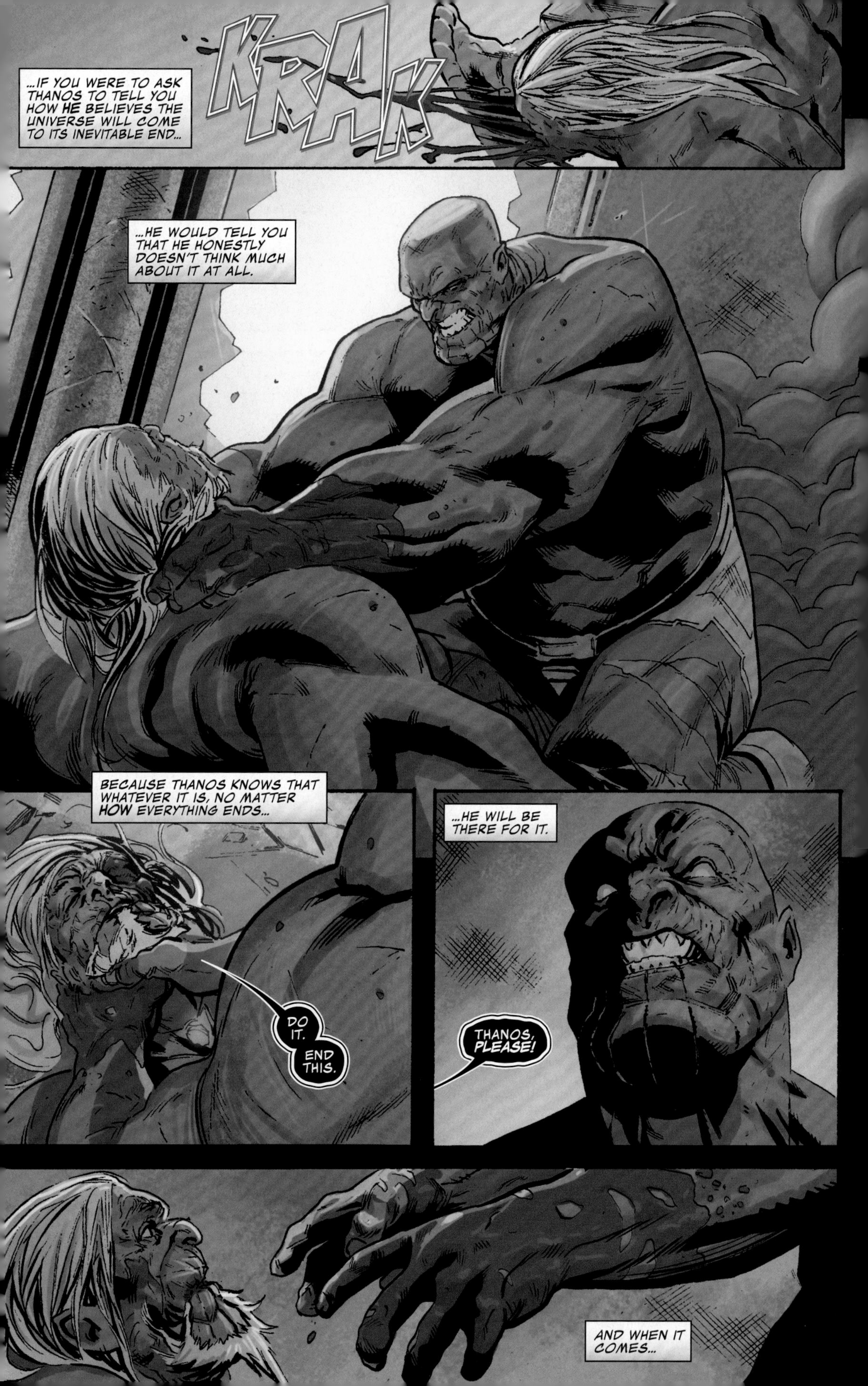
KRAK
...IF YOU WERE TO ASK THANOS TO TELL YOU HOW HE BELIEVES THE UNIVERSE WILL COME TO ITS INEVITABLE END...
...HE WOULD TELL YOU THAT HE HONESTLY DOESN'T THINK MUCH ABOUT IT AT ALL.
BECAUSE THANOS KNOWS THAT WHATEVER IT IS, NO MATTER HOW EVERYTHING ENDS...
DO IT.
END THIS.
...HE WILL BE THERE FOR IT.
THANOS, PLEASE!
AND WHEN IT COMES...

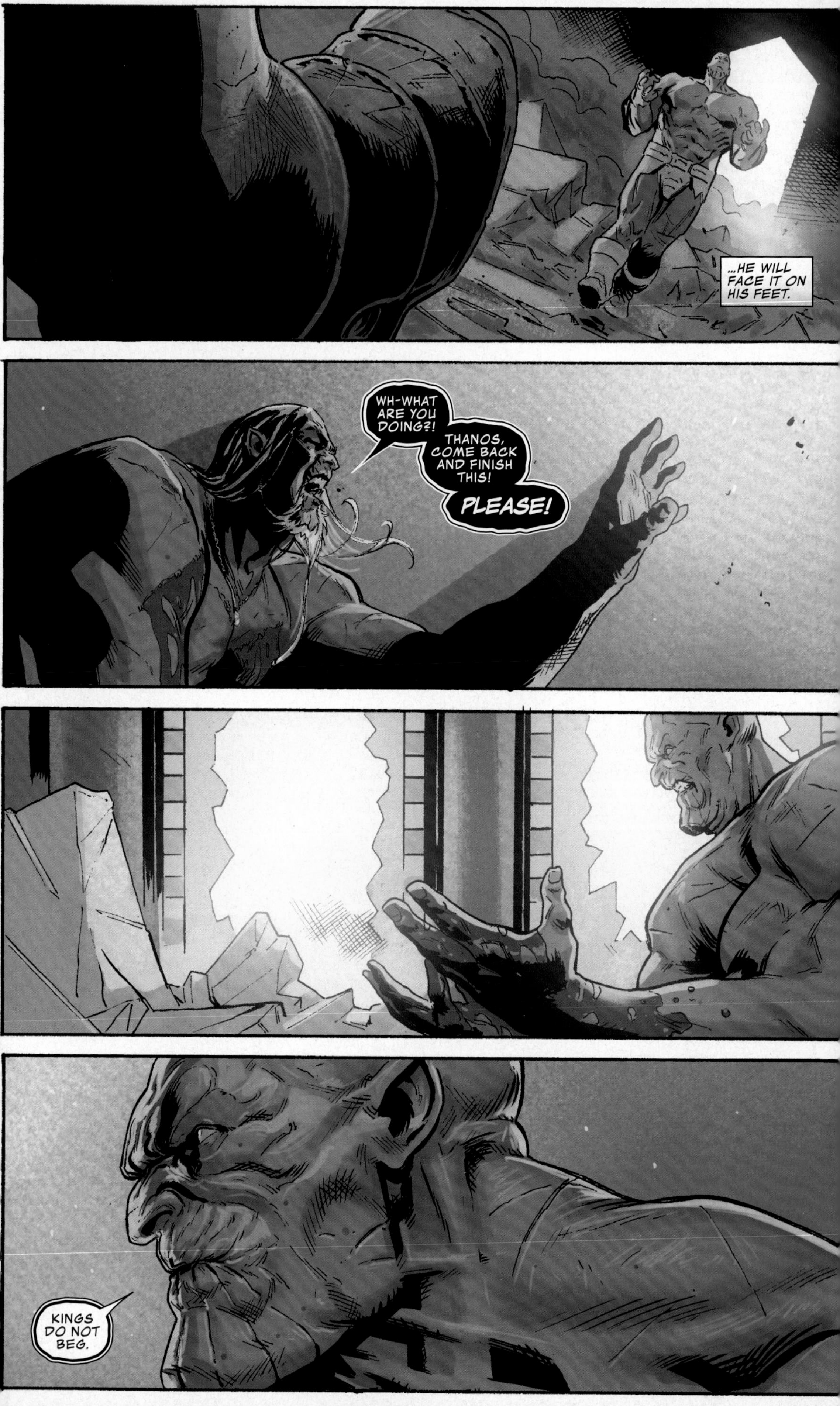

...HE WILL FACE IT ON HIS FEET.
WH-WHAT ARE YOU DOING?!
THANOS, COME BACK AND FINISH THIS!
PLEASE!
KINGS DO NOT BEG.

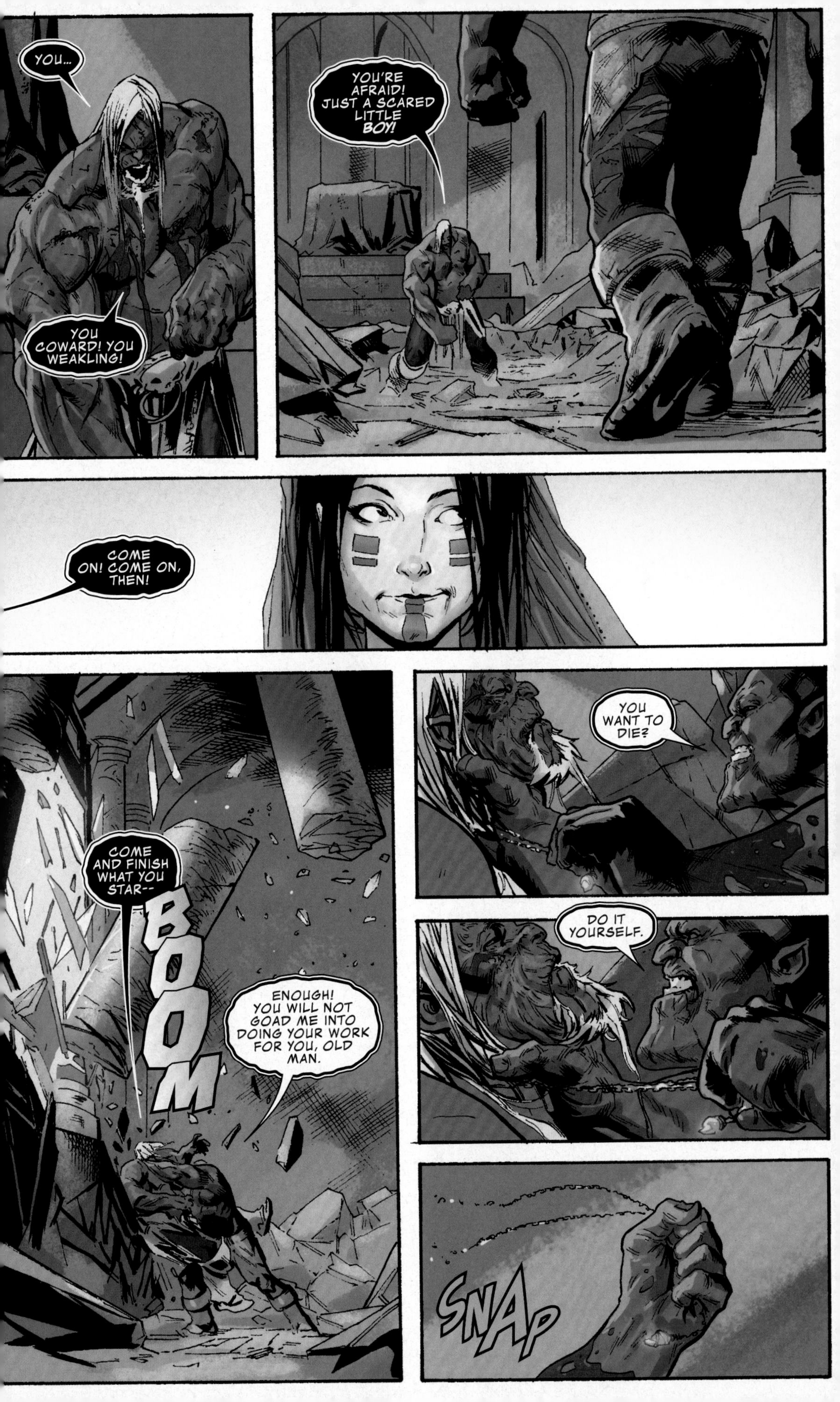
YOU...
YOU COWARD! YOU WEAKLING!
YOU'RE AFRAID! JUST A SCARED LITTLE BOY!
COME ON! COME ON, THEN!
COME AND FINISH WHAT YOU STAR--
BOOM
ENOUGH! YOU WILL NOT GOAD ME INTO DOING YOUR WORK FOR YOU, OLD MAN.
YOU WANT TO DIE?
DO IT YOURSELF.
SNAP

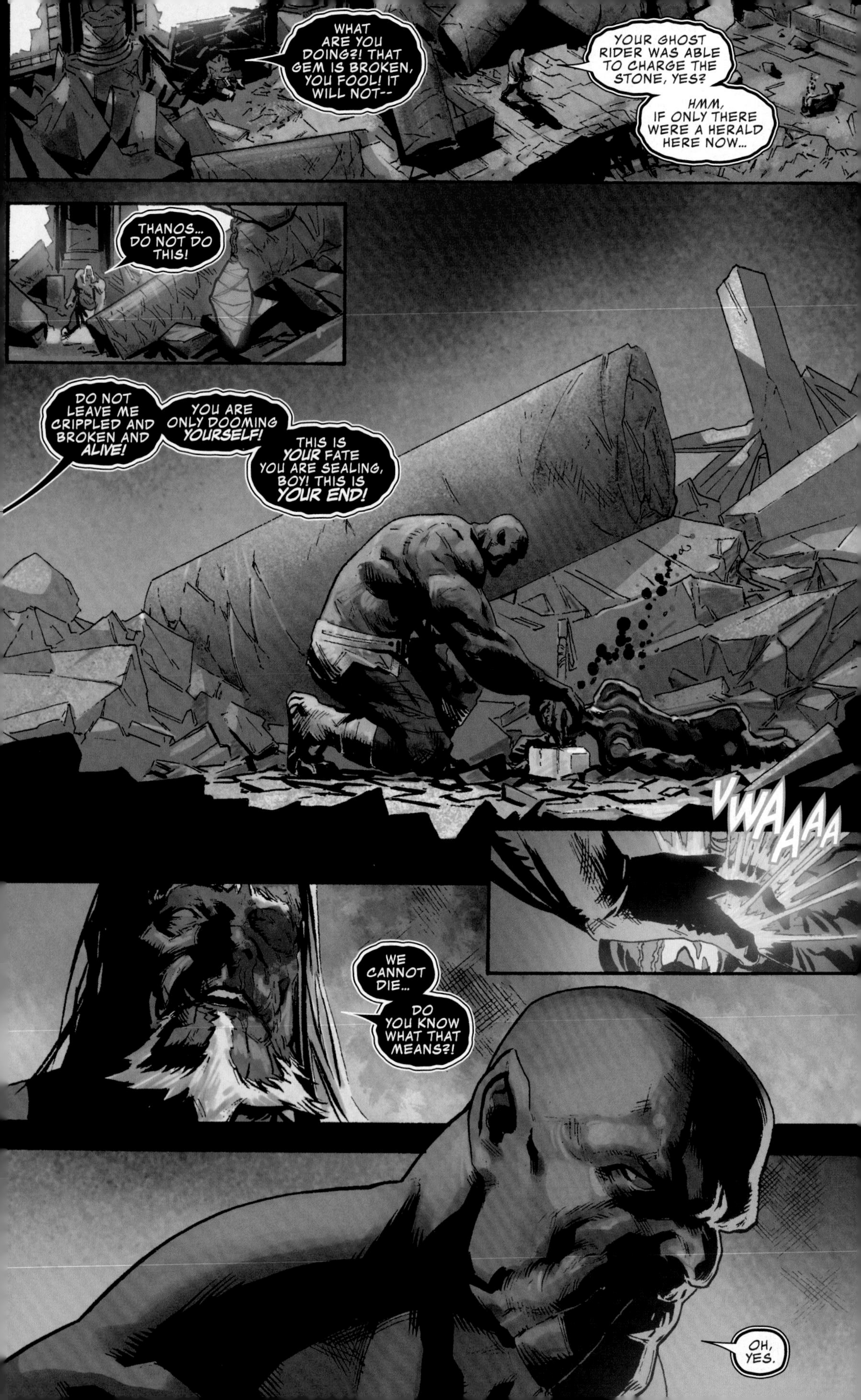
WHAT ARE YOU DOING?! THAT GEM IS BROKEN, YOU FOOL! IT WILL NOT--
YOUR GHOST RIDER WAS ABLE TO CHARGE THE STONE, YES?
HMM, IF ONLY THERE WERE A HERALD HERE NOW...
THANOS... DO NOT DO THIS!
DO NOT LEAVE ME CRIPPLED AND BROKEN AND ALIVE!
YOU ARE ONLY DOOMING YOURSELF!
THIS IS YOUR FATE YOU ARE SEALING, BOY! THIS IS YOUR END!
VWAAAAA
WE CANNOT DIE...
DO YOU KNOW WHAT THAT MEANS?!
OH, YES.

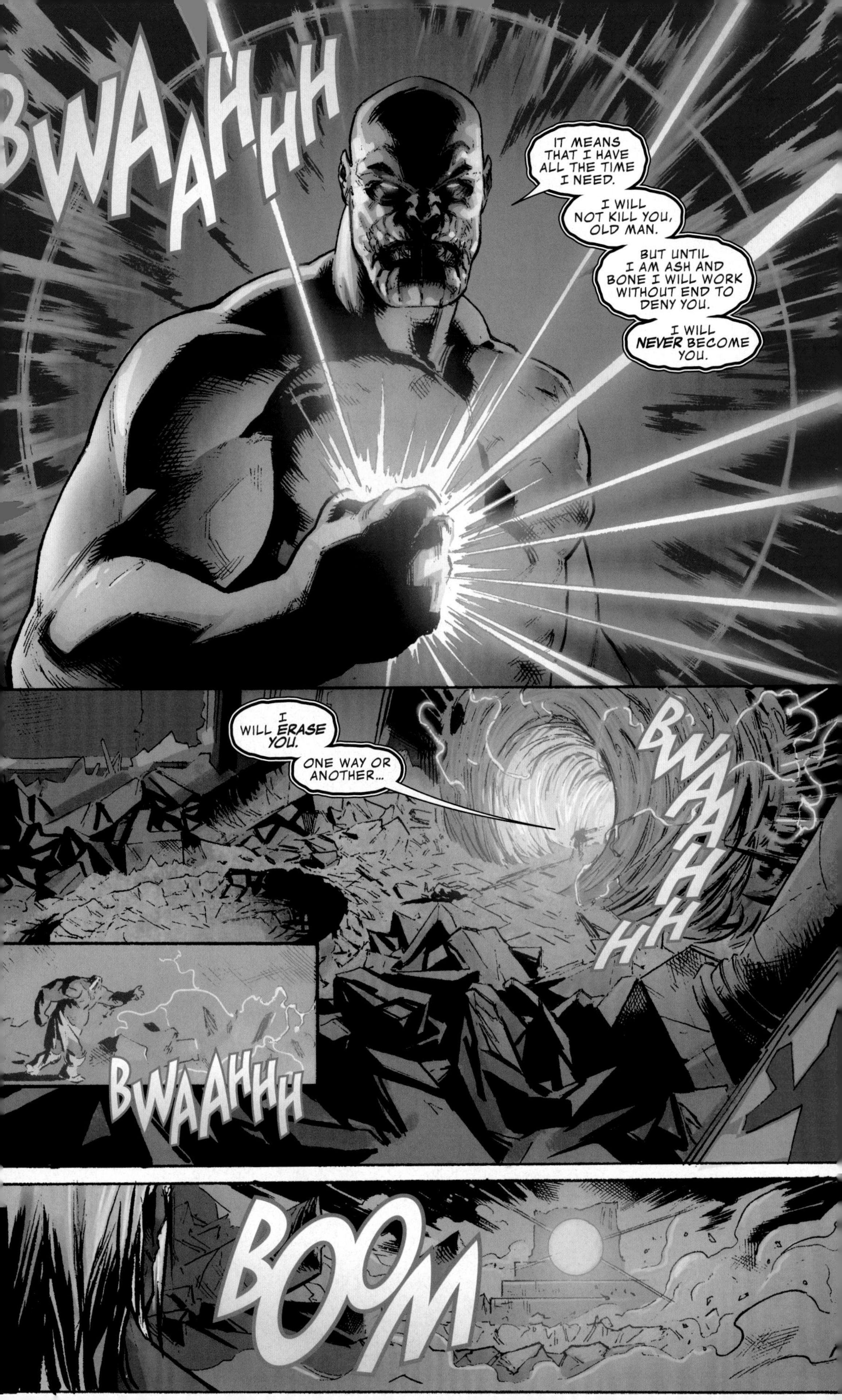
BWAAHHH
IT MEANS THAT I HAVE ALL THE TIME I NEED.
I WILL NOT KILL YOU, OLD MAN.
BUT UNTIL I AM ASH AND BONE I WILL WORK WITHOUT END TO DENY YOU.
I WILL NEVER BECOME YOU.
I WILL ERASE YOU.
ONE WAY OR ANOTHER...
BWAAAHHHH
BWAAHHH
BOOM

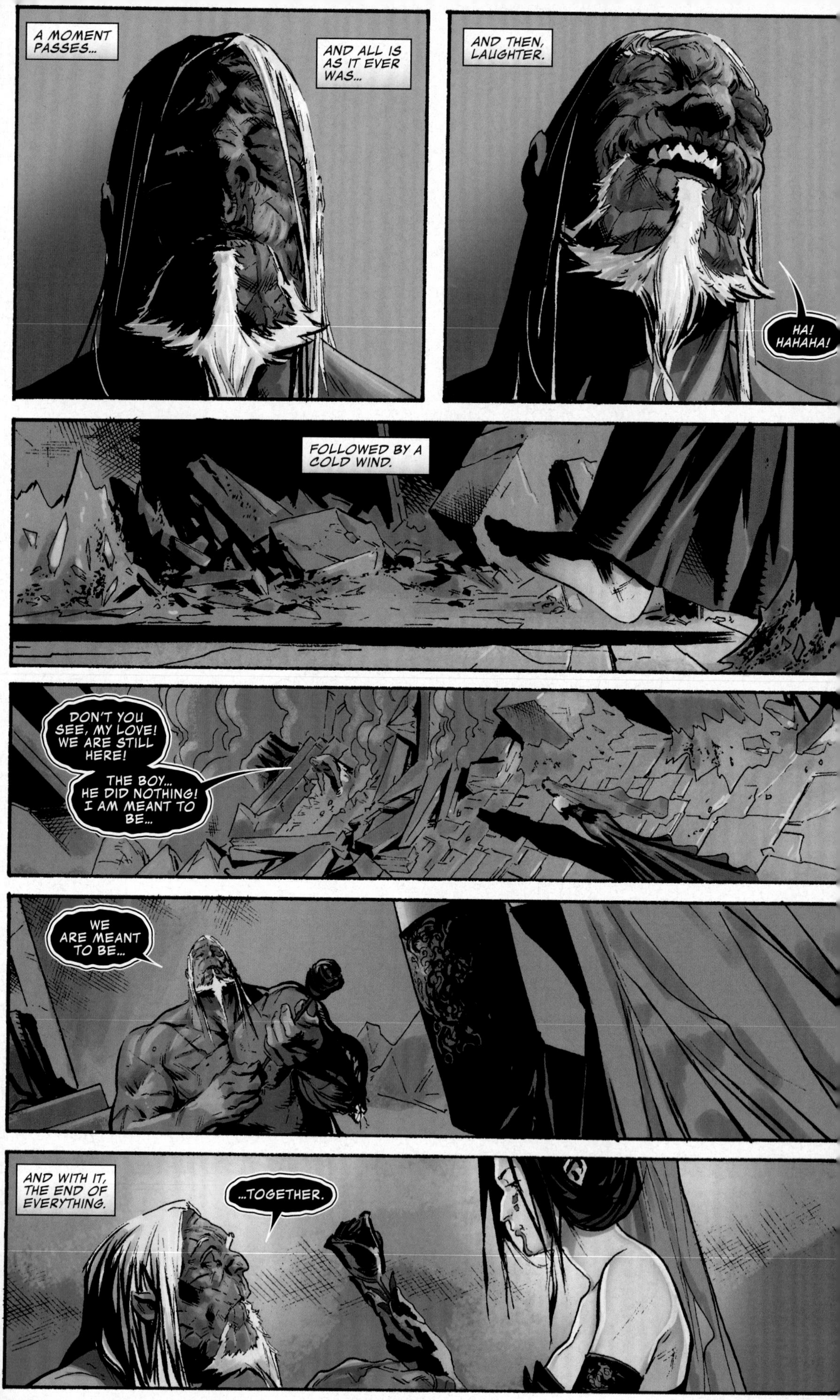

A MOMENT PASSES...
AND ALL IS AS IT EVER WAS...
AND THEN, LAUGHTER.
HA! HAHAHA!
FOLLOWED BY A COLD WIND.
DON'T YOU SEE, MY LOVE! WE ARE STILL HERE!
THE BOY... HE DID NOTHING! I AM MEANT TO BE...
WE ARE MEANT TO BE...
AND WITH IT, THE END OF EVERYTHING.
...TOGETHER.

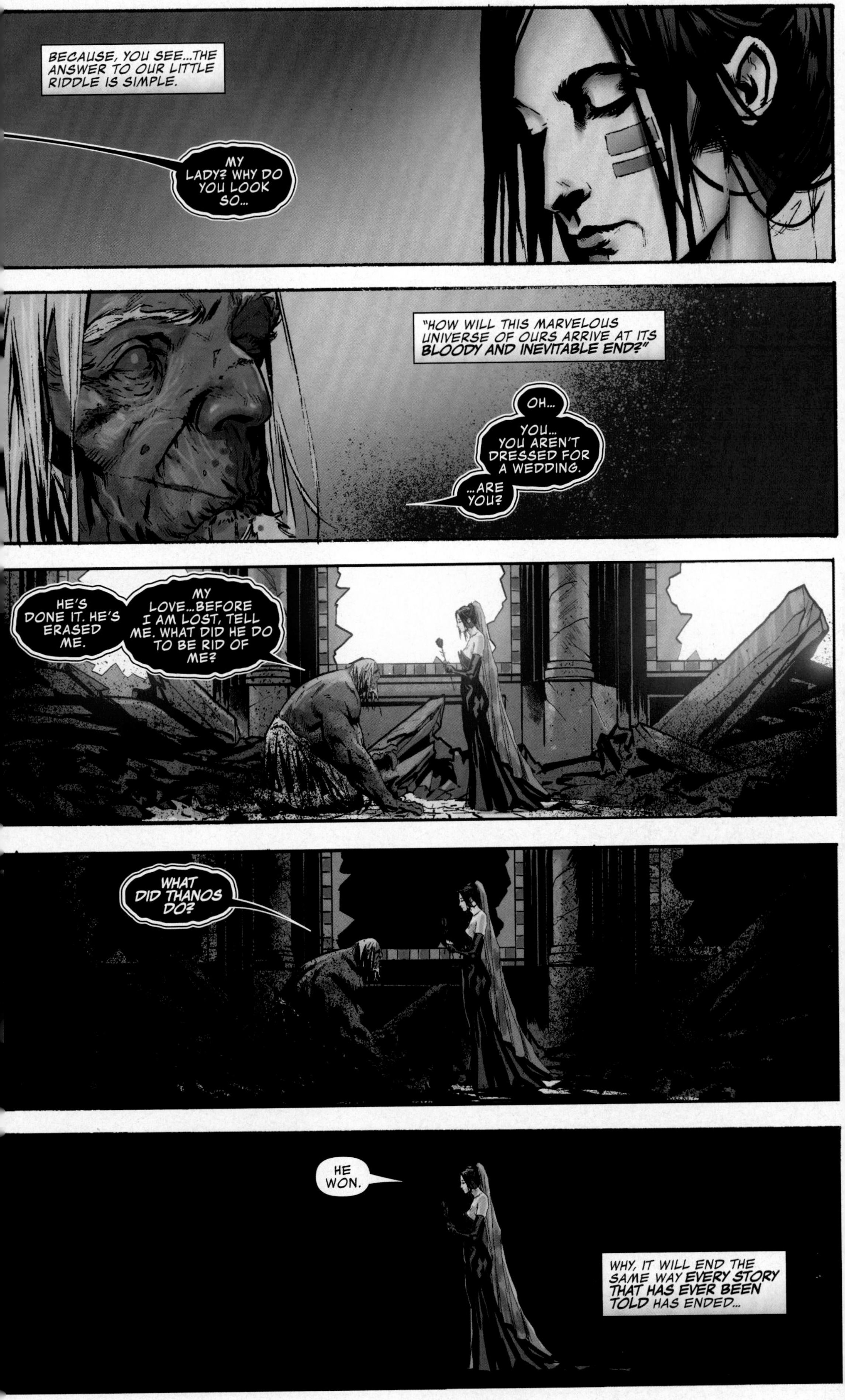
BECAUSE, YOU SEE...THE ANSWER TO OUR LITTLE RIDDLE IS SIMPLE.
MY LADY? WHY DO YOU LOOK SO...
"HOW WILL THIS MARVELOUS UNIVERSE OF OURS ARRIVE AT ITS BLOODY AND INEVITABLE END?"
OH...
YOU... YOU AREN'T DRESSED FOR A WEDDING.
...ARE YOU?
HE'S DONE IT. HE'S ERASED ME.
MY LOVE...BEFORE I AM LOST, TELL ME. WHAT DID HE DO TO BE RID OF ME?
WHAT DID THANOS DO?
HE WON.
WHY, IT WILL END THE SAME WAY EVERY STORY THAT HAS EVER BEEN TOLD HAS ENDED...

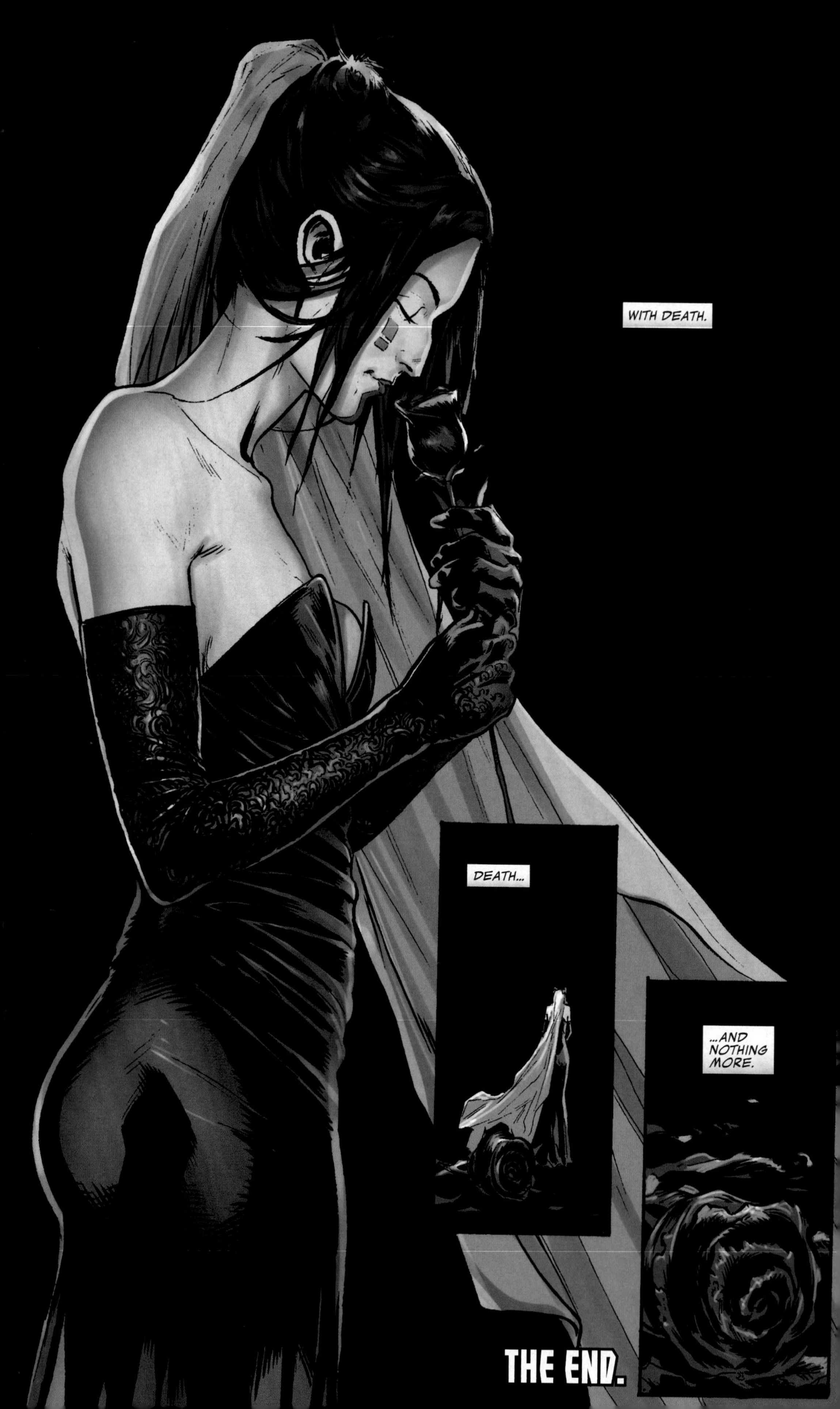
WITH DEATH.
DEATH...
...AND NOTHING MORE.
THE END.

Hey there, True Believers! Donny Cates here.

Let me begin by thanking all of you for going on that insane ride with us. I think I'm supposed to be the one on the team who's like...good with words and stuff, but honestly, I am struck by a lack of ability to properly express how grateful we are to you for taking the chance on us, and for sticking with us month after month.

Now, with that out of the way... What the hell, man?! THANOS is ending? What's that all about?!

Well, if you'll calm down and stop yelling at me, I'll tell you! When Jordan D. White (who, ironically, I used to intern for!) called me and offered me THANOS, I was outof-my-mind excited. I don't know if you can tell or not, but I'm KIND OF a big fan of that guy. I immediately said yes, and then spent about three days in a cosmic-fueled haze, plotting out the story you just read. I then turned in this insane document outlining every inch of THANOS WINS, and then...braced for impact.

See, here's the secret of what you just read: I honestly didn't think they'd let me do it. At all.

When I started writing my outline, I wanted to pitch the most insane, brazen, out-of-this-world story I could come up with. I wanted to blow the doors off of this thing. But not because I thought these ideas would end up on the page, but because I wanted to show Marvel the kind of thing I was attracted to. What I was capable of. I wrote the pitch KNOWING IN MY HEART that they would come back and say, "Hey, this is fun, but the Silver Surfer with Thor's hammer? Hulk as a dog? FRANK CASTLE IS WHAT NOW???" and then I'd have a fun laugh, and then go back and change a bunch of stuff to calm it down.

Now, I say that not because Marvel is some evil empire that hates fun, but because... well, who the hell was I to come in and do all this big stuff?! I thought surely they would tell me that there were other plans for this character, or that this beat was too hardcore and this and that and so on and etc... Again, at the time I was just some shmuck with a cool indie book about big swords in Texas. No way they were gonna let me burn the universe down.

But then Jordan called me and said, "Hey this is all cool. Let's do it." And I was FLOORED. Wait, I thought, ALL of it? I can do ALL OF IT? I went from being incredibly excited to dumbfounded and terrified all within the span of a few minutes. But then something incredible happened. Geoff Shaw, my *God Country* and *Buzzkill* partner in crime and best buddy, joined the project. That was when I knew this thing might actually work.

Add in the incredible colors of Antonio Fabela, the killer lettering from Clayton Cowles and the steady hands of Jordan D. White and Annalise Bissa, and...damn. We had ourselves one fine-looking book. And then you all read it. And you liked it. And now we are here.

At the end of everything.

Why is that happening? Well, let me dispel some rumors. THANOS was NOT canceled. This end is part of a larger plan for the Mad Titan that will spill out as the months unfold.

I mean...you guys, come on. There's Infinity Gems in play right now in the Marvel Universe. And with a certain Mad Titan now on a quest to change the course of history...well...

If I were you, I would PAY ATTENTION TO INFINITY COUNTDOWN...

'Nuff said, amiright?

So yeah, this wasn't some evil plan. This wasn't dictated to us by some unseen evil hand. This was our call. Geoff and I have a new thing coming. Stay tuned. And Thanos... Well, he tends to win, right? I sure as hell wouldn't bet against him.

Also check out THANOS ANNUAL #1, coming soon, for clues as to the goings-on of a certain Cosmic Ghost Rider. After all...his story is just beginning. Even though...he died? Well, if history is any indication, death doesn't seem to slow Frank Castle down one bit.

And I promise, that series is JUST as bananas as this one has been. Maybe even more so!

Okay, folks. That's my time. Again, I can't thank you all enough for hanging out with us and enjoying the series as much as you have. I think I can speak for the whole team when I say it's been surreal and overwhelming and just...so much damn fun.

And hey, that's kind of the point, right?

Until next time.

Excelsior!

-Donny

ANNUAL 1

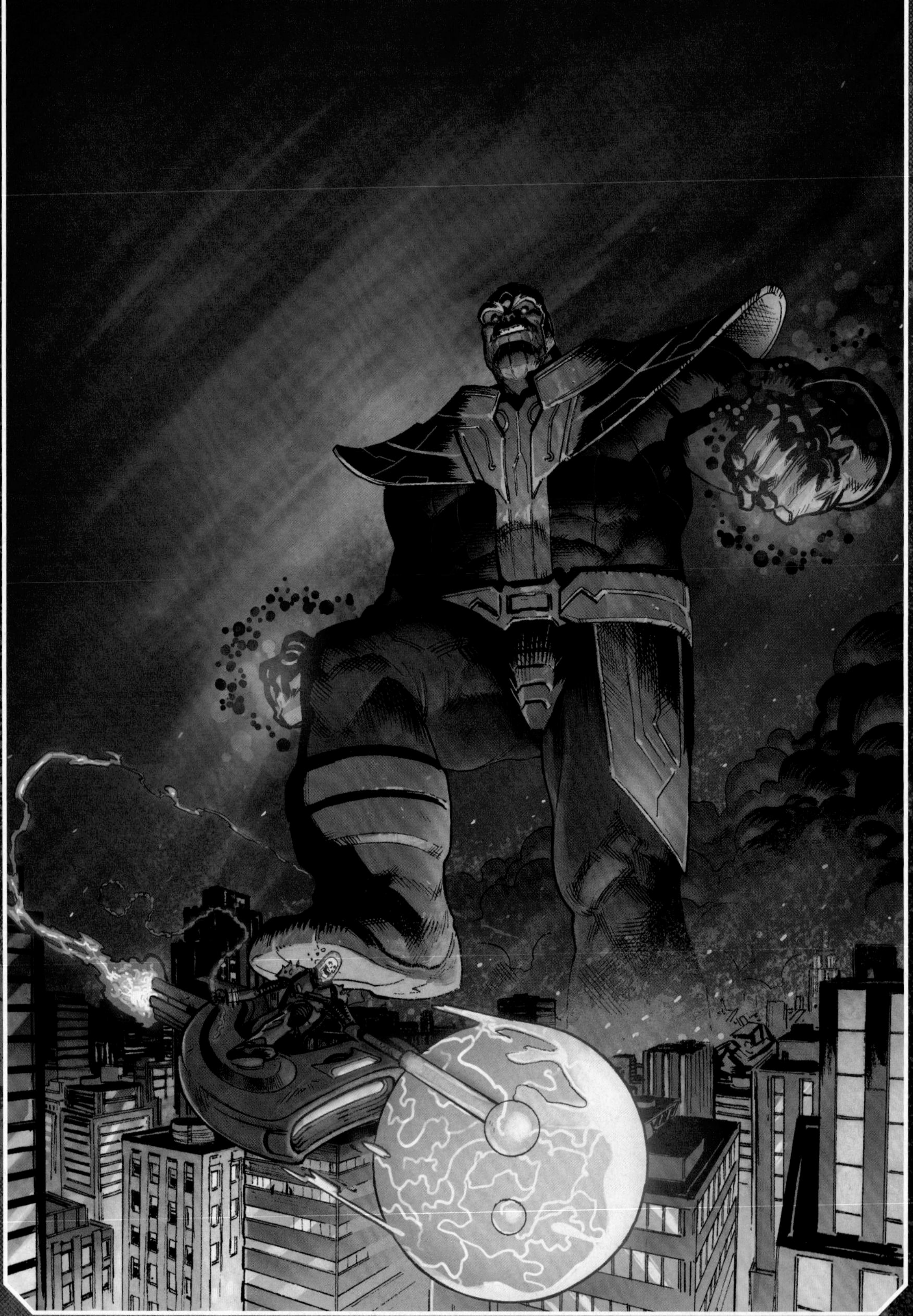

A total obsession with power drives him...to control the forces of the universe.
He is the Mad Titan. He is...

THANOS

A full chronicle of Thanos' evildoing might take days...weeks...years, even, to explore. Therefore, presented here are choice selections from that chronicle of cruelty...an annotated anthology of Thanos' most malevolent moments!

'TITAN'S GREATEST DAD'
DONNY CATES, GEOFF SHAW & ANTONIO FABELA

'WHAT TO GET FROM THE MAN WHO TAKES EVERYTHING'
CHRIS HASTINGS, FLAVIANO & FEDERICO BLEE

'EXHIBITION'
KIERON GILLEN, ANDRE ARAUJO & CHRIS O'HALLORAN

'MY LITTLE THANOS'
KATIE COOK & HEATHER BRECKLE

'THAT TIME THANOS HELPED AN OLD LADY CROSS THE STREET!'
RYAN NORTH, WILL ROBSON & RACHELLE ROSENBERG

'THE COMFORT OF THE GOOD'
AL EWING & FRAZER IRVING

VC's CLAYTON COWLES
letterer

GEOFF SHAW & ANTONIO FABELA
cover artists

MIKE DEODATO & EDGAR DELGADO
variant cover artists

ANNALISE BISSA
assistant editor

JORDAN D. WHITE
editor

C.B. CEBULSKI
editor in chief

JOE QUESADA
chief creative officer

DAN BUCKLEY
president

ALAN FINE
exec. producer

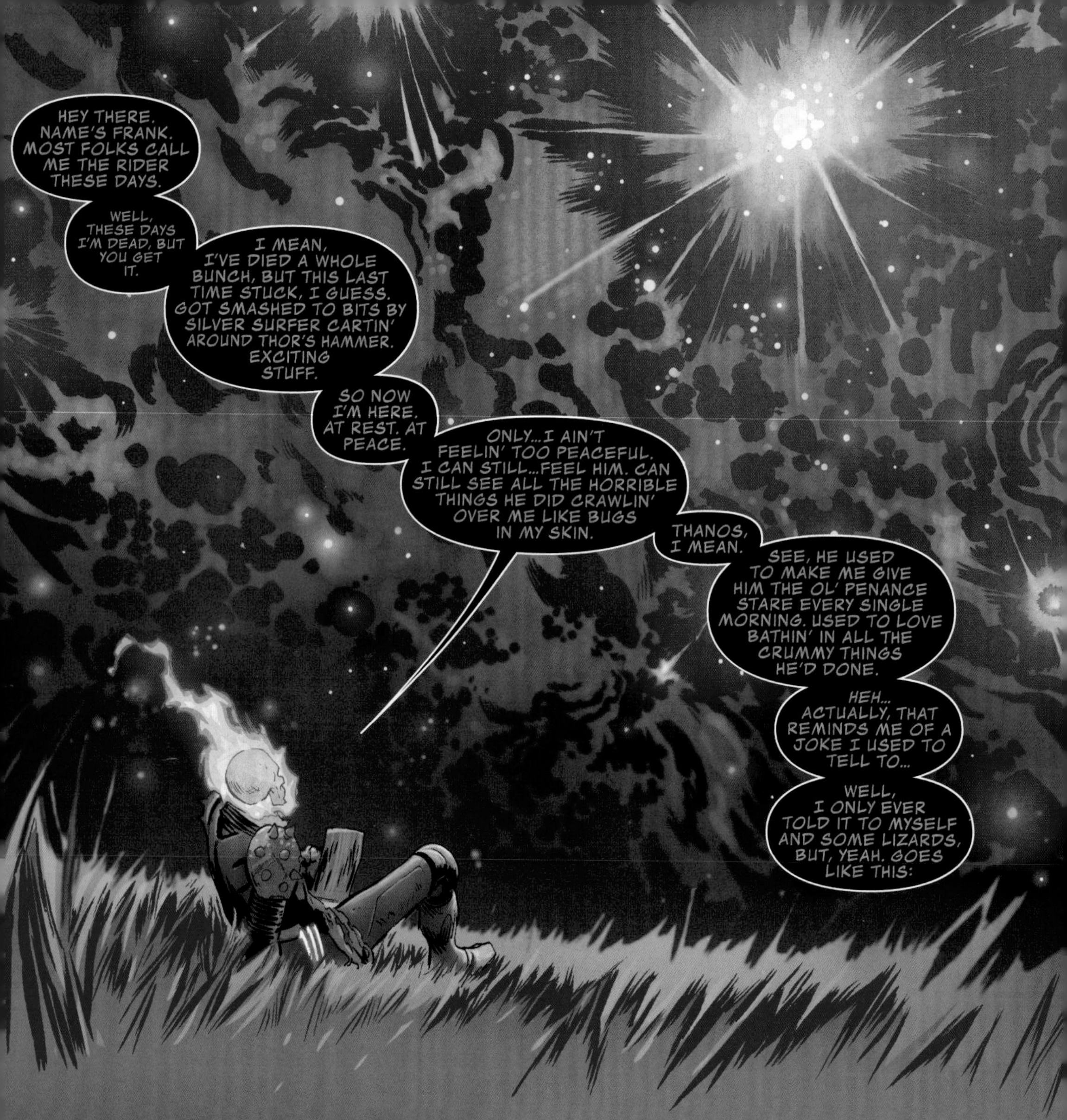
HEY THERE. NAME'S FRANK. MOST FOLKS CALL ME THE RIDER THESE DAYS.
WELL, THESE DAYS I'M DEAD, BUT YOU GET IT.
I MEAN, I'VE DIED A WHOLE BUNCH, BUT THIS LAST TIME STUCK, I GUESS. GOT SMASHED TO BITS BY SILVER SURFER CARTIN' AROUND THOR'S HAMMER. EXCITING STUFF.
SO NOW I'M HERE. AT REST. AT PEACE.
ONLY...I AIN'T FEELIN' TOO PEACEFUL. I CAN STILL...FEEL HIM. CAN STILL SEE ALL THE HORRIBLE THINGS HE DID CRAWLIN' OVER ME LIKE BUGS IN MY SKIN.
THANOS, I MEAN.
SEE, HE USED TO MAKE ME GIVE HIM THE OL' PENANCE STARE EVERY SINGLE MORNING. USED TO LOVE BATHIN' IN ALL THE CRUMMY THINGS HE'D DONE.
HEH... ACTUALLY, THAT REMINDS ME OF A JOKE I USED TO TELL TO...
WELL, I ONLY EVER TOLD IT TO MYSELF AND SOME LIZARDS, BUT, YEAH. GOES LIKE THIS:

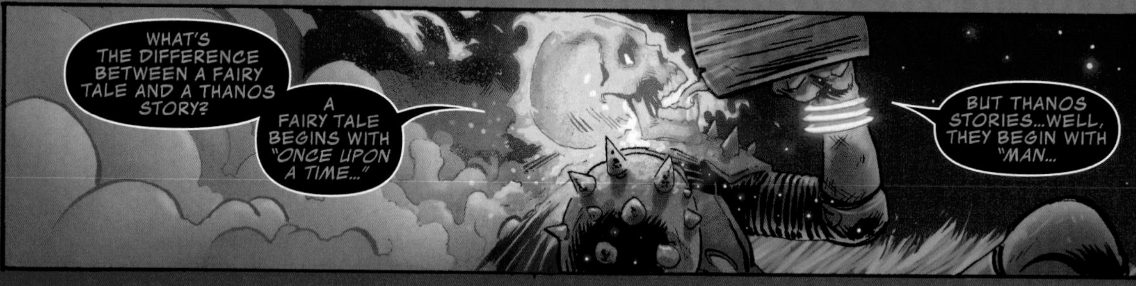
WHAT'S THE DIFFERENCE BETWEEN A FAIRY TALE AND A THANOS STORY?
A FAIRY TALE BEGINS WITH *"ONCE UPON A TIME..."*
BUT THANOS STORIES...WELL, THEY BEGIN WITH *"MAN...*

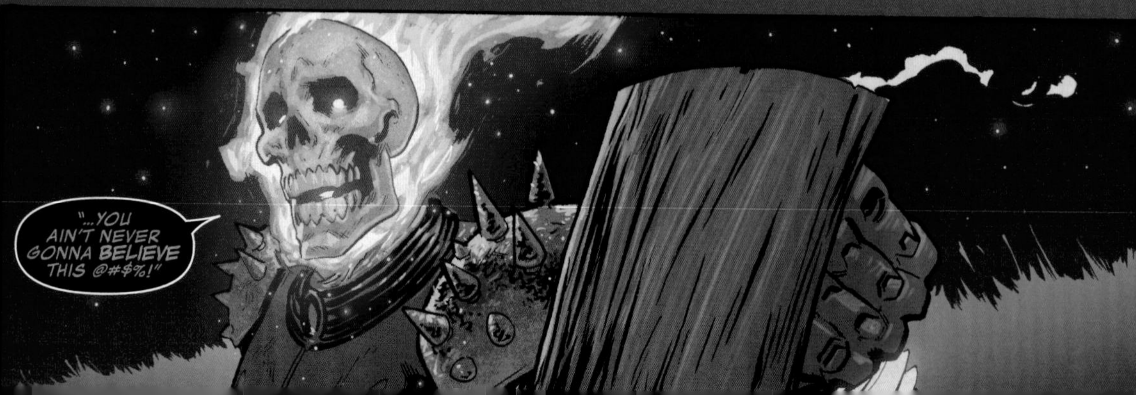
"...YOU AIN'T NEVER GONNA **BELIEVE** *THIS @#$%!"*

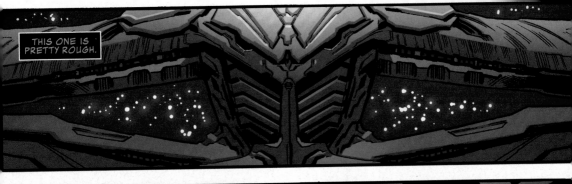

THIS ONE IS PRETTY ROUGH.

IT TAKES PLACE A LONG, LONG TIME AGO...

SEE, THANOS USED TO HOLD THESE LITTLE MAKESHIFT FIGHTING TOURNAMENTS ON HIS SHIP, THE SANCTUARY II.

AND NO, I DON'T KNOW WHAT HAPPENED TO SANCTUARY I. GO ASK HIM.

THEY WERE MORE OR LESS BLOOD SPORT DISGUISED AS TRAINING EXERCISES...

...A MURDER PIT FOR A CLASSROOM...

...FOR HIS DAUGHTER. GAMORA.

MAY I BE DONE YET, "FATHER"?

NO.

ANOTHER.

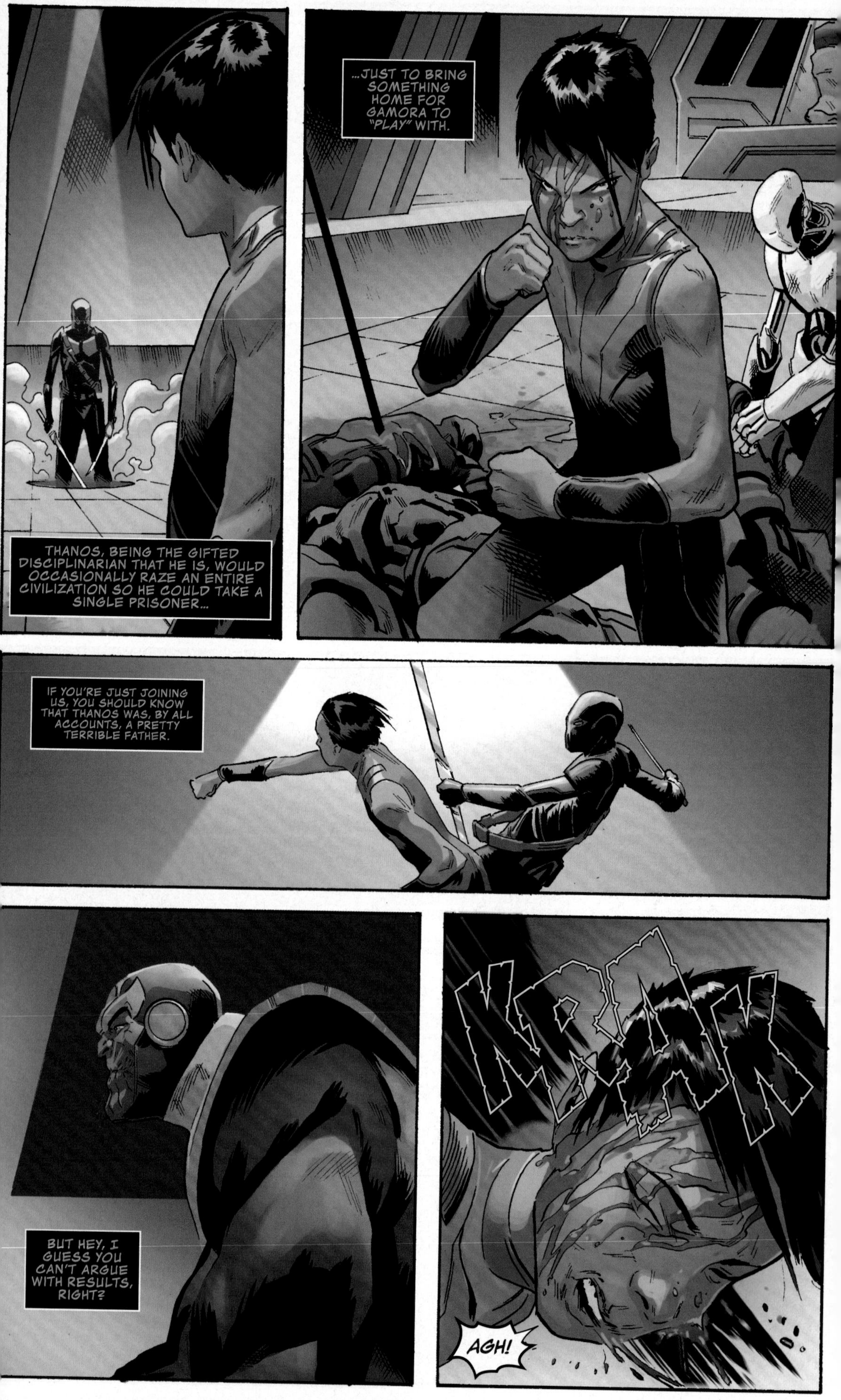
THANOS, BEING THE GIFTED DISCIPLINARIAN THAT HE IS, WOULD OCCASIONALLY RAZE AN ENTIRE CIVILIZATION SO HE COULD TAKE A SINGLE PRISONER...
...JUST TO BRING SOMETHING HOME FOR GAMORA TO "PLAY" WITH.
IF YOU'RE JUST JOINING US, YOU SHOULD KNOW THAT THANOS WAS, BY ALL ACCOUNTS, A PRETTY TERRIBLE FATHER.
BUT HEY, I GUESS YOU CAN'T ARGUE WITH RESULTS, RIGHT?
KRAAK
AGH!

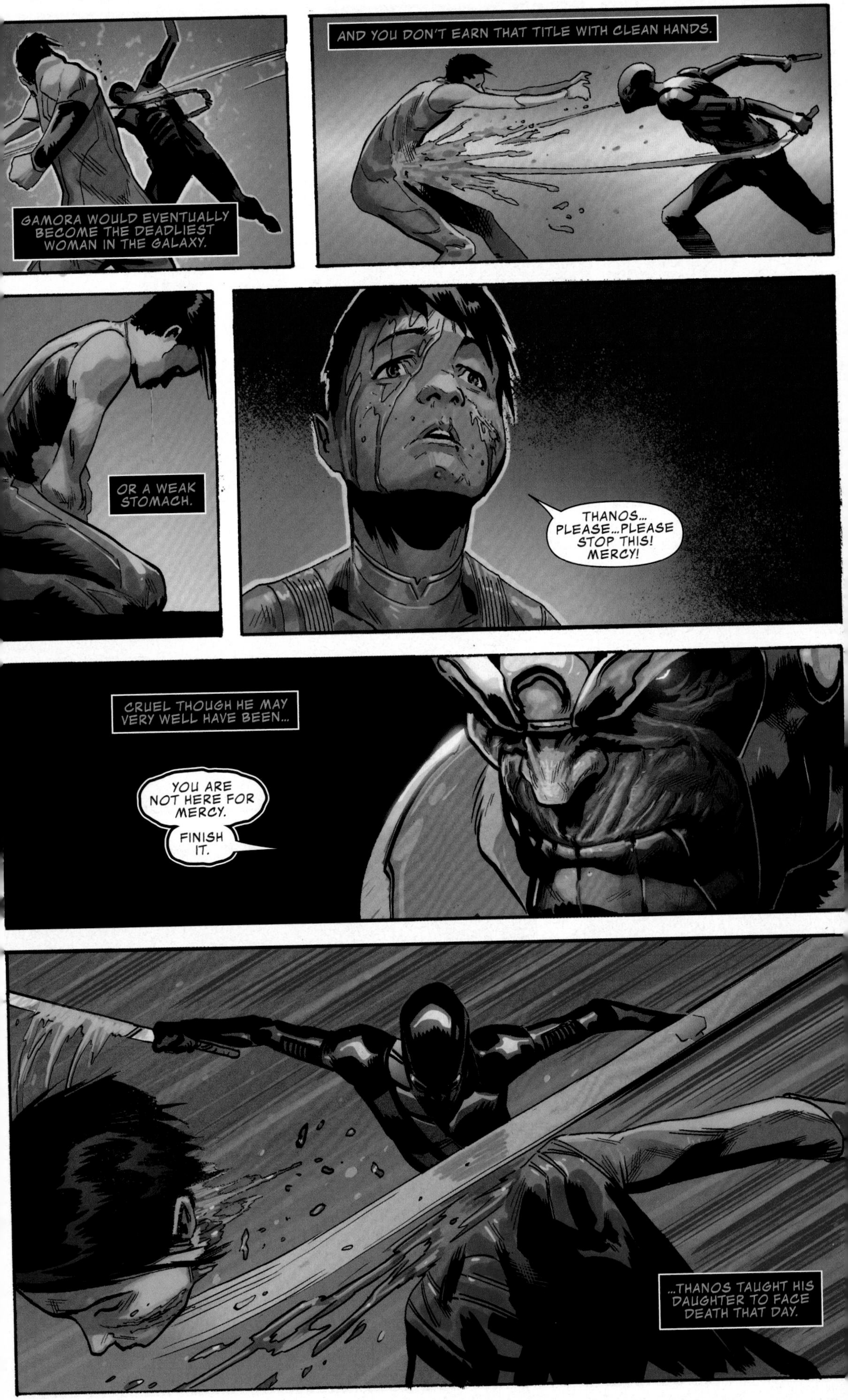
GAMORA WOULD EVENTUALLY BECOME THE DEADLIEST WOMAN IN THE GALAXY.
AND YOU DON'T EARN THAT TITLE WITH CLEAN HANDS.
OR A WEAK STOMACH.
THANOS... PLEASE...PLEASE STOP THIS! MERCY!
CRUEL THOUGH HE MAY VERY WELL HAVE BEEN...
YOU ARE NOT HERE FOR MERCY.
FINISH IT.
...THANOS TAUGHT HIS DAUGHTER TO FACE DEATH THAT DAY.

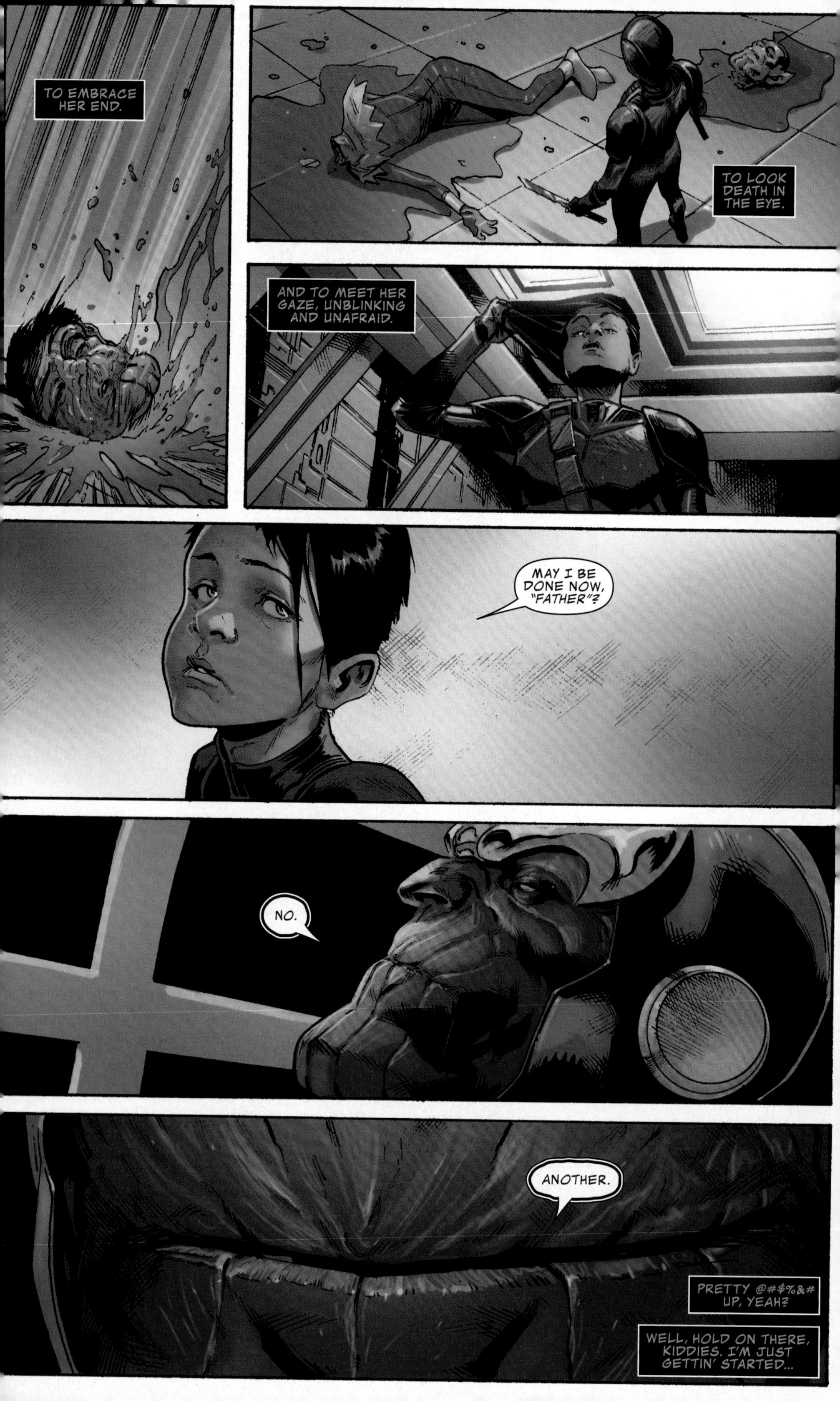
TO EMBRACE HER END.
TO LOOK DEATH IN THE EYE.
AND TO MEET HER GAZE, UNBLINKING AND UNAFRAID.
MAY I BE DONE NOW, "FATHER"?
NO.
ANOTHER.
PRETTY @#$%&# UP, YEAH?
WELL, HOLD ON THERE, KIDDIES. I'M JUST GETTIN' STARTED...

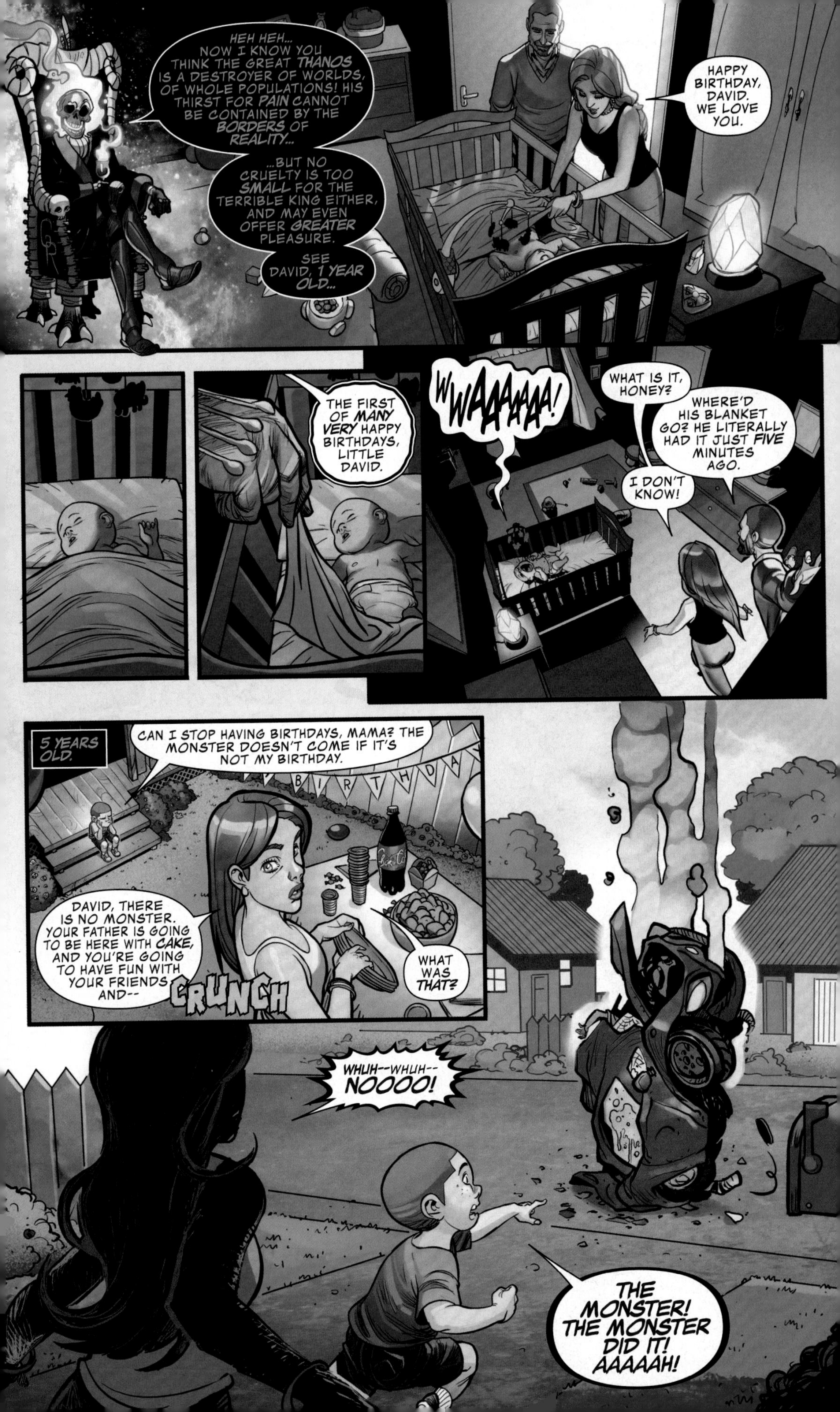
HEH HEH... NOW I KNOW YOU THINK THE GREAT THANOS IS A DESTROYER OF WORLDS, OF WHOLE POPULATIONS! HIS THIRST FOR PAIN CANNOT BE CONTAINED BY THE BORDERS OF REALITY...
...BUT NO CRUELTY IS TOO SMALL FOR THE TERRIBLE KING EITHER, AND MAY EVEN OFFER GREATER PLEASURE.
SEE DAVID, 1 YEAR OLD...
HAPPY BIRTHDAY, DAVID. WE LOVE YOU.
THE FIRST OF MANY VERY HAPPY BIRTHDAYS, LITTLE DAVID.
WWAAAAAAA!
WHAT IS IT, HONEY?
WHERE'D HIS BLANKET GO? HE LITERALLY HAD IT JUST FIVE MINUTES AGO.
I DON'T KNOW!
5 YEARS OLD.
CAN I STOP HAVING BIRTHDAYS, MAMA? THE MONSTER DOESN'T COME IF IT'S NOT MY BIRTHDAY.
DAVID, THERE IS NO MONSTER. YOUR FATHER IS GOING TO BE HERE WITH CAKE, AND YOU'RE GOING TO HAVE FUN WITH YOUR FRIENDS AND--
CRUNCH
WHAT WAS THAT?
WHUH--WHUH--NOOOO!
THE MONSTER! THE MONSTER DID IT! AAAAAH!

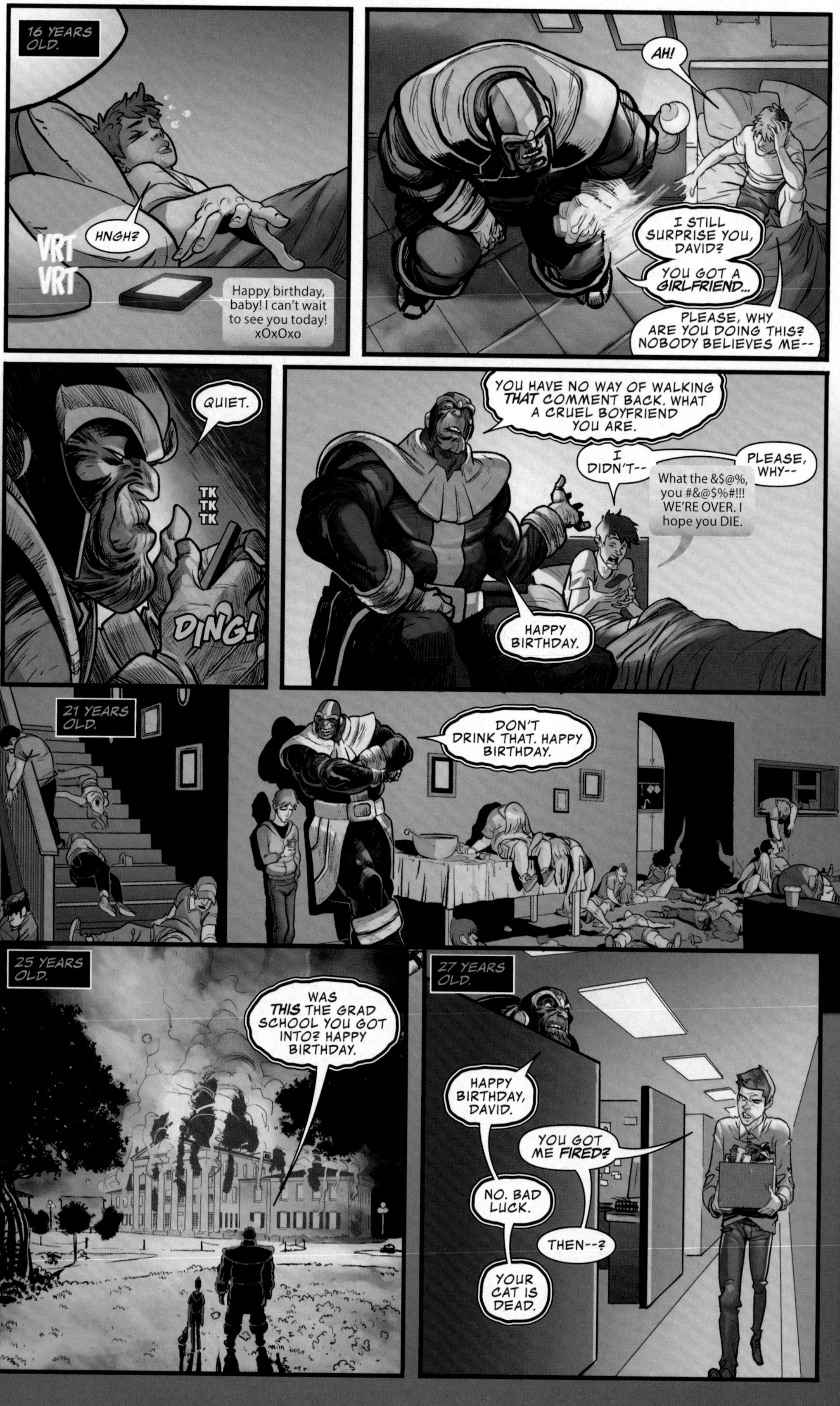
16 YEARS OLD.
HNGH?
VRT VRT
Happy birthday, baby! I can't wait to see you today! xOxOxo
AH!
I STILL SURPRISE YOU, DAVID?
YOU GOT A GIRLFRIEND...
PLEASE, WHY ARE YOU DOING THIS? NOBODY BELIEVES ME--
QUIET.
TK TK TK
DING!
YOU HAVE NO WAY OF WALKING THAT COMMENT BACK. WHAT A CRUEL BOYFRIEND YOU ARE.
I DIDN'T--
PLEASE, WHY--
What the &$@%, you #&@$%#!!! WE'RE OVER. I hope you DIE.
HAPPY BIRTHDAY.
21 YEARS OLD.
DON'T DRINK THAT. HAPPY BIRTHDAY.
25 YEARS OLD.
WAS THIS THE GRAD SCHOOL YOU GOT INTO? HAPPY BIRTHDAY.
27 YEARS OLD.
HAPPY BIRTHDAY, DAVID.
YOU GOT ME FIRED?
NO. BAD LUCK.
THEN--?
YOUR CAT IS DEAD.

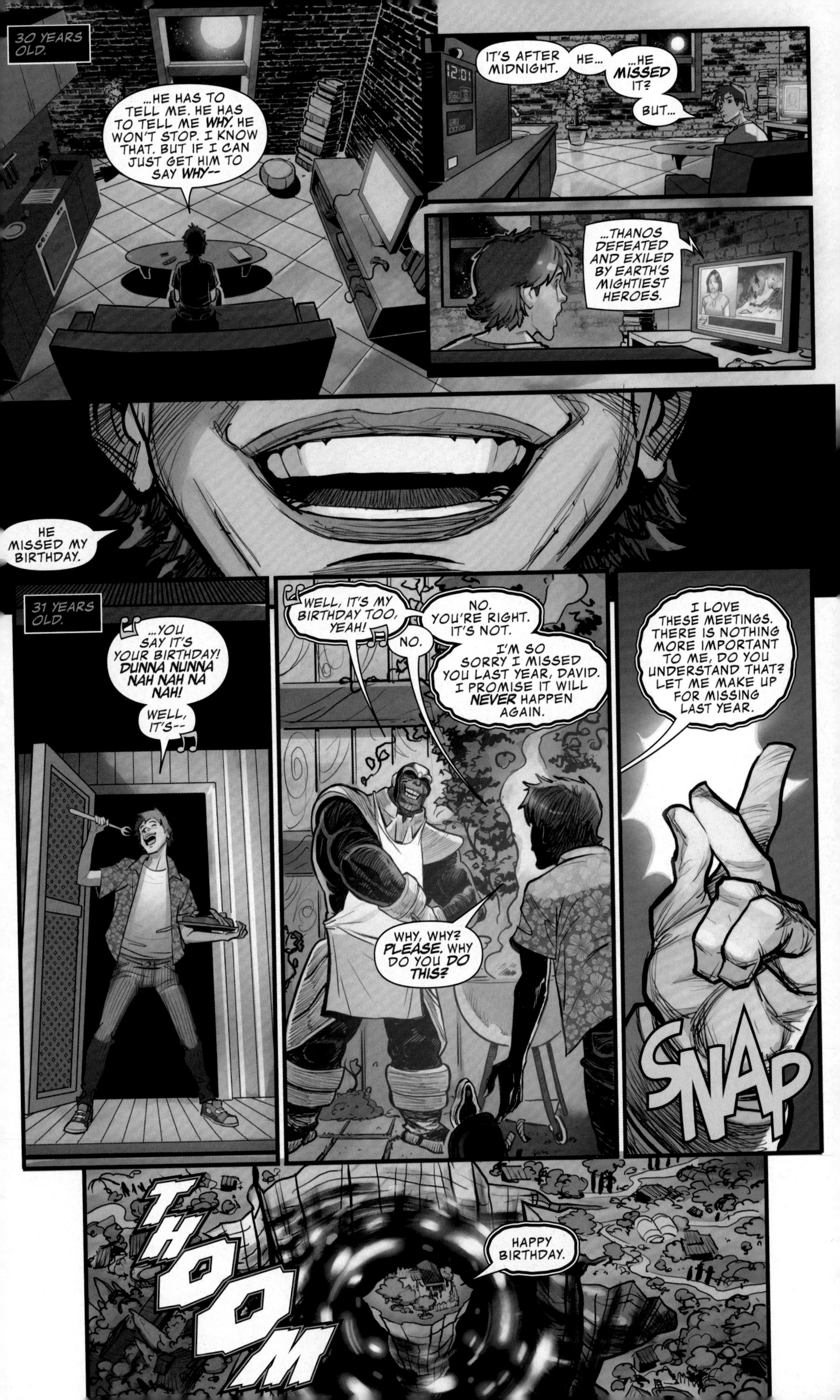

30 YEARS OLD.
...HE HAS TO TELL ME. HE HAS TO TELL ME WHY. HE WON'T STOP. I KNOW THAT. BUT IF I CAN JUST GET HIM TO SAY WHY--
IT'S AFTER MIDNIGHT.
HE...
...HE MISSED IT?
BUT...
...THANOS DEFEATED AND EXILED BY EARTH'S MIGHTIEST HEROES.
HE MISSED MY BIRTHDAY.
31 YEARS OLD.
...YOU SAY IT'S YOUR BIRTHDAY! DUNNA NUNNA NAH NAH NA NAH!
WELL, IT'S--
WELL, IT'S MY BIRTHDAY TOO, YEAH!
NO.
NO. YOU'RE RIGHT. IT'S NOT.
I'M SO SORRY I MISSED YOU LAST YEAR, DAVID. I PROMISE IT WILL NEVER HAPPEN AGAIN.
WHY, WHY? PLEASE. WHY DO YOU DO THIS?
I LOVE THESE MEETINGS. THERE IS NOTHING MORE IMPORTANT TO ME, DO YOU UNDERSTAND THAT? LET ME MAKE UP FOR MISSING LAST YEAR.
SNAP
THOOM
HAPPY BIRTHDAY.

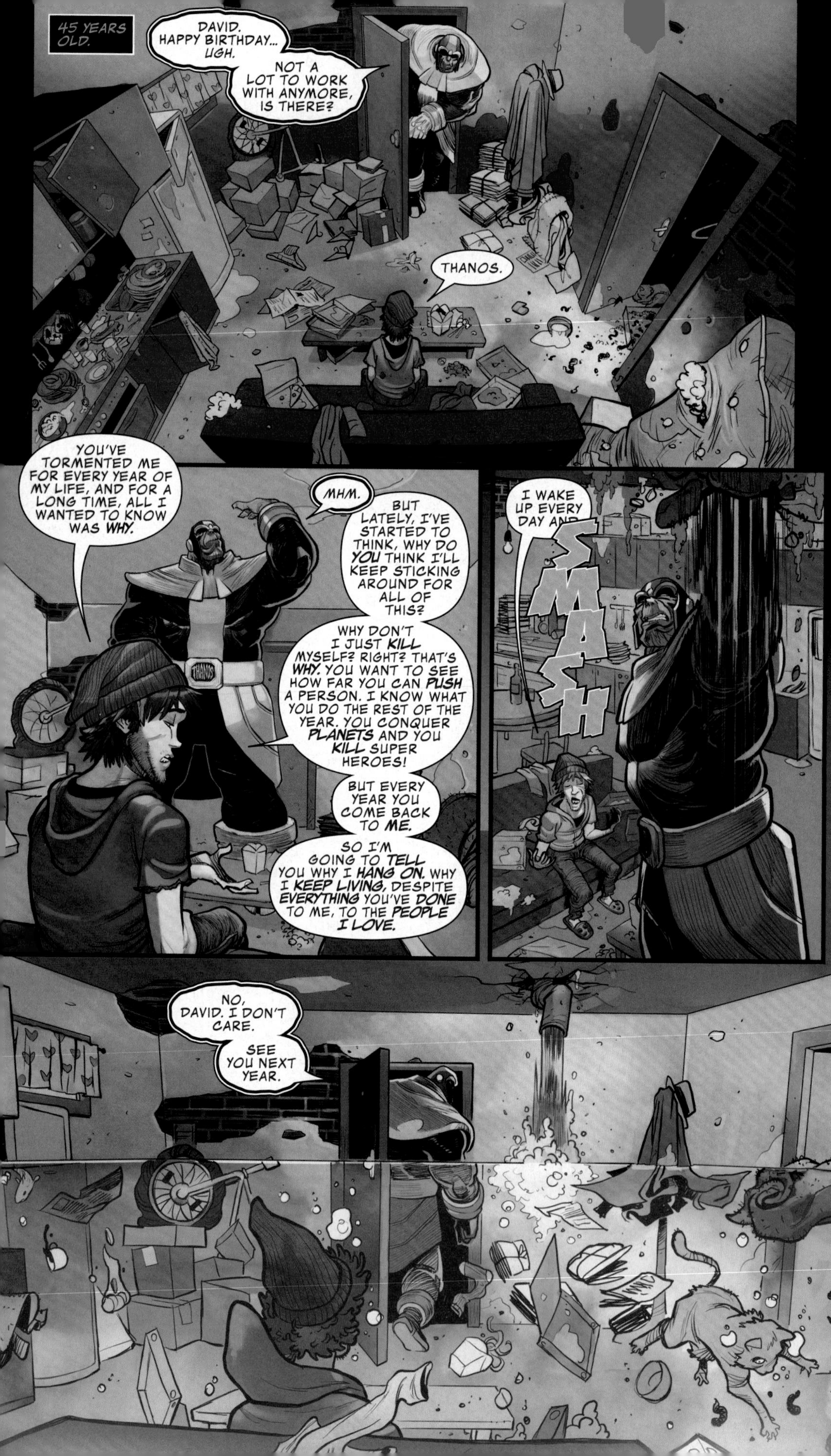
45 YEARS OLD.
DAVID. HAPPY BIRTHDAY... UGH.
NOT A LOT TO WORK WITH ANYMORE, IS THERE?
THANOS.
YOU'VE TORMENTED ME FOR EVERY YEAR OF MY LIFE, AND FOR A LONG TIME, ALL I WANTED TO KNOW WAS WHY.
MHM.
BUT LATELY, I'VE STARTED TO THINK, WHY DO YOU THINK I'LL KEEP STICKING AROUND FOR ALL OF THIS?
WHY DON'T I JUST KILL MYSELF? RIGHT? THAT'S WHY. YOU WANT TO SEE HOW FAR YOU CAN PUSH A PERSON. I KNOW WHAT YOU DO THE REST OF THE YEAR. YOU CONQUER PLANETS AND YOU KILL SUPER HEROES!
BUT EVERY YEAR YOU COME BACK TO ME.
SO I'M GOING TO TELL YOU WHY I HANG ON. WHY I KEEP LIVING, DESPITE EVERYTHING YOU'VE DONE TO ME, TO THE PEOPLE I LOVE.
I WAKE UP EVERY DAY AND
SMASH
NO, DAVID. I DON'T CARE.
SEE YOU NEXT YEAR.

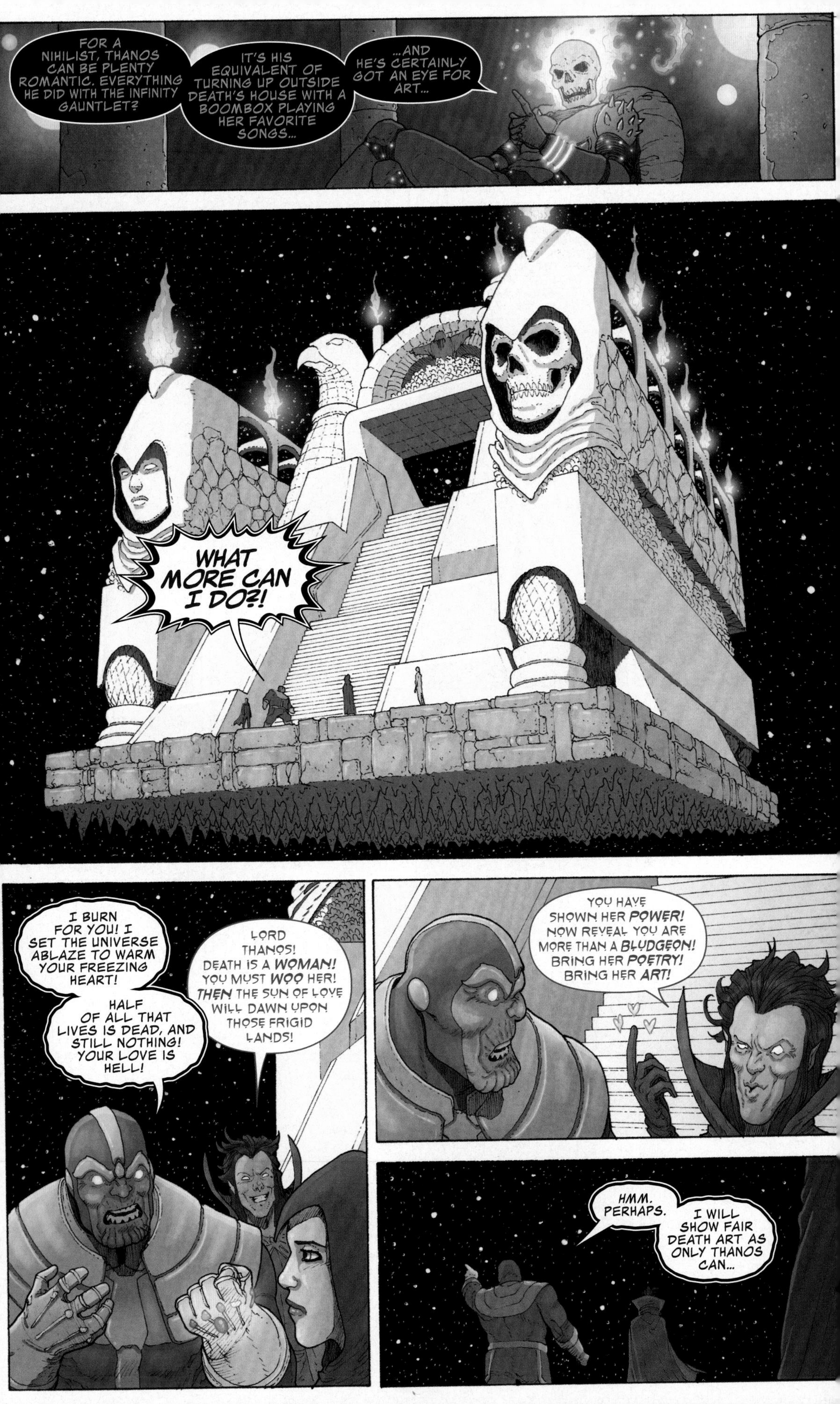
FOR A NIHILIST, THANOS CAN BE PLENTY ROMANTIC. EVERYTHING HE DID WITH THE INFINITY GAUNTLET?
IT'S HIS EQUIVALENT OF TURNING UP OUTSIDE DEATH'S HOUSE WITH A BOOMBOX PLAYING HER FAVORITE SONGS...
...AND HE'S CERTAINLY GOT AN EYE FOR ART...
WHAT MORE CAN I DO?!
I BURN FOR YOU! I SET THE UNIVERSE ABLAZE TO WARM YOUR FREEZING HEART!
HALF OF ALL THAT LIVES IS DEAD, AND STILL NOTHING! YOUR LOVE IS HELL!
LORD THANOS! DEATH IS A WOMAN! YOU MUST WOO HER! THEN THE SUN OF LOVE WILL DAWN UPON THOSE FRIGID LANDS!
YOU HAVE SHOWN HER POWER! NOW REVEAL YOU ARE MORE THAN A BLUDGEON! BRING HER POETRY! BRING HER ART!
HMM. PERHAPS.
I WILL SHOW FAIR DEATH ART AS ONLY THANOS CAN...

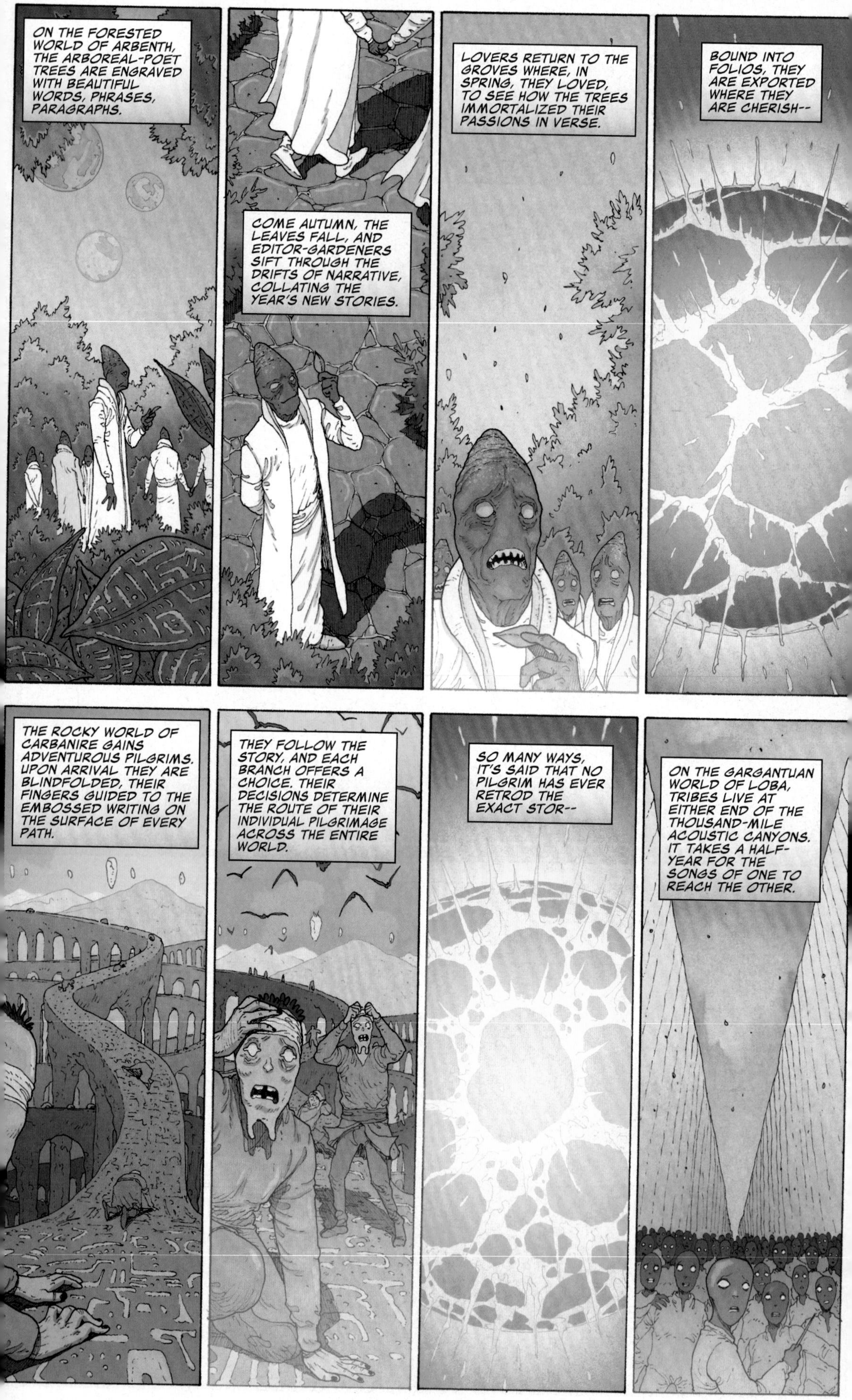
ON THE FORESTED WORLD OF ARBENTH, THE ARBOREAL-POET TREES ARE ENGRAVED WITH BEAUTIFUL WORDS, PHRASES, PARAGRAPHS.
COME AUTUMN, THE LEAVES FALL, AND EDITOR-GARDENERS SIFT THROUGH THE DRIFTS OF NARRATIVE, COLLATING THE YEAR'S NEW STORIES.
LOVERS RETURN TO THE GROVES WHERE, IN SPRING, THEY LOVED, TO SEE HOW THE TREES IMMORTALIZED THEIR PASSIONS IN VERSE.
BOUND INTO FOLIOS, THEY ARE EXPORTED WHERE THEY ARE CHERISH--
THE ROCKY WORLD OF CARBANIRE GAINS ADVENTUROUS PILGRIMS. UPON ARRIVAL THEY ARE BLINDFOLDED, THEIR FINGERS GUIDED TO THE EMBOSSED WRITING ON THE SURFACE OF EVERY PATH.
THEY FOLLOW THE STORY, AND EACH BRANCH OFFERS A CHOICE. THEIR DECISIONS DETERMINE THE ROUTE OF THEIR INDIVIDUAL PILGRIMAGE ACROSS THE ENTIRE WORLD.
SO MANY WAYS, IT'S SAID THAT NO PILGRIM HAS EVER RETROD THE EXACT STOR--
ON THE GARGANTUAN WORLD OF LOBA, TRIBES LIVE AT EITHER END OF THE THOUSAND-MILE ACOUSTIC CANYONS. IT TAKES A HALF-YEAR FOR THE SONGS OF ONE TO REACH THE OTHER.

CHOIRS THE SIZE OF CITIES SERENADE ONE ANOTHER ACROSS SEASONS. PEACE AND JOY IS--

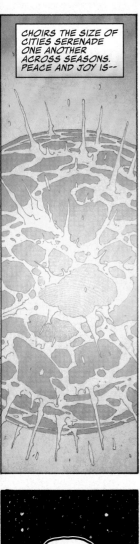

ACROSS MILLIONS OF YEARS, INIX WAS HAND-CARVED TO BE A SCULPTURE PLEASING TO ALL EYES, BEST VIEWED FROM ORBIT, WHERE--

SHEEKA GLIFF, THE SILVERED LAND, A CLOCKWORK PARADISE WHERE FILIGREE BIRDS SIP FROM PLATINUM BLOOMS AND--

ARCO PRIME, THE THEATER BIOME, WHERE EVERY CELL IS A STAGE, AND NANO-ACTORS PERFORM BENEATH EXPECTANT MICROSCOPES. THE--

SEE, MY LOVE?

ALL THAT ART.

IT FUELS MY GREATER WORK.

IT SHOWS WHAT ALL THIS ART TRULY IS...

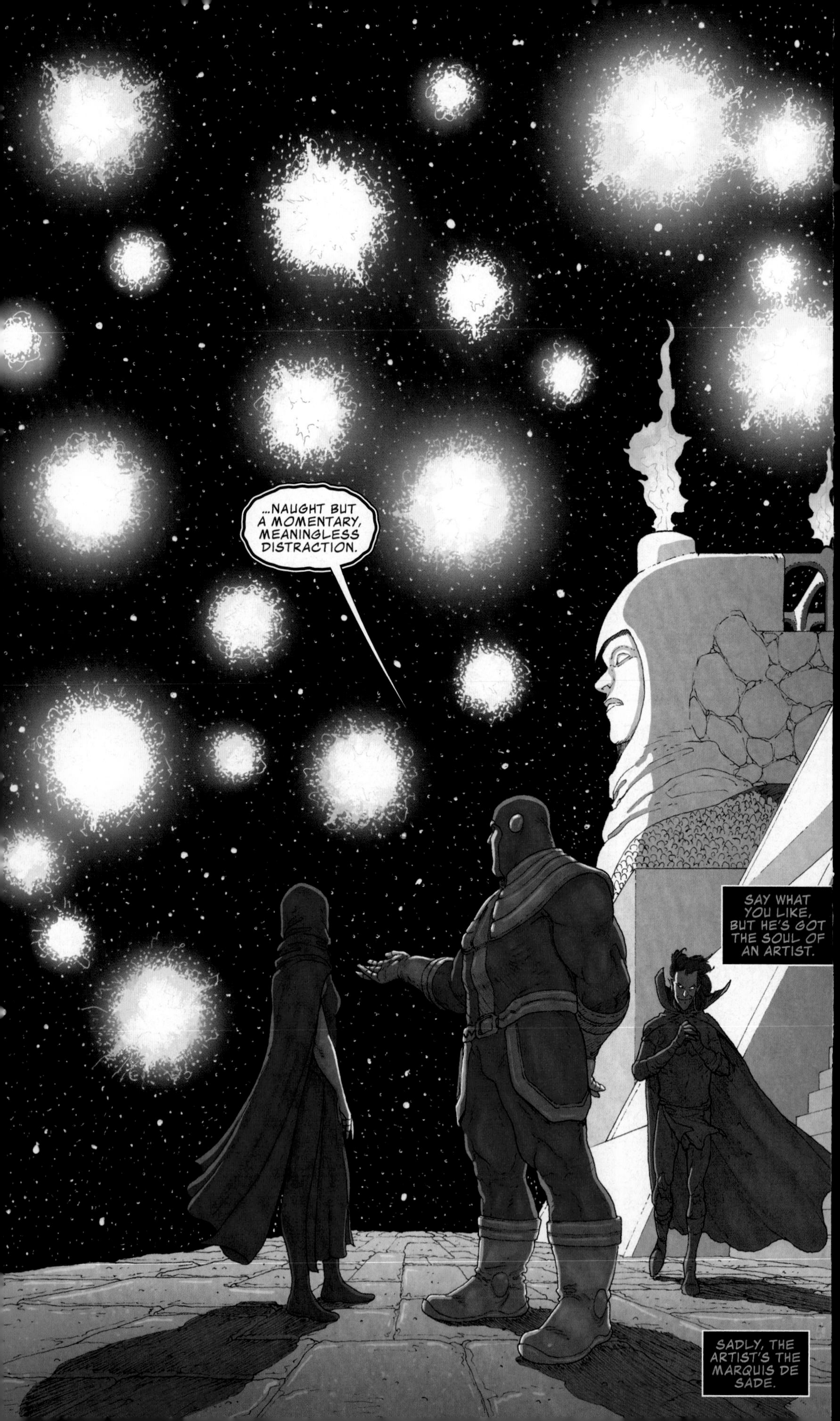
...NAUGHT BUT A MOMENTARY, MEANINGLESS DISTRACTION.
SAY WHAT YOU LIKE, BUT HE'S GOT THE SOUL OF AN ARTIST.
SADLY, THE ARTIST'S THE MARQUIS DE SADE.

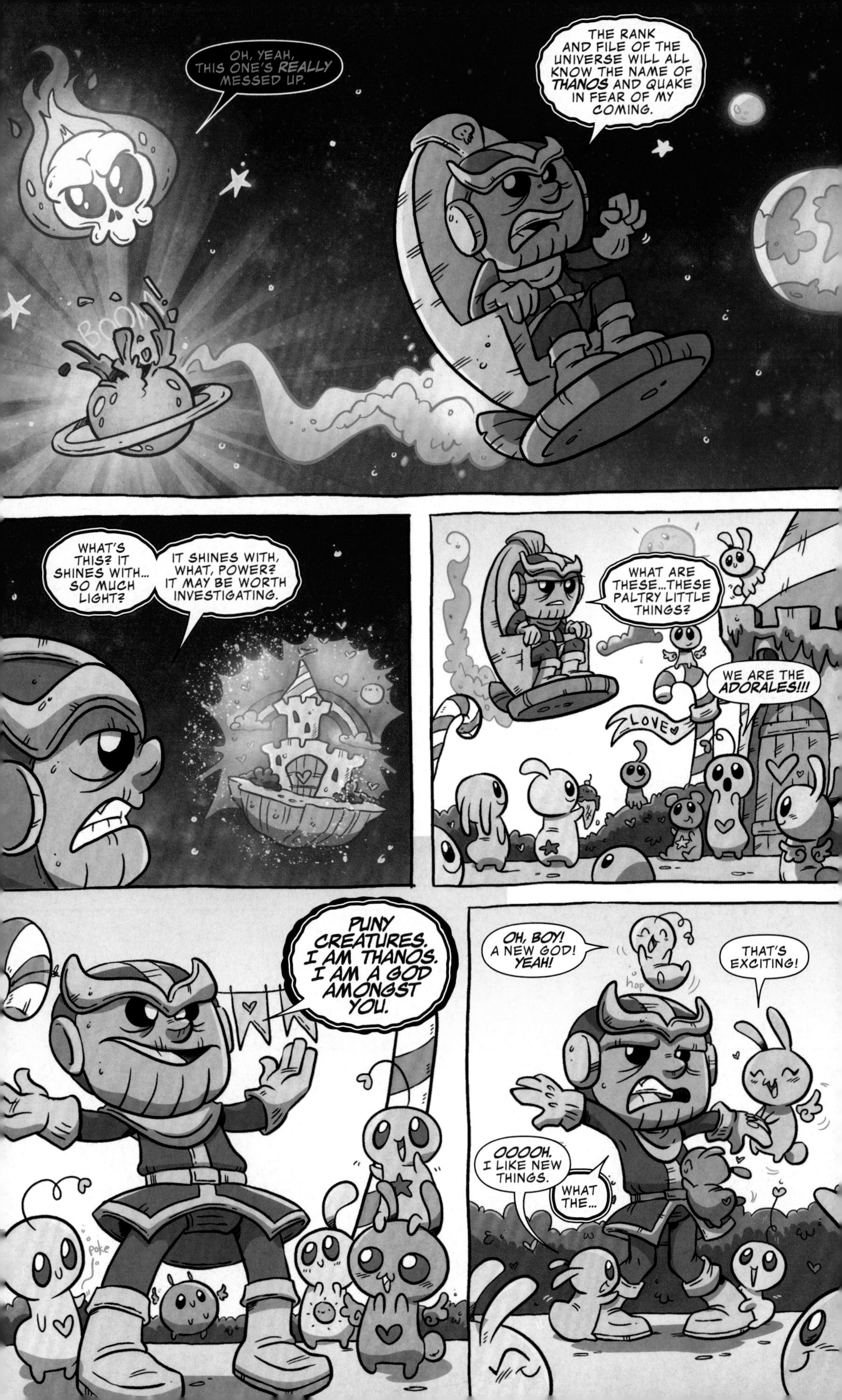
OH, YEAH, THIS ONE'S REALLY MESSED UP.
THE RANK AND FILE OF THE UNIVERSE WILL ALL KNOW THE NAME OF THANOS AND QUAKE IN FEAR OF MY COMING.
BOOM!
WHAT'S THIS? IT SHINES WITH... SO MUCH LIGHT?
IT SHINES WITH, WHAT, POWER? IT MAY BE WORTH INVESTIGATING.
WHAT ARE THESE...THESE PALTRY LITTLE THINGS?
WE ARE THE ADORALES!!!
LOVE
PUNY CREATURES. I AM THANOS. I AM A GOD AMONGST YOU.
poke
OH, BOY! A NEW GOD! YEAH!
hop
THAT'S EXCITING!
OOOOH. I LIKE NEW THINGS.
WHAT THE...

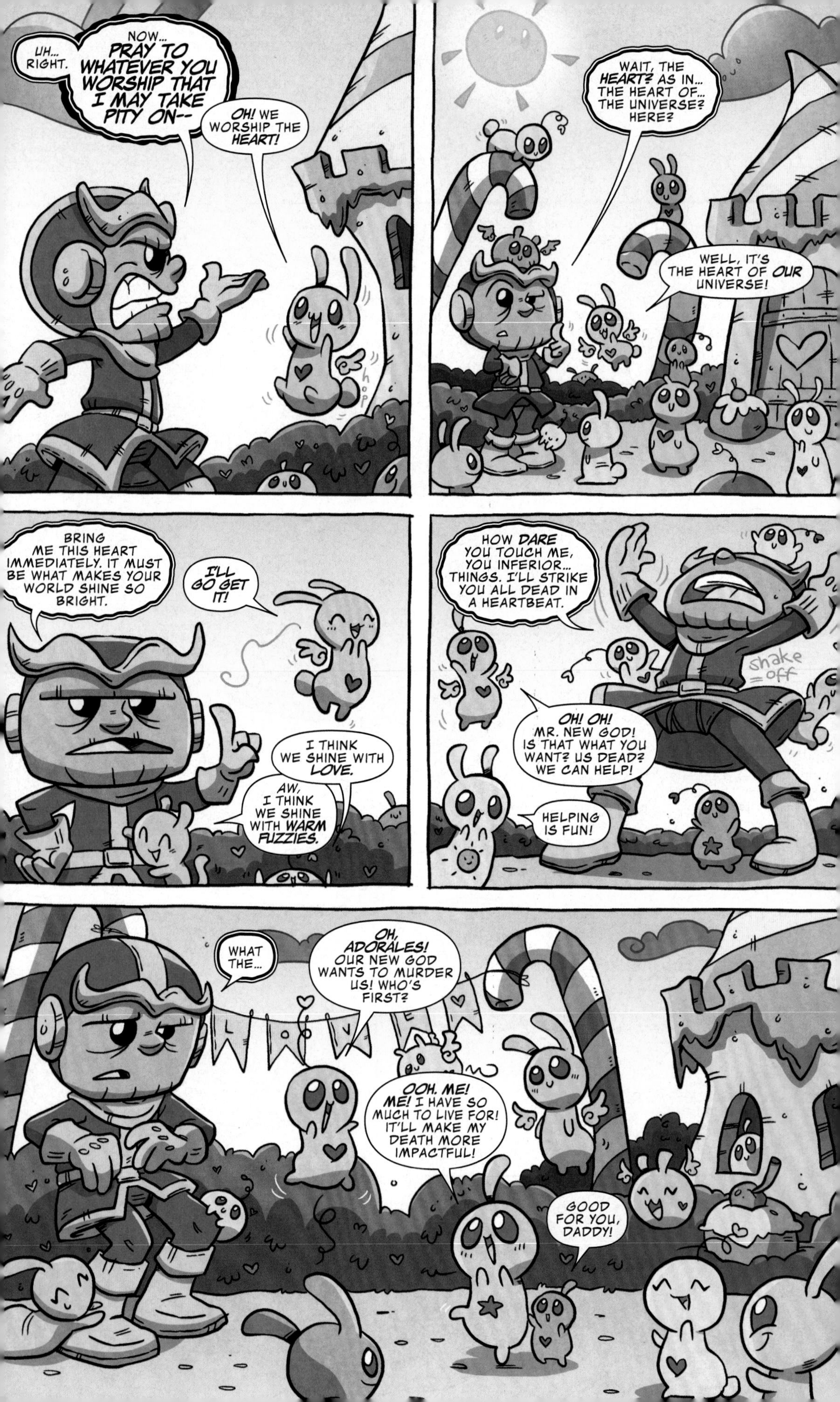

UH... RIGHT.
NOW... PRAY TO WHATEVER YOU WORSHIP THAT I MAY TAKE PITY ON--
OH! WE WORSHIP THE HEART!
hop
WAIT, THE HEART? AS IN... THE HEART OF... THE UNIVERSE? HERE?
WELL, IT'S THE HEART OF OUR UNIVERSE!
BRING ME THIS HEART IMMEDIATELY. IT MUST BE WHAT MAKES YOUR WORLD SHINE SO BRIGHT.
I'LL GO GET IT!
I THINK WE SHINE WITH LOVE.
AW, I THINK WE SHINE WITH WARM FUZZIES.
HOW DARE YOU TOUCH ME, YOU INFERIOR... THINGS. I'LL STRIKE YOU ALL DEAD IN A HEARTBEAT.
shake off
OH! OH! MR. NEW GOD! IS THAT WHAT YOU WANT? US DEAD? WE CAN HELP!
HELPING IS FUN!
WHAT THE...
OH, ADORALES! OUR NEW GOD WANTS TO MURDER US! WHO'S FIRST?
OOH. ME! ME! I HAVE SO MUCH TO LIVE FOR! IT'LL MAKE MY DEATH MORE IMPACTFUL!
GOOD FOR YOU, DADDY!

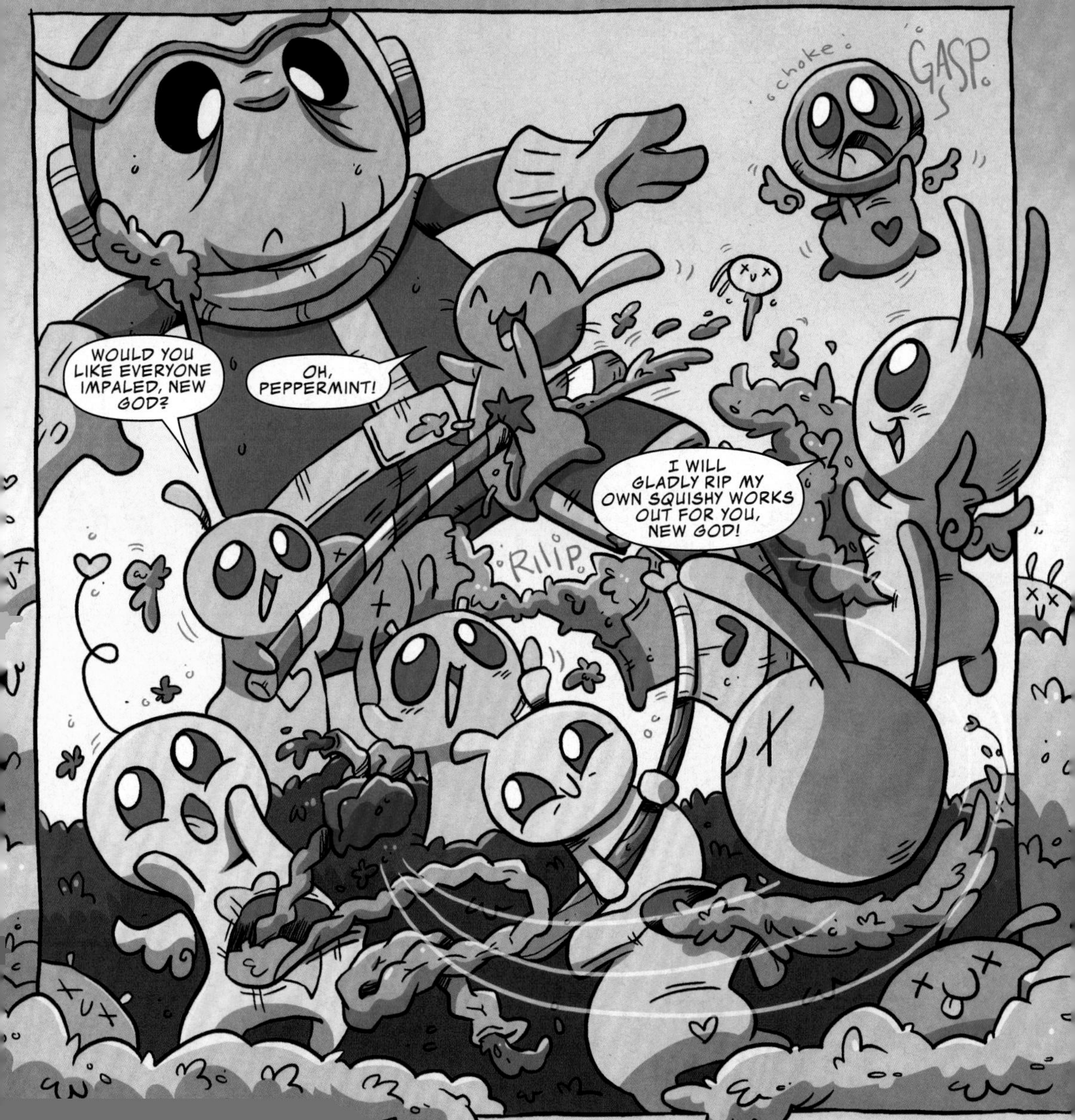
choke
GASP
WOULD YOU LIKE EVERYONE IMPALED, NEW GOD?
OH, PEPPERMINT!
I WILL GLADLY RIP MY OWN SQUISHY WORKS OUT FOR YOU, NEW GOD!
RIIIP

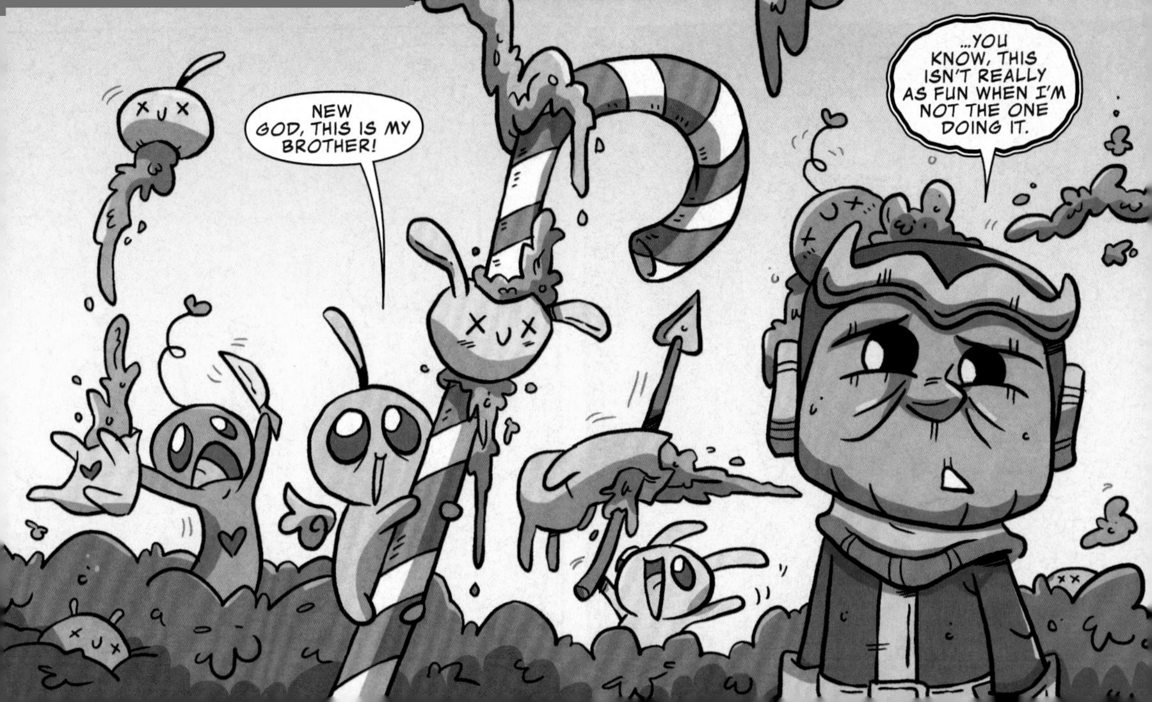
NEW GOD, THIS IS MY BROTHER!
...YOU KNOW, THIS ISN'T REALLY AS FUN WHEN I'M NOT THE ONE DOING IT.

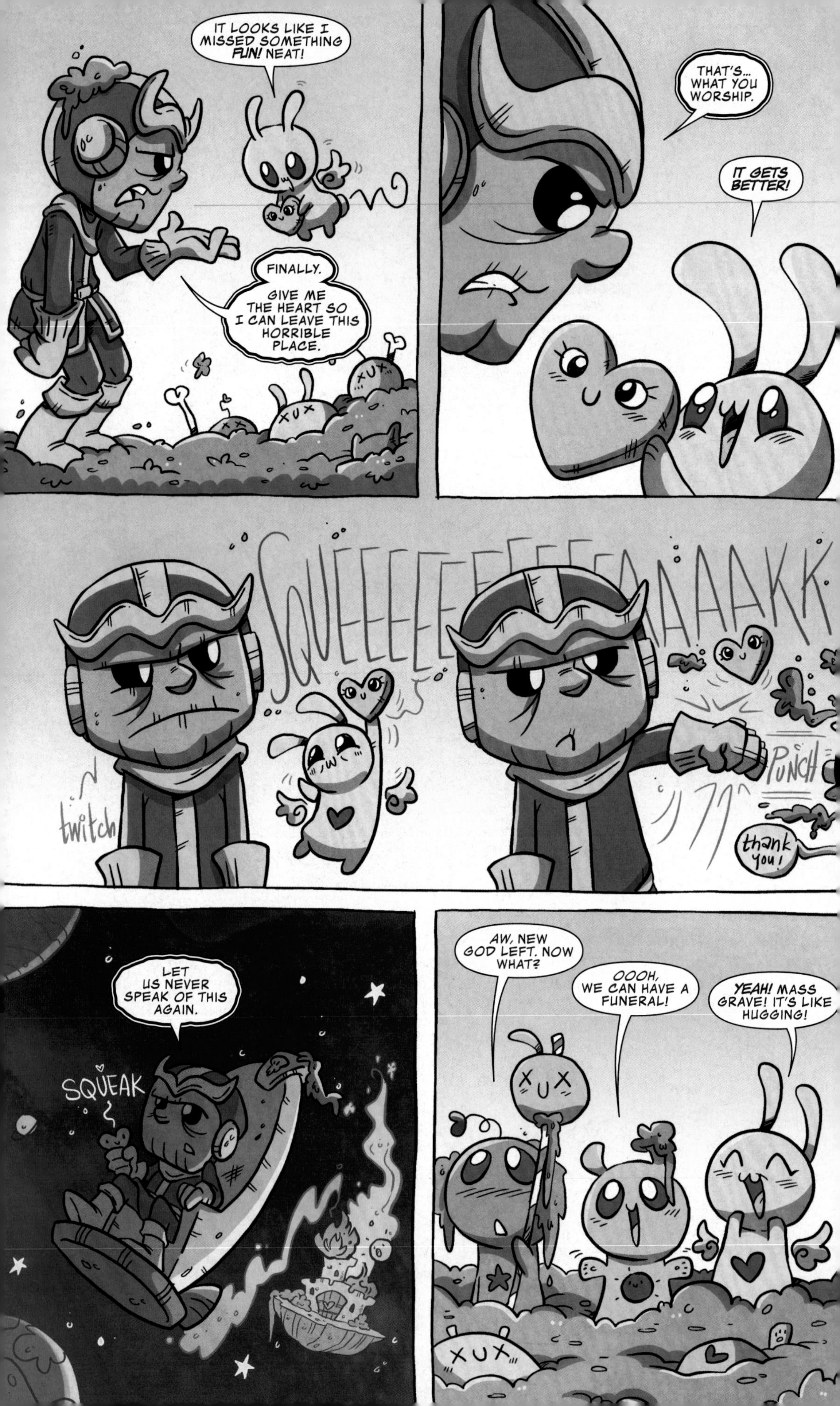
IT LOOKS LIKE I MISSED SOMETHING FUN! NEAT!
FINALLY.
GIVE ME THE HEART SO I CAN LEAVE THIS HORRIBLE PLACE.
THAT'S... WHAT YOU WORSHIP.
IT GETS BETTER!
SQUEEEEEEEEEEAAAAKK
twitch
PUNCH
thank you!
LET US NEVER SPEAK OF THIS AGAIN.
SQUEAK
AW, NEW GOD LEFT. NOW WHAT?
OOOH, WE CAN HAVE A FUNERAL!
YEAH! MASS GRAVE! IT'S LIKE HUGGING!

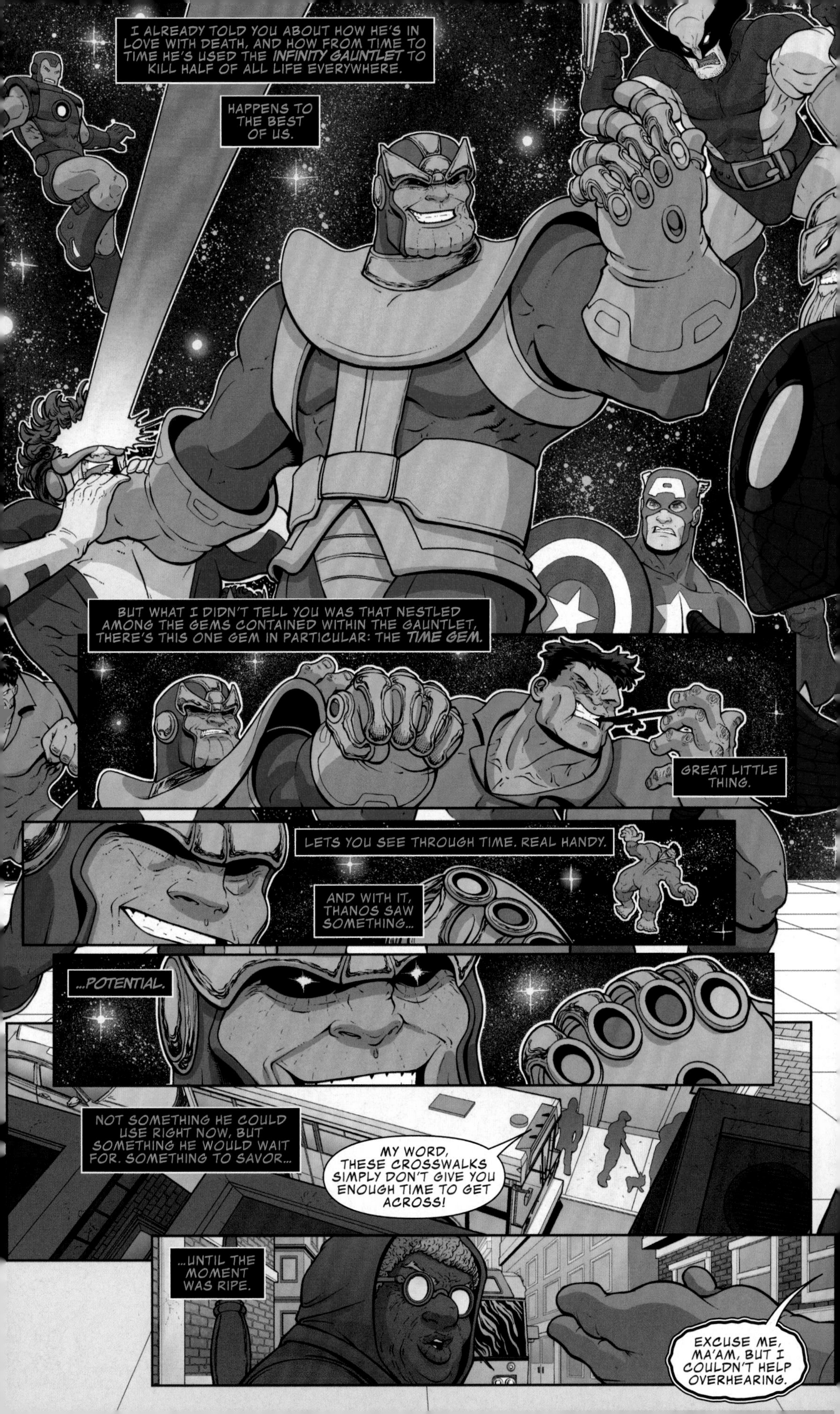

I ALREADY TOLD YOU ABOUT HOW HE'S IN LOVE WITH DEATH, AND HOW FROM TIME TO TIME HE'S USED THE *INFINITY GAUNTLET* TO KILL HALF OF ALL LIFE EVERYWHERE.
HAPPENS TO THE BEST OF US.
BUT WHAT I DIDN'T TELL YOU WAS THAT NESTLED AMONG THE GEMS CONTAINED WITHIN THE GAUNTLET, THERE'S THIS ONE GEM IN PARTICULAR: THE *TIME GEM*.
GREAT LITTLE THING.
LETS YOU SEE THROUGH TIME. REAL HANDY.
AND WITH IT, THANOS SAW SOMETHING...
...POTENTIAL.
NOT SOMETHING HE COULD USE RIGHT NOW, BUT SOMETHING HE WOULD WAIT FOR. SOMETHING TO SAVOR...
MY WORD, THESE CROSSWALKS SIMPLY DON'T GIVE YOU ENOUGH TIME TO GET ACROSS!
...UNTIL THE MOMENT WAS RIPE.
EXCUSE ME, MA'AM, BUT I COULDN'T HELP OVERHEARING.

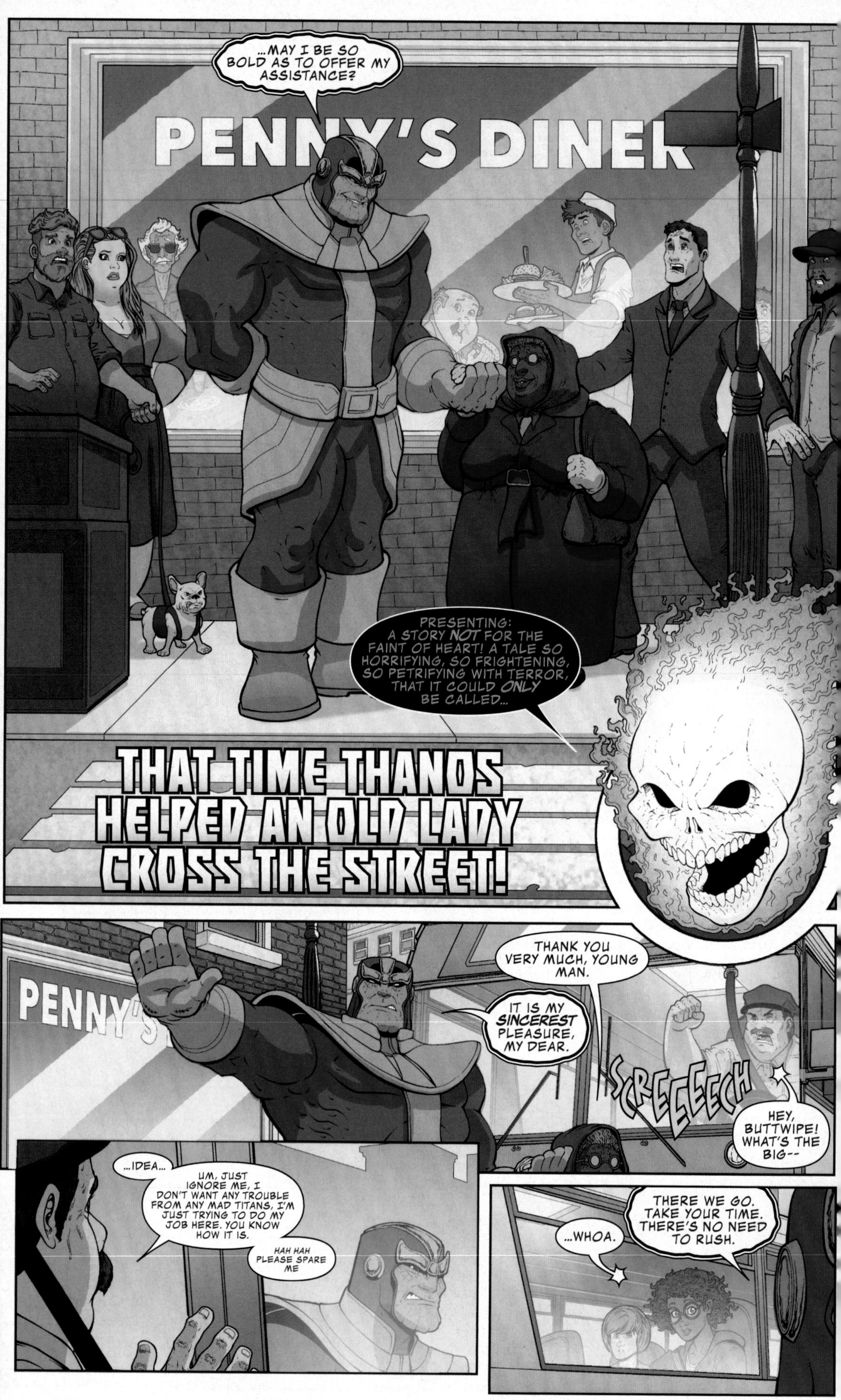
...MAY I BE SO BOLD AS TO OFFER MY ASSISTANCE?
PENNY'S DINER
PRESENTING: A STORY NOT FOR THE FAINT OF HEART! A TALE SO HORRIFYING, SO FRIGHTENING, SO PETRIFYING WITH TERROR, THAT IT COULD ONLY BE CALLED...
THAT TIME THANOS HELPED AN OLD LADY CROSS THE STREET!
PENNY'S
THANK YOU VERY MUCH, YOUNG MAN.
IT IS MY SINCEREST PLEASURE, MY DEAR.
SCREEEECH
HEY, BUTTWIPE! WHAT'S THE BIG--
...IDEA...
UM, JUST IGNORE ME, I DON'T WANT ANY TROUBLE FROM ANY MAD TITANS, I'M JUST TRYING TO DO MY JOB HERE. YOU KNOW HOW IT IS.
HAH HAH PLEASE SPARE ME
...WHOA.
THERE WE GO. TAKE YOUR TIME. THERE'S NO NEED TO RUSH.

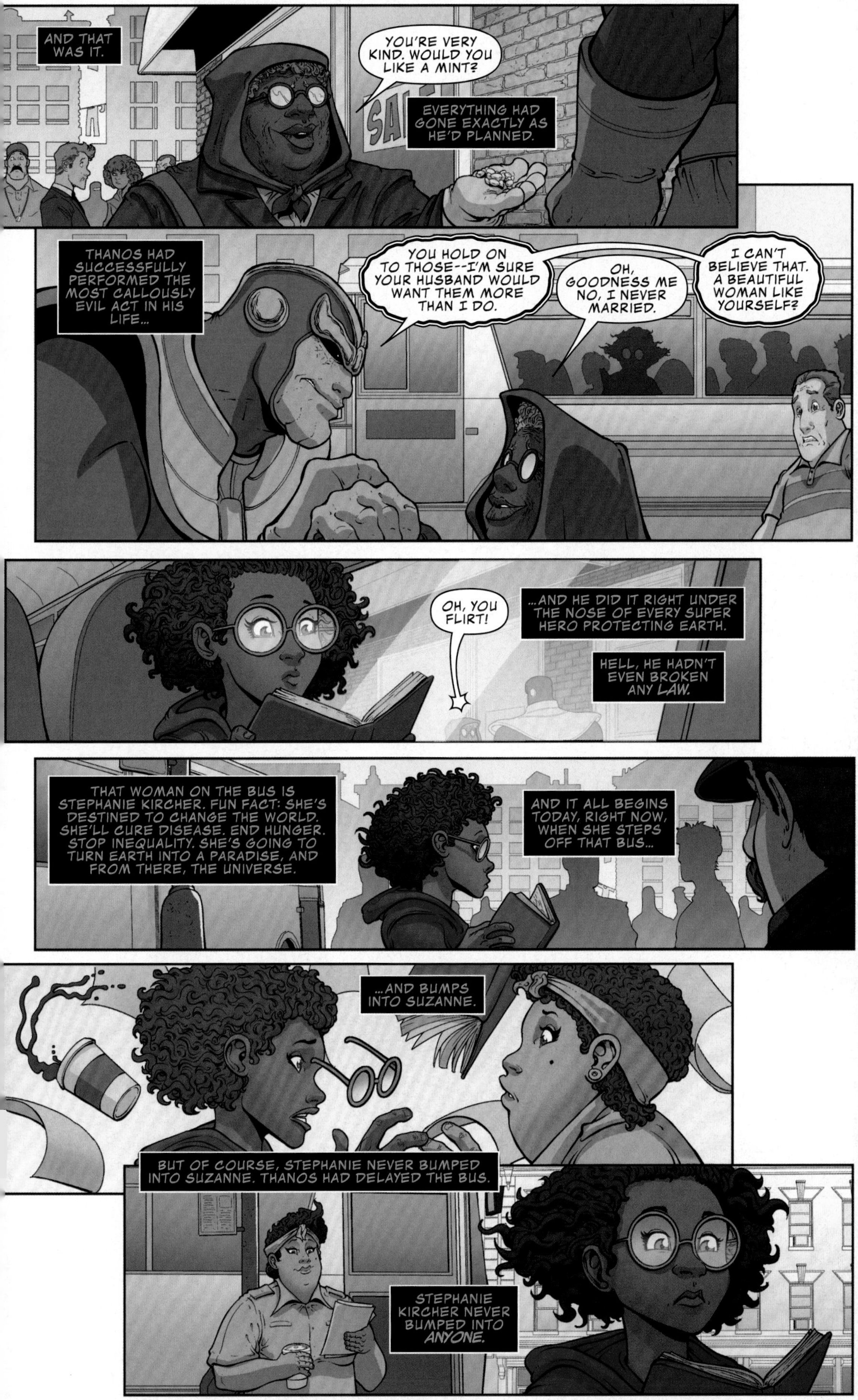
AND THAT WAS IT.
YOU'RE VERY KIND. WOULD YOU LIKE A MINT?
EVERYTHING HAD GONE EXACTLY AS HE'D PLANNED.
THANOS HAD SUCCESSFULLY PERFORMED THE MOST CALLOUSLY EVIL ACT IN HIS LIFE...
YOU HOLD ON TO THOSE--I'M SURE YOUR HUSBAND WOULD WANT THEM MORE THAN I DO.
OH, GOODNESS ME NO, I NEVER MARRIED.
I CAN'T BELIEVE THAT. A BEAUTIFUL WOMAN LIKE YOURSELF?
OH, YOU FLIRT!
...AND HE DID IT RIGHT UNDER THE NOSE OF EVERY SUPER HERO PROTECTING EARTH.
HELL, HE HADN'T EVEN BROKEN ANY LAW.
THAT WOMAN ON THE BUS IS STEPHANIE KIRCHER. FUN FACT: SHE'S DESTINED TO CHANGE THE WORLD. SHE'LL CURE DISEASE. END HUNGER. STOP INEQUALITY. SHE'S GOING TO TURN EARTH INTO A PARADISE, AND FROM THERE, THE UNIVERSE.
AND IT ALL BEGINS TODAY, RIGHT NOW, WHEN SHE STEPS OFF THAT BUS...
...AND BUMPS INTO SUZANNE.
BUT OF COURSE, STEPHANIE NEVER BUMPED INTO SUZANNE. THANOS HAD DELAYED THE BUS.
STEPHANIE KIRCHER NEVER BUMPED INTO ANYONE.

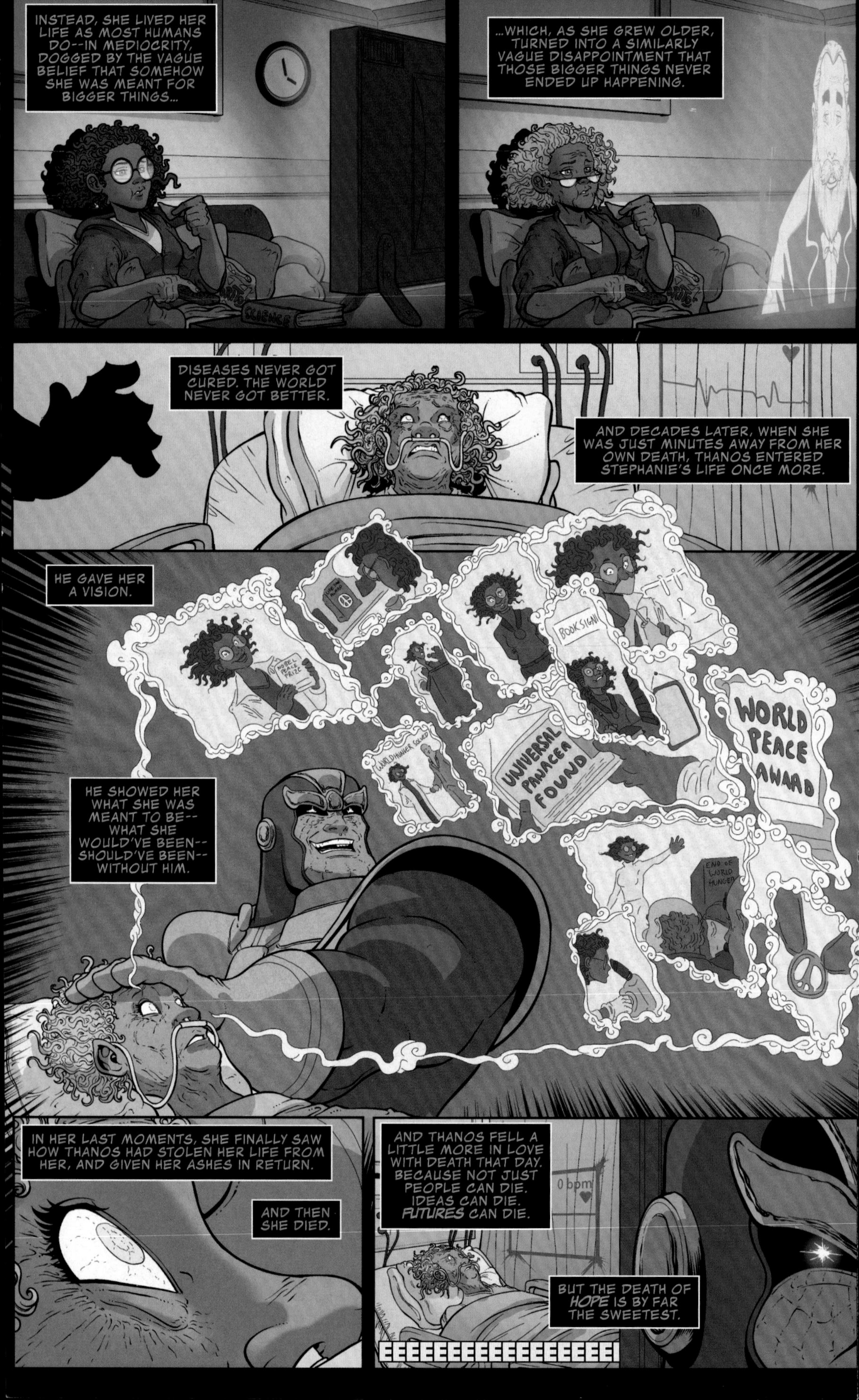
INSTEAD, SHE LIVED HER LIFE AS MOST HUMANS DO--IN MEDIOCRITY, DOGGED BY THE VAGUE BELIEF THAT SOMEHOW SHE WAS MEANT FOR BIGGER THINGS...
SCIENCE
...WHICH, AS SHE GREW OLDER, TURNED INTO A SIMILARLY VAGUE DISAPPOINTMENT THAT THOSE BIGGER THINGS NEVER ENDED UP HAPPENING.
DISEASES NEVER GOT CURED. THE WORLD NEVER GOT BETTER.
AND DECADES LATER, WHEN SHE WAS JUST MINUTES AWAY FROM HER OWN DEATH, THANOS ENTERED STEPHANIE'S LIFE ONCE MORE.
HE GAVE HER A VISION.
NOBEL PEACE PRIZE
BOOK SIGNI
UNIVERSAL PANACEA FOUND
WORLD PEACE AWARD
HE SHOWED HER WHAT SHE WAS MEANT TO BE-- WHAT SHE WOULD'VE BEEN-- SHOULD'VE BEEN-- WITHOUT HIM.
IN HER LAST MOMENTS, SHE FINALLY SAW HOW THANOS HAD STOLEN HER LIFE FROM HER, AND GIVEN HER ASHES IN RETURN.
AND THEN SHE DIED.
AND THANOS FELL A LITTLE MORE IN LOVE WITH DEATH THAT DAY. BECAUSE NOT JUST PEOPLE CAN DIE. IDEAS CAN DIE. *FUTURES* CAN DIE.
0 bpm
BUT THE DEATH OF *HOPE* IS BY FAR THE SWEETEST.
EEEEEEEEEEEEEEEEEEI

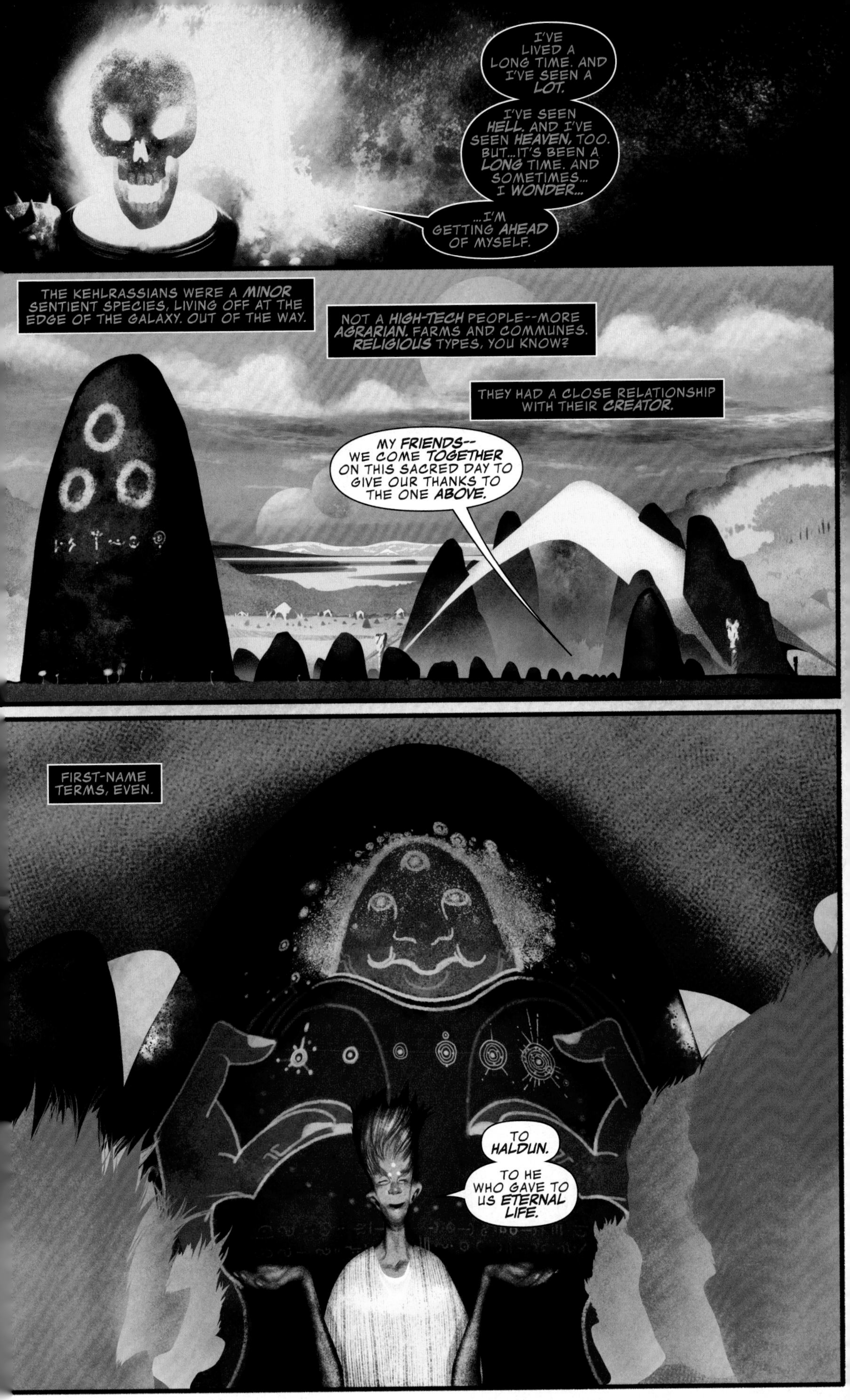

I'VE LIVED A LONG TIME. AND I'VE SEEN A LOT.
I'VE SEEN HELL, AND I'VE SEEN HEAVEN, TOO. BUT...IT'S BEEN A LONG TIME. AND SOMETIMES... I WONDER...
...I'M GETTING AHEAD OF MYSELF.
THE KEHLRASSIANS WERE A MINOR SENTIENT SPECIES, LIVING OFF AT THE EDGE OF THE GALAXY. OUT OF THE WAY.
NOT A HIGH-TECH PEOPLE--MORE AGRARIAN. FARMS AND COMMUNES. RELIGIOUS TYPES, YOU KNOW?
THEY HAD A CLOSE RELATIONSHIP WITH THEIR CREATOR.
MY FRIENDS-- WE COME TOGETHER ON THIS SACRED DAY TO GIVE OUR THANKS TO THE ONE ABOVE.
FIRST-NAME TERMS, EVEN.
TO HALDUN.
TO HE WHO GAVE TO US ETERNAL LIFE.

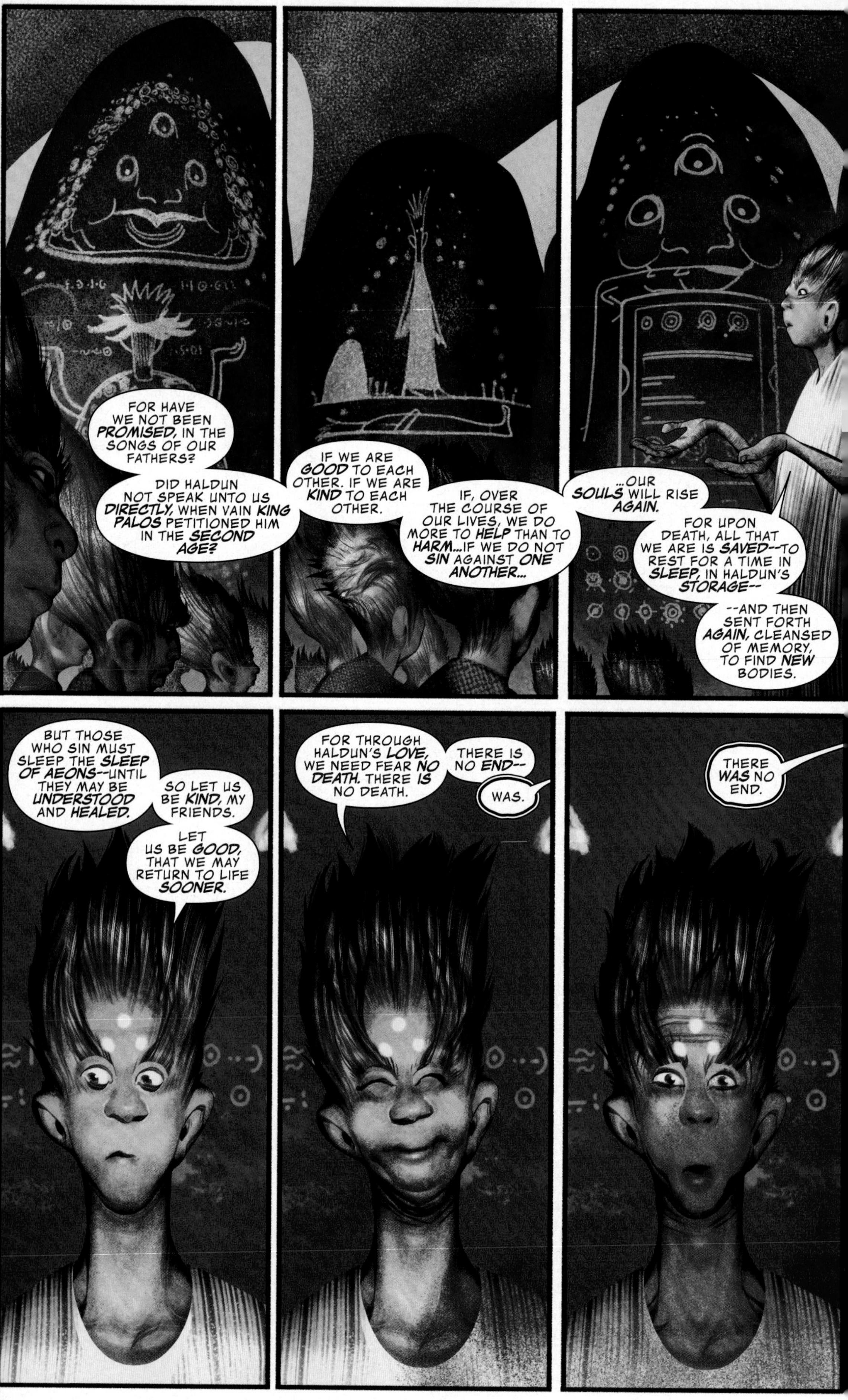
FOR HAVE WE NOT BEEN PROMISED, IN THE SONGS OF OUR FATHERS?
DID HALDUN NOT SPEAK UNTO US DIRECTLY, WHEN VAIN KING PALOS PETITIONED HIM IN THE SECOND AGE?
IF WE ARE GOOD TO EACH OTHER. IF WE ARE KIND TO EACH OTHER.
IF, OVER THE COURSE OF OUR LIVES, WE DO MORE TO HELP THAN TO HARM...IF WE DO NOT SIN AGAINST ONE ANOTHER...
...OUR SOULS WILL RISE AGAIN.
FOR UPON DEATH, ALL THAT WE ARE IS SAVED--TO REST FOR A TIME IN SLEEP, IN HALDUN'S STORAGE--
--AND THEN SENT FORTH AGAIN, CLEANSED OF MEMORY, TO FIND NEW BODIES.
BUT THOSE WHO SIN MUST SLEEP THE SLEEP OF AEONS--UNTIL THEY MAY BE UNDERSTOOD AND HEALED.
SO LET US BE KIND, MY FRIENDS.
LET US BE GOOD, THAT WE MAY RETURN TO LIFE SOONER.
FOR THROUGH HALDUN'S LOVE, WE NEED FEAR NO DEATH. THERE IS NO DEATH.
THERE IS NO END--
WAS.
THERE WAS NO END.

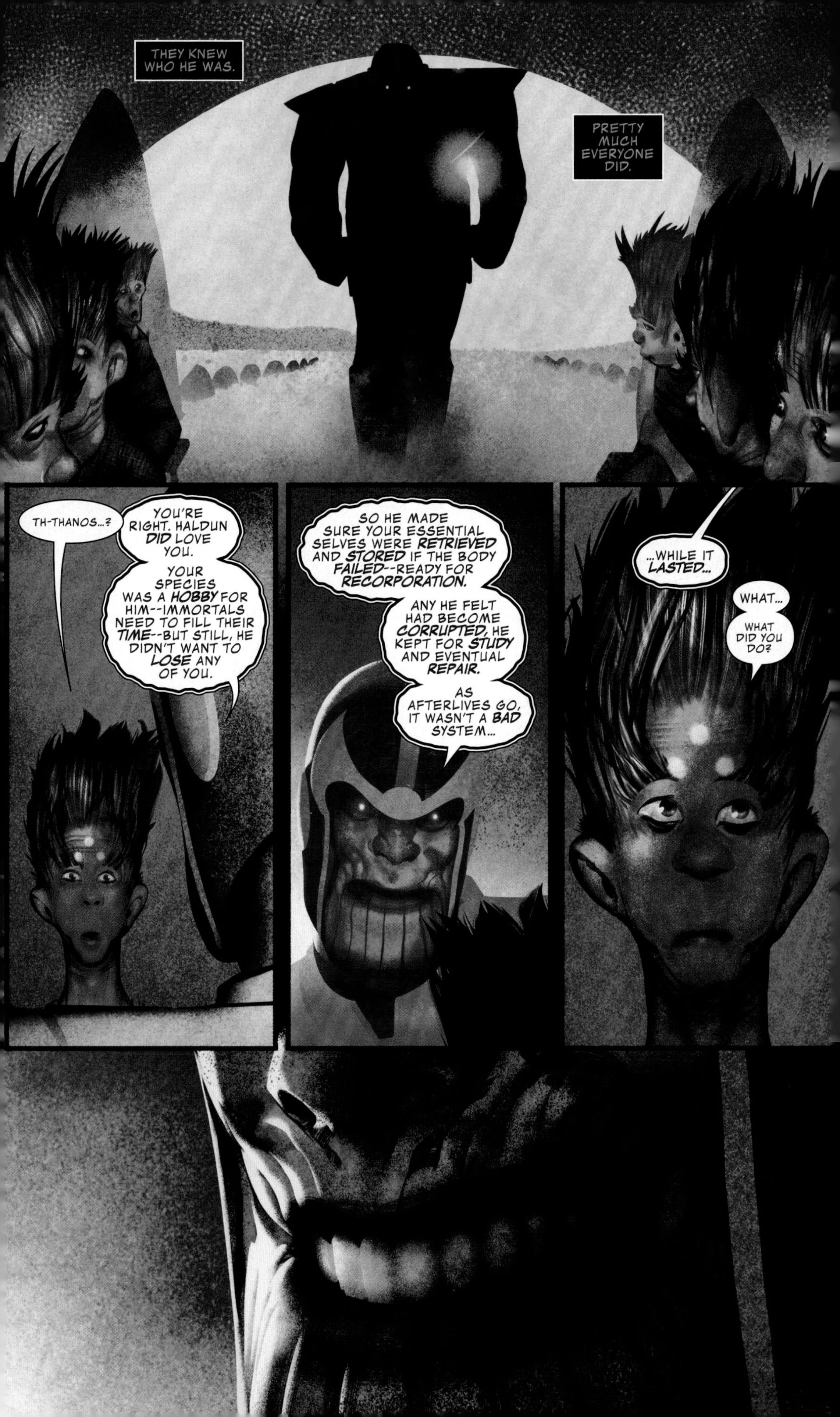
THEY KNEW WHO HE WAS.
PRETTY MUCH EVERYONE DID.
TH-THANOS...?
YOU'RE RIGHT. HALDUN DID LOVE YOU.
YOUR SPECIES WAS A HOBBY FOR HIM--IMMORTALS NEED TO FILL THEIR TIME--BUT STILL, HE DIDN'T WANT TO LOSE ANY OF YOU.
SO HE MADE SURE YOUR ESSENTIAL SELVES WERE RETRIEVED AND STORED IF THE BODY FAILED--READY FOR RECORPORATION.
ANY HE FELT HAD BECOME CORRUPTED, HE KEPT FOR STUDY AND EVENTUAL REPAIR.
AS AFTERLIVES GO, IT WASN'T A BAD SYSTEM...
...WHILE IT LASTED...
WHAT...
WHAT DID YOU DO?

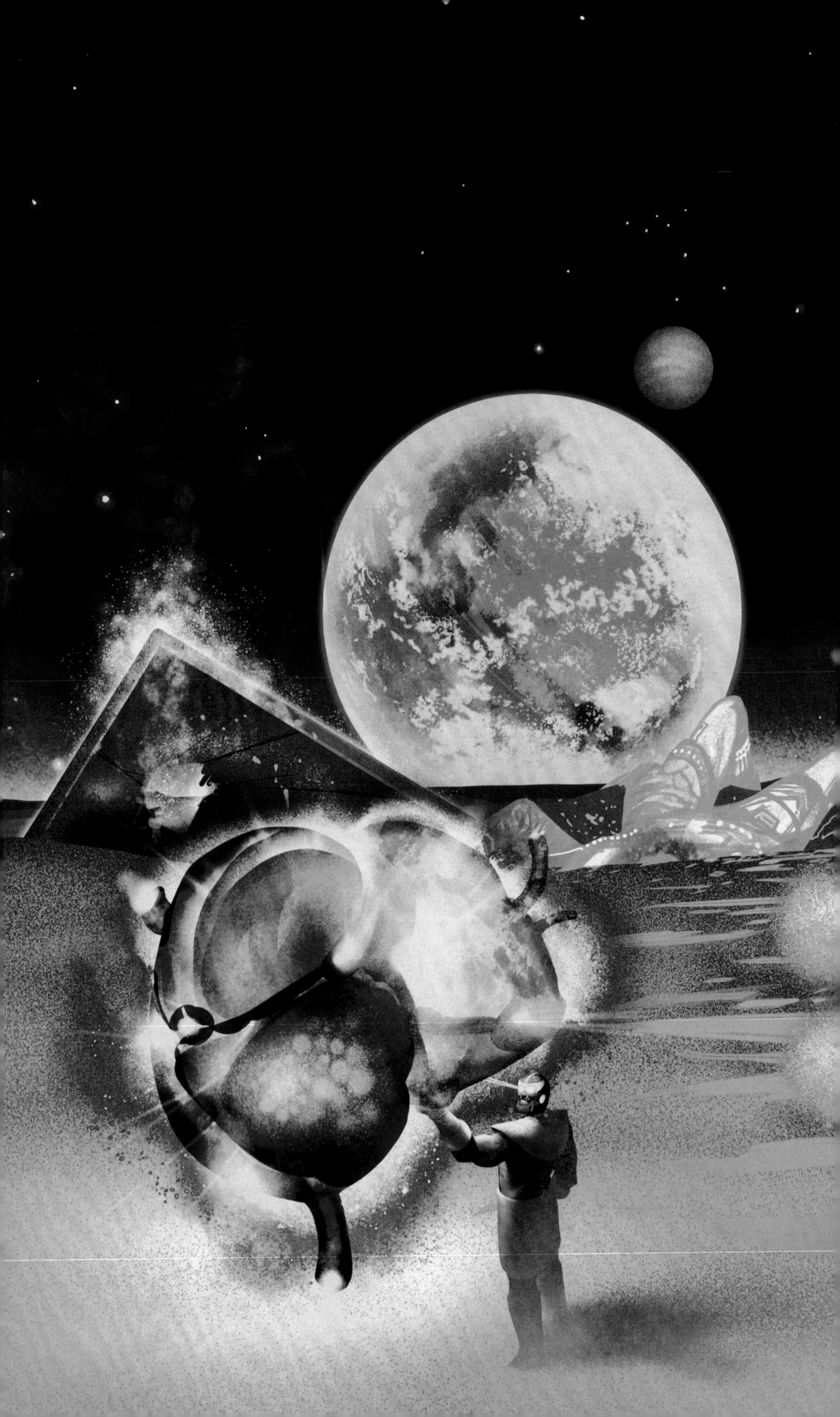

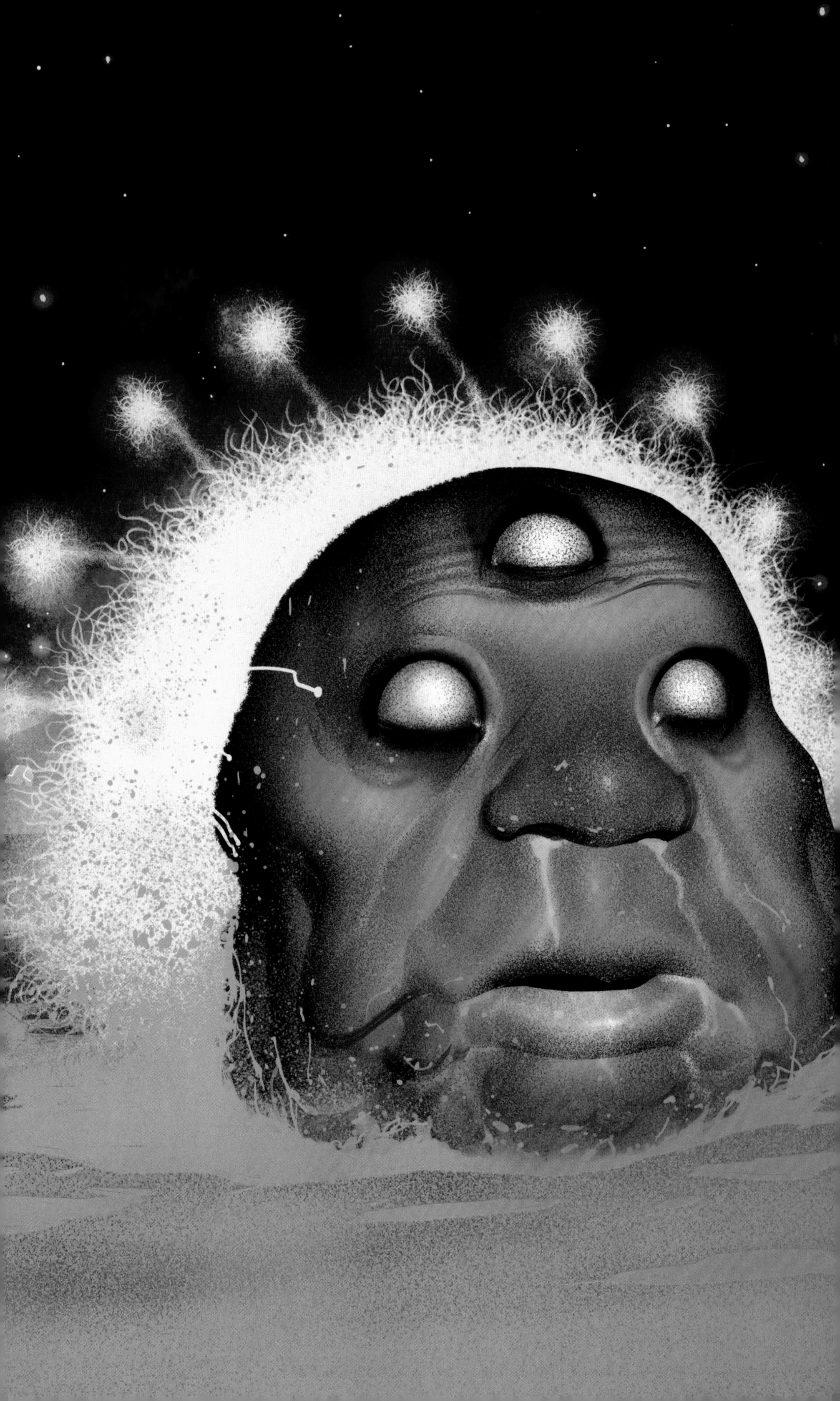

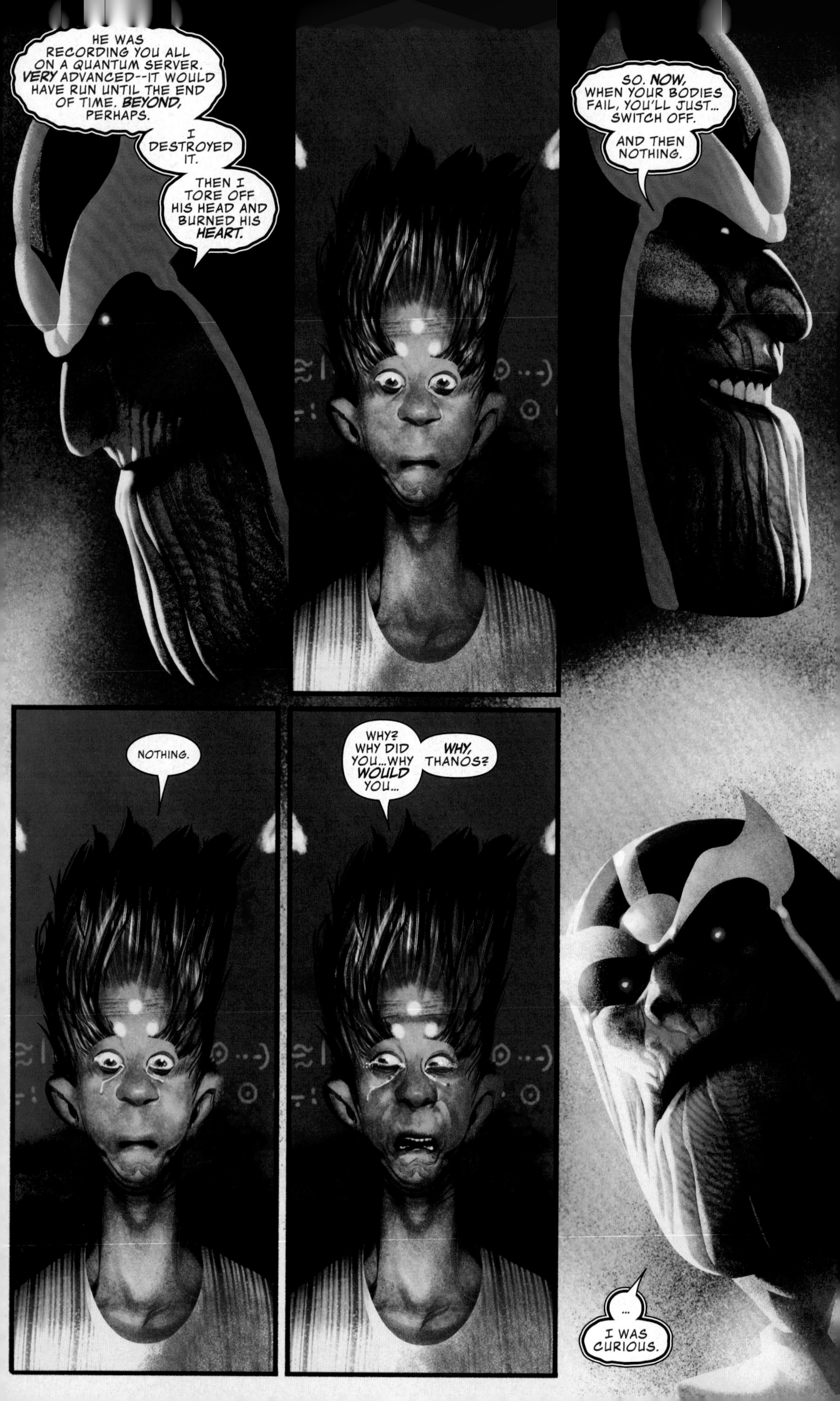
HE WAS RECORDING YOU ALL ON A QUANTUM SERVER. VERY ADVANCED--IT WOULD HAVE RUN UNTIL THE END OF TIME. BEYOND, PERHAPS.
I DESTROYED IT.
THEN I TORE OFF HIS HEAD AND BURNED HIS HEART.
SO. NOW, WHEN YOUR BODIES FAIL, YOU'LL JUST... SWITCH OFF.
AND THEN NOTHING.
NOTHING.
WHY? WHY DID YOU...WHY WOULD YOU...
WHY, THANOS?
...
I WAS CURIOUS.

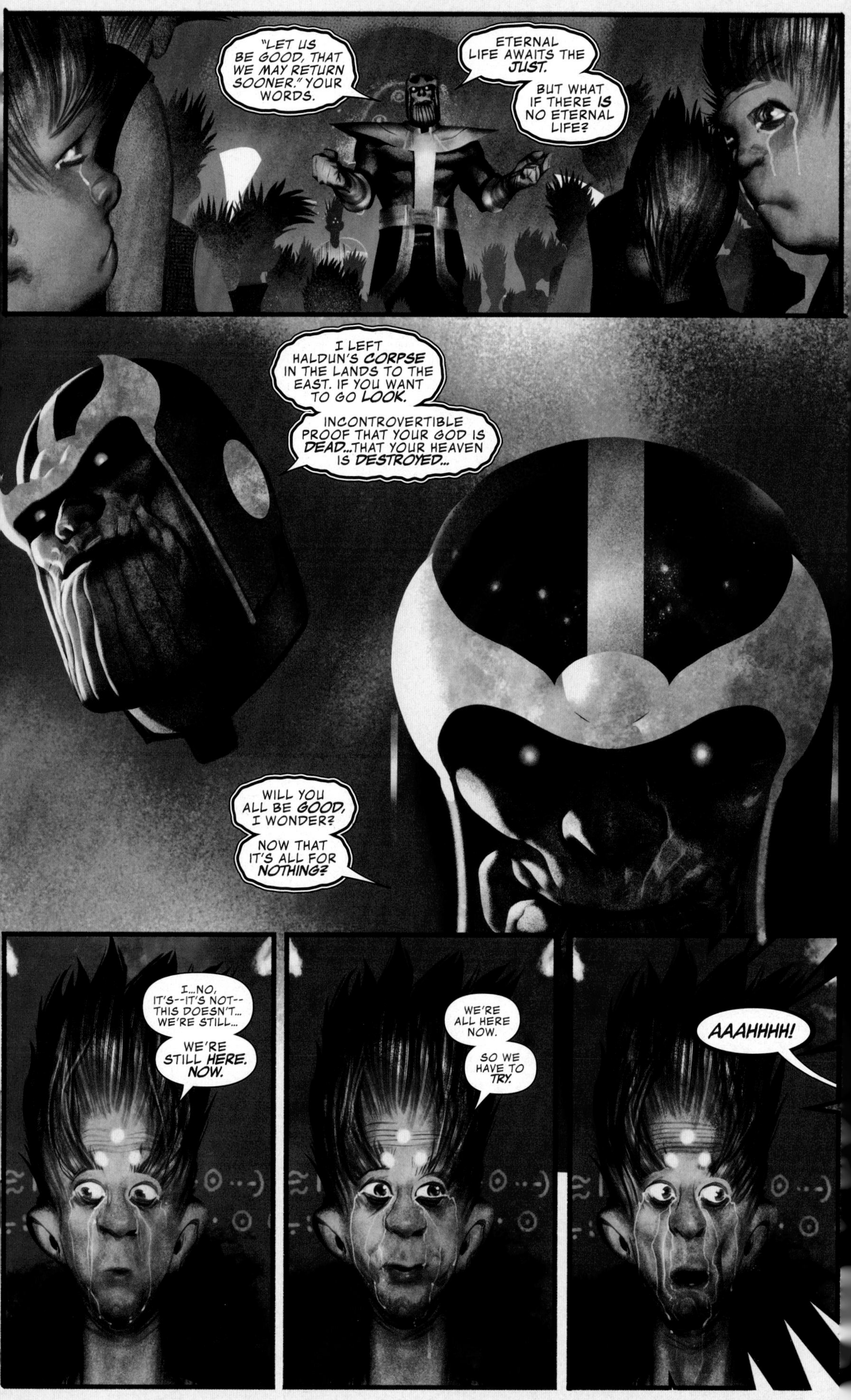
"LET US BE GOOD, THAT WE MAY RETURN SOONER." YOUR WORDS.
ETERNAL LIFE AWAITS THE JUST.
BUT WHAT IF THERE IS NO ETERNAL LIFE?
I LEFT HALDUN'S CORPSE IN THE LANDS TO THE EAST. IF YOU WANT TO GO LOOK.
INCONTROVERTIBLE PROOF THAT YOUR GOD IS DEAD...THAT YOUR HEAVEN IS DESTROYED...
WILL YOU ALL BE GOOD, I WONDER?
NOW THAT IT'S ALL FOR NOTHING?
I...NO, IT'S--IT'S NOT--THIS DOESN'T... WE'RE STILL...
WE'RE STILL HERE. NOW.
WE'RE ALL HERE NOW.
SO WE HAVE TO TRY.
AAAHHHH!

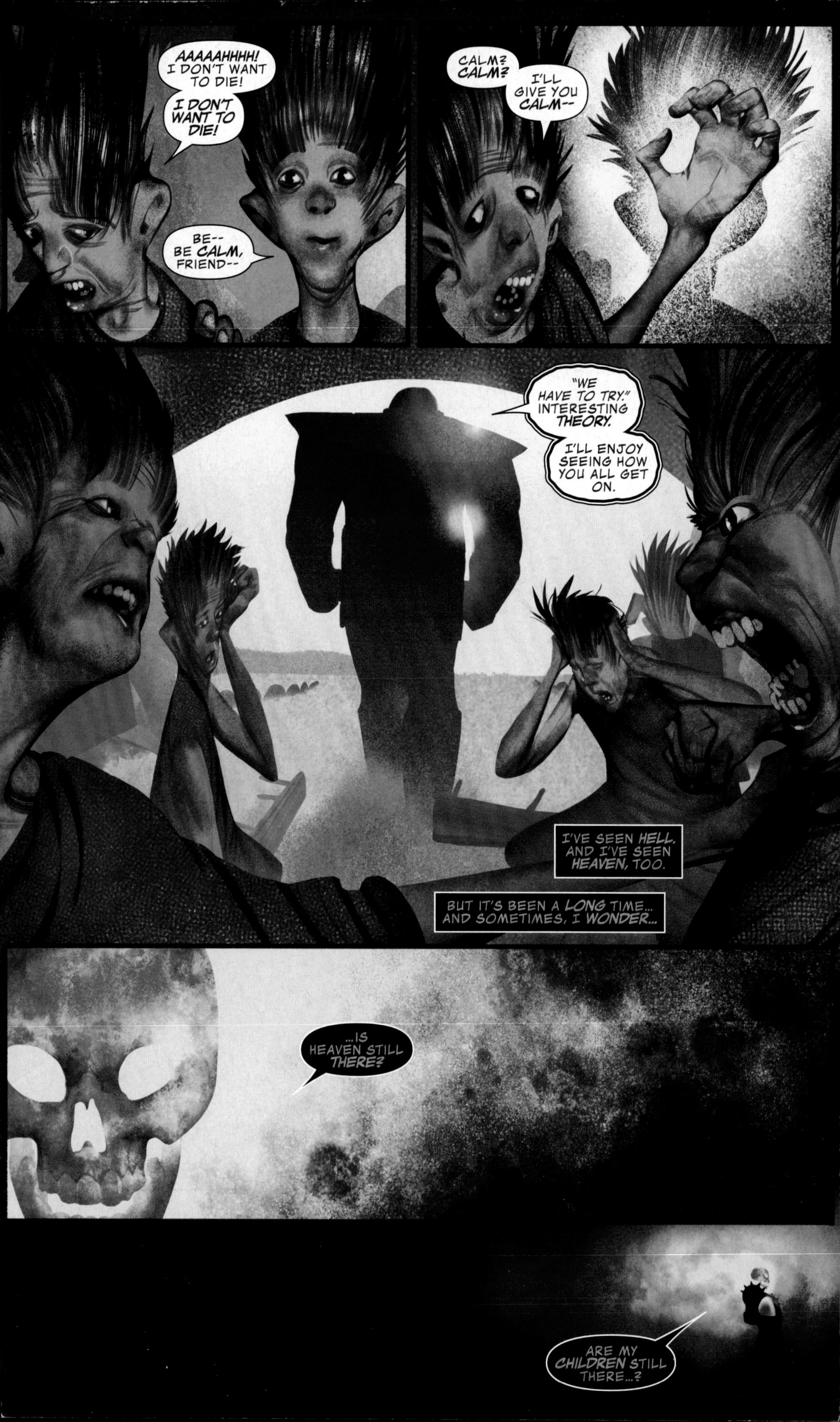
AAAAAHHHH! I DON'T WANT TO DIE!
I DON'T WANT TO DIE!
BE-- BE CALM, FRIEND--
CALM? CALM?
I'LL GIVE YOU CALM--
"WE HAVE TO TRY." INTERESTING THEORY.
I'LL ENJOY SEEING HOW YOU ALL GET ON.
I'VE SEEN HELL. AND I'VE SEEN HEAVEN, TOO.
BUT IT'S BEEN A LONG TIME... AND SOMETIMES, I WONDER...
...IS HEAVEN STILL THERE?
ARE MY CHILDREN STILL THERE...?

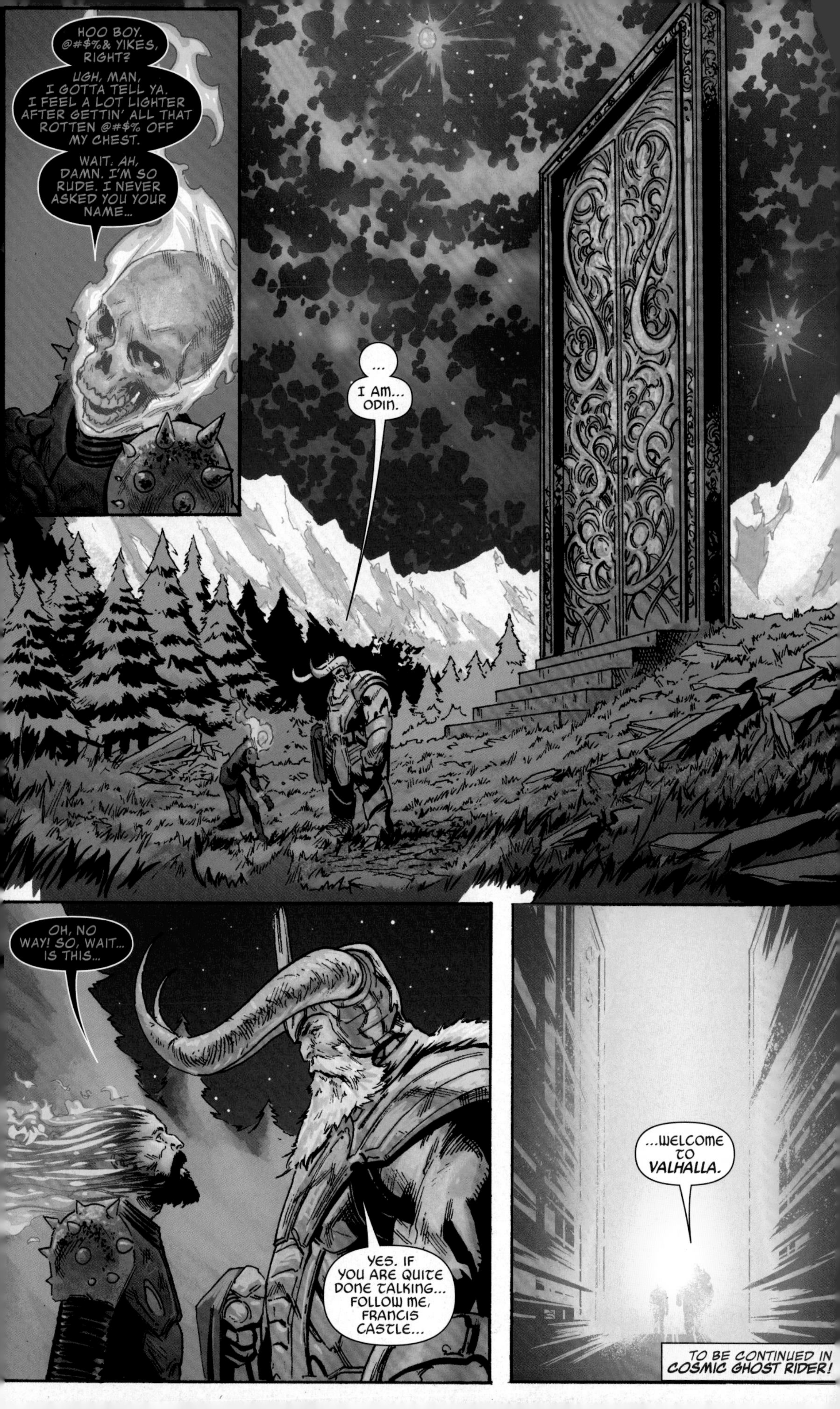
HOO BOY. @#$%& YIKES, RIGHT?
UGH, MAN, I GOTTA TELL YA. I FEEL A LOT LIGHTER AFTER GETTIN' ALL THAT ROTTEN @#$% OFF MY CHEST.
WAIT. AH, DAMN. I'M SO RUDE. I NEVER ASKED YOU YOUR NAME...
...
I AM... ODIN.
OH, NO WAY! SO, WAIT... IS THIS...
YES. IF YOU ARE QUITE DONE TALKING... FOLLOW ME, FRANCIS CASTLE...
...WELCOME TO VALHALLA.
TO BE CONTINUED IN COSMIC GHOST RIDER!

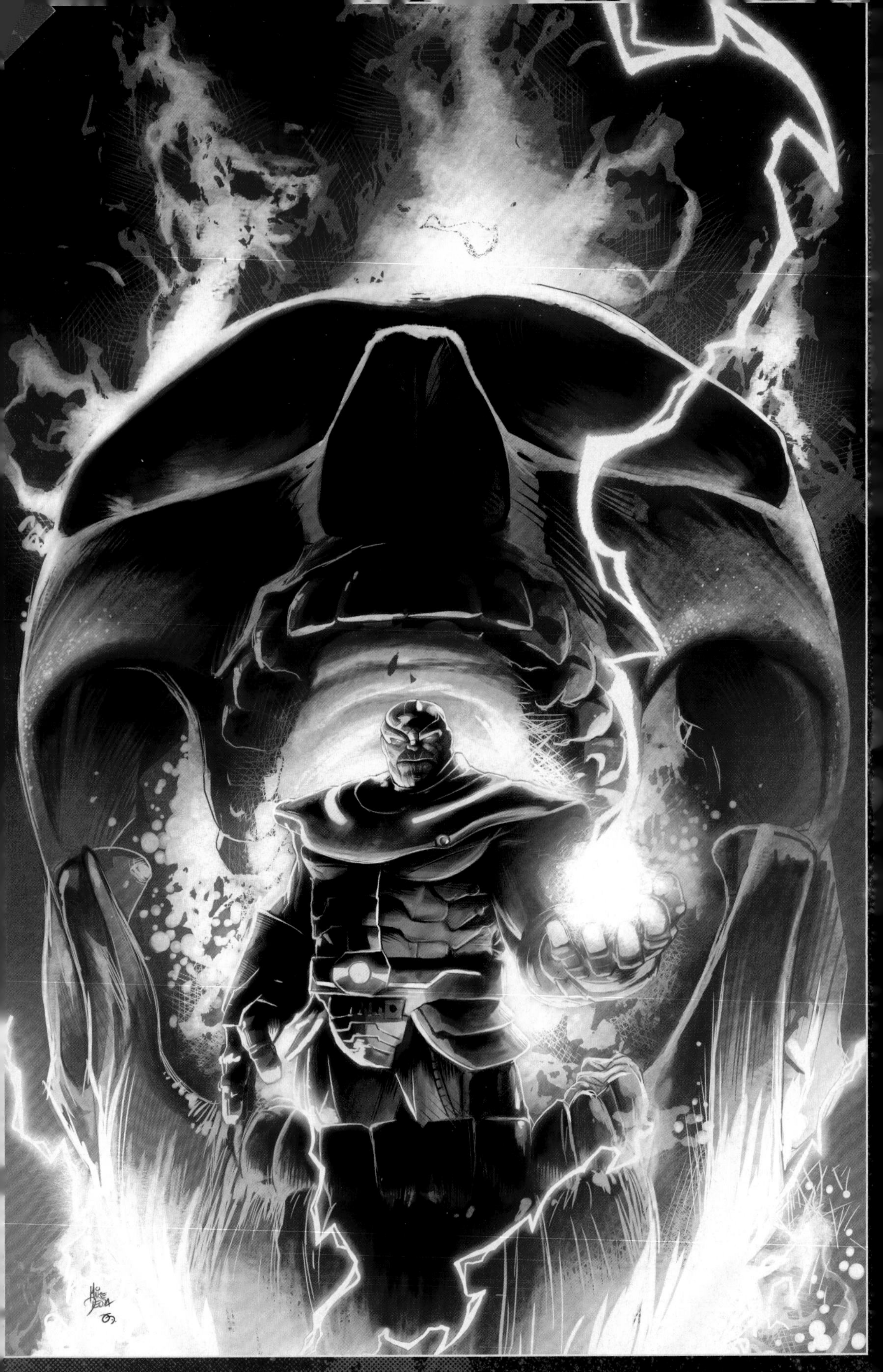

MIKE DEODATO JR. & EDGAR DELGADO

ANNUAL NO. 1 VARIANT